Jewellery

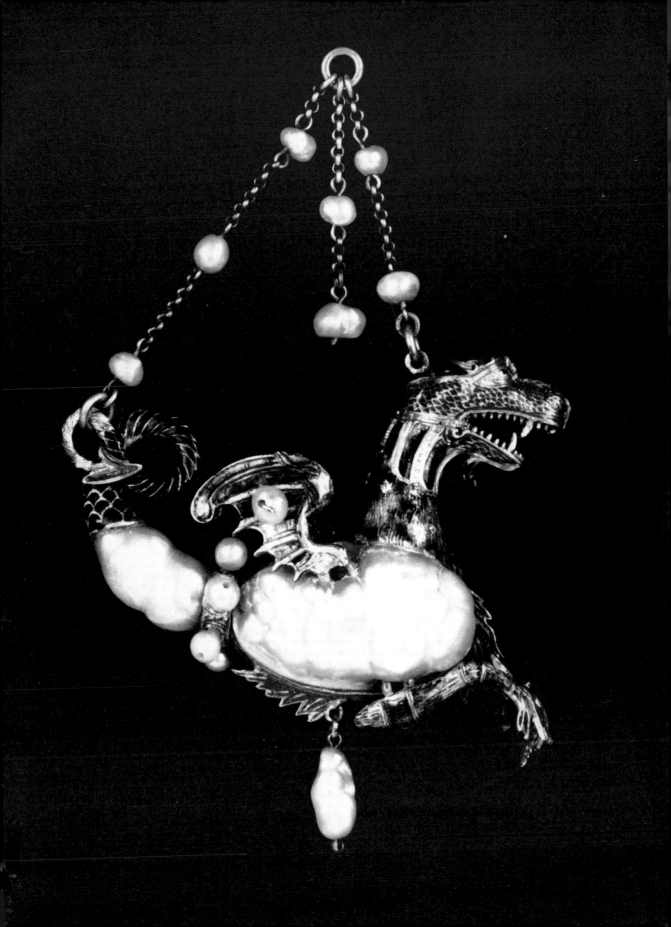

Jewellery
THROUGH 7000 YEARS

Published for The Trustees of the British Museum by British Museum Publications Limited

© 1976, The Trustees of the British Museum
ISBN 0 7141 0054 4 cased
ISBN 0 7141 0055 2 limp
Published by British Museum Publications Ltd
6 Bedford Square, London, WC1B 3RA

Designed by Patrick Yapp

Set in Monotype Garamond 156
Printed in Great Britain by
Balding & Mansell Ltd, London and Wisbech

Contents

Preface

The aim has been to bring together here jewellery from all the major phases of man's history. This selection, made entirely from the collections of the British Museum, ranges in date from about 5000 BC to the middle of the nineteenth century and has been deliberately restricted to approximately 500 items.

Although the Museum's collections of antiquities come from almost every part of the world and span the years from the Stone Age to the last century, there is inevitably no even distribution, either in quantity or quality. This is, of course, due to the accident of survival and of archaeological rediscovery and of opportunity for acquisition; consequently, some areas and periods are noticeably more richly represented than others. Nevertheless, the scope extends beyond Europe and the ancient cultures of Western Asia to India, Tibet and the Far East and includes certain areas of Africa and of Central and Southern America.

Jewellery for personal adornment is the main theme, but, in addition, amuletic (protective) jewellery – in so far as it can be specifically recognized – is treated separately. The use of cameos in jewellery and the role of finger-rings are two further facets which have been singled out for individual consideration, partly because both have histories peculiar to themselves and partly because both present special problems of display and illustration.

I am deeply grateful to the Director, Sir John Pope-Hennessy, for his support and to the Keepers and staff of the eight Departments contributing to this rich assemblage of precious material. In particular, I wish to thank my colleagues, who have given me, so generously and unsparingly, of their time and expertise during the preparations both for the Exhibition and for the production of this Catalogue, and who have written the commentaries and catalogue entries on items from the collections in their care: Carol Andrews (Egyptian Antiquities); Malcolm McLeod (Ethnography, Africa, Ashanti); Elizabeth M. Carmichael and Penny K. Bateman (Ethnography, the Americas); John Picton (Ethnography, Africa, Benin); Reynold Higgins (Greek and Roman); Richard Camber (Medieval and Later Antiquities, Early Christian and Byzantine); Leslie Webster and Dafydd Kidd (Medieval and Later Antiquities, Anglo-Saxon and Migration periods); John Cherry (Medieval and Later Antiquities, Medieval); Ralph Pinder-Wilson (Oriental Antiquities, Islamic); Jessica M. Rawson (Oriental Antiquities, Far Eastern); Wladimir Zwalf (Oriental Antiquities, India and Tibet); Mansel Spratling (Prehistoric and Romano-British Antiquities); and Julian E. Reade (Western Asiatic Antiquities).

I would also like to express my appreciation of the work of Geoffrey Pickup, Elizabeth Robertson and their colleagues in the Design Office, of the staff of the Photographic Service, and of the British Museum Publications Ltd; my special thanks go to my young temporary assistant, Peter Clifford, and to the staff of my own Department who have helped in so many different ways.

HUGH TAIT
Deputy Keeper of Medieval & Later Antiquities
30 July 1976

7

Introduction

Jewellery was man's answer to the profound human need for self-adornment and, consequently, is one of the oldest forms of decorative art. For the past seven thousand years, its history – albeit interrupted and incomplete – can be traced from the centres of the earliest known civilizations in Mesopotamia (Iraq) and Egypt to its universality in modern times. A panoramic survey of this kind highlights both the inventiveness of man's imagination and, at the same time, the basic, almost primitive qualities that remain consistent factors throughout the long story.

Man's recognition of the intrinsic beauty of certain materials, minerals and especially gold, has led to their constant use in totally unconnected civilizations separated by vast barriers of time and space. That these basic materials were from the earliest times fashioned to beautify the human form seems beyond doubt, but at what stage jewellery began to serve man's superstitious need to protect himself from the multitude of frightening ills that befell him and were beyond his comprehension cannot be established; in the absence of supporting archaeological or written evidence, the little carved stone pendants representing animals and objects (no. 331) which have been found in Mesopotamia and date from about 5000 BC, cannot be regarded as amulets with certainty but, like so much jewellery through the ages, they were probably worn for both decorative and amuletic purposes.

Again, no date can be put on the first use of jewellery to proclaim the wearer's wealth and social status. While man was making jewellery from objects that were available for all to wear, such as shells or pebbles, it could have no such function; but, clearly, at some very early stage in man's history, relatively scarce materials, such as gold and lapis-lazuli, began to be selected and fashioned for this purpose. During the formative early period of Egypt's history (about 3000 BC) a simple form of gold jewellery incorporating stones or rare minerals was undoubtedly being made (no. 6) but so little has survived or been recovered that its use, its quality and its extent are still conjectural.

The oldest and most spectacular examples are to be found, not in Egypt but farther to the east, in ancient Babylonia (Iraq), where, on the site of the Biblical city of Ur of the Chaldees, the Royal Tombs, especially the tomb of Queen Pu-abi, have yielded a fantastic profusion of gold jewellery dating from about 2500 BC when Ur was the most powerful city-state in Mesopotamia. These discoveries, made between 1922 and 1934, proved the existence of jewellery of very high quality and diversity: hair-ornaments in sheet gold, cut to resemble flowers; earrings and complicated gold chains and necklaces of carnelian, lapis-lazuli, agate and gold; even finger-rings inlaid with lapis-lazuli within a sophisticated scale-pattern of gold cells (nos. 11–14). Two of the most important techniques in the history of jewellery, filigree and granulation, were used in the making of this royal jewellery from Ur; at the present, these pieces are the earliest recorded use of these techniques but their skilful application suggests that the Sumerians may have been employing them for some considerable time. It is important to remember that all the metals used, together with the carnelian and lapis-lazuli, must have been imported by the Sumerians.

The Sumerians with their knowledge of writing and the engraved seal, of the wheel, and of the skills required to smelt and fashion metals (including gold) into weapons, utensils and ornaments enabled them to make great progress towards establishing a settled social order when most peoples of the world were still living in a primitive state. It is, therefore, not surprising to find the art of the Sumerian goldsmith spreading widely over the lands of Western Asia and northwards to the Mediterranean areas of Turkey where, on the site of Homer's Troy, fine gold jewellery of approximately 2500–2300 BC was excavated. The movement westwards may have continued, for in the islands of southern Greece, the Cycladic Islands, and in Crete, gold jewellery of a slightly later date and less spectacular nature has been found.

Although the tenuous thread is now broken, there was probably a fairly continuous development in different parts of the Eastern Mediterranean and in Western Asia. In the Nile valley, where one of the more stable cultures of ancient history was being simultaneously developed, jewellery had, by the XIIth Dynasty (about 1900 BC) begun to play a most important role, having already acquired elaborate amuletic, social and decorative functions (nos. 22–26, 339).

The Minoan culture on the island of Crete reveals in its jewellery strong influences from both Egyptian and Western Asiatic civilizations. From about 1700 BC, Cretan jewellery has survived in sufficient quantity to state that the techniques of filigree, granulation and repoussé work had been most successfully mastered and combined with novel designs (nos. 31–34) so that when, about 1550 BC the Minoan culture was transplanted to the Greek mainland and the city of the Mycenae rose to power, the Mycenaeans seem to have adopted Minoan jewellery forms and techniques. After the fall of Knossos (about 1400 BC), the Mycenaeans became the undisputed heirs of the Minoan cultural heritage and their jewellery (no. 39) reflects this continuity but also begins to develop a character of its own.

In northern Europe, the absence of written evidence makes the subject more difficult to trace but by about 2000 BC the craft of metalworking had been introduced. Though a few splendid items of gold jewellery, like the gold lunula (no. 45) and the gold cape from Mold in Wales (no. 59), have survived from the period about 1800–1400 BC – contemporary with the construction of Stonehenge – it is not until the succeeding centuries that the development of jewellery during the European Bronze Age becomes more easy to chart. Although there is nothing yet excavated which might be identified as a 'palace' of a chieftain, the quantity of metalwork, both weapons and ornaments, found in the burials indicates the privileged status of these leaders. Their metal workers, using both gold and bronze, produced jewellery of good quality and bold design (no. 70). The trading contacts that provided the impetus had been established with the Eastern Mediterranean by about 2000 BC and brought jewellery, such as faience beads, into Central Europe whilst gold was exported to the Mycenaean world.

Towards the period 1100–1000 BC there is evidence of widespread disruption, which not only affected the higher civilizations to the south-east, including the Mycenaeans and the Hittites, but also the flourishing barbarian Bronze Age society in Central Europe. The subsequent emergence of the Urnfield culture has been regarded as 'proto-Celtic', whereas the peoples of the Hallstatt culture (about 700–500 BC) and the succeeding La Tène culture are accepted as fully Celtic. The Celts were never a nation in the usual sense of the word but they established a stylistic tradition that persisted in parts of Europe throughout the Roman period and reappeared in the succeeding centuries before the emergence of medieval society in Western Europe. Whilst much of their jewellery was essentially functional – pins (no. 69) and brooches (nos. 131–144), for example – the ornamentation lavished on it is often remarkable for its inventiveness and complexity. Perhaps the single item of jewellery most readily associated with the Celts is the torc (nos. 111–125). These massive neck-pieces and armlets, with their very distinctive circlet shapes and terminals of varying design, may have their ancestry in Asian sources and it is interesting to see that they are not wholly unknown even in Egypt (no. 28).

Celtic craftsmen were using red enamel, as well as red coral inlay, to decorate their bronze jewellery, as early as 400 BC; certainly, throughout the Roman period, champlevé enamelling was carried on in those Celtic areas which had in most instances become the northern provinces of the Roman Empire (nos. 145–6). Although the Romans noted this practice of 'the barbarians in

the ocean' (according to the Greek philosopher, Philostratus, writing in the second century AD), they do not seem to have adopted it. They do seem, however, to have acquired a taste for colour in their jewellery, especially for polished gemstones of different hues and for cameos – no doubt, from their contacts with Western Asia – and this legacy was to have a lasting effect on the history of European jewellery.

The inlaying of jewellery with richly coloured stones, especially garnets, was a striking feature of the Migration period (fourth to eighth centuries AD) following upon the collapse of the Roman Empire. This practice, combined with the re-emergence of Celtic enamelling and an obsessive use of surface ornamental detail, made North European jewellery of this period among the most colourful and the most intricate (nos. 197–202).

In China, the early stages in the development of jewellery are obscure but the working of jade seems to be an ancient tradition. Pendants in the form of animals, carved in jade and turquoise, have survived from the Shang and Eastern Chou dynasties (thirteenth to tenth centuries BC) and are thought to have had amuletic properties. Jade was not only highly regarded in ancient China as a beautiful stone but it was from early times thought to possess special qualities of a quasi-magical or spiritual nature and no doubt its rarity and the difficulty of getting supplies of it, made it a most precious material – rather as gold had become in the Mediterranean lands.

The item of Chinese jewellery worn by men that has mostly survived from the centuries BC is the belt-hook, and the artistic carving of the early jade belt-hooks is of the highest order, both technically and artistically. Jewellery for women was principally concerned with the adornment of the hair, both pins and combs, and, to some extent, earrings. In the period between about AD 500–1000 the Japanese seem to have worn jewellery to a very limited extent, mainly beads, but thereafter there is no evidence that jewellery played any significant part in their adornment. In China the hair ornaments become more delicate and elaborate, and by the Ming dynasty head-dresses for the ladies have become fragile and intricate creations of pierced and finely worked gold.

Simultaneously, in the ancient civilizations of central and southern America, jewellery was being produced in great quantities mainly using gold, but, as in the Mayan jewellery of about AD 600–1000, also jade. The present state of knowledge concerning the histories of the ancient cultures of America before the arrival of the Spaniards in the sixteenth century is too incomplete to permit of any form of precise dating. Consequently, chronological sequences are very approximate but it is interesting to note that much of the jewellery is designed to embellish parts of the human face, not only earrings but nose-ornaments, lip-pieces and ear-flares. The large gold pectoral ornaments display the greatest variety of skills, having anthropomorphic or zoomorphic subjects executed in relief, with openwork, filigree and applied elements cast as a rule by the *cire-perdue* (lost wax) process. The functions of this jewellery are totally undocumented but much of it may have served more than a purely decorative purpose.

With the Spanish conquests stretching from Peru in the south to Mexico in the north, the production of this remarkable jewellery came abruptly to an end. Back in Europe, the Spanish court, enriched by its territories in the New World and their plentiful supplies of gold and emeralds, began to set the fashion and, by the middle of the sixteenth century, was leading Europe into its last great epoch of formal ostentatious display, in which the art of the goldsmith-jeweller played such a spectacular and vital role. But, probably for the first time, jewellery was being designed on an international scale by artists and men who were not practising goldsmiths. The princes of northern Europe, wishing to keep abreast with the latest fashions of the Renaissance courts of Italy, expected their court painters and artists to provide drawings and designs for jewellery in the new styles – and Hans Holbein at the court of Henry VIII in England was no exception (no. 287). The contemporary development of the art of engraving provided an excellent means for mass reproduction of these designs and they were soon being sold and distributed throughout the workshops of the goldsmiths and jewellers of Europe. This speedy dissemination of styles brought about a greater unity in the field of European jewellery and it is only in exceptional cases that the nationality of court jewellery of the sixteenth century can with certainty be identified. Furthermore, the leading goldsmiths/jewellers also moved from one court to another, according to the chance of patronage, and the constant exchange of ideas on techniques and styles was thereby fostered. The role of the gifted artist in the creation of jewellery went even further, for during the late sixteenth and early seventeenth centuries, miniaturists, like Nicholas Hilliard, often provided the major element in the jewel – the portrait – and demanded that it was an integrated part of the whole design and colour scheme of the jewel into which it was set. No finer example than the famous Lyte Jewel (no. 298) has survived and, by a miracle of good fortune, it has reached us complete with its unbroken pedigree, its royal history and a painting of its first owner, proudly wearing it in 1611 (no. 299). Few personal jewels can offer us such a richly documented story. Although princely gifts of gold chains to reward loyal service had been the standard practice since the Middle Ages and was to die out only in the eighteenth century, when, significantly, the gold snuff-box took the place of jewellery, grateful monarchs have rarely given to humble subjects a present more exquisite in form than the Lyte Jewel.

Crowns and sceptres, mitres and crosiers, rings of investiture and high office, etc., are all jewels made specifically to denote rank and, as such, have been deliberately excluded. Whilst some of the jewellery described here dating from prehistoric and early times may have been worn for that purpose, the evidence is inconclusive.

Personal jewellery from the earliest periods was undoubtedly already being used as an indication of status and, even in medieval Europe, this attitude was still so strongly held that laws and decrees were proclaimed both in England and on the Continent controlling the freedom of the individual in this respect and permitting only certain classes of society to wear certain categories of jewellery.

The use – or misuse – of jewellery by man is an elusive subject, but no matter whether a piece of jewellery was originally chosen for its amuletic purpose, its attractiveness or its social cachet, it probably always had one special quality – it could be used as a form of currency, almost as an investment. Few branches of the decorative arts have such diverse and complex uses – or, indeed, such a long history.

HUGH TAIT

Notes on the Catalogue

Abbreviations

Departments:

EA :	Egyptian Antiquities
ETH :	Ethnography
G & R :	Greek and Roman Antiquities
M & L :	Medieval and Later Antiquities
OA :	Oriental Antiquities
P & D :	Prints and Drawings
P & RB :	Prehistoric and Romano-British Antiquities
WAA :	Western Asiatic Antiquities

Measurements:

all dimensions are in centimetres.

H :	height
L :	length
W :	width
D :	diameter
T :	thickness
WT :	weight (in grammes)

The Colour Plates

List of Colour Plates

PLATE 1
Sumerian:
about 2500 BC
Catalogue No. 11

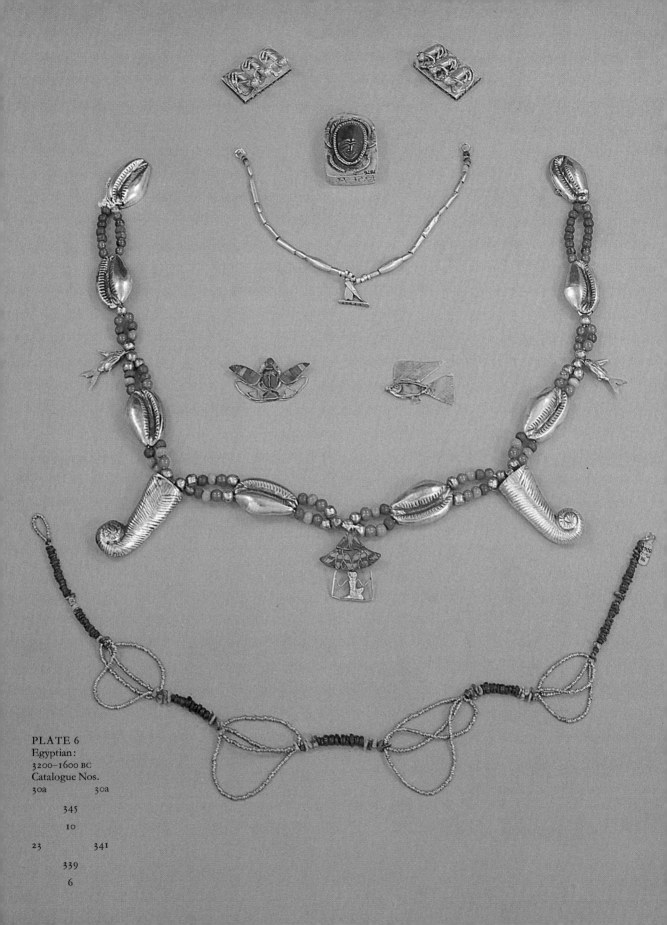

PLATE 6
Egyptian:
3200–1600 BC
Catalogue Nos.

30a		30a
	345	
	10	
23		341
	339	
	6	

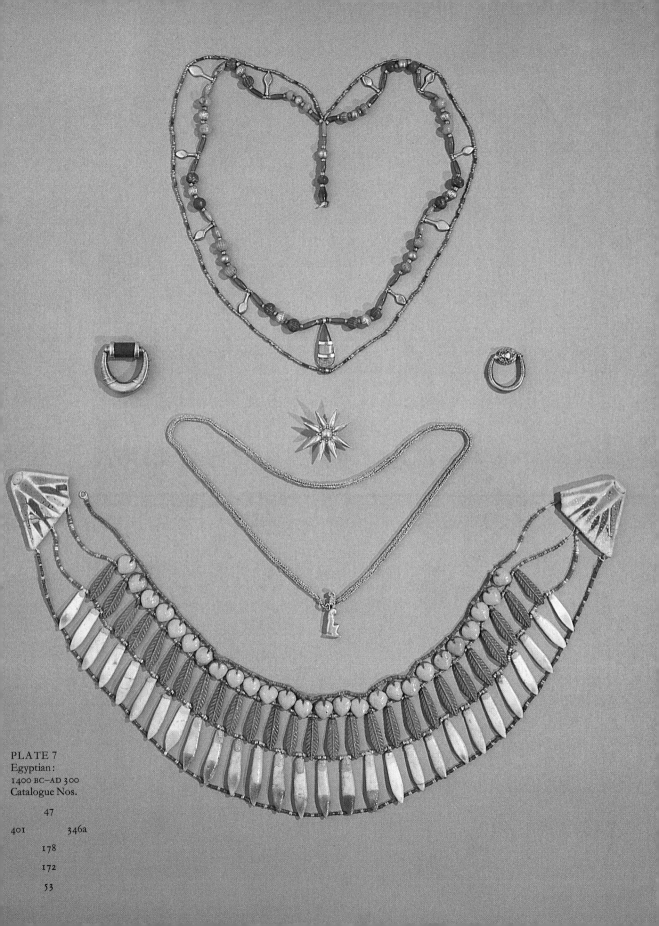

PLATE 7
Egyptian:
1400 BC–AD 300
Catalogue Nos.

47
401   346a
178
172
53

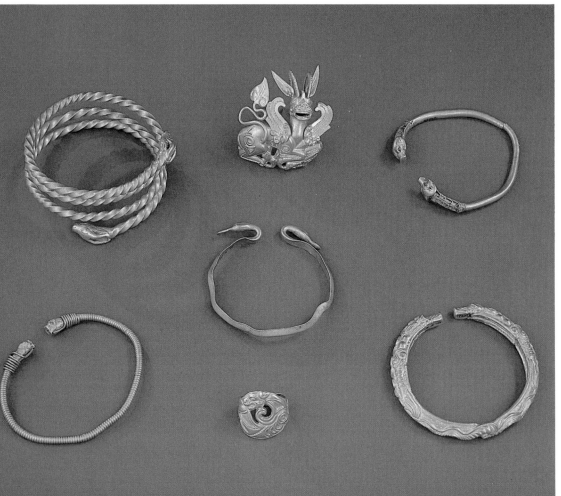

◁
PLATES 8, 9
Oxus Treasure:
Persian
5th–4th century BC
Catalogue Nos.

      109a

      109d

109c   109b ii

      109b iii

109b i   109b iv

      109f

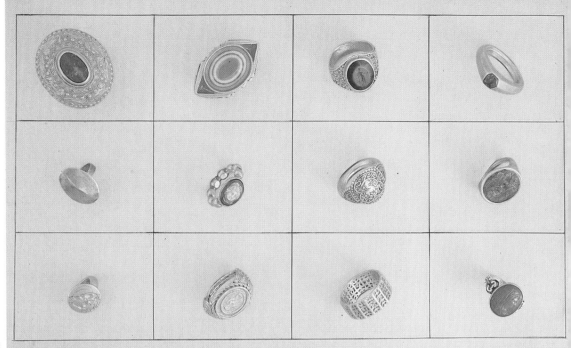

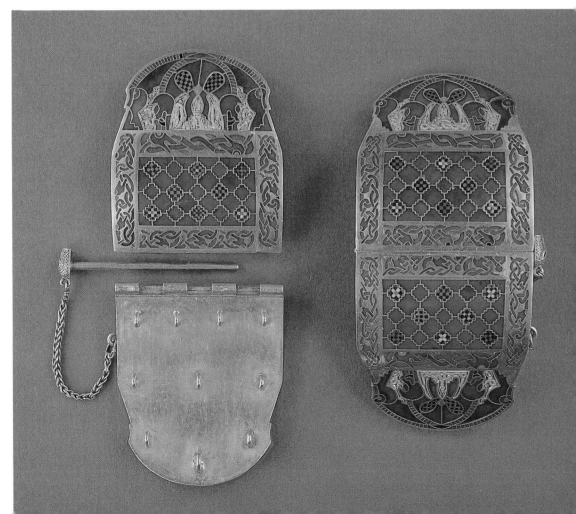

PLATE 12
Benin Ivories:
16th century AD
Catalogue
No.324b

PLATE 13
Celtic Bronzes:
1st–2nd century
AD
Catalogue Nos.
146   145

PLATE 14
Anglo-Saxon
silver:
9th century AD
Catalogue
No.207

PLATE 15
Byzantine Chain:
about AD 600
Catalogue
No.190

◁

PLATES 18, 19
Medieval Cameo
Pendant:
Catalogue
No.386
(*front and back*)

PLATE 20   ▷
The 'Dunstable'
Swan Jewel:
15th century AD
Catalogue No.268

PLATE 21   ▷
Renaissance
Cameo:
Catalogue
No.392

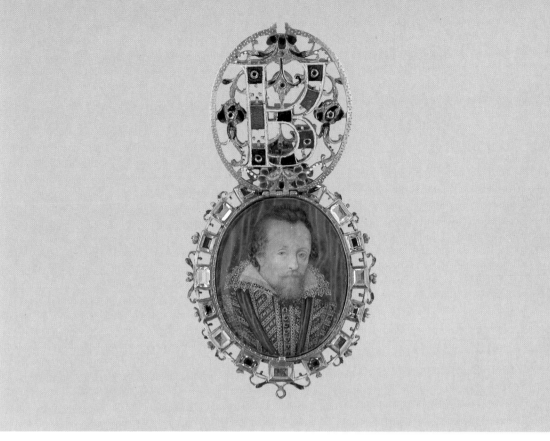

PLATE 27
Pre-Columbian
America:
6th–16th century AD
Catalogue
No.247

The Catalogue

1
The Middle East

5000-2000 BC

Western Asia

Beads are among the commonest objects found during excavations at prehistoric sites in Western Asia; they were presumably used for the same general range of decorative purposes as they are today. The demand for exotic materials, out of which beads and other items of jewellery could be made, was probably a significant factor in the growth of extensive trading networks in prehistoric and early historic times. Meanwhile the invention of glazed faience, a forerunner of glass, made it possible to imitate scarce varieties of coloured stone at relatively low expense.

A vast amount of jewellery was found in graves at the Sumerian city of Ur, in what is now southern Iraq. Several of the earlier graves, which date from about 2500 BC, were mass interments, with one principal occupant and many other attendants. These are usually regarded as royal graves, in which the king, queen, or other dignitary, was accompanied to the next world by an appropriate retinue. The men and women buried there may then have been wearing Sumerian court dress, of which jewellery was an important part.

The position of the jewellery on the skeletons enabled the excavator, Sir Leonard Woolley, to reconstruct the essential appearance of many pieces, and restring them accordingly, though some may once have been attached to clothes or cloth backings. The main materials used were gold, silver, carnelian, and lapis-lazuli. All four seem to have been abundant, though they must have been imported into Mesopotamia. The Sumerian sources of metal are unknown, but may have lain in the highland territories of Iran or Anatolia; the lapis-lazuli came from Badakhshan, in the far east of modern Afghanistan, and some at least of the carnelian originated in the Indus valley area. Agate, a stone with bands of varying shades and whose use distantly foreshadows the development of

the cameo, is rare in the royal graves but becomes more common later.

Great care was evidently taken by the Sumerians to alternate and balance the different colours of stone and metal. The workmanship is excellent, but the shapes and ornamentation are relatively restrained. Filigree work and small-scale inlay are scarce; a crude type of granulation is occasionally found. Items of jewellery, comparable in style and technology to those from Ur, have been excavated elsewhere in Western Asia, though different areas had their local traditions. J.E.R.

Egypt

During Egypt's Predynastic and Early Dynastic Period some of the standard forms of pharaonic jewellery and its techniques of manufacture were evolved. Even before the First Dynasty natural pebbles and bone had been supplemented by small gold and finely worked stone beads; glazed stone, especially steatite, was a substitute for more precious materials. The ivory bangles, massive glazed steatite girdle and forehead ornament are typical of the Predynastic Period; the diadem is unique. An ivory *serekh*-bead illustrates the type of bracelet, composed of many such beads, worn by Early Dynastic royalty. Necklaces of the period seem to have been formed from a single string of beads.

It was not until the Fourth Dynasty (about 2613–2494 BC) that the broad collar (*wesekh*), composed of many strands of beads, came into being. By this time anklets and diadems, girdles and belts, bangles and bracelets were all in use. During the Old Kingdom there was a considerable increase in the number of materials used: glazed composition becomes commoner, gold beads and amulets more numerous and often quite large.

Purely funerary diadems composed of a band of

metal with attached repoussé discs continue during the First Intermediate Period, a time of civil war and disruption from which jewellery of only the cheapest materials and crudest workmanship has usually survived. The gold bangle and gold and silver bracelet-spacers are uncommon but date towards the end of the period.

C.A.

1

1 Necklace Halaf Period about 5000 BC
Arpachiya, Iraq.

Flakes of obsidian polished on one side, holes drilled at either end; one bead of dark unbaked clay, perforated through its length; cowrie-shells with backs removed; and one black stone pendant or whetstone. The shells originally held red pigment, and traces of bitumen are around the outside. Present stringing corresponds to arrangement observed during excavation. L 5·80 (largest obsidian).

The obsidian probably derived from the Lake Van area, while the cowrie-shells must have travelled from the Red Sea or the Persian Gulf. The clay bead is apparently an imitation of obsidian.
Bibliography: Mallowan and Rose (1935), p. 97.
WAA 127814.

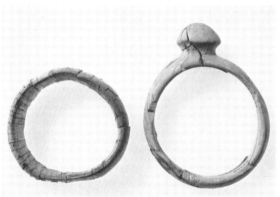

2 △   ▽ 3

2 Two Bangles Egyptian, Badarian about 4000 BC
Excavated at Mostagedda, Egypt, grave 2211, by British Museum in 1928.

(a) Ivory, slightly oval in shape, broken and repaired. Outer face convex, inner flat. D (external) 5·5; H 2·1.
(b) Ivory, with round-topped, waisted knob at top, carved from same piece of ivory. Outer rim bevelled; inside face vertical. Broken and repaired. D (external) 6; H 1·6.

Grave of child aged about three. Two of five such bangles found on the wrists. This type of bangle is typical of the Badarian culture; they seem to have been worn by males only.
Bibliography: Brunton (1937), pp. 40, 53, pl. XXV, 9, 12; Grave register, pl. IX.
EA 62221; 62223.

3 Girdle Egyptian, Badarian about 4000 BC
Excavated at Mostagedda, Egypt, grave 592, by British Museum in 1928.

Bright green glazed steatite, short and standard cylinder beads, strung closely together in nine separate rows: each of eight bone spacer-beads pierced by three holes. L 131·5; L (spacers) 2·2.

Found over the knees of a slightly bearded male. Similar massive bead girdles seem always to be found

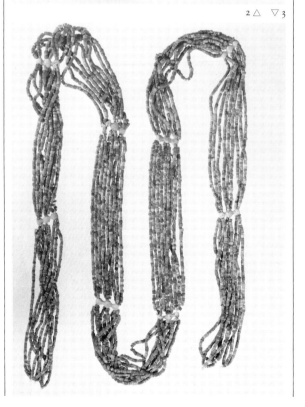

on male bodies. The spacer-beads are amongst the earliest known.

Bibliography: Brunton (1937), pp. 37, 51, 52, 60, 61, pl. XXIII, 4; Grave register, pl. VIII; Bead corpus, pl. XXXIX, 95.C.4; H. C. Beck, 'Notes on Glazed Stones', *AE* (1934), p. 70, fig. 1.

EA 62150.

4 Necklace Egyptian, Badarian about 4000 BC
Excavated at el-Badari, Egypt, grave 5449, during 1922–5.

Short cylindrical beads of green glazed steatite, carnelian barrel and disc beads and carnelian drop pendant. L 36·6; L (pendant) 2.

Found on a male. The shape of the pendant is typical of the period.

Bibliography: G. Brunton and G. Caton-Thompson, *The Badarian Civilisation* (London, 1928), Grave register, pl. VII; Bead corpus, pls. XLIX, 75.B.15; L, 86.F.14, P.8, R.14; 89.C.18.

EA 59687. Given by British School of Archaeology in Egypt.

5 Forehead Ornament Egyptian, Nagada I about 3500 BC
Excavated at Mostagedda, Egypt, grave 1890, by British Museum in 1929.

Shell, in form of open hoop with knob carved at one end; other sharpened to point. D (external) 5·5; T 0·4.

From the grave of a female, found lying just in front of the eyes. Other examples have been found with males as well as females. It seems that they were ornaments, probably charms, or possibly tribal or class distinctions; they were not for the suspension of face veils.

Bibliography: Brunton (1937), pp. 73, 88, pls. XL, 40, XLII, 37; Grave register, pl. XXXI.

EA 63088.

6 Diadem Egyptian, Nagada II about 3200 BC
Excavated at Abydos, Egypt, grave 1730, in 1925–6.

Turquoise, garnet, gold, malachite and jadeite. On one end, loop of gold beads. Beads and chips of stone on single string sections between gold beads arranged generally in order turquoise, garnet, turquoise but include beads and chips of jadeite and malachite among turquoise beads. Extra section of garnet beads at each end of diadem. Gold beads made from very narrow strips of metal turned up into rings; a few are soldered. Apart from uneven chips there are turquoise and jadeite cylindrical disc beads, garnet cylindrical, truncated convex bicone and barrel beads and malachite cylindrical disc beads. L 31·2.

4

7 △   ▽ 9

From the undisturbed burial of a woman. At the back of the head had been the string only which disappeared under the tresses. The beaded part in front went from ear to ear and seemed to hold a piece of cloth like a veil over the face.

Bibliography: H. Frankfort, 'The Cemeteries of Abydos: work of the season 1925–26', *JEA* 16 (1930), p. 214, pl. xxx, 1; Egypt Exploration Society, *Exhibition of Antiquities from Abydos and Tell el-Amarna 1925–6. Exhibited at the Rooms of the Society of Antiquaries, Burlington House, July 5th–24th, 1926* (London, 1926), p. 8, group III, A; H. R. Hall, 'Recent Egyptian Accessions', *BMQ* 1 (1926), p. 65, pl. xxxva; Wilkinson (1971), p. 11.

EA 37532. Given by Egypt Exploration Society.

Colour plate 6

7 Necklace Jamdat Nasr Period about 3000 BC
Ur, Iraq.

Beads of shell, mother-of-pearl, stone, and faience. L 8·67 (largest shell).

The people buried in the Jamdat Nasr graves at Ur, from one of which this comes, generally used locally available materials of this kind for their jewellery.

Bibliography: Woolley (1955), p. 203 (U 19247).

WAA 123596.

8 Necklace Egyptian, Nubian A-Group
about 3100 BC
Excavated at Faras, Nubia, Cemetery 3, grave 31 during 1910–12.

Beads, truncated bicones and barrels of garnet and carnelian arranged in separate groups, except for single garnet bead among carnelian. L 67·5.

The carnelian was apparently at the back of the neck reaching to the front where the garnets began.

Bibliography: F. Ll. Griffith, 'Oxford Excavations in Nubia', *Liverpool Annals* 8 (1921), p. 15.

EA 51178. Given by University of Oxford.

9 Bracelet Bead Egyptian, Ist Dynasty, Djer
about 3000 BC
Excavated at Abydos, Egypt, tomb of king Djer, in 1900.

Ivory, in form of *serekh* with panels of palace-façade and dots above it incised. Falcon on top in archaic crouched position; *serekh* pierced from side to side by two holes. H 1·6; W 0·8.

The *serekh* is a rectangular frame at the bottom of which is a design of recessed panelling such as is found in façades of early brick tombs and in false doors of the Old Kingdom. On top of the rectangular frame is perched the falcon of Horus. Within the frame is usually written the Horus name of the king; in this case there is only a dotted design. *Serekhs* occur as beads in bracelets of contemporary date and various materials: gold and turquoise *serekhs* were found on the arm of a queen of Djer (see Aldred (1971) pl. 1, top); blue glazed composition *serekhs* were found in a First Dynasty mastaba tomb at Giza.

Bibliography: W. M. F. Petrie, *The Royal Tombs of the Earliest Dynasties* (London, 1901), pp. 17, 37: duplicate in lapis-lazuli, pl. xxxv, 81; *BM Guide* (1904), p. 51, no. 107; *ibid.* (1922), p. 285, no. 107.

EA 35528. Given by Egypt Exploration Fund.

10 Necklace (Part) Egyptian, IVth Dynasty
about 2550 BC
Excavated at Mostagedda, Egypt, grave 312 by British Museum, in 1928.

Stone and gold beads and falcon amulet of gold. Stone short and long cylinders are turquoise. Gold beads are long and short cylinders and long convex bicones made from thin sheet gold folded over with rough joins where one side overlaps other. Body of falcon cast; legs are sheet gold made separately and joined to base-plate, itself a separate piece of gold. Feathering incised on legs and body; tail feathers also distinguished. Suspension loop soldered to back of head. L 17; H (falcon) 1·2; L (base-plate) 1·4.

Part of a necklace from the burial of a woman. Later the falcon amulet seems to be connected with Chapter LXXVII of the Book of the Dead: 'Spell for taking on the form of a falcon of gold'. This is an early example of an amulet frequently reproduced in stone and glazed composition.

Bibliography: Brunton (1937), p. 94, pl. LV, 1; Tomb register, pl. XLV; Bead register, pl. XLIX; Bead corpus, pl. LVII, 45.B.4.

EA 62444.

Colour plate 6

11 Court Jewellery Sumerian about 2500 BC
Ur, Iraq.

Mounted on a model, the following items: hair-ornament with three gold rosette finials fixed to modern shaft; gold hair-ribbons; three head-dresses of lapis-lazuli and carnelian beads, one with narrow leaf-shaped gold pendants, another with broad leaf-shaped gold pendants, and third with circular gold pendants having lapis-lazuli centres fastened with gold wire; pair of gold earrings; choker of alternating gold and lapis-lazuli triangles; three necklaces, one of gold and lapis-lazuli fluted beads, another of varied gold and carnelian beads, and third of biconical lapis-lazuli beads; silver dress-pin with lapis-lazuli head. H 65 (total).

This model combines items from several bodies, but the general effect must be approximately correct. Jewellery of this kind was worn by many of the attendant women buried side by side in the royal graves, and was found in position on their heads and shoulders. These items derive mainly from graves PG 1234, 1236, and 1237.
Bibliography: Woolley (1934), pp. 238–242; Maxwell-Hyslop (1971), pp. 3–13; Nissen (1966), pp. 116–8.
WAA 122411–3 (combined); 122364; 122310; 122311 and 122325 (combined); 122312; 122414–5; 122343; 122335; 122318 A; 1929, 10–17, 320; 121441.

Colour plate 1

12 Female Jewellery Sumerian about 2500 BC Ur, Iraq.

(a) Head-dress; pendants of sheet gold attached to strings of lapis-lazuli and carnelian beads. L 36·5.

The way in which head-dresses of this kind were worn is demonstrated on the model (no. 11); they were common in the royal grave PG 1237 and elsewhere. The pendants may represent young leaves of the tree *populus euphratica*.
Bibliography: Woolley (1934), p. 118 (part of U 12383); Maxwell-Hyslop (1971), pp. 3–4.
WAA 122368.

(b) Pair of spiral gold hair-rings. D 3·61; 3·58.

These rings were found with the skull of Queen Pu-abi, in grave PG 800, and it is thought that tresses of hair were passed through them. They can hardly have been earrings as Pu-abi already had a pair of these. Spiral rings were sometimes found, however, close to the ears on other bodies, and may have served various functions.
Bibliography: Woolley (1934), pp. 85, 241 (U 10942).
WAA 121361.

(c) Gold toggle-pin with incised spiral pattern on head. L 2·11.

This apparently belonged to a spare head-dress which was placed in Queen Pu-abi's grave beside her body. The quadruple spiral pattern on the head of the pin, while not new in 2500 BC, was to have a long subsequent history: similar or related designs were employed on the jewellery of Troy about 2000 BC and in Bronze Age Europe. See also no. 12 (f) and (g).
Bibliography: Woolley (1934), p. 89 (U 10984); Mallowan (1947), p. 172.
WAA 121372.

(d) Pair of gold earrings. Each incorporates two hollow crescents of sheet gold, soldered together, with curved pin from one crescent reaching over to fit into socket at end of second. L 7·2; 6·6.

Earrings of this kind (see Colour Pl. 1) were standard items of jewellery worn by women in the royal graves; this pair belonged to an attendant in PG 1237. Smaller varieties of crescent-shaped earrings became popular later; for a particularly elaborate example, see no. 41.
Bibliography: Woolley (1934), pp. 118, 241; Maxwell-Hyslop (1971), p. 4–5.
WAA 122365–6.

(e) Choker; alternating gold and lapis-lazuli triangular beads. Gold beads made from sheet metal folded in half and hammered on rods so as to leave channels for string; lapis-lazuli ones are single pieces drilled horizontally. L 22·5.

This is another standard piece of equipment from the royal grave PG 1237, and was worn around the neck as shown on no. 11. (Colour Pl. 1).
Bibliography: Woolley (1934), pp. 119, 369 (part of U 12424); Maxwell-Hyslop (1971), pp. 6–7.
WAA 122392.

(f) Gold and lapis-lazuli beads and pendants. Middle of central pendant made from two lengths of gold wire, partly twisted round each other, with four ends coiled into cones; group has been attached to a ring, itself attached to a suspender of folded and hammered sheet gold. Each of the smaller gold pendants has a single cone of gold wire attached to a similar suspender; the lapis-lazuli pendants imitate this shape. Some of the gold wire melted during assembly. L 17.

These beads were found together with no. 12 (g) and (h) in the ruins of the royal grave PG 580, and have been arbitrarily restrung; there is another example of lapis-lazuli imitating gold in no. 12 (h). The spiral cones are an elaboration of the flat spiral ornament seen in no. 12 (c) and (g).
Bibliography: Woolley (1934), p. 547 (part of U 9656); Culican (1964), p. 41; Maxwell-Hyslop (1971), pp. 10–12.
WAA 121425.

(g) Gold, carnelian and lapis-lazuli beads and pendants arbitrarily restrung. Gold items include biconical beads made from coiled wire, hollow bud-shaped pendants, and double spiral made from single piece of wire. L 18.
WAA 121426.

(h) Gold and lapis-lazuli beads and pendants, arbitrarily restrung. Gold leaf-shaped pendants made from three pieces: flat leaf; spine, which is a strip of

12c

12a

12i △   ▽ 12b

12e △   ▽ 12f,g,h

metal folded to form one loop at top; second short strip of metal, rolled to form upper loop. L 18. WAA 121424.

(i) Bull pendant, white shell with vertical perforation. L 3·5.

Large animal pendants of this nature, which were rare outside the royal graves, were either used as parts of head-dresses or were attached to the dress-pins with which clothes were fastened. This example was found out of position in what may have been a royal grave, PG 55.
Bibliography: Woolley (1934), pp. 375, 527 (U 8033). WAA 120851.

13 Male Jewellery Sumerian about 2500 BC Ur, Iraq.

(a) Head-dress; cloisonné gold roundel, with carnelian and lapis-lazuli inlay, and gold cap on central lapis-lazuli boss. Loops, inserted between sheet gold backing and outermost wire ring, attach roundel to string of beads: carnelians, in groups of four; quadruple lapis-lazuli spacer beads; gold spacer beads each made from four separate beads soldered together. Two further gold roundels, detached, have concentric rings of wire filled with openwork filigree in double rosette pattern that may have once held inlay. D (cloisonné disc) 4·5; D (filigree discs) 4·9, 4·1.

All three ornaments were found on the head of one man, buried in PG 1133, but it was not clear how the openwork roundels were attached to the remainder of the head-dress.
Bibliography: Woolley (1934), pp. 167, 574 (U 11806–7). WAA 122206–8.

(b) Head-dress; central lapis-lazuli bead, with others of carnelian and chalcedony on either side, attached to gold chain made by 'loop-in-loop' method. L 55.

This was around the head of one of Queen Pu-abi's male attendants in grave PG 800. Very similar head-dresses, with three large beads and gold chains, were regularly worn by men in the royal graves. Their function may have been to keep head-cloths in position, as do the twisted cords worn by modern Arabs.
Bibliography: Woolley (1934), pp. 89, 243 (U 10873). WAA 121487.

14 Dress-pins Sumerian about 2500 BC Ur, Iraq.

(a) Gold toggle-pin, carnelian head with gold caps. L 26·9.

This was worn by a woman, the principal occupant of the royal grave PG 1054; her cylinder-seal (compare

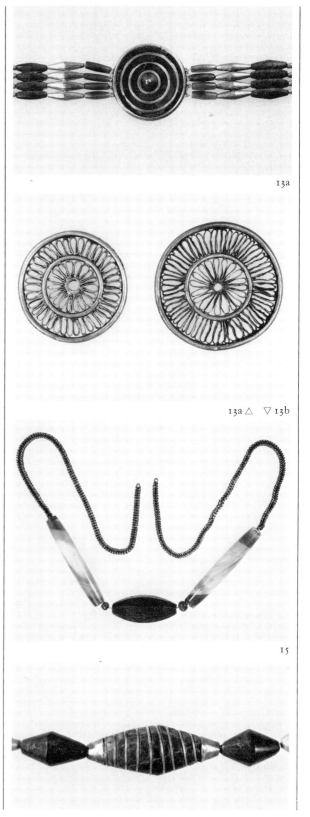

13a

13a △   ▽ 13b

15

40

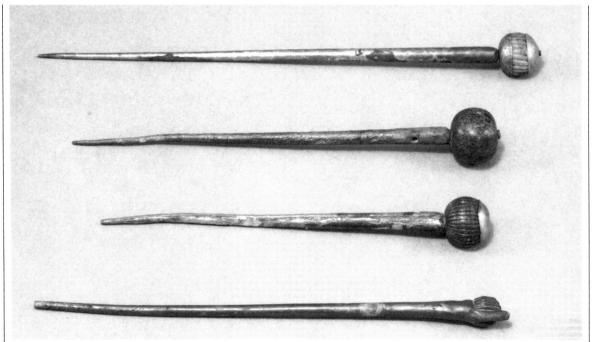

14b,c,d,e

no. 400) had been attached to it by a string, but it presumably also functioned, like the simpler toggle-pins nos. 14 (b)–(e), as a fastener for clothes.
Bibliography: Woolley (1934), pp. 106, 239, 310 (U 11903).
WAA 122204.

(b) Gold or electrum toggle-pin. Head is fluted lapis-lazuli bead, capped with separate pieces of gold. L 21.
Bibliography: Woolley (1934), p. 536 (U 8680).
WAA 120663.

(c) Silver toggle-pin with lapis-lazuli head. L 17.
Bibliography: Woolley (1934), p. 66 (part of U 10824).
WAA 121443.

(d) Silver toggle-pin with gold-capped lapis-lazuli head; point missing. L 14·7.
Bibliography: Woolley (1934), p. 119 (part of U 12406).
WAA 122347.

(e) Silver toggle-pin. Head in shape of fist, with hole passing through it; point missing. L 17·2.
Bibliography: Woolley (1934), pp. 148, 527 (U 8014); Maxwell-Hyslop (1971), p. 13.
WAA 120699.

15 Beads Sumerian about 2300–2100 BC
Ur, Iraq.

Gold and lapis-lazuli beads, arbitrarily restrung. Central lapis-lazuli bead has gold caps at either end, and gold wire inlaid in spiral around it. L 24.

Beads embellished with gold caps became increasingly fashionable in the later third millennium BC. It is unusual to find a stone inlaid with gold, rather than gold inlaid with stones.
Bibliography: Woolley (1934), p. 543 (duplicate of U 9281).
WAA 120583.

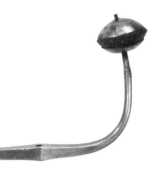

14a

16 Male Jewellery Sumerian about 2100 BC
Ur, Iraq.

(a) Frontlet of undecorated sheet gold, with hole for attachment at either end. L 14·25.

This frontlet was one of six worn on the head of the man buried in grave PG 1422; other items of jewellery found with him included no. 16(b)–(e), and a single hair-ring of the same type as no. 12(b). This man was alone in his grave; his rich jewellery suggests that he was a person of considerable importance.
Bibliography: Woolley (1934), pp. 184–7, 593 (part of U 12463); Maxwell-Hyslop (1971), pp. 65–68.
WAA 122243.

(b) Gold earring or hair-ring, made of sheet metal probably hammered over bitumen core; originally one of pair. W 3·39.

16b

Bibliography: Woolley 1934, p. 583 (part of U 12467).
WAA 122217.

(c) Necklace of carnelian and hollow gold beads. L 31.
Bibliography: Woolley (1934), p. 584 (U 12476).
WAA 122433.

(d) Gold pendant representing goat, with horizontal perforation; originally hung from necklace. H 2·34.
Bibliography: Woolley (1934), p. 583 (U 12469).
WAA 122202.

(e) Pair of hollow bracelets; hammered sheet gold. D 8·9; 8·7.
Bibliography: Woolley (1934), p. 583 (part of U 12472).
WAA 122213–4.

17 Head-band Rosettes Egyptian, First Intermediate Period about 2150 BC
Excavated at Matmar, Egypt, grave 509 by British Museum, during 1929–31.

16c △   ▽ 16d

Eleven green glazed composition pierced rosettes, each with central black-coloured boss. Radiating from bosses are slit-shaped perforations. Around rim of each rosette is rope-pattern. At back, loop for suspension. D 1·9.

Fifteen rosettes were discovered, four have remained in Cairo. From the burial of a child of about three years of age. Although found at the neck they almost certainly came originally from a head-band: cf. the diadem of Sit-Hathor-Iunet in G. Brunton, *Lahun, I, the Treasure* (London, 1920), pl. v.
Bibliography: Brunton (1948), pp. 35, 47, pl. XXXII, 79; Tomb register, pl. XXVI; Bead register, pl. LXXII; 'The Brunton Archaeological Expedition', *BMQ* 6 (1931), p. 29.
EA 63709.

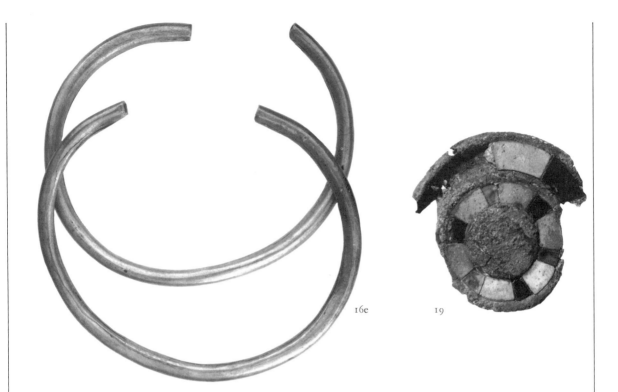

16e   19

18 Bangle Egyptian, First Intermediate Period
about 2100 BC
Excavated at Mostagedda, Egypt, grave 544 by
British Museum, in 1928.

Gold, made from two pieces of wire knotted in centre
to produce reef knot and soldered at ends into loops.
D 4·6; H 0·2.

From the body of a female; one of two such bangles
found, one on each wrist. The knot-clasp amulet
based on the reef knot became one of the most popular amulets of the Middle Kingdom.
Bibliography: Brunton (1937), pp. 101–2, 110, pl.
LXVII, 3; Tomb register, pl. XLVIII.
EA 62468.

19 Head-band Disc Egyptian, First Intermediate
Period about 2100 BC
Excavated at Matmar, Egypt, grave 306 by British
Museum, during 1929–31.

Copper worked in repoussé, hollows inlaid with segments of carnelian and green and black glazed composition. One black and two green inlays alternate
with red between each two green inlays. Inlays very
thin slivers mounted on bed of cement. On reverse,
rings for suspension have corroded away. D (max.
extant) 4·8.

The disc was found wrapped in a piece of cloth behind the neck of a child of three years. It was probably
intended to be sewn on to a cloth head-band or
attached to a metal diadem. Apparently the ornament
was damaged when buried.
Bibliography: Brunton (1948), pp. 38, 50; pl. XLI, 9;
Tomb register, pl. XXVIII; *cf*. E. Chassinat and Ch.
Palanque, 'Une Campagne de Fouilles dans la Nécropole d'Assiout, *MIFAO* 24 (1911), pl. XXVI.
EA 63438.

20 Bracelet Egyptian, First Intermediate Period
about 2070 BC
Excavated at Matmar, Egypt, grave 313 by British
Museum, during 1929–31.

Four rows of carnelian disc beads joined by four
spacer-bars. One of spacers is of gold; two of others
are of silver and have four rings. Third silver spacer-
bar has only three rings, repaired with gold one to
make four rings. Remaining beads are gold and
carnelian discs and six long cylindrical beads of green
glazed composition. L 14; L (spacers) 0·8.

From the left wrist of a woman. Silver is not a common material in this period.
Bibliography: Brunton (1948), pp. 38, 47; pl. XXXII,
150.95.F; Tomb register, pl. XXVIII; Bead register,
pl. LXXIII.
EA 63444.

2

The Middle East, Eastern Mediterranean and the British Isles

2000-1400 BC

Egypt

In Egypt, the Middle Kingdom (about 2040–1730 BC) marks a high point in the art of the Egyptian jeweller. Goldworking in every technique is carried out including ajouré, granulation, repoussé and chasing. Silver becomes more common although still rarer and more highly prized than gold. Cloisonné work is developed to sophisticated levels: an ornament spelling out a royal name (23) gives some idea of the excellence reached in the making of contemporary inlaid pectorals. Carnelian, amethyst, garnet, lapis-lazuli, green felspar and turquoise are the lapidary's favourite stones. Bracelets made from brightly-coloured beads with spacers are popular, as are *wesekh*-collars of cylinders and discs with two semi-circular terminals. Strings of metal-capped beads, often graded in size, first appear now. Gold sphinxes probably have the same significance as gold lions, later given as honorific decorations. Metal oyster-shells, usually amuletic, may have a military significance when bearing a royal name. Beadmakers and workers in precious metals worked side by side: a wall-painting from a Theban tomb, although New Kingdom in date (late fifteenth century BC) is identical with Middle Kingdom scenes in showing men drilling stone beads with multiple bow-drills and another threading a bead collar alongside a metalworker holding tongs and a blow-pipe as he anneals gold.

During the troubled Second Intermediate Period graves again contain jewellery of the poorest materials; it is not until just before the beginning of the XVIIIth Dynasty that gold returns in any quantity. The gold cats on royal bracelet spacers may have an honorific significance. A contemporary scarab-ring looks back to the Middle Kingdom for its gold mounting-plate and forward to the New Kingdom for its twisted wire shank decoration and added gold legs. During the late Middle Kingdom and Second Inter-

mediate Period the Pan-Grave culture from Nubia produces forms of non-Egyptian tradition which are to survive: earrings now appear in quantity but are not common among native Egyptians before the mid-XVIIIth Dynasty. Torcs, always rare in Egypt before the Coptic Period, are typical of the culture, as are armlets of mother-of-pearl plaques.

C.A.

21 Bead Collar and Bracelets Egyptian, XIth Dynasty about 2020 BC
Excavated at Deir el-Bahri (near Thebes), Egypt, tomb 3, in 1903.

(a) Broad collar of five rows of beads, two semi-circular terminals and seven mummiform pendants, all of glazed composition, either blue, white or purplish in colour. Four rows of vertical cylindrical beads connected only at ends, longer beads in centre of collar, shorter towards sides. Topmost row: single string of cylinder beads strung lengthwise. In centre of each row short loop of blue glazed composition disc beads. Mummiform pendants attached to bottom row. Two semi-circular terminals undecorated having ridge along underside pierced by six holes through which thread holding rows of beads is knotted. L (outermost row) 41·6; H (collar) 18·3; D (terminals) 5·5.

(b) Pair, each of two tubular silver wires joined together on one side for distance of 2·5. At opposite side to this join are two knobs forming part of clasp; on one wire are two knobs, on other one. Bracelet closed by pushing one tube over tube projecting from knob. D (maximum) 8; T (wire) 0·2.

(c) Pair, one of silver gilt and one of silver, each made of silver tube formed from thin sheet metal rolled over and joined along inner face. Each end of tube has two rings slipped over it. On one bracelet

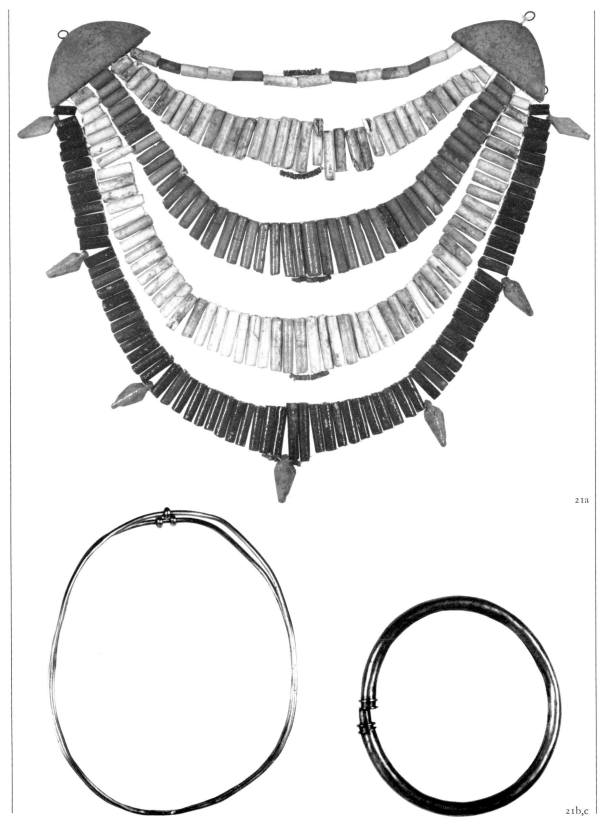

21a

21b,c

45

push-fit end can be seen clearly: closed end of tube was pushed into open end. External D (silver) 5·8, (gilt) 5·6; internal D (silver) 4·9, (gilt) 4·8.

(a) Purplish colour of the outermost row is not common until the XVIIIth Dynasty; it comes from oxide of manganese. The collar is characteristic of burials of the period.

(b) and (c) Two pairs of three found on the body of a woman. Presumably both of (c) were originally gilded. Silver becomes a little more common during the Middle Kingdom.

Bibliography: E. Naville, *The XIth Dynasty Temple at Deir el-Bahari*, London, 1907, p. 44; pl. x; *BM Guide* (1922), p. 221, no. 1.

EA 40928; 40930; 40931. Presented by Egypt Exploration Fund.

22 Sphinx Spacer-beads Egyptian, XIIth Dynasty
about 1950–1900 BC

Two thin gold-foil recumbent sphinxes, each on small rectangular pedestal with curved back edge. Sphinxes made with a punch in shaped mould; whole of each side made in one piece including pedestal: join visible down centre of nose and middle of back. Base-plate, slightly turned up at edges, added at bottom. Sphinxes have human heads and lions' bodies. Each wears beard on chin and *nemes*-head-dress with uraeus composed of gold wire curving across top of head in four loops. Beards composed of cylindrical tube, slightly corrugated, which rests on another small tube set at right angles and provides passage for stringing thread. Thus protects figure itself from being rubbed by thread or wire as does collar of gold wire at back of figure around hole where thread or wire would emerge. Sphinxes' tails made of wire and arranged around right haunch; thickened at extremity into small knob. L (bases) 2·6; 2·5.

Sphinx beads which can be dated come from the XIIth and XVIIth Dynasties, the New Kingdom and the Late Period but the uraeus with up to four curves in its body is characteristic of the time of Sesostris I.

Bibliography: *BM Guide* (1904), p. 216, nos. 176–7; *ibid.* (1922), p. 90, nos. 176–7.

EA 30486–7.

23 Inlaid Ornament Egyptian, XIIth Dynasty, Sesostris II about 1885 BC

Electrum winged scarab holding sun's disc, inlaid with carnelian, in forefeet and *kha*-sign, inlaid with green felspar above and carnelian below, in back feet. *Kha*-sign is flanked by two papyrus heads, inlaid with green felspar, whose wire stems surround and unite three bottom symbols. These two wires curve around underneath but do not reach as far as base of papyrus heads. Scarab's head and wing-cases are inlaid with

lapis-lazuli, its back with green felspar. Only four legs represented, made of flat wire, rectangular in section, soldered to underside of body. Notched forelegs hold circular cloison of sun's disc. Wings are filled with strips of carnelian, green felspar (missing on left side and replaced recently by green-painted inlay), lapis-lazuli, carnelian and green felspar, all arranged side by side, with lapis-lazuli at one wing tip and dark-blue glazed composition at other. These strips are not set in cloisons but set side by side held in position by glue or cement. Reverse undecorated, being smooth except for body of scarab which has four grooves across it imitating underside of beetle. Tubes, incised to represent separate rings, soldered to underside of wings at slight angle. H 1·8; L (wing) 1·5; L (scarab) 1.

The design represents the prenomen of Sesostris II, Khakheperre. Each of the cloisons seems to have been made from a single piece of electrum folded up in a mould. The tubes on the underside could have been used for sewing the ornament to a cloth or for a suspension wire or thread. A virtual duplicate consisting of a winged scarab, head missing, with *kha*-sign below and lotus flowers under the wings was found in tomb A 124 at el-Riqqa on the chest of a male: see R. Engelbach, *Riqqeh and Memphis* VI (London, 1915), pl. I, 1.

Bibliography: *BM Guide* (1922), p. 96, no. 668; Wilkinson (1971), p. 90.

EA 54460.

Colour plate 6

24 Metal-capped Beads Egyptian, XIIth Dynasty
about 1900–1800 BC

(a) Thirty-nine bright-blue glazed composition ball beads capped at each end with silver and gold knot-clasp amulet. Some beads have very glossy surface. Caps are discs of silver with central hole over which tube is soldered. Tubes cover inner cylinder comprising rolled piece of copper stuck into opening of bead. One bead has cap missing: only tube remains. Knot-clasp stamped in two halves; on underside of one half a flat plate is cut by central groove; on flat underside of other half, mounted on strip of gold, a flange fits into groove and joins two halves together. L 72·8; L (knot-clasp) 1·4.

(b) Forty long convex bicone beads of amethyst with gold-foil caps, graded in size, and uninscribed amethyst scarab. Gold-foil caps made from pieces of sheet gold folded in at boring at each end of beads. On beads with missing caps glue visible which once held foil in place. Back of scarab divided into three sections by incised lines. Head is indicated and legs shown by rough incisions. L 69·5; max. L (beads) 2·4; L (scarab) 2·5.

(a) Said to come from Thebes, Egypt. Knot-clasp amulets are characteristic of the XIIth Dynasty. Identical ones of gold have been found in the burials of Sit-Hathor, Meret, Khnemet, Senebtisi and Sit-Hathor-Iunet.

(b) Gold- and silver-capped beads are typical of Middle Kingdom jewellery. The scarab is also of a type characteristic of the period.

Bibliography: (a) *Salt Collection* (1835), lot 60; *BM Guide* (1922), p. 100, no. 763; (b) *BM Guide* (1922), p. 95, no. 599.

EA 3084; 32220.

25 Oyster-shell Pendant Egyptian, XIIth Dynasty about 1950–1800 BC

Thin sheet gold, hollow on inside. Ring at top has broken away and been carelessly re-soldered. Upper surface inscribed with name Senusert (Sesostris) in cartouche. H 4·9; W (max.) 4·3.

The shell represented is probably *Avicula (Meleagrina) margaritacea*. Gold and electrum oyster-shells inscribed with the prenomen of XIIth Dynasty kings are not rare (cf. Petrie (1914), pl. XIV, 112c; R. Engelbach, *Riqqeh and Memphis*, VI, London, 1915, pl. I, no. 4; W. C. Hayes, *The Scepter of Egypt*, I, New York, 1953, fig. 149). However it is doubtful if the inscription in this instance is authentic: the fourth and fifth signs are orthographically peculiar. The later addition of the inscription does not invalidate the authenticity of the shell itself: uninscribed metal oyster-shells are a popular amulet of the Middle Kingdom. H. E. Winlock (*Studies Presented to F. Ll. Griffith*, London, 1932, 388–91) believed that inscribed natural oyster shells were military decorations; perhaps the metal ones were also.

Bibliography: *Catalogue of the Egypt Exploration Society's Exhibition of the results of the recent excavations at Amarna and Armant and a loan exhibition of Egyptian Jewellery. Wellcome Historical Medical Museum, 8th September to 3rd October, 1931* (London, 1931), p. 38, no. 72. EA 65281. Sir Robert Mond Bequest.

26 Bracelet Egyptian, Middle Kingdom about 2000–1800 BC

Said to be from Thebes, Egypt.

Six strings of stone beads threaded between five metal spacer-bars. Latter made in two halves, each decorated with three horizontal and six vertical knobs representing multiple beads. Four are electrum; one having seven divisions and made from gilded silver is probably modern. Beads oblate, spherical, standard and long truncated convex bicone in shape made from amethyst, carnelian, lapis-lazuli, green felspar and turquoise. Two large spherical beads, one at each

24a △ ▽ 25

47

26

end, are green glazed quartz although much of glaze is rubbed away. L 23·8; H (spacers) 1·8: D (quartz beads) 1.

The narrow cigar-shaped beads and spacers of this type are found in jewellery of the New Kingdom as well as the Middle Kingdom but glazed quartz is relatively uncommon after the XIIth Dynasty.
Bibliography: *Salt Collection* (1835), lot 640.
EA 3082.

27 Openwork Plaque Egyptian, XIIth Dynasty, Ammenemes IV about 1795 BC
Gold, representing king Ammenemes IV (Makherure), offering vase of unguent to Atum, god of the setting sun. Frame composed of two uprights supporting sign for heaven with bar along bottom. Atum wears double crown with uraeus, is bearded and wears collar and tunic with straps over his shoulders. From his belt hangs tail, now broken. Front of his kilt is tied in 'Girdle of Isis' knot, the *tit*. In his right hand he carries *ankh*-amulet and in his left *was*-sceptre King wears *khat* bag-wig with uraeus, collar and kilt with elaborate apron. Between the two figures are signs for 'giving unguent'; above Atum signs for 'Atum, Lord of Heliopolis', and above king 'the Good God, Makherure'. There is solder in some places, notably at Atum's feet. On reverse there is no surface decoration. Three pins are soldered onto this side: one in centre of heaven-sign, one at top of legs of each figure. H 2·8; W 3; T 0·05.

The technique is true ajouré (cutting out from a piece of sheet metal). There are no rings for suspension on this object and although it is usually called a pectoral in descriptions of it there is little reason to suppose it was one. It is more likely to have been the covering for a cylindrical amulet (cf. WAA 27381, *BM Guide* (1922), p. 218, no. 18) or the decoration from a small box or ointment vase, held in position by the three pins on the reverse.
Bibliography: A. Moret, *Académie des Inscriptions et Belles Lettres, Comptes Rendus des Séances de l'Année, 1928* (Paris, 1928), p. 34; H. R. Hall, 'An Open-work Gold Plaque of Amenemhet IV', *BMQ* 4 (1929), p. 1, pl. 1a; *BM Guide* (1964), pp. 40, 211; E. Feucht-Putz, *Die Königlichen Pektorale. Motive, Sinngehalt und Zweck* (Bamberg, 1967), pp. 38–9, no. 7.
EA 59194. Given by Birmingham Jewellers' and Silversmiths Association.

28 Torc and Earrings Egyptian, Pan-Grave about 1800–1500 BC
Excavated at Mostagedda, Egypt, grave 3120 by British Museum, in 1929.

48

(a) Thick silver wire, ends being beaten out into wide thin flange and then curled up. Max. internal D 14·1; T (wire) 0·3.

(b) Silver, pair of hoop-style made from thick wire. Ends overlap slightly and have been drawn into blunt point. Max. internal D 3·6; T (wire) 0·3.

(a) Torcs are not a common form of jewellery in Egypt before Coptic times but the Pan-Grave people were of Nubian descent, influenced by Black African traditions.

(b) One of two pairs of earrings found on the ears. Earrings were not worn with any regularity in Egypt before the mid-XVIIIth Dynasty. Both torc and earrings come from the grave of an oldish female.

Bibliography: **(a)** Brunton (1937), pp. 116, 129, pls. LXXIV,3,ab, LXXV,16; Tomb register, pl. LXX.

(b) *ibid.*, pp. 116, 129, pls. LXXIV,3,ab, LXXV,17; Tomb register, pl. LXX.

EA 63211; 63213.

29 Bracelet Egyptian, Pan-Grave
about 1800–1500 BC
Excavated at Hu, Egypt, grave X 58, in 1898–9.

Formed from twenty-seven oblong strips of mother-of-pearl pierced by holes at top and bottom bored from both sides. L 16·6; L (longest plaque) 2·6; W (max.) 0·8.

A characteristic form of Pan-Grave jewellery, these armlets seem often to have been worn in threes on the forearms. They have been rethreaded in the ancient manner.

Bibliography: W. M. F. Petrie, *Diospolis Parva, The cemeteries of Abadiyeh and Hu, 1898–9* (London, 1901), p. 46; pl. XL.

EA 30849. Given by Egypt Exploration Fund.

30 Two Spacer-bars and Scarab-ring Egyptian, XVIIth Dynasty, Nubkheperre Inyotef
about 1650 BC
(a) Possibly from the tomb of Queen Sobkemsaf at Edfu, Egypt; **(b)** Said to be from Thebes, Egypt.

(a) Gold, from bracelet. On top of flat box enclosed at ends but open at sides recline three cats, heads erect, facing forward. Through width of box between upper and lower plates run twelve tubes, made from rolled up strips of gold not completely joined, for threading. Cats' legs and tails made from beaten gold wire; bodies and heads probably not cast but hand-made; ears added separately. Inscription roughly incised on base between horizontal lines: 'The Good God, Lord of the Two Lands, Inyotef, given life. The Great Royal Wife, who has assumed the Beautiful White Crown, Sobkemsaf, living.' The other inscribed on base: 'The Good God, Lord of the Two Lands, Nubkheperre, given life forever. The Great Royal Wife, who has assumed the Beautiful White Crown, Sobkemsaf, living.' L (base) 3; W 1·8; Total H 1·2.

Colour plate 6

(b) Lapis-lazuli scarab with details of head only marked, set in gold funda. Three holes drilled each side of scarab and two more, one at each end. Former holes for legs of gold wire which are joined to rim of funda, itself made from plate of sheet gold with rim around. At either end of funda are soldered rings to protect ends of scarab. Shank goes under scarab between its body and funda. Thin twisted gold wire is wound around upper part of shank at both sides of scarab; one of wires goes through scarab to hold it in position. Base of funda inscribed with name 'Inyotef', not in cartouche. External D (shank) 2·6; L (funda) 1·6; H (scarab and funda) 0·9.

Nubkheperre Inyotef was one of the earliest Theban princes to reject Hyksos suzerainty: see W. C. Hayes, *CAH*, II, 1, Cambridge, 1973, pp. 70–1. For similar spacer-bars with cats cf. Aldred (1971), pl. 84.

Bibliography: **(a)** *Catalogue of an Exhibition of Ancient Egyptian Art, Burlington Fine Arts Club* (London, 1922), p. 18; pl. L; H. E. Winlock, *The Rise and Fall of the Middle Kingdom in Thebes* (New York, 1947), p. 112; pl. 47; *BM Guide* (1964), p. 211; Wilkinson (1971), p. 94; pl. XXVIIB.

(b) *Catalogue of an Exhibition of Ancient Egyptian Art, Burlington Fine Arts Club* (London, 1922), p. 18; pl. L; H. E. Winlock, 'The Tombs of the Kings of the Seventeenth Dynasty at Thebes', *JEA* 10 (1924), p. 233, note 5.

EA 57699–700; 57698. Given by C. W. Dyson Perrins.

27

30b

Minoan and Mycenaean Jewellery

The art of making gold jewellery seems to have reached Greek lands about 2400 BC. Tombs in Crete of this date have yielded diadems, hair ornaments, beads and bracelets of sheet metal, and quite elaborate chains, chiefly of the loop-in-loop variety. These forms derive ultimately from Babylonian prototypes.

About 2000 BC the more sophisticated techniques of filigree and granulation were introduced into the island of Crete from Western Asia. No. 31, of the 17th century BC is a good example of these techniques. A richer source of Minoan jewellery of this period is the so-called Aegina Treasure, a large collection of personal ornaments and gold plate acquired in 1892 and said to come from the island of Aegina (nos. 32–34).

Minoan jewellery gives place about 1450 BC to Mycenaean. The Mycenaean culture, which takes its name from the key site of Mycenae, was to a large extent a mainland Greek offshoot of the Minoan culture. The principal difference in the jewellery of the two cultures is that the Mycenaean is more plentiful but less adventurous in content than the Minoan. Rightly did Homer call Mycenae 'rich in gold'. The Mycenaeans obviously had a richer source of gold to draw on but this source has not yet been established.

Pure Mycenaean jewellery is poorly represented in the British Museum, for nearly all of it is in Greek museums. From Cyprus, however, we have a large collection of jewellery, part Mycenaean and part Oriental, chiefly from the Museum's excavations at Enkomi at the end of the last century. This jewellery comprises for the most part simple funerary diadems and mouthpieces (no. 35), earrings of several forms (nos. 36–38) with occasionally beads and pendants of higher quality (no. 40).

The Minoan–Mycenaean world ended about 1100 BC and gold jewellery of any quality was absent from Greek lands until about 850 BC.

R.H.

31 Pendant Minoan 17th century BC
Crete

Gold, in form of bee. Body and wings decorated with filigree and granulation. Eyes probably inlaid. H 1.9.
Bibliography: *BMCJ*, no. 1239.
G & R 75.4–6.2.

32 Pendant Minoan 17th century BC
Said to be from Aegina.

A Nature-god stands on a field with lotuses, holding in either hand a water-bird. Behind him are two curved objects, probably composite bows. Five discs hang from the pendant. H 6.

There is Egyptian influence to be seen here.
Bibliography: *BMCJ*, no. 762; *GRJ*, p. 64.
G & R 92.5–20.8

33 Pectoral Minoan 17th century BC
Said to be from Aegina.

Gold. Curved plate ending in human heads in profile. Ten discs hang below. Eyes and eyebrows formerly inlaid. W 10.8.

Much Egyptian influence is exhibited.
Bibliography: *BMCJ*, no. 761, *GRJ*, p. 65, pl. 4A.
G & R 92.5–20.7.

34 Earring Minoan 17th century BC
Said to be from Aegina.

Gold. Within a hoop in the form of a double-headed snake are a pair of monkeys and above them a pair of greyhounds; from the circumference hang owls and discs on chains. Carnelian beads threaded in various places. D 6.5 (hoop).
Bibliography: *BMCJ*, no. 765, *GRJ*, p. 65, pl. 4B.
G & R 92.5–20.13.

35 Funerary Mouth-piece Cypro-Mycenaean 14th or 13th century BC
Excavated at Maroni, Cyprus, in 1897.

Gold, embossed with spirals and rosettes. L 10.
Bibliography: *BMCJ*, no. 188.
G & R 98.12–1.74.

36 Pair of Earrings Cypro-Mycenaean 14th or 13th century BC
Enkomi, Cyprus (Tomb 24), excavated 1896.

Gold, of 'leech' shape. H 4.5; 4.7.
Bibliography: *BMCJ*, nos 328–9; *GRJ*, p. 88, pl. 12H.
G & R 97.4–1.34 and 35. Turner Bequest.

37 Pair of Earrings Cypro–Mycenaean 14th or 13th century BC
Enkomi, Cyprus (Tomb 92), excavated 1896.

Gold, in form of circular hoop made from two strips twisted round each other. D 2.5.
Bibliography: *BMCJ*, nos. 348–9; *GRJ*, p. 88, pl. 12D.
G & R 97.4–1.480 and 481. Turner Bequest.

38 Pair of Earrings Cypro–Mycenaean 14th or 13th century BC
Enkomi, Cyprus (Tomb 61), excavated 1896.

Gold. Hoop of thin wire threaded with stylised figure of bull's head. H 3.2.
Bibliography: *BMCJ*, no. 525; *GRJ*, p. 88, pl. 12G.
G & R 97.4–1.239 and 240. Turner Bequest.

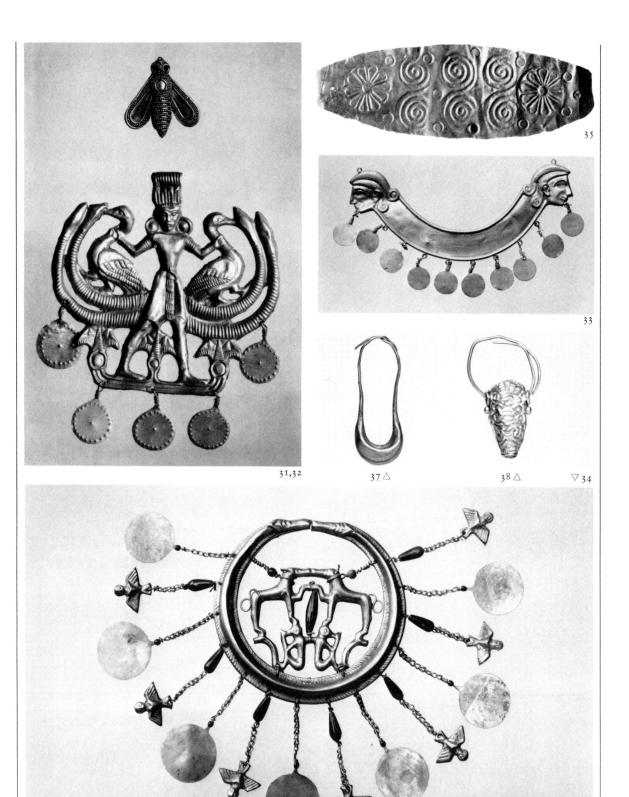

35

33

31,32

37 △

38 △   ▽ 34

51

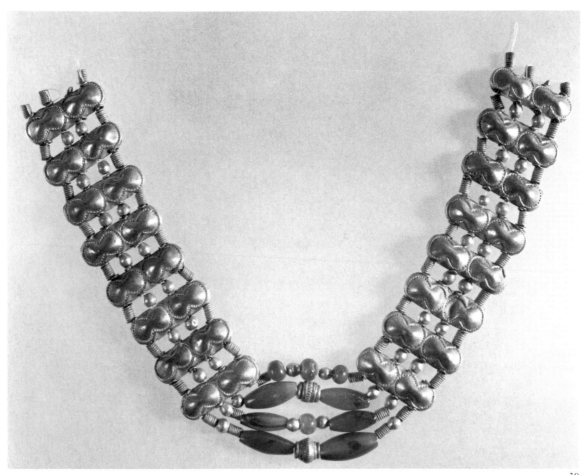

39 Necklace Cypro-Mycenaean 14th century BC
Enkomi, Cyprus (Tomb 93), excavated 1896.

Gold. Sixteen doubled shield-shaped beads, with
other beads of gold and carnelian. H. 3·5 (shield
beads).
Bibliography: *BMCJ*, no. 580.
G & R 97.4–1.604. Turner Bequest.

40 Pendant Cypro–Mycenaean 14th century BC
Enkomi, Cyprus (Tomb 67), excavated 1896.

Gold, in form of pomegranate. Fine granulation.
H 3·6.
Bibliography: *BMCJ*, no. 623; *GRJ*, p. 75.
G & R 97.4–1.356. Turner Bequest.

Western Asia

In the centuries after 2000 BC, the miniature techniques of goldworking, especially filigree and granulation, became popular on jewellery throughout
Western Asia. Craftsmen, especially on the Mediterranean coast, amalgamated skills and fashions of

40

diverse origins, and some of the finest pieces of jewellery come from tombs and hoards excavated in this area, notably at Tell el-'Ajjul in southern Palestine. An innovation is the use of thin sheets of gold soldered together back to back, giving an air of solidity to objects which are really hollow.

J.E.R.

41 Earrings Old Babylonian Period about 1900 BC
Ur, Iraq.

Pair of crescent-shaped gold earrings decorated below with embossed spikes and, at either end, with circular filigree cloisons and granulation. H 3·33; 3·14.
Bibliography: Maxwell-Hyslop (1960), pp. 112–4; Woolley and Mallowan (1976), p. 232 (U 10405 A).
WAA 121416.

42 Necklace Hittite about 1700–1500 BC
Gold necklace of wire with pendants in shape of hawks; each hawk originally had three disc pendants attached, several are missing. W 13·1.
Bibliography: Barnett (1960), p. 29; Porada (1976), p. 52.
WAA 132116.

43 Pendants Palestine about 1600 BC
Tell el-'Ajjul, Palestine.

(a) Gold pendant or earring made from two sheets of gold soldered together back to back, joint being covered by wire to which clusters of granules are attached. Front sheet convex, and decorated with filigree and granulation. W 4·57.
Bibliography: Petrie (1934), p. 6, no. 28; Maxwell-Hyslop (1971), pp. 116–7; Stewart (1974), pp. 30–33.
WAA 130762.

(b) Gold pendant or earring, resembling no. 43(a), but more crudely worked, with granulation attached to bosses on surface. W 3·61.
Bibliography: Petrie (1934), p. 6, no. 30.
WAA 130763.

(c) Gold pendant or earring of sheet metal cut in shape of hawk, with granulated and filigree decoration. W 3·38.
Bibliography: Maxwell-Hyslop (1971), p. 118.
WAA 130764.

(d) Gold pendant or earring in shape of winged disc with oval above and small discs at angles of wings, all originally inlaid with blue glass; underneath is stylized animal-head with horns. W 3·81.
Bibliography: Petrie (1934), p. 7, no. 52; Maxwell-Hyslop (1971), pp. 118–20.
WAA 130767.

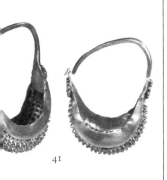

41

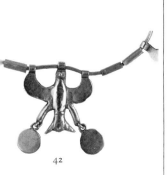

42

43a

43b

43c

43d

The British Isles

By about 2000 BC the craft of metalworking had been introduced into the British Isles, working copper and gold in the first instance. The first items to be made of metal were prestige goods, for chieftains and their families, such as basket earrings and lunulae. As metalworking intensified, so new techniques were discovered, and new metals created by the deliberate addition to copper first of arsenic, later of tin. In the centuries following 2000 BC, when these events were taking place, chieftains managed to amass a great deal of wealth, by controlling the long-distance trade in the necessary raw materials, and were able to divert much effort towards the manufacture of luxury items in various materials, many of them now used for the first time. One of these was jet; the Melfort necklace bears witness to the skill with which it was worked. Like many others of these luxury items, this necklace was placed in a grave with the dead.
M.S.

44

44 Earrings (Pair) British Early Bronze Age
about 2100–1800 BC
Excavated at Boltby Scar Camp, North Yorkshire, England, in 1939.

Sheet gold; half-tubular with rounded sides and ends; a hook arises from centre of one side and curves round to meet other; decorated around edge, in repoussé relief beaten up from inside, with spaced bosses flanked by ridges. L 3·2 and 3·1; W 1·3 and 1·3; WT 1·2 and 1·1.

The earliest goldwork in Britain consisted of jewellery hammered out into thin foil, and decorated with simple geometric designs. Earrings of the 'basket' type are rare finds, and are associated with 'Beaker' pottery.
Bibliography: Brailsford (1953), p. 34; Butler (1963), p. 187.
P & RB 1940.4–4.1–2.

45 Lunula Irish Early Bronze Age
about 1800–1500 BC
Found in Ireland.

Sheet gold flat crescentic neckring with rounded rectangular terminals twisted at right angles to the plane of the crescent; the geometric zoned ornament, executed by chasing and scoring, is symmetric about vertical axis and concentrated towards terminals; outer edge trimmed down in antiquity, removing most of outer ornamental border; when terminals overlapped to close ring (effected with thong?), lunula becomes conical (both inner and outer edges

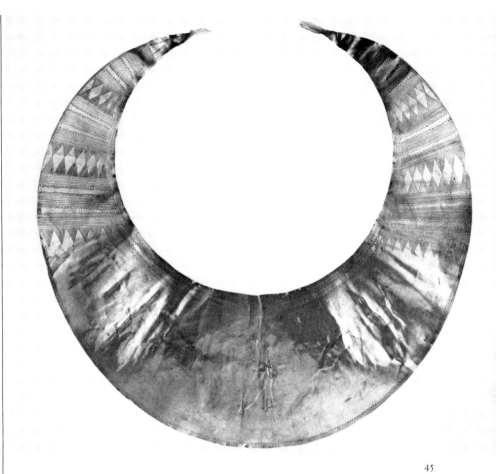

45

forming near-true circles) and rides well on the base of the neck. W 23·7; WT 81·2.

More than one hundred lunulae have been recorded in north-western Europe, the great majority of them in Ireland. Not all of them were made in Ireland; there is some evidence for their manufacture elsewhere, for example in Brittany. In contrast to other jewellery of the period, lunulae are never found in graves but occur as isolated finds, occasionally in small hoards. Their ornamental repertoire derives from contemporary pottery. A number of styles has been recognised on lunulae, among them the 'Classical' to which the present specimen belongs. The arrangement of the ornament on the lunulae is probably matched on the contemporary spacer-bead jet necklaces from northern Britain, e.g. from Melfort (no. 46).

Bibliography: Craw (1928–9), fig. 11.36; Sandars (1968), pp. 161, 162, pl. 170; Taylor (1970), pp. 54, 72, no. NLI 26.

P & RB 45.1–22.1.

46

46 Necklace North British Early Bronze Age
about 1800–1500 BC
Melfort, Argyll, Scotland.

Jet necklace-components comprising:
(a) small triangular toggle with V-perforation drilled in from basal edge; H 1·0; W 2·8.
(b) two triangular terminals, each originally with single perforation at apex and four perforations drilled in from lower edge at an oblique angle so that they emerge from back 8 mm. from edge; decorated in pointillé technique with triangular motifs within a larger triangular frame, and inverted triangle at apex of frame. H 5·3 and 4·7; W 3·4 and 3·0.
(c) six trapeze-shaped spacer-beads ornamented in two styles, three in one, three in other – both in pointillé technique: one style corresponds to style of (b), with filled triangles and reserved (plain) lozenges; other has plain zigzags reserved against filled triangles; perforations drilled through from long side to long side: first style of beads has two beads with four perforations on one side and five on other (one of the four bifurcating to become five), and one with five perforations on one side and eight on other; second style has one bead with five perforations on both sides, and other two beads have five perforations on one side and nine on other; largest bead 5·0 by 2·4.
(d) fifty-one fusiform or elongated barrel-shaped beads of various dimensions, the longest 2·8.

The necklace components are made from two varieties of jet (here called A and B): A is generally well preserved with shiny polish, and is black in colour; B has a crazed surface, poorly preserved, is brown in colour. Twenty-two of the elongated beads are of jet A, 29 of jet B. The triangular toggle and the three spacer-beads with reserved zigzag designs are of jet A, the triangular terminals and the other three spacer-beads of jet B.

Like all surviving jet necklaces, this specimen was found in conditions that did not permit detailed observations to be made regarding its probable original design. However, such necklaces, when found, normally consist of six trapeze-shaped spacer-beads, a pair of triangular terminals, a triangular toggle, and a varying number of fusiform beads. The present specimen is thus no exception. However, incomplete necklaces are also known from certain burials, particularly in northern and eastern England where the type is exceptional rather than quite common as it is in Scotland; the combination of spacer-beads with two different designs, coupled with the fact that these designs differ on beads of two different materials, and that the fusiform beads are also of the same two different materials, suggests that parts of two necklaces were put together just or some time before burial. It is generally assumed that these necklaces were laid out to imitate the contemporary lunulae (see no. 45), with the decorated spacer-beads close to the triangular terminals, and the fusiform beads separating the spacer-beads and filling up the central part of the necklace.

Found in a cist (stone-lined grave) with a pair of bronze armlets (now in the National Museum of Antiquities of Scotland, Edinburgh) on a skeleton.
Bibliography: Proceedings of the Society of Antiquaries of Scotland, Vol. 19 (1884–5), pp. 134–6; Callander (1915–16); Craw (1928–9); Smith (1920), p. 100, fig. 104; Brailsford (1953), p. 36, pl. VII.1; *BMG* (1976), p. 161, fig. 12.

P & RB 90.4–10.1.

Egypt

1500-900 BC

In form and technique New Kingdom jewellery is generally similar to that of the Middle Kingdom except that coloured glass is often used in imitation of stone and that both ear-plugs and earrings become far more common. The varied forms of the latter include leech shapes and open hoops, some with suspension loops; others are made from triangular-sectioned tubes. Heavy gold *shebyu*-collars and hollow gold *awaw*-bangles, few of which have survived, can be seen depicted on the black granite torso of a late XVIIIth Dynasty official (no. 51) and both these and gold flies were honorific decorations, first awarded during the early XVIIIth Dynasty.

Broad collars show considerable variation, especially during the Amarna Period when floral elements of multicoloured glazed composition become popular. Gold floral and inlaid elements from collars and nasturtium-seed beads from a girdle, all found in a royal XVIIIth Dynasty burial, have been combined in a double string. Gold and stone pendants, beads and a scarab have been restrung in the fashion of late XVIIIth Dynasty royal jewellery. A gold torc is rare. A pair of gold and inlay bracelets date to the end of the New Kingdom but their tradition can be traced back to the Middle Kingdom.

C.A.

47 Necklace Egyptian, XVIIIth Dynasty, Tuthmosis III, about 1480 BC
Tomb of the Three Princesses at Thebes, Egypt.

Beads and pendants at present strung as necklace. Two strings separated by ten gold *nefer*-signs, seven with remains of decayed inlay, three with plain gold fronts, and single large gold drop-shaped pendant inlaid with carnelian, green glazed steatite and decayed glass or glazed composition, probably once green or blue in colour. Base-plates of closed *nefer*-signs have holes to allow for escaped air. Drop pendant comprises base-plate with rim added; two bands of gold divide it into three zones for inlaying. Outer string comprises small short cylinders of gold, carnelian and blue glass. Two short barrels of red jasper at top and bottom of drop-shaped pendant. Inner string consists of twelve groups of three beads, always gold in centre flanked by two lapis-lazuli or blue glass beads, or two green felspar or turquoise-blue glass beads: many are nasturtium-seed beads, others spherical or oblate. These groups separated by long bicones of carnelian, red jasper, green felspar and turquoise-blue glass. All beads separated from one another by one or more gold short cylinders. Gold beads formed from strips of metal folded over. Pendant string contains beads of carnelian, lapis-lazuli, gold and turquoise-blue glass. L (outer row) 65·5; L (inner row) 58·5; L (drop pendant) 2·7.

See Aldred (1971), pls. 65, 66 for identical beads and pendants from the same tomb. The nasturtium-seed beads probably originally came from a girdle: cf. Wilkinson (1971), pl. XLVIIA, from the same tomb.
Bibliography: *Catalogue of the Egypt Exploration Society's Exhibition of the results of the recent excavations at Amarna and Armant and of a loan exhibition of Egyptian Jewellery. Wellcome Historical Medical Museum, 8th September to 3rd October, 1931* (London, 1931), p. 42, no. 127; H. E. Winlock, *The Treasure of Three Egyptian Princesses* (New York, 1948), pp. 19–22, 37.
EA 66827. Formerly in Captain E. G. Spencer-Churchill Collection.

Colour plate 7

48 Glass Ear Ornaments Egyptian, XVIIIth to XIXth Dynasties about 1400–1300 BC
(g) Excavated at el-Amarna, main town, Egypt, in 1921–2; (h) Excavated at Mostagedda, Egypt, grave 5110 by British Museum, in 1929.

(a) Earplug of papyrus-column form. Shaft opaque dark blue, glossy surface. Flat capital edged with dark-green thread. Pierced vertically. H 2·8.
(b) Earplug of papyrus-column form. Opaque dark blue, glossy surface. Yellow spiral encircles shaft and continues on to capital. Pierced vertically. H 2·7.
(c) Earplug of palm-column form in dark blue, once glossy now filmed. Shaft and capital, in form of four foliations, virtually covered with elaborate chevron pattern in opaque white and yellow. Pierced vertically. H 2·7.
(d) Earplug in papyrus-column form in turquoise-blue. White spiral encircles shaft and runs onto capital. Both base of shaft and edge of capital outlined with opaque yellow threads. Pierced vertically. H 2·8.
(e) Earring pendant in form of pomegranate, one of pair with EA 48064. From heavy loop in opaque turquoise-blue hangs inverted pomegranate of same material as body, glossy surface. Yellow thread encircles centre of body and outlines foliations. H 2·4; D 1·2.
(f) Penannular earring formed from cane of dark blue, circular in section, drawn into open-ended circle; ends drawn into two vertical hoops. Prefabricated twisted cord of opaque white and dark blue decorates outer circumference. Piece of gold wire threaded through loops and ends twisted together. D 2·5.
(g) Penannular earring, formed from cane of translucent palest green, circular in section, drawn into circle with open sheared ends. D 2·2.
(h) Pair of penannular earrings, each composed of twisted thread of opaque turquoise-blue and dark brown. Narrow opening. D (larger) 1·8; D (smaller) 1·6.
(i) Earring pendant of opaque yellow in penannular form built on metal wire, still in place. Suspension loop of body material. Three prefabricated twisted cords of opaque white and semi-translucent pale blue run around outer circumference of thick crescent from open end to open end where they form two vertical hoops, one now damaged. H 2·4; D 1·7.

(a)–(d) Although these objects are identical in shape with glazed composition earplugs of similar date they are pierced as though for stringing. The hole through the shaft is probably due to the manufacturing method; even if it is intentional for stringing, these pieces could have been earring pendants on a thin metal ring. (e) These pairs of pendants seem to have been worn from metal rings which passed through the ear lobes. (f) Originally this type of earring would have been worn with a bar passing through the loops and a hole in the ear lobe: cf. Aldred (1971), pl. 68. (g)(h) Worn by stretching the flesh of the lobe so as to pass through the open end. The pair come from a child's burial. (i) Possibly worn on a ring of metal which passed through the lobe. Cf. *Salt Collection* (1835), lot 618.
Bibliography: (a)–(c) Cooney (1976), nos. 986, 994, 995. (e) *ibid.*, no. 1019; *Sale Catalogue of the Athanasi Collection of Egyptian Antiquities*, London, March 13th 1837, lot 358. (f) Cooney (1976), no. 999. (g) *ibid.*, no. 1006. (h) *ibid.*, no. 1010; Brunton (1937), pl. LXXX, 19; Tomb register, pl. LXXVIII. (i) Cooney (1976), no. 1032.
EA 29255; 29263; 29264; 68531; 2895; 14508, formerly in the Castellani Collection; 57516, given by the Egypt Exploration Society; 63347; 64186, given by Professor Percy E. Newberry.

49 Fly Pendants Egyptian, New Kingdom about 1550–1300 BC
(a) Pair of gold flies. Gold foil moulded over core which still remains. Both identical and have same details of eyes, ridging around neck, curved stripes over rump and striations on folded wings on both sides. Ring soldered to head. L 2; W (max) 1·2.
(b) Thirty-eight gold fly pendants cast solid, upper side decorated, underside flat and many oblate and spherical beads of garnet. L 24; L (flies) 1·4; W (across end) 0·6.

(a) Gold flies may have originally been solely military awards but probably came to be a decoration for which any courtier was eligible: see Wilkinson (1971), 98–9. (b) Fly pendants which are undoubtedly ancient are hollow not cast, yet in form these pendants are typical and identical with other fly amulets in different materials.
Bibliography: (a) H. R. Hall, 'Egyptian Antiquities from the Maxwell Collection', *BMQ* 4 (1930), p. 104; pl. LVIII. (b) I. E. S. Edwards, 'The Late Sir Robert Mond's Bequest', *BMQ* 14 (1940), p. 5; pl. VI.
EA 59416–7. Given in memory of Sir John Maxwell by Committee members of Egypt Exploration Society; 65279. Sir Robert Mond Bequest.

50 Collar Egyptian, XVIIIth Dynasty about 1500–1320 BC
Excavated at Abydos, Egypt, tomb 101A, in 1925–6.

Four rows of glass and glazed composition beads separated by twelve bone spacer-bars each with ten perforations, three glass eye-beads and fifteen glazed composition pendants. Beads, mostly disc, short cylinders and short barrels, arranged generally in

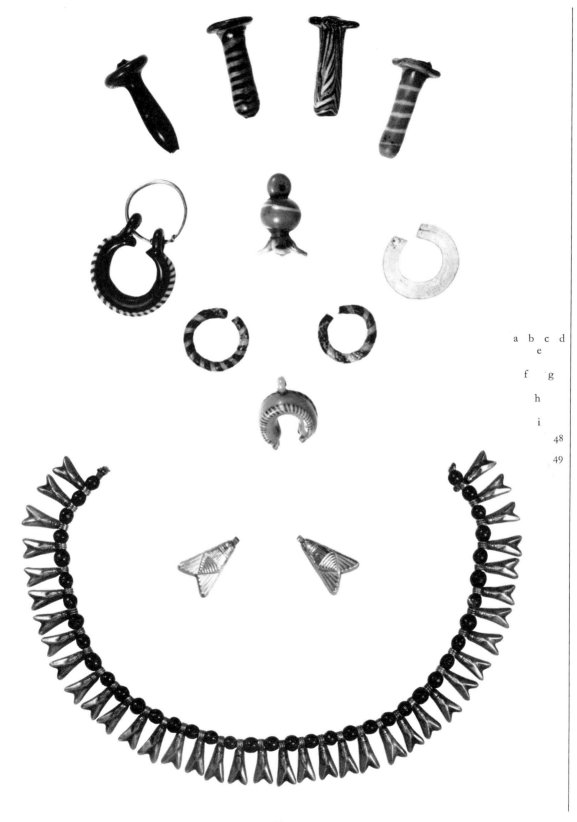

a b c d
    e
f   g
    h
    i
        48
        49

groups of one colour: blue, yellow, orange, blue and white, with one string of red and same arrangements repeated in reverse order to end of row. Blue pendants flat-backed lotus-seed vessels. Red, white and blue eye-bead at each end and central white and black spot bead. L (top row) 28·8; L (bottom row) 35·4; L (spacers) 3·7.

Obviously the collar is missing six rows of beads to judge from the number of perforations in the spacers. There would also presumably have been a terminal, probably lunate in shape, at each end.
Bibliography: H. R. Hall, 'Recent Egyptian Accessions', *BMQ* I (1926), pl. xxxv, b.
EA 58610. Given by Egypt Exploration Society.

51 Collar and Armlets Egyptian, XVIIIth Dynasty about 1500–1320 BC
(a) Three rows of gold ring beads strung tightly together. Terminals consist of five rings soldered together into tube, three tubes thus formed being soldered side by side. Pierced cup with ring set at right angles to rim soldered at one end of each tube. When two terminals were brought together rings in cups would be in alignment, allowing gold locking pin to be inserted. Attached to each terminal are two loop-in-loop gold chains each ending in lapis-lazuli bell-shaped bead. L (outermost string) 19·4; L (innermost row) 17·8; L (terminals) 0·9.

(b) Two hollow gold armlets. Strip of thin sheet gold equal in length to proposed external diameter of armlet is beaten into shape on wooden ring and its two ends soldered together in step-shaped join so as to form three-sided hoop with internal face open. Onto this open face is placed strip of thin sheet gold joined at top and bottom to hoop by soldering. One of armlets badly crushed at one side. D (external) 11·9; D (internal) 8; H 1·9.

A torso of a late XVIIIth Dynasty official, carved in black granite (EA 66718) indicates how these items would have been worn;
(a) This type of collar, sometimes with four strings, was part of an honorific decoration and was called in Egyptian a *shebyu*-collar. Few in gold have survived.
(b) Also part of an honorific decoration and very rare, these gold armlets were called in Egyptian *awaw*-bangles.
Bibliography: (a) *BM Guide* (1922), p. 100, no. 791; Wilkinson (1971), p. 108; (b) Wilkinson (1971), p. 101.
EA 14693; 66840/1. Formerly in Castellani Collection.

52 Beads and Floral Pendants Egyptian, XVIIIth Dynasty, Amarna Period about 1380–1350 BC El-Amarna, Egypt.

(a) One tier of collar composed of glazed composition beads and floral pendants. Beads are bright blue cylinders. Green date palm leaves alternate with yellow and blue mandrake fruits and red and mauve poppy petal pendants. All pendants have suspension loops at top and bottom so as to join two rows of collar. L 28·7; L (palm leaf) 2·6.
(b) Another tier of floral collar with bright blue glazed composition cylinder beads. Yellow, white and mauve lotus petals alternate with mandrake fruit, corncockle pendants and palm leaves, all of various colours, and individual lotus flowers and buds, thistles, bunches of grapes and unique leafy branch or multiple jasmine blossom pendant. Suspension loops at top and bottom. L 29·5; L (lotus petal) 3·4.
(c) Third tier of floral collar. This time there are bright blue glazed composition disc beads as well as cylinders. Between every green date palm leaf is a grape bunch and a daisy. The grape bunches are either blue or red; the daisies are either white with yellow centres or else all blue. All are of glazed composition. Suspension loops at top and bottom. L 32·2; L (palm leaf) 2·9.

Some of the bunches of grapes do not have a lower suspension loop, presumably they were intended for the lowest row of the collar. Originally pendants of the same height would all have been strung in a single row. All were made in moulds and are flat-backed. Most of the glaze is still very bright. These floral collars, so characteristic of the Amarna Period, imitate garlands of real flowers.
Bibliography: cf. W. M. F. Petrie, *Tell el-Amarna* (London, 1894), pls. XVIII–XX.
EA 57884; 57885; 57886. Formerly in Bethell Collection.

53 Collar Egyptian, XVIIIth Dynasty, Amarna Period about 1380–1350 BC Excavated at El-Amarna, Egypt, House S 35.4, during 1926–9.

Three rows of pendants, interspersed with beads and two lotus terminals, all of glazed composition. Top row of yellow and blue mandrake fruit, middle of green date palm leaves and lower of yellow, white and mauve lotus petals. Beads between pendants are all tiny discs of red, blue, mauve or yellow. Terminals, of lotus shape, are inlaid with red, yellow, blue and green glazed composition to indicate petals. L 52; H 7·5; W (terminals) 5·2.

The glaze is still very bright. The collar was found apparently complete but the order of stringing could not be determined.
Bibliography: J. D. S. Pendlebury, *The City of Akhenaten*, II (London, 1933), pp. 44, 78, pl. XXXVI, 1; S. R. K. Glanville, 'Egyptian Antiquities from el-Amarna and Armant', *BMQ* 4 (1929), p. 77; *BM Guide* (1964), p. 198.
EA 59334. Given by Egypt Exploration Society.

Colour plate 7

54 Torc Egyptian, New Kingdom
about 1400–1200 BC
Composed of thin gold discs strung tightly together on thick cord. At each end gold cup with hole in base through which cord passes. External D 15·1; internal D 13·4.

The torc has the appearance of the scaley body of a snake. The cord is original.
Bibliography: *BM Guide* (1874), p. 71, erroneously numbered 3354; *ibid.* (1879), p. 72, erroneously numbered 3354.
EA 3359. Formerly in Anastasi Collection.

54

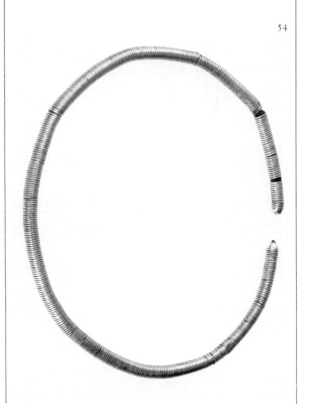

55 Earrings Egyptian, New Kingdom
about 1500–1200 BC

(a) Electrum, leech or boat-shaped. Piece of sheet metal was folded over shaped core and joined along inner circumference and possibly along outer. Joins masked by wire notched to indicate beading. Wire passing through ear is attached at top. W 1·9; H 2·9; T (max.) 0·8.

(b) Gold, formed from sheet metal cut into two circles and raised by beating to form one side of hoop. Two halves soldered together, line being visible on inside but masked on outside by 'rope braid' decoration. Loops to hold pin which passed through lobe of ear were soldered on either side of central depression allowing room for ear-tip. Ends covered with piece of metal, one pierced with escape hole for air. D (external) 3·4; T (max.) 1·1.

(c) Gold, pair of ribbed earrings made from six separate tubes, triangular in section, soldered together. Tubes made by folding metal over wire and pressing or hammering to make ribbed edge on exterior; wire then removed. On one side of hoop thus formed from soldered tubes, two central tubes are longer by 2·3 cm. and are decorated on outer circumference with 4 cm. of twisted gold wire. Ends of tubes finished with plate of gold covering holes. External D 4·6; H 1·3.

(d) Gold, pair of ribbed earrings made from five tubes of sheet metal, triangular in section. Central tube is longer at one end and on either side of it gold wire has been soldered. Flower with five rounded petals soldered at point where outer tubes end: made in two pieces, moulded front and flat back-plate, soldered at circumference. D (external) 2·8; H 1; D (rosette) 0·9.

(a) This type of earring appears to date usually to the late XVIIIth Dynasty. (b) This form is identical with glass penannular earrings. (c)–(d) Cf. Aldred (1971) pl. 48; H. E. Winlock, *The Treasure of Three Egyptian Princesses* (New York, 1948), pl. VIII, B. This seems to have been one of the most popular types of earring during the XVIIIth Dynasty and was evidently worn by women rather than men, often a pair in each lobe.
Bibliography: (a) Cf. H. Schäfer, G. Möller and W. Schubart, *Ägyptische Goldschmiedearbeiten. Königliche Museen zu Berlin. Mitteilungen aus der ägyptischen Sammlung* (Berlin, 1910), pl. 14, no. 90. (b) Cf. Vernier (1927), pl. XXIX, 52.355.
EA 2864, formerly in Anastasi Collection; 14346; 54315–6, Franks Bequest; 54317–8, Franks Bequest.

56 Earring Egyptian, XIXth Dynasty,
Queen Tausert about 1209–1200 BC
From tomb 56, Valley of the Kings, Thebes, Egypt.

Gold, barrel-shaped open hoop with inlaid cartouche of Queen Tausert formed in two hollow halves of thin sheet gold, triangular in section, soldered so that two points form upper and lower rims of earring. Two plates cover hollow ends, each with escape hole for air. On outer surface of ring is sunken plate roughly rectangular in section in which are set gold strip cloisons forming feather-topped cartouche containing name Tausert. Most of inlay material missing but remainder appears to be decomposed glass. Green material is adhesive. D (external) 2·4; D (internal) 0·7; H 1·6; L (inlaid section) 2·2.

This earring is one of a pair; the other is in Cairo, see Vernier (1927), pl. XXVI, 52.331. It came from excavations in tomb 56 of the Valley of the Kings. Tausert was one of the last rulers of the XIXth Dynasty: see R. O. Faulkner, *CAH*, II, 2 (Cambridge, 1975), p. 239.
Bibliography: Wilkinson (1971), p. 155.
EA 54459.

57 Bracelet and Necklace Egyptian,
XVIIIth Dynasty about 1370–1350 BC
(a) Collection of gold, carnelian and glazed composition beads and lapis-lazuli scarab now strung as bracelet. Gold beads are long truncated convex bicones, cylinders and discs and three large short truncated convex bicones all formed from thin sheet metal folded over and joined along one edge. Carnelian beads of same shapes. There are number of blue glazed composition short cylinders; other glazed composition beads, red, yellow, green and blue are all disc beads. Lapis-lazuli scarab set in gold; gold wire outlines thorax and wing-cases. Legs hold bar consisting of six rings for threads. Hairs on legs indicated by chased lines. L 19·1; L (scarab) 2·8; W (bracelet) 1·7.

(b) Collection of beads and pendants now strung in two rows. Top row: green glass barrel beads, long truncated convex bicones of gold, single gold short cylinder and carnelian bell-shape at either end. Lower row: long and short barrels of carnelian and red jasper, short cylinders of blue glazed composition and discs and two spherical beads of gold. Upper row of drop-shaped pendants made of sheet gold base-plate to which was soldered convex upper plate. Air-hole in each base-plate. Rings soldered at top and bottom. Lower row corncockle pendants have gold calyx made from two pieces of gold foil over core with bracts indicated, bound at top and bottom by band of gold. Flower with serrated edge is blue glazed composition held in position by gold spike. Suspension ring soldered to base ring of calyx. L (lower row) 34; L (drop pendants) 2·2.

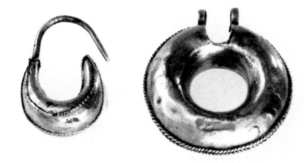

56 △　▽ 55c,d

(a) Collection of loose beads, pendants and a scarab strung in the fashion of royal jewellery of the end of the XVIIIth Dynasty (cf. Wilkinson (1971), pl. xxix, E). (b) An identical corncockle of gold and glazed composition is in the Metropolitan Museum, New York.
EA 65616; 65617.

58 Pair of Bracelets Egyptian, XXIInd Dynasty, Sheshonq I about 940 BC
Said to come from Sais, Egypt.

Gold with lapis-lazuli and blue glass inlay. Each has panel containing raised gold figure of Harpocrates seated on lotus, flanked by uraei wearing sun discs. Details of Harpocrates' body and those of uraei are chased. Panel framed at each side by vertical pattern and above by gold tubes between strips of inlay. Remaining part of each bracelet decorated with chevron pattern formed of gold alternating with inlays.

Although most of inlays lost, to judge from pale blue cement which remains they were dark blue. However there are traces of red inlay between tips of lotus flowers. Bracelet opened by hinge composed of three striated tubes along edge of main panel and secured by pin. Identical inscription incised inside each bracelet reads: 'Made for the King's-Son-of-Ramesses, Leader of the entire army, Nemareth, justified, his mother [being] daughter of the Great Chief of the Meshwesh, Penreshnes.' D 6·4; H 4·2.

The technique of decorating a surface with cut out and chased figures surrounded by inlay is found in the early XVIIIth Dynasty. Prince Nemareth was a son of Sheshonq I, founder of the XXIInd Dynasty: see K. A. Kitchen, *The Third Intermediate Period in Egypt*, (Warminster, 1973), p. 290, section 246.
Bibliography: *BM Guide* (1922), p. 89, nos. 134–5; *ibid.* (1964), p. 211; Wilkinson (1971), p. 172; pl. LXII,A.
EA 14594–5.

58

4

Europe and Western Asia

1400-600 BC

North-west Europe

The great gold cape from Mold in North Wales (no. 59) represents the culmination of the north-west European Early Bronze Age metalworking tradition in its mastery of the techniques of beating out and embossing sheet gold on a large scale. From then on, that is, from about 1500 BC, attention was diverted for the most part in temperate Europe towards different techniques of working gold: casting, twisting bars, and making wire.

In contrast to the Continent, very little of the 'jewellery' from Britain and Ireland has been found in burials, so there is more than a suspicion that much of what scholars have long accepted as jewellery may never have been so intended or used; pieces such as the bronze 'Sussex-loop armrings' (no. 70), the gold 'dress-fastener' (no. 80), the 'hair-ring' (no. 73), the gold 'sleeve-fastener' (no. 76), and so on, may also have been used as 'special-purpose' currency for quite specific kinds of contracts and transactions. Numerous hoards of bronze and gold ornaments (rarely mixed) have been found, one of them, of gold, from Ireland, weighing about 5 kg (and possibly much more); two 'bracelets' (no. 78) from this find are included. A major invention of this period was the brooch, of safety-pin type (*fibula*). The four in this section (nos. 61–63) give some indication of the interest that began early and ran right down through later prehistoric into historic times in Europe (see also below in **7** and **8**). The delicacy of one from Holstein (no. 61) contrasts vividly with the extraordinary exuberance of the one from Moravia (no. 63), while the pair of gold wire from Hungary (no. 62), together with other ornaments from the same find, show how a consistent style could be created from such simple techniques as wire-making, twisting, and the creation of spirals. Indeed, all four brooches, together with a neckring from Denmark

(no. 64) and a Central European armlet (no. 60), represent in various ways the pleasure taken in the spiral motif in the European Bronze Age.
M.S.

59 Cape British Early Bronze Age about 1400 BC
Found with a necklace of amber beads on the skeleton of a man under a cairn called Bryn-yr-ellyllon at Mold, Flintshire, Wales, in 1833.

Sheet gold; curved lower edge, rising at arms and sagging front and back; near-circular opening for neck at top; incomplete, in several pieces, largest comprising front, smallest a tiny fragment; in present reconstruction a small piece has been added to complete circuit at back; ornament in bands (more at front than at back) following neck opening, and comprising ridges and lines of larger or smaller bosses, beaten up from inside in repoussé technique; at each side a triangular panel is included to compensate for 'dead' space caused by rise of cape over shoulder; larger bosses of four designs: conical, crested lenticular, pyramidal and rectangular; smaller of two: conical and domed; the crested lenticular bosses merge into each other; larger bosses (except in lateral triangular panels) ringed by dotted lines made with centre-punch from front; same decorative technique used to edge many of the ridges and, inside, to highlight the interfaces on the pyramidal and rectangular bosses; perforations along upper and lower edges and at various points over surface, and fragments of sheet bronze, attest to existence of bronze frame to which cape attached by rivets, and to ancient repairs of cracks; two surviving fragments probably formed part of a pair of shoulder-straps recorded at time of discovery. Reconstructed H 25·5; W 46·2.

This unique object, with its banded ornament suggesting the fall of a cloth cape, represents the apogee of sheet gold working at the close of the British Early Bronze Age. As it is unique, it is not easy to place in its precise cultural milieu; scholars have found it difficult to resolve the chronological contradictions to which their stylistic and technical analogies have led them. Some of the parallels drawn are not so very close (e.g. the north European embossed gold vessels of Montelius Period III), but, when discounted, the chronological problems begin to melt away; the closest both in Britain (the Melfort armlets) and on the Continent (the Schifferstadt cone) belong to the mid-second millennium BC.

Broken up on discovery, the fragments were dispersed, some of them being remodelled as parts of pieces of small jewellery; the present fragments have been acquired by the Museum at various dates since 1836. Some recently acquired pieces are not included in the reconstruction.

Bibliography: Gage (1836); Smith (1920), pp. 93–4, fig. 98, pl. VII; Davies (1949), pp. 256–63, fig. 94; Grimes (1951), pp. 86, 199, no. 588, pl. IX; Brailsford (1953), p. 36, pl. VIII.2; Powell (1953); Powell (1966), pp. 152–5, ills. 145–7; Burgess (1974), pp. 197, 311, note 207.

P & RB 36.9–1; 56.10–14.1; 57.12–16.1; 77.5–7.1; 81.5–14.1; 81.5–16.1–2; 83.12–7.1; 1927.4–6.1; P1972.6–1.1–4.

Colour plate 2

60 Armring Central European Middle Bronze Age
about 13th century BC

Bronze, with geometric chased or scored ornament on hoop, and chased nicks on spiral terminals. D 12·2 by 10·5; WT 278·9.
P & RB P1974.12–1.269. Formerly in Pitt Rivers Collection.

61 Brooch North European Middle Bronze Age
about 12th century BC
Holstein, Germany.

Bronze; two-part construction; head-spiral, bow, catch and foot-spiral made of wire; pin (? cast in a mould) threaded on before head-spiral coiled up; bow and catch ornamented with grooving in imitation of twisted work; chased nicks on beginnings of spirals. L 7·0; WT 5·8.

One of the earliest types of brooch in Europe.
Bibliography: Smith (1920), p. 133, fig. 140a.
P & RB 68.12–28.341. Formerly in collection of G. Klemm of Dresden.

62 Suite Central European Late Bronze Age
about 11th–9th century BC

Banks of the Danube between Duna-Földvár and Paks, Hungary.

Suite of jewellery made of gold wire comprising:
(a), (b) pair of 'Posamenterie' brooches, each of composite construction: a single wire forms large foot-spiral, catch, bow (where it is twisted), figure-of-eight head, four-coil spring, and pin; attached to bow by three strips of gold are four lengths of wire, two a side, with spiral terminals. L 7·7 and 7·8; WT 28·1 and 26·3.
(c) four-armed piece with spiral terminals branching from central plate through which there is a slot for attaching the piece on to a rod; probably mounted with similar pieces to form a ? pectoral ornament. H 5·1; W 11·9; WT 30·3.
(d), (e) pair of loop-pendants each with two spiral terminals and twisted loop. W 5·0 and 4·6; WT 14·6 and 14·3.

One of the finest groups of gold-wire Late Bronze Age jewellery of the 'Posamenterie' style discovered in Central Europe.

Collection of S. Egger of Vienna; sold at Sotheby's on 25 June 1891 (lots 112–5); Pitt Rivers Collection until acquired by the Museum in 1974.
Bibliography: *British Museum Report of the Trustees 1972–1975*, p. 50, pl. VIII; for Posamenterie brooches, see von Merhart (1947), and for objects similar to the ? pectoral ornament-fragment, see Vinski (1959), and Hartmann (1970), pls. 48–9.
P & RB P1974.12–1.342–6.

63 Brooch Central European Late Bronze Age
about 10th century BC
Sechovic wood, near Tisnov (near Přerov), Moravia, Czechoslovakia.

Bronze; two-piece construction; ring-headed pin made separately and threaded on before head wound up into spiral; spirals at both ends have simple chased ornament, laid out in segments and executed before coiling; oval plate has chased linear and dotted ornament and simple repoussé bossing. L 35·3; L (pin) 25·7; WT 334·7.
A particularly large specimen of the rare *Blechblattbügel* type of brooch, made in an early phase of the Urnfield period. Found with a twisted bronze bracelet of uncertain type (Greenwell coll. lot 526; present location unknown).

Collection of Canon William Greenwell; sold at Sotheby's on 24 June, 1918 (lot 506).
P & RB 1964.12–6.113. Bequeathed by C. T. Trechman, 1964.

60

61

62

63

64 Neckring North European Late Bronze Age
8th century BC
Isle of Fyn (Fünen), Denmark.

Bronze, cast, mock-torsion ring with oval plates leading through loops, which hook together, to wrought spiral terminals; on plates now barely visible chased design. D 20·9 by 18·4; WT 232·3.

A type of neckring worn by high-ranking women throughout southern Scandinavia in the penultimate phase of the Bronze Age (Montelius V); for the type, see Baudou (1960), pp. 55–6, pl. XI: type XVIC2.
P & RB 69.7–24.69.

65 Neckring North European Late Bronze Age
7th–6th century BC
Haldensleben, East Germany.

Bronze, wrought, with ten changes of direction of twist; of cruciform section except for terminals which are of rectangular section, in opposing planes, and stepped to secure tight rabbet joint. D 16·1 by 15·1; WT 185·0.

The *scharflappig* variety of *Wendelring*, a type of neck-ring worn by high-ranking women in the final phase of the Bronze Age and earliest phase of the Iron Age in the northern half of Germany and southern Scandinavia.
Collection of Canon William Greenwell.
Bibliography: Smith (1920), p. 139; for the type, see Baudou (1960), p. 57, pl. XI: type XVID2.
P & RB WG1188. Given by J. Pierpont Morgan, 1909.

66 Collar Iberian Late Bronze Age
about 7th century BC
Near Sintra, Portugal.

Gold; three swelling bars joined at ends; (?)chased chevron and zigzag zoned ornament in middle and on either side; each of four lotus-like cups attached by spike-headed rivet to central bar, after chased ornament at sides had been executed; curved rectangular link has projections either end, one acting as hinge, other as hook, and has five parallel longitudinal ridges, outer and central simply ornamented with chased oblique lines; collar designed for neck of English collar-size 12–13, therefore presumably for child or woman. D 13·1; WT 1262.

The finest Late Bronze Age neckring from Iberia, with features of the design reflecting both local traditions and connexions as far afield as southern Scandinavia.
Bibliography: Smith (1920), p. 158, fig. 168; Powell (1966), pp. 181–2, ill. 180; Hawkes (1971).
P & RB 1900.7–27.1.

67 Pin Later Tumulus Culture (Central Europe)
about 13th century BC
From Hallstatt, Upper Austria.

Cast bronze; biconical circular head with running S-scroll ornament on end-face, scalloped design underneath, and pair of grooves around edge; lengths of spiral grooving intermittently down stem; oblique perforation through head from centre of end-face to top of stem. L 39·7; D 5·5; WT 257·8.
P & RB 1939.5–1.3.

68 Dress-Pin North French Middle Bronze Age
about 1200–1000 BC
Ramsgate, Kent, England.

Cast bronze; head circular with low dome; below chased or scored ornament extends to point just below swelling which is transversely perforated; perforation probably for thread which helped to secure it to clothing. L 27·4; D (head) 1·6; WT 53·5.

One of a small group of 'Picardy' pins imported from north-east France into south-east England together with a group of armrings decorated in similar style; see Rowlands (1971).
Bibliography: Hawkes (1942), pp. 26, 28–9, 33, no. 7, fig. 2.3.
P & RB 1954.10–2.4.

69 Pin Alpine and North Italian Early Iron Age
about 7th century BC
From the cemetery at Hallstatt, Upper Austria.

Cast bronze, with elaborately modelled head, and with separately made (also cast bronze) and similarly ornamented ferrule to protect point of pin. L (pin) 40·6; L (ferrule) 3·8; combined L 49·0; D (pin-head) 1·8; L (modelled section of pin) 9·2; WT (pin) 81·1; WT (ferrule) 9·8.

Collected by Sir John Lubbock at Hallstatt in the 1860s; presented by his son, the second Lord Avebury, in 1916.
Bibliography: Read and Smith (1916), pp. 154–6, fig. 18.
P & RB 1916.6–5.300–1.

70 Armrings British Middle Bronze Age
12th century BC
Found in a mound at Hollingbury Hill, Brighton, Sussex, in 1825.

Bronze; each wrought from bar, one of diamond, other of rounded section. D (greatest) 8·3; 8·2; WT 168·1; 238·6.

Two of a group of four 'Sussex loops' from a hoard

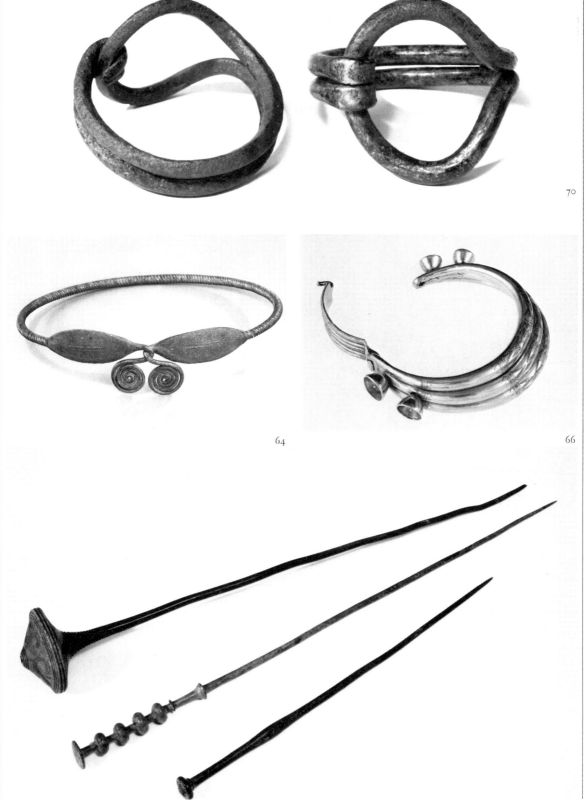

70

64

66

69

67,68,69

of bronzes which also contained three coiled finger-rings, a torc and a palstave. It is a type only found in Sussex, normally in pairs, in hoards assigned to the 'Ornament Horizon' of the southern British Middle Bronze Age, a period when large numbers of personal ornaments (armrings, bracelets, finger-rings, pins and torcs) were hoarded. This hoard came to light within the ramparts of the later hillfort of Hollingbury, which probably developed from an earlier palisaded settlement with which the hoard of bronzes may well be associated.

Bibliography: *Archaeological Journal* 5 (1848), pp. 323–5, fig; Curwen (1937), pp. 177, 218–9, table I, no. 5; Brailsford (1953), p. 34, fig. 13.4; Brown and Blin-Stoyle (1959), p. 203; Smith (1959), p. 153; for the site, see Curwen (1932), and Bradley (1971).
P & RB 53.4–12.16–17.

71 Torc Middle Bronze Age about 1200–900 BC
Borders of Glamorgan with Brecknockshire, Wales, 1838.

Gold; twisted bar of cruciform section with plain terminals of circular section soldered on and bent backwards; torc re-wound up into 3½ coils since discovery. L 11·6; WT 231·5.

The 'Tara' type of torc, found in Britain, Ireland and northern France. Although it is generally held that all those found outside Ireland were exported from there, it may be noted that the Irish specimens are never found coiled up, but the British usually are. The terminals of the Irish specimens are hooked to each other. If these torcs were used as jewellery, which is actually by no means certain (for they might also, or otherwise, have been used as a special purpose currency), then a difference in use is likely: in Ireland worn about the neck, in Britain about the arm.

Bibliography: Smith (1865), p. 1140, fig; Crawford (1911–12), p. 46; Wheeler (1925), pp. 171–2; Hawkes (1932); Maryon (1938); Grimes (1951), pl. IX; Savory (1958), p. 8; Eogan (1964), p. 281
P & RB 38.1–28.1

72 Torc Irish Later Bronze Age about 1200–900 BC
Inishowen, Co. Donegal, Ireland.

Gold; twisted ribbon with sample hook-terminals ending in tiny knob-finials. D (closed) 11·7; WT 12·3.

This type of torc, in bronze or gold, was in fashion in Britain and Ireland at the close of the second millennium BC; all the Irish specimens are of gold, and date to the first, 'Bishopsland' phase of the Later Bronze Age there.

Collection of Canon William Greenwell.
Bibliography: *J. Arch. Ass. Irel.*, 4th series, VI, p. 180;

71 △   ▽ 72

for the type, see Eogan (1964), pp. 280–1.
P & RB WG2. Given by J. Pierpont Morgan, 1909.

73 'Hair-ring' ('Ring-money')
Irish Later Bronze Age about 1200–800 BC
Fuaraig Glen, Glen Avon, Banffshire, Scotland.

Sheet gold wrapped around hollow (?)copper(-alloy)
penannular ring, with tapered ends. D 3·0 by 2·7;
WT 24·3.

Such rings are variously interpreted as 'ring-money',
that is, as a form of currency, or, on analogy with
contemporary Egyptian rings of the same design, as
'hair-rings'. Probably imported into Scotland from
Ireland. For the type, see Armstrong (1933), pp. 34–5;
Hawkes (1961), pp. 453–4; Eogan (1964), p. 272.
 Collection of Canon William Greenwell.
Bibliography: Coles (1959–60), p. 91.
P & RB WG23. Given by J. Pierpont Morgan, 1909.

74 Earring Irish Later Bronze Age
about 1200–1000 BC
Gold; twisted bar with plain, tapered terminals.
D 2·5 by 2·3; WT 7·3.

One of a small group of earrings from western
Europe apparently influenced by contemporary designs in the Near East; see Hawkes (1961); Eogan
(1964) p. 272, fig. 3. This example appears to have
been found in Ireland; precise findplace unknown.
P & RB 74.3–3.9.

75 Earring Middle Bronze Age about 1200–1000 BC
Dinnington, Northumberland.

Gold; twisted bar with plain, tapered terminals.
D 2·6 by 2·3; WT 15·3.
As preceding earring (no. 74).
 Collection of Canon William Greenwell.
P & RB WG22. Given by J. Pierpont Morgan, 1909.

76 'Sleeve-Fastener' Irish Later Bronze Age
8th–7th century BC
Found near Tara Hill, Co. Wexford, Ireland.

Gold; swelling hoop, partly ornamented (inner face
plain) with longitudinal grooving ending close to
each terminal in finely cross-hatched band bordered
on each side by three parallel grooves; plain disc-
terminals. W 2·3; D (terminals) 1·6; WT 38·7.

An Irish type, found outside Ireland only in western
Scotland. Conventionally considered to have been
used like a modern cuff-link, with the hoop projecting
outside the sleeve; however, such a use is precluded
on certain specimens owing to the size of the terminals which are sometimes very large, and some-

73

74,75 △   ▽ 76

times very small. Perhaps simply used as a special purpose currency. For the type, see Wilde (1862), p. 65; Armstrong (1933), pp. 30, 65–8, pl. XIV.141–74; Hawkes and Clarke (1963), p. 223, fig. 52.4; Eogan (1964), p. 304.
Bibliography: Brailsford (1953), p. 36, fig. 14.4.
P & RB 49.3–1.8.

77 'Lock-ring' Irish Later Bronze Age
8th–7th century BC
Cheesburn, Northumberland.

77

Gold; triangular section penannular ring, longitudinally grooved on all three faces; end-faces plain. D 1·8; WT 4·7.

An Irish type, exported to Britain. Manner of use uncertain. For the type, see Savory (1958), pp. 14–5; Hawkes (1961), p. 454; Eogan (1964), p. 304.
  Collection of Canon William Greenwell.
P & RB WG20. Given by J. Pierpont Morgan, 1909.

78 Bracelets (Two) Irish Late Bronze Age
8th–7th century BC
Ballykitty, near Newmarket-on-Fergus, Co. Clare, Ireland.

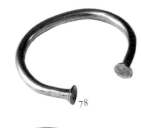

78

Gold; penannular hoops of circular section with expanded terminals, flat on thinner, dished on fatter bracelet. W 6·8 and 8·5; WT 65·3 and 238·2.

Found in a very large hoard of gold ornaments in March 1854; other pieces from the hoard are in the British Museum and in the National Museum of Ireland in Dublin. The bracelets are of 'Covesea' type which is found throughout Britain and Ireland.
Bibliography: Armstrong (1917); Armstrong (1933), p. 17; Proudfoot (1955); Hawkes and Clarke (1963); Eogan (1964), pp. 304–6.
P & RB 57.6–27.1 and 3.

79 Bracelet Late Bronze Age 8th–7th century BC
Morvah, Cornwall.

Gold; hollow; slightly swelling hoop of oval section, decorated on outer face with seven zones of chased or engraved triangles defined by transverse grooves; conical ('trumpet-mouth') terminals. W 8·3; WT 69·9.

From a hoard of six gold bracelets, two like the present specimen, the other three of different types.
Bibliography: Smith (1920), p. 52; Hencken (1932), pp. 92–3, fig. 26.3; Brailsford (1953), p. 36, fig. 14.1; Proudfoot (1955); Hawkes and Clarke (1963), pp. 230, 246, fig. 53.3.
P & RB 85.6–13.3.

79 △   ▽ 80

80 'Dress-fastener' Irish Later Bronze Age
8th–7th century BC
Gold; swelling hoop with open conical ('trumpet-mouth') terminals decorated externally with four concentric chased grooves close to rims. w 11·7; terminals' D 4·6 and 4·7; WT 73·7.

An Irish type characteristic of the final, 'Dowris' phase of the Bronze Age. The precise manner of use of these objects is uncertain; indeed, they may have been designed as currency rather than jewellery. Said to have been found in Ireland.
Bibliography: Smith (1920), pp 109–10, fig. 116 ('Tullamore, King's County'); Hawkes and Clarke (1963), p. 245 ('Tullamore, Co. Offaly'); for the type, see Armstrong (1933); Eogan (1964), p. 302.
P & RB 34.12–22.1.

81a

Western Asia

The bronze pins of Luristan, dating from about 1000 to 700 BC, represent an unusual development of jewellery. Pins had been used to fasten clothes since at least the Sumerian period (about 2500 BC) and were to remain popular until they were superseded by the brooch. In Luristan, however, some pins reach an extraordinary size, and it is probable that these were not really designed for wearing at all, but were manufactured specifically as votive jewellery, for dedication in temples. The decorative patterns on these pins, though often reminiscent of later nomadic work from Central Asia, mostly seem to be stylized and distorted versions of standard Mesopotamian and Elamite motifs.

J.E.R.

81c

81 Dress-pins Luristan about 1000–700 BC

(a) Cast bronze pin with head representing lion. L 16·9.
Bibliography: Moorey (1971), p. 194–5.
WAA 130683. Raphael Bequest.

(b) Iron pin with cast head of base silver, representing hero wrestling with two animals. L 22·45.
Bibliography: Barnett (1963), p. 98; Moorey (1971), p. 202.
WAA 132927.

(c) Cast bronze pin with head in shape of winged monster. L 33·9.
Bibliography: Hančar (1934), p. 108; Moorey (1971), p. 197–8.
WAA 132057.

(d) Cast bronze pin, head disc-shaped and decorated with pattern of arcaded buds and pomegranates. L 41·45.
Bibliography: Moorey (1971), p. 212–3; (1974), p. 33.
WAA 132025.

81d

(e) Much restored head of cast bronze pin, originally attached to iron shank. Openwork decoration principally represents horned figure struggling with two animals. H 22·45.
Bibliography: Moorey (1971), p. 200; Barnett and Curtis (1973), p. 124.
WAA 135124.

82 Fragment of belt Iran about 8th–7th century BC Ziwiye, Iran.

Gold sheet, embossed and chased with pattern of lions' masks linked by looped tendrils which enclose figures of stags and goats. H 8·5.

This is part of a wide belt which would have been

81b

81e

sewn on to a leather or cloth backing. Belts of this kind were used principally in the kingdom of Urartu and its provinces. Comparable stylized animals recur on later metalwork from what is now the southern USSR, tribes from which penetrated Anatolia and Iran in the eighth and seventh centuries BC.
Bibliography: Godard (1950), p. 56; Barnett (1963), p. 98–9.
WAA 132825.

83 Bracelet Iran about 7th century BC
Gold bracelet, hollow; one section in form of two ducks back to back, made separately from main hoop. D 9·67.
Bibliography: Ghirshman (1950), p. 192.
WAA 135588.

83

82

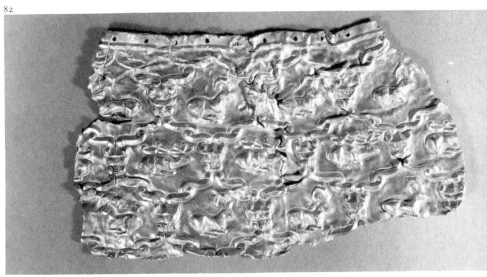

84 Silver hoard Iran about 600 BC
Tepe Nūsh-i Jān, Iran.

Group of spiral pendants, rings, and scraps. w (largest pendant) 4·0.

This material, with much more of similar nature, was found concealed beneath a floor. It demonstrates what must have been the usual fate of ancient jewellery, being cut up or melted down to serve as currency when it fell out of fashion or its owners needed to realize their capital. This economic function of jewellery was particularly important before the invention of coinage. The spiral pattern on the pendants in the hoard is a survival of a type also found in the royal graves of Ur; see no. 12(g).

Bibliography: Stronach (1969), pp. 15–16; Bivar (1971). WAA 135072–4, 6–8, 135082–5.

5

Phoenician, Greek, Etruscan and Persian lands

850-325 BC

Phoenician

The Phoenicians, in the early first millennium BC, carried the jewellery of Western Asia throughout the Mediterranean. They were both traders and colonists, and it is sometimes hard to distinguish between their own work and that of the native Europeans who learned from them. Jewellery from the graves at Tharros, in Sardinia, seems to be true Phoenician work. Much of it is extremely intricate, in the Tell el-'Ajjul tradition (no. 43), with sumptuous effects achieved at relatively small expense; colourful glass necklaces were also popular. A distinctive characteristic of the Phoenician style is the use of motifs derived from Egypt. Many of these had originally had an amuletic value, and presumably retained it for the Phoenicians, but the patterns have often been misunderstood or transformed into shapes and combinations which would have been unacceptable in Egypt itself.

J.E.R.

85 Bracelet Phoenician about 7th–6th century BC
Gold spacer-beads, each consisting of four single beads soldered together, on either side of ivory button in gold mount. Button has rosette carved on one side, and fictitious Egyptian cartouche on other. Bracelet fastened by insertion of pin through hinges at back. L 10·0.

Bracelets with central rosette ornaments, much like the modern wristwatch in general effect, became common under the Assyrian Empire, and are shown on sculptures. The spacer-beads on the strap of this piece recall those on the Ur head-dress, no. 13a.

Bibliography: Marshall (1911), p. 155, no. 1538.
WAA 135782. Castellani collection.

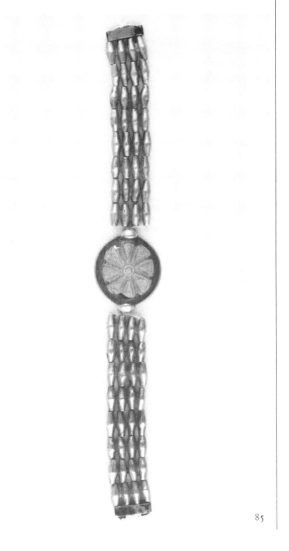

85

86 Jewellery from Graves Phoenician
about 7th–6th century BC
Tharros, Sardinia.

(a) Bracelet, incomplete, consisting of oblong gold plaques attached to one another by hinges swivelling on silver pins. Separate pieces of embossed gold, with granulation, representing floral motifs, soldered on to plaques. L 13·2.

The wide spread of Phoenician jewellery is evident from the places in which comparable bracelets have been found: they include Syria, Cyprus, Malta, Tunisia, and Spain.
Bibliography: Marshall (1911), p. 156, no. 1542; Pisano (1974), pp. 56–7.
WAA 133392 (part).

(b) Necklace of glass beads and gold pendants. Central pendant, flat plaque to which embossed decora-tion applied, shows *uraeus* cobras on either side of bottle-shaped motif, probably divine symbol. L 33·0.
Bibliography: Marshall (1911), p. 157, no. 1547; Pisano (1974), p. 61.
WAA 133334.

(c) Earrings, gold, each consisting of open hoop with flat cruciform ornament attached below. H 5·2; 5·0.

Earrings of this general shape appear in ninth-century Assyria, when they are shown among items of tribute imported from Syria. They have been found at many Mediterranean sites. The cruciform ornament is per-haps derived from the Egyptian *ankh*, a symbol of life.
Bibliography: Marshall (1911), pp. 152–3, nos. 1501, 1499; Pisano (1974), p. 49.
WAA 133529; 133530.

86a △   ▽ 86c

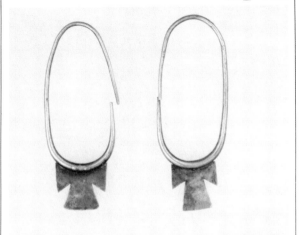

The Orientalizing Period in Greek Jewellery

The Mycenaean world came to an end about 1100 BC, to be succeeded by some two to three centuries of great poverty, when artistic creation was at a low ebb, and articles of jewellery were rare indeed. About 850 BC, however, contacts with Western Asia were resumed. The jewellery in this age of Greek revival, which lasted until about 600 BC, was again plentiful and of the highest quality.

From 850 to 700 BC we see the production of superb goldwork at certain important centres such as Knossos in Crete, Corinth, and Athens. It is probable that immigrant goldsmiths from Phoenicia, which was famed at this date for its craftsmen, settled at these places, set up workshops, and taught the secrets of their trade to local apprentices. Much of this jewellery rather puzzlingly recalls that of the Mycenaean period, some five centuries earlier. We know that there can have been no continuity of tradition in Greek lands, and the only possible explanation is that in the late Bronze Age Mycenaean fashions had found their way to the coasts of the Levant, where they were kept alive by the Phoenicians and reintroduced to the Greek world when it was once more in a position to enjoy the luxuries of life. Our principal source in the British Museum for the ninth and eighth centuries BC is a collection formed, probably from excavations in Athens, by the seventh Earl of Elgin in the early 1800s (see nos. 88, 89).

In the seventh century BC the best jewellery now comes from the Islands and Asia Minor. Among the most important sources are the cemeteries of Camirus in Rhodes, excavated in the 1860s (see nos. 91–93) and the Temple of Artemis at Ephesus, excavated in 1904–5 (see no. 94).

Closely related to the Rhodian tradition is an exquisite class of rosettes (no. 90) made for attachment to diadems of cloth or leather. Most surviving examples have been found on the island of Melos, and that is doubtless where they were made. They are decorated with human and animal heads, insects, and flowers.

The jewellery from Ephesus was excavated on the site of the early Temple of Artemis (the Roman Diana). Although deposited as a votive offering to the goddess, it was originally made to be worn. This jewellery falls almost entirely within the seventh century. The style has much in common with contemporary Rhodian jewellery, but, as might be expected, the oriental element is stronger.

R.H.

87

90

92

94

87 Earring Greek 8th century BC
Athens.

Gold. Crescent formerly inlaid (inlay now missing) and decorated with very fine granulation; hung with four gold chains. H 4·7.
Bibliography: *BMCJ*, no. 1240; *GRJ*, p. 98, pl. 13D.
G & R TB116. Burgon Collection.

88 Pair of Earrings Greek 8th century BC
Gold. Disc with fine granulation and central inlay (now missing). From back springs curved 'stalk' on end of which is a double-pyramidal inlaid finial (inlay also missing). D 2·9 (stud).
Bibliography: *GRJ*, p. 99, pl. 13E.
G & R 1960.11–1.18–19. Collection of the seventh Earl of Elgin.

Colour plate 3

89 Pair of Fibulae Greek 8th century BC
Gold. Catch-plates engraved with deer on one side and swastika on the other. L 6.
Bibliography: *GRJ*, p. 100, pl. 14B.
G & R 1960.11–1.46–47. Collection of the seventh Earl of Elgin.

Colour plate 3

90 Rosette Greek 7th century BC
Gold. Rosette with six petals, decorated alternately with female head and rosette. Lion's head in centre. Rich granulation. D 4·3.

Runner on back indicates use as diadem-ornament.
Bibliography: *BMCJ*, no. 1230.
G & R 84.8–4.2.

91 Relief Plaques Greek 7th century BC
Camirus, Rhodes.

Gold. Seven relief plaques, forming pectoral ornament. Each depicts two human heads, shown frontally. Rich granulation. W 2·7 (central plaque), 2·2 (other plaques).
Bibliography: *BMCJ*, no. 1103; *GRJ*, p. 112, pl. 18E.
G & R 61.11–11.2.

92 Relief Plaque Greek 7th century BC
Camirus, Rhodes.

Gold relief plaque. Winged goddess with lions. Flower and hawks, in the round, above. Rich granulation. H 5·2.
Bibliography: *BMCJ*, no. 1107; *GRJ*, p. 112, pl. 19E.
G & R 61.4–25.3.

93 Relief Plaques Greek 7th century BC
Camirus, Rhodes.

Gold. Set of seven pectoral ornaments. Winged goddess with lions. Rich granulation. H 4·2 (plaques).
Bibliography: *BMCJ*, nos. 1128–30; *GRJ*, p. 112, pl. 20.
G & R 61.11–11.1, 3–4.

94 Brooch Greek 7th century BC
Excavated at Ephesus, Temple of Artemis, by D. E. Hogarth, in 1904.

Gold. In form of hawk. H 3·1.
Bibliography: *BMCJ*, no. 1037.
G & R 1907.12–1.9.

93 △   ▽ 91

Etruscan

The identity of the Etruscans is still a mystery, but, according to the most likely theory, their forebears entered Italy from Asia Minor in the late eighth century BC or earlier, and settled in that part which is still known after them as Tuscany. The period of their greatest power covers the seventh and sixth centuries BC. The decline began shortly after the beginning of the fifth century BC, and continued till the middle of the third, when the Etruscan cities were absorbed by the growing power of Rome.

Etruscan jewellery is best considered in two phases: Early Etruscan, of the seventh to fifth centuries BC, and Late Etruscan, 400 to 250 BC. After 250 BC there was still plenty of jewellery being made in Etruria, but it was now purely Hellenistic in style.

Early Etruscan jewellery is characterized by its abundance, its technical perfection, and its variety. The technical knowledge reached the Etruscans from the same Phoenician sources as supplied the Greeks, but the Etruscans made different use of it. Granulation was the decorative process *par excellence*, and its possibilities were developed to a far higher degree than in Greece. Not only were the grains disposed in simple patterns, but whole scenes were portrayed in silhouettes of granulation, or, by a reversed process, the figures were in relief and the background granulated; alternatively the whole surface was covered with 'gold dust'.

Filigree was at first used sparingly, but on occasion was applied in open-work patterns without a background, an extremely difficult process.

Towards the end of the seventh century, Greek influence first made itself felt, not so much in the forms of the jewellery as in new decorative motifs and technical innovations, such as an increased use of filigree and the introduction of inlay and enamelling. These changes should probably be explained by the arrival of immigrant Greek goldsmiths.

The Etruscans loved colour and their necklaces of delicately granulated gold beads frequently included also glass and faience beads of Phoenician origin.

Late Etruscan jewellery, of about 400 to 250 BC, is completely different in form and in execution, consisting as it does of large convex surfaces of sheet gold. Decoration is meagre: filigree and granulation were occasionally used, but in general, the goldsmith restricted himself to embossed patterns of the simplest kind. The repertoire was as limited as the style: flimsy wreaths for burial with the dead, earrings, necklaces, bracelets and finger-rings. After this poverty-stricken art the adoption of Hellenistic fashions comes as a pleasant surprise.

R.H.

95 Fibula Etruscan 7th century BC
The Roman Campagna.

Gold. Bolt-fibula composed of four curved tubular rods with female heads as finials. Four transverse plates each decorated with four figures in the round of crouching sphinxes. L 12·1 (closed).

For a description of the bolt-fibula, see *GRJ*, p. 147.
Bibliography: *BMCJ*, no. 1370; *GRJ*, p. 147.
G & R 67.5–8.485. Blacas Collection.

96 Fibula Etruscan about 700 BC
Gold. Leech-shaped, with cross-bar with attached spirals at foot and flat oval sheath beyond it, set at right-angles to the bow. Engraved decoration throughout. L 7·4.

This form is Villanovan in origin.
Bibliography: *BMCJ*, no. 1373; *GRJ*, p. 147.
G & R 94.5–7.3.

97 Fibula Etruscan 7th century BC
Vulci, or perhaps Cerveteri.

Gold. Serpentine fibula, covered with designs in superfine granulation and with figures in the round, also richly granulated of lions, lions' heads, horses' heads and sphinxes. L 18·6.
Bibliography: *BMCJ*, no. 1376; *GRJ*, p. 145, pl. 37C.
G & R 62.5–12.16. Blayds Collection.

98 Pair of Bracelets Etruscan 7th century BC
Tarquinii.

Gold. Front decorated in superfine granulation with patterns and human figures. Back decorated with embossed patterns and figures. L 16·5.
Bibliography: *BMCJ*, nos. 1358–9; *GRJ*, p. 143, pl. 35.
G & R 1358F and 1359F. Franks Bequest, 1897.

Colour plate 5

99 Comb-Fibula Etruscan 7th century BC
Silver, parcel-gilt. Central element is a richly decorated tube with wire running down each side. Two comb-like elements, originally sewn to opposing corners of cloak were hooked over side-wires, to fasten the cloak on the shoulder. L 12·4.
Bibliography: *BMCJ*, no. 1372; *GRJ*, p. 147, pl. 38B.
G & R 40.2–12.1.

100 Necklace Etruscan 7th century BC
Gold and glass. Composed of gold beads, many decorated with filigree and granulation; coloured glass beads; and coloured glass pendant in form of grotesque human head. H 3·1 (pendant).

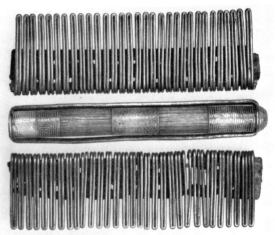

96 △   ▽ 97   99 △   ▽ 95

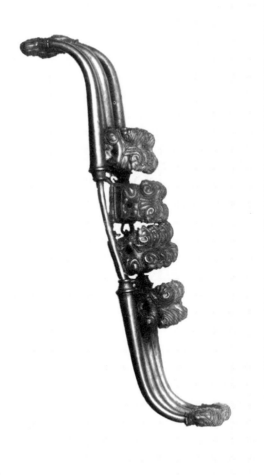

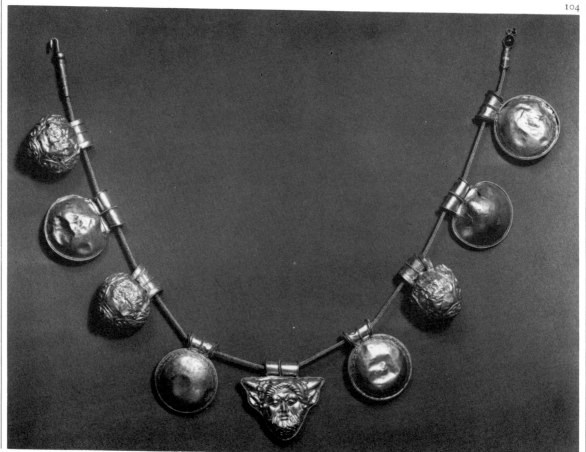

The pendant is probably Phoenician work, exported to Etruria in antiquity.
Bibliography: BMCJ, no. 1450.
G & R 72.6–4.644. Castellani Collection.

101 Earrings Etruscan 6th century BC
Chiusi.

Gold, *a baule* type. Composed of strip bent round almost in circle; gap bridged by wire which also passed through ear-lobe. Richly decorated with repoussé ornament, granulation and filigree. L 1·9.

A baule is the name given to this class by the Italians from its resemblance to a valise.
Bibliography: BMCJ, nos. 1303–4; GRJ, p. 38, pl. 32A, B.
G & R 72.6–4.467. Castellani Collection.

102 Necklace Etruscan 6th century BC
The Tuscan Maremma.

Gold. Strap-necklace hung with heads of river-god, sirens, flowers, buds and scarabs. L 27·6.
Bibliography: BMCJ, no. 1461; GRJ, p. 142, pl. 33.
G & R 56.6–25.17.

Colour plate 5

101 △　▽ 105

103 Ear Stud Etruscan 6th century BC
Gold. Richly decorated with filigree, granulation and inlay. Projection in back for insertion in ear-lobe. D 6·8.
Bibliography: BMCJ, no. 1419; GRJ, p. 138, pl. B2.
G & R 81.5–28.2. Bale Collection.

Colour plate 5

104 Necklace Etruscan 4th century BC
Tarquinii.

Gold cord, threaded with nine *bullae*: five lens-shaped, three heart-shaped and embossed, and one as head of river-god. L 46·2.
Bibliography: BMCJ, no. 2271; GRJ, p. 152, pl. 44.
G & R 72.6–4.643. Castellani Collection.

105 Earring Etruscan 3rd century BC
Found in Perugia in 1869.

Gold. Tubular hoop, masked in front by shield-shaped plate from which hangs pendant in shape of woman's head and smaller pendants in shape of jars. H 10·7.
Bibliography: BMCJ, no. 2262; GRJ, p. 151, pl. 42C.
G & R 84.6–14.10. Castellani Collection.

The Classical Period of Greek Jewellery

Between 600 and 475 BC, jewellery was very rare in Greece (due it would seem, to the scarcity of gold), but after the Persian wars it became rather more plentiful. The character of Classical jewellery follows closely from what little we know of the Archaic period. The workmanship is fine, but less fine than in the seventh century. Filigree was used in decorative patterns, and enamel was becoming more popular. Granulation was rarely used; inlay of stone or glass even more rarely. Towards the end of the period, however, we first find engraved stones in the bezels of finger-rings. In general, the sculptural forms of the gold were left to speak for themselves, diversified only by the above-mentioned processes.

The forms were very varied. Naturalistic wreaths developed in the fifth century and flourished in the fourth, and diadems continued in many varieties. Earrings proliferated; human figures, some of great elaboration, which were to be typical of the Hellenistic period, made their first appearance as adjuncts to earrings about the middle of the fourth century. Beads and pendants of types already familiar are found in this period, altered to suit the taste of the new age. Elaborate necklaces were made, with interlocking beads; and acorns, birds and human heads were popular as pendants. Bracelets took the form of spirals or penannular hoops with elaborate finials. Finger-rings are found in several varieties, some containing seal-stones, some purely decorative in purpose.

In general, the comparative scarcity of classical jewellery is compensated for by its very high quality. R.H.

106 Pair of Earrings Greek 5th century BC
Eretria, Euboea.

Gold. Crescent-shaped member hangs from an enamelled rosette. From crescent hang cockle-shell pendants on chains, and a siren sits on it. Decorated with filigree and green enamel. H 6.
Bibliography: *BMCJ*, nos. 1653–4; *GRJ*, p. 122, pl. 24A. G & R 93.11–3.1.

107 Earrings Greek 5th century BC
Amathus, Cyprus; excavated, 1894 with funds from Turner Bequest.

Gold-plated bronze. Pair of spiral earrings ending in griffin's head. Griffin's collars and tail of spiral decorated with blue and green enamel. D 2·9.

A Greek Cypriot speciality.
Bibliography: *BMCJ*, nos. 1646–7; *GRJ*, p. 124, pl. 25E. G & R 94.11–1.450–451.

108 Necklace Greek 4th century BC
Tarentum.

Gold. Composed of interlocking rosettes and other ornaments, from which hang flower-buds and female heads. Filigree decoration. L 30·6.
Bibliography: *BMCJ*, no. 1952; *GRJ*, p. 127, pl. 28. G & R 72.6–4.667.

Colour plate 4

107 △   ▽ 106

Persian Lands

Phoenicia, from the eighth to the fourth centuries BC, came to be dominated politically by empires based further east, in Mesopotamia and Iran. The jewellery of these areas, as represented here, though influenced from the west in some respects, tends to be technically simpler but, because of the lavish use of gold, more imposing in its general effect. The Oxus Treasure, from which our examples are drawn, has an obscure history: it was found somewhere on the Oxus River, about 1877, and was carried by merchants to India where most of it was eventually bought by a British official. It is not clear, however, whether it came from a single hoard. Even if there was only one, it may incorporate the contents of a temple treasury which had accumulated over two or more centuries. One possibility is that much of the jewellery was hidden about 330 BC, when the Greek army of Alexander the Great was advancing into Central Asia, and that it represents offerings deposited during the period of the Persian Empire.

The Oxus Treasure bracelets are mostly in a tradition which the Persians had inherited from Mesopotamia or Elam; comparable objects, hoops ending in elegant animal heads, can be seen on Assyrian sculptures of the ninth century BC. The Greek historians commented several times on the remarkable quantities of gold worn, in various forms, by the Persian kings and their high officials and bodyguards; they refer, not only to the bracelets and torcs, but also to appliqué ornaments sewn on to clothes.

While much of the Oxus Treasure jewellery looks as if it might equally well have been found much further to the south-west, closer to the ancient centres of civilization, a few pieces belong stylistically to quite another world, the nomadic culture of Central Asia which is frequently called Scythian. A characteristic of the nomadic style was to take animal motifs and distort them in such a way that the shape of the animal was secondary both to the shape of the object it was decorating and to the general decorative effect. These distorted animals, like the Oxus Treasure itself, have a disputed history, but jewellery incorporating them is found over a long period and a vast geographical area, from Europe to the borders of China. We include examples on a gold belt from Ziwiye in Iran (no. 82) of the eighth or seventh century BC, and on a belt-clasp from Georgia (no. 129), which may be as late as the third century AD. A finger-ring from the Oxus Treasure demonstrates how this stylistic approach could successfully be applied to the manufacture of small-scale jewellery.

J.E.R.

109 The Oxus Treasure Persian Empire

about 5th–4th century BC
Oxus River (Amu Darya) area, Russian Turkestan.

The following is a selection of the major items of jewellery:

(a) Pair of gold armlets. Each hoop almost solid metal at back, but becomes tubular towards ends which are embossed in the shape of winged monsters, with hindquarters and legs represented in relief on surface of hoop. Hollows chased into horns, faces, and bodies of the monsters originally inlaid; wings and upper parts decorated with applied gold cloisons, also for inlay. H 12·8; 12·4.

These magnificent but impractical armlets may have been designed for use on ceremonial occasions. The monsters are a distinctively Persian development of the old Mesopotamian griffin; this variety has horns, high ears, the body and forelegs of a lion, and the wings, head, and hindlegs of an eagle.

Bibliography: Dalton (1964), pp. 32–4, no. 116; Barnett (1968), pp. 40–43.
WAA 124017. Franks Bequest; L 1155, on loan from the Victoria and Albert Museum.

Colour plate 8

109a

109e i

109e ii

109e iii

(b) Four gold bracelets:
(i) with ribbed hoop and lion's head ends; wire emerges from each lion's mouth, and is wound seven times around neck. D 7·9.
(ii) with ram's head ends, decorated with turquoise inlay in applied cloisons. D 7·25.
(iii) with duck's head ends. D 7·5.
(iv) cast and chased to represent two animals, probably stylized griffins, with tails interlocked at back of hoop while heads form ends. D 7·9.
Three of these bracelets are evidently Persian in inspiration, though they may have been locally made, but the fourth shows the adaptation of a Persian motif to the requirements of nomadic art.
Bibliography: Dalton (1964), pp. 36–8, nos. 124, 133, 142, 145.
WAA 124026; 124036; 124045; 124048. Franks Bequest.

Colour plate 9

(c) Torc, spirally fluted gold hoop with goat's head ends. Present arrangement, with hoop twisted into three rings, may be modern alteration; should probably be single ring, worn around neck. D 8·6.
Bibliography: Dalton (1964), p. 38, no. 138.
WAA 124041. Franks Bequest.

Colour plate 9

(d) Head ornament, convex gold plaque, elaborately embossed and chased to represent stylized griffin. Two pins, presumably for attachment, extend horizontally from back. Originally inlaid. L 6·15.

The function of this unique object is unclear, but it may have been designed to fasten a turban. The griffin is still identifiable, but the tail now ends in a leaf while the legs, which are bent without regard for anatomy, end in hooves rather than claws.
Bibliography: Dalton (1964), p. 11, no. 23; Barnett (1968), pp. 44–5.
WAA 123924. Franks Bequest.

Colour plate 9

(e) Five gold dress ornaments:
(i) Openwork roundel showing sphinx whose wing terminates in griffin's head. D 5·0.
(ii) Roundel showing head of Egyptian god Bes; four holes for attachment in border. D 4·35.
(iii) Bird's head with curved beak emerging from serpentine body; loops for attachment at back. L 3·35.
(iv) Roundel showing lion's head; gold wire, for attachment, soldered across back. D 4·15.
(v) Roundel showing beardless head, with design of dolphins round edge; gold wire, for attachment, soldered across back. D 4·15.

109e iv

109e v

(f) Finger-ring, gold, open work, representing a highly stylized and distorted lion; originally inlaid. B 3·6 (bezel).

Colour plate 9

This group incorporates decorative motifs derived from Mesopotamia, Syria, Egypt and Greece, as well as the Oxus River area itself, all territories which were under Persian control or influence. The cosmopolitan nature of the Oxus Treasure jewellery, and indeed of other objects from the Oxus Treasure, has caused considerable confusion among scholars attempting to assess its date and origin.
Bibliography: Dalton (1964), pp. 14–17, 29–30, nos. 26, 32, 39–41, 111.
WAA 123927; 123933; 123940–123942; 124012. Franks Bequest.

Colour plate 9

110 Necklace Persian Empire about 4th century BC Pasargadae, Iran.

Part of necklace of gold and pearl beads, with one gold bell-shaped pendant. D 0·50 (largest pearl).

These beads came from a large hoard of jewellery which was probably hidden about 330 BC, when Alexander's Greeks were advancing through Iran. Pearls, presumably from the Persian Gulf, first appear to have become fashionable about this time, and these are among the earliest surviving examples.
Bibliography: Stronach (1965), pp. 32–40.
WAA 135089.

110

6

Torcs in Celtic Europe

500-1 BC

The torc (or neckring) is often regarded, with good reason, as the principal piece of jewellery of the Celts. While torcs are mentioned by Classical writers as worn by Celtic warriors in battle, when found in graves they occur only around the necks of women or girls. Those torcs that occur in hoards, as at Snettisham and Ipswich, may never have been used as neckrings at all, but simply as special-purpose currency. M.S.

111 Torc Early La Tène about 4th century BC
From a grave at Courtisols, dép. Marne, France.

Bronze, cast, penannular hoop, with touching hollowed buffer terminals each ornamented with pair of beaded ridges; three circular collars either side of terminals have sinuous grooves around them and beaded ridges on each side. D 14·9 by 13·8; WT 244·3.
Bibliography: Morel (1898), pl. 37.3; Smith (1905), p. 56, fig. 51.9; Smith (1925), p. 63, fig. 60.9.
P & RB ML1710. Collection of L. Morel, of Reims, 1901.

112 Torc Early La Tène 4th–3rd century BC
Found in France.

Gold, cast, plain oval penannular hoop; beaded ridges flank globes adjoining conical hollowed out terminals. D 16·7 by 13·8; WT 391·9.
Bibliography: Smith (1905), p. 56; Smith (1925), p. 62; Jacobsthal (1944), no. 39.
P & RB 67.5–8.477.

113 Torc Early La Tène 4th–3rd century BC
Courtisols, dép. Marne, France.

Bronze, cast, penannular ring with touching buffer terminals; very abraded relief scroll ornament around terminals; on ring on either side of terminals pair of highly stylised human faces framed by fleshy S-scrolls in relief; panel of abraded relief ornament also at back of ring. D 14·5 by 15·6; D (terminals) 3·3; WT 275·0.

A type of woman's neckring only found in Champagne and with close stylistic links with the Avon Fontenay torc (no. 118).
Bibliography: Morel (1898), pl. 37.4; Smith (1905), p. 63; Smith (1925), p. 66; Jacobsthal (1944), no. 208; Favret (1950), p. 448, fig. 12.7; Megaw (1965–66), pp. 116–17, 134–9, figs. 2J, 4G, pl. 12.3–4; Powell (1966), p. 218, ill. 212; Megaw (1970), no. 119.
P & RB ML1711. Collection of L. Morel, of Reims, 1901.

114 Torc and Bracelets Early La Tène
4th century BC
Sheet gold torc and pair of bracelets; hollow, filled with unidentified non-metallic core; repoussé relief ornament: rosettes on faces of terminals, intertwined floral patterns (flowers, leaves and stems) around terminals (and collars on torc) and adjacent parts of hoops. Torc: D 14·8 by 13·8; WT 105·3; bracelets: D 7·8 by 6·5 and 7·8 by 6·1; WT 19·2 and 19·2.
The design of the torc and bracelets finds its closest analogy in pieces from the richly furnished princess's burial of the fourth century BC at Waldalgesheim on the Middle Rhine (after which is named one of the styles of early Celtic art on the European mainland). However, whereas the ornament on the latter pieces also derives from the floral patterns of Classical art in the Mediterranean world and represents a masterly transformation into a coherent style by a craftsman confident of his ability, that of the present pieces, on the other hand, is far less assured, very fussy and somewhat confused. Its wiriness recalls more precisely the filigree-work of contemporary Greek and Etruscan jewellery.

III △ ▽ II4

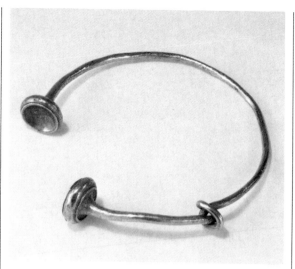

Bibliography: Smith (1931); Jacobsthal (1944), nos. 45, 56; Jope (1971), p. 176.
P & RB 1930.4–11.1 (torc); 1929.12–21.1 and 1930.4–11.2 (bracelets).

115 Torc La Tène Iron Age 4th–1st century BC
Gold; knot in hoop; 'buffer' terminals hollowed out front and back, with beaded ridge around each face.
D 15·1; WT 189·9.

Findplace unknown but found with two others before 1846. Completely plain 'buffer-terminal' torcs had such a long vogue in the La Tène Iron Age that it is impossible to specify the date and region of manufacture of this specimen. The knot is unparalleled on any other torc, and its purpose quite unknown.

Bibliography: Birch (1846), p. 31, fig; Smith (1905), p. 56; Smith (1925), p. 62; Jacobsthal (1944), no. 40.
P & RB

115

116 Torc Early La Tène about 4th century BC
Probably found in Champagne, France.

Cast bronze, mock-torsion ring, with beading on spiral edge; two flat oval terminals overlap and are secured by rivet with conical head once inlaid at top (probably with coral imported from Mediterranean); around rivet-head are horizontal grooves. D 22·6 by 22·0; WT 259·6.

Bibliography: Smith (1905), p. 55, fig. 61.8; Smith (1925), p. 61, fig. 60.8.
P & RB ML 1819. Collection of L. Morel, of Reims, 1901.

117 Torc Early La Tène about 4th century BC
Pleurs, dép. Marne, France.

117 △   ▽ 118

Bronze, cast in two pieces; circular hoop with detachable segment secured by mortise-and-tenon joints; of tripartite design with three regularly-spaced collars flanked by beaded ridges alternating with circular projections flanked by three spheres; bands of Xs outlined by grooves either side, executed in uncertain technique, flank the two projections at either end of the detachable segment. D 19·2; WT 452·1.

A type of torc worn by high-ranking women in Champagne during the Early La Tène period.

Bibliography: Morel (1898), pl. 25.3; Smith (1905), pp. 55–6, fig. 51.2; Smith (1925), pp. 62–3, fig. 60.2; Jacobsthal (1944), pl. 263. P43.
P & RB ML1621. Collection of L. Morel, of Reims, 1901.

118 Torc Early La Tène 4th–3rd century BC
Avon Fontenay, dép. Aube, France.

Bronze, cast in two pieces, with closing link joined by mortise-and-tenon at either end; ring with tripartite design: three knobs each with fleshy relief S-coil, and three panels of intertwined fleshy relief scrolls (some within borders which continue round back of ring) from which very stylised human faces stare out. D 15·5; WT 264·1.

Neckrings of this type are only found in Champagne, where they were worn by high-ranking women, but the ornament, a development of the 'Waldalgesheim' style, is of a kind more widely distributed, throughout much of Western and Central Europe north of the Alps.

Bibliography: Morel (1898), pl. 37.2; Smith (1905), pp. 55, 63, fig. 50; Smith (1925), pp. 61, 66, fig. 59; Jacobsthal (1944), no. 241; Favret (1950), p. 446, fig. 11.3; Megaw (1965–66), p. 143, pl. 11.4; Megaw (1970), no. 122.

P & RB ML1709. Collection of L. Morel, of Reims, 1901.

119 Torc Castro Culture 2nd–1st century BC
Gold; hollow sheet 'double hour-glass' terminals slotted onto solid penannular hoops of diamond section; terminals flat-faced with six-petal rosette executed by stamping with bobbles at centre and at outer ends of petals. W 14·1; WT 119·5.

Torcs of this type belong to the Galician Castro Culture of north-western Iberia, which probably developed in the mid-first millennium BC and lasted until the Roman Conquest in the first century BC – for the type, see Lopez Cuevillas (1951), pp. 20–51, figs. 3–30. The culture was Celtic; the Celts are generally considered to have arrived in Iberia from France early in the first millennium BC.

Bibliography: Almagro Gorbea (1962), pl. 11; Raddatz (1969), pp. 172–97 (type A1).

P & RB 1960.5–3.1.

120 Torc Castro Culture 2nd–1st century BC
Gold; hollow sheet 'double hour-glass' terminals slotted on to solid penannular hoops of diamond section; terminals have conical indentation in end-face with spike rising from base. W 15·5; WT 201·0.

For torcs of this type see note in previous entry (no. 119).

Bibliography: Almagro Gorbea (1962), pl. 1; Raddatz (1969), p. 197, no. 34a.

P & RB 1960.5–3.2.

120, 119

121 Torc, Bracelets, Armlet Iberian Iron Age
about 100 BC
From a hoard of silver objects found at Córdoba, Spain, in January 1915.

(a) Silver torc, repaired since discovery, with biconical mouldings on hoop, and biconical terminals bent backwards; inner faces of terminals have chased ladder pattern forming base of frieze of triangles at apices of which are chased circles; fine line either side of carination on each terminal. H 18·8; W 16·2; WT 143·6.

(b) Silver bracelet; broad hoop, smooth inside; four ridges outside; inner two obliquely nicked with tracer, and border simply ornamented frieze of dot-and-circle motifs linked by oblique strokes that runs short distance round from terminals; chevron band across neck of each animal-head terminal simply modelled, in great part by chasing alone. D 9·2; W 1·8; WT 66·5.

(c) Silver bracelet; plain hoop of circular section with very worn snake-head terminals. D 10·1; WT 70·5.

(d) Silver armlet; when found, this piece had two perforated coins each linked by length of chain to one terminal; terminals are simple loops with quadruple-ridge moulding; long plain neck between terminals and main part of armlet made of two rods twisted together with two twisted wires; rods swell in thickness towards centre; most of this wire now missing. Possibly originally neckring later coiled up. D 11·0; WT 214·6.

These items of jewellery come from one of many hoards of silver – comprising jewellery, coinage, ingots, and vessels – buried in Iberia during the third to first centuries BC.
Bibliography: Hildburgh (1922); Raddatz (1969), pp. 208–10, pls. 5–6.
P & RB 1932.7–6.2.5.19.22.

122 Torc British Later Iron Age 1st century BC
Found at Ken Hill, Snettisham, Norfolk in 1950 (Hoard D).

Gold alloy; made of two bars of circular section twisted together; ends of bars coiled into circular terminals; coiled, tapered strip of gold alloy (same metal as torc itself) threaded through one of terminals. D 21·2 (torc), 4·6 (coil); WT 1062·3.

The Snettisham Treasure came to light during the period 1948 to 1973; this torc, of the 'loop-terminal' type, comprises Hoard D. The enormous amount of precious metal found there represents without doubt the treasury of an Iron Age chieftain; some of the finds from the site, including an unfinished torc, indicate that torcs were made there. The purpose of

the ring threaded through the terminal of this torc may have been to round up its weight to a specific value; this value represents a simple multiple of a unit of weight recently recognized to have been used by the prehistoric Celts. This suggests that the torc had not only symbolic value (as an indicator of the social standing of the owner) but was also valued for its precise metal content; in this sense it may be considered as both currency and jewellery. The same appears to be true of many other finds of torcs from Britain which were either so manufactured as to have a precisely calculated weight (compare the Needwood Forest torc, no. 123, which weighs precisely two-fifths of the present Snettisham torc), or combined with others to achieve the same result (compare the six torcs from Ipswich (no. 124), whose combined weight is four and one-sixth times as much as the combined weight of the complete and broken torcs and bracelet that make up Snettisham Hoard E, no. 125).
Bibliography: Brailsford (1953), p. 66, pl. XVII.1; Clarke (1954), pp. 46–7, no. 13, pp. 48–51, 56, no. 16, pl. X; Spratling (1973), p. 120.
P & RB 1951.4–2.1.

123 Torc British Late Iron Age 1st century BC
Found in Greaves Wood, Needwood Forest, Staffordshire, England, in 1848.

Gold-silver-copper alloy; simple loop terminals, ornamented with bobbles along outer edges, lines of dot-facets and crimped ridges (last two done with blunt centre-punch), cast on to ends of wires; dot-facets run short way along some of wires from their ends; hoop comprises eight strands of wires (each strand made of four wires twisted together) twisted together in pairs. D (greatest) 18·0; WT 425·7.

The loose weave and the precise arrangement of the strands on this torc set it apart from the rest of the British series; the unusual design of the terminals is most nearly paralleled on another Staffordshire torc – from Glascote, now in the Birmingham City Museum & Art Gallery (Painter [1971]) – which suggests that both were made in that part of the country. The present torc weighs precisely two-fifths of the loop-terminal torc with make-weight from Snettisham (no. 122), suggesting that it too was intended as much as currency as a prestigious piece.
Bibliography: Ellis (1849); Leeds (1933), p. 467, pl. LXXXI.2; Hawkes (1936); Brailsford (1953), p. 66, pl. XV.2; Clarke (1954), pp. 64, 65; Fox (1958) p. 37, pl. 25a; Powell (1966), p. 218, ill. 211; Painter (1971), pp. 308–9, 310, 311, pl. LXIVb; Spratling (1973), p. 120.
P & RB. Collection of HM the Queen in right of the

Duchy of Lancaster. Deposited on permanent loan by HM King Edward VIII, 1936.

124 Torcs (six) South British Late Iron Age
1st century BC
Ipswich, Suffolk, England.

Gold-silver-copper alloys of varying proportions; all are of wrought metal with cast-on terminals; twisted rods all faceted, probably by swaging; five of the torcs (a)–(e) have two rods twisted together and simple loop-terminals; the sixth (f) has four rods twisted together in pairs – twist of pairs against each other is in opposite direction to that used to form each pair, thus giving unusually tight weave – and ring-terminals; each terminal has triple ring moulding (outer rings faceted, inner rounded) separated by tiny beaded ridges and quadruple ridged collar of which inner pair obliquely worked in different directions in herring-bone effect; torc (b) broken into two equal halves in antiquity, repair being just visible as slight unevenness in faceting of rods; torcs (b)–(e) have relief decoration with some chased and/or engraved detailing; different finishes were given to the terminals of the torcs. (a) D 18·8; WT 932·6; (b) D 19·7; WT 1044·1; (c) D 18·7; WT 858·1; (d) D 18·7; WT 915·1; (e) D 18·1; WT 867·8; (f) D 18·8; WT 880·5.

Torcs (a)–(e) were found together in 1968, and torc (f) separately and a short distance away in 1970; possibly all from one hoard, though possibly from more than one as at Snettisham, Norfolk (nos. 122 and 125), where at least six hoards have been brought to light. The five loop-terminal torcs (a)–(e) are paralleled by finds elsewhere, notably at Snettisham (Burns (1971)), while torc (f) is most closely matched by a torc from Ulceby-on-Humber (Leeds (1933) pl. LXXX, lower). Torcs (b)–(e) have been claimed as unfinished on the grounds that their ornament represents different stages in the production of relief work like that on the bracelet and ring-terminal torc from Hoard E at Snettisham (no. 125, a–b). This view, however, overlooks the various kinds of finishes and techniques of surface modelling employed on relief work in the British later Iron Age. Moulds for producing pony-harness decorated in the same style as that represented by the finds from Snettisham mentioned above (from Gussage All Saints, Dorset), show the ornament there to be fully modelled in wax before casting. There thus seems no reason for regarding any of the Ipswich torcs as anything other than finished.
Bibliography: Owles (1969); Megaw (1970), no. 292 (= torc b); Brailsford and Stapley (1972); Spratling (1973), pp. 123–4; Brailsford (1975), pp. 44–52, figs. 59–76, pl. IV.
P & RB 1969.1–3.1–5; P1971.2–3.1.

124

96

125 Hoard South British Late Iron Age
1st century BC
Found on Ken Hill, Snettisham, Norfolk, England, in 1950 (Hoard E).

Hoard of gold-alloy objects comprising:
(a) Ring-terminal torc, with hollow terminals ornamented in relief; on them also chased hatching and lines of dots, and crimped ridges, all executed with same blunt centre-punch; terminals soldered on to ends of hoop which comprises eight strands twisted together as tube, each strand consisting of eight wires twisted together; small worn coin contained in one of terminals. D 19·5; WT 1085·3.
(b) Bracelet, hollow, with relief, engraved and chased ornament along its two panels; ornament is symmetrical about groove formed by junction of panels; badly damaged on discovery. D 9·5 by 7·5 by 1·7; WT 110·9.
(c) About half of buffer-terminal torc with pair of twisted rods forming hoop, and large circular terminal dished on both faces; deliberately cut up in antiquity; on discovery threaded through bracelet and terminals of the complete torc. 10·8 by 6·2; D (terminal) 3·5; WT 123·6.

Whereas the bracelet and buffer-terminal torc-fragment are unique, the complete torc is the finest yet discovered of a group distributed from southern Scotland to Hengistbury Head on the Dorset coast. The style of ornament on the complete torc and bracelet is matched on the damaged Sedgeford and other torcs, and on contemporary bronze pony-harness. Since the total weight of these three pieces from Snettisham bears a direct relationship to a unit of weight used in later prehistoric Europe, it is likely that they were deliberately assembled, and the incomplete torc trimmed down, as a unit of currency.

Bibliography: Brailsford (1953), pp. 66–8, frontispiece and pl. XVII.2–3; Clarke (1954), p. 59, no. 14, pp. 63–8, fig. 12, pls. XV, XVI; Fox (1958), pp. 45–8, figs. 32–4; Allen (1961), p. 160; Sandars (1968), p. 265, pl. 296; Megaw (1970), no. 291; Brailsford (1975), pp. 55–61, figs. 77–89, pls. V–VII.
P & RB 1951.4–2.2–4.

125c

7

China, Western Asia, Celtic Europe, Mexico and Peru

600 BC-AD 400

China

The belt-buckles from the Ordos region (no. 126) provide a specific link between the Far East and more western areas of Asia. Both the themes of animals and the manner of execution are closely associated with similar belt-plaques from the Scythian and Russian Steppe areas. Although schematized the kneeling horse or mule shows an attention to realistic representation in which it is unlike the mainstream of Chinese art. However, this emphasis on the belt and its ornaments probably exerted an influence on Chinese habits of dress. In China proper it was the belt-hook which became the main vehicle for ornament. Belt-hooks functioned as buckles for belts with a stud on their back fastening the hook to one end of the belt, a ring or some other loop at the other end of the belt then went over the actual hook. The earliest examples were fine castings but relatively unornamented. Three of the more elaborately decorated types known (no. 127) clearly go a long way beyond what is functionally necessary.

J.M.R.

126 Two Belt-Plaques China 3rd–2nd century BC
Ordos type

(a) Silver belt-plaque in shape of stylized tiger in profile, flat, with details of ear, eye and jaw in low relief; two round holes forming paws and possibly used for suspending chains, tail openwork sequence of loops. L 16·5.

(b) Silver belt-plaque in shape of kneeling horse shown in profile, details of ears, mane and hooves cast in geometric stylized sunken elements. Hollow, with impression of coarse textile on underside; hook as part of belt fastening attached above mouth, pierced on hind quarters with two holes. L 13·5.

The Ordos region is the name given to the area inside the loop of the Yellow River where it turns inside Mongolia. The art of the nomadic peoples of this area reflects their concern with horses and hunting, and shows important relationships with the work of peoples living further to the west.
Bibliography: Jettmar (1967), pl. 27; Talbot Rice (1957); pls. 61, 62.
OA 1937.4–16.209; 1945.10–17.215. Bequeathed by O. C. Raphael.

127 Three Belt-hooks China 4th–1st century BC
Eastern Chou and Han Dynasty

(a) Slender bronze belt-hook consisting of pair of parallel bars joined at centre and at one end by group of curved elements, inlaid with turquoise, forming fish between two confronted birds; hook highly arched with stud below centre; small dragon's head at end forms hook. L 24·8.

Han dynasty, 3rd–1st century BC.
Bibliography: Hansford (1957), no. A45, p. 67, pl. XXIV.

(b) Gilt-bronze belt-hook with oval body inlaid with coiled dragon of white jade with elaborate forked tail; plain bar joins body to hook made from dragon's head. Round stud for attaching hook to belt lies behind oval body. L 9·5.

Han dynasty, 2nd–1st century BC.
Bibliography: Ayers and Rawson (1975), no. 119; Gure (1964), pl. 3 (2); Watson (1963), pl. 26 (b).

(c) Dark green jade belt-hook with grey flecks, altered in places to white by calcification; consisting of arched bar of rectangular cross-section tapering towards hook formed from simplified dragon's head,

126a

127 △   ▽ 126b

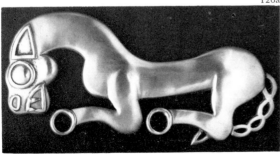

rectangular stud on the lower side; decoration of three groups of squares on upper. L 15·6.

Eastern Chou or Han period, 4th–3rd century BC.
Bibliography: Ayers and Rawson (1975), no. 167.
OA 1973.7–26.42; 1936.11–18.254; 1945.10–17.87.

128 Belt-hook China 1st–2nd century AD
Han Dynasty
Bronze belt-hook in shape of prowling animal with hook attached by bar to collar around neck; round stud for attachment to belt at back. L 7·5.

This piece is said to have been found in eastern Siberia. Whether made there or exported from the north-west of China it illustrates the contact between China and Siberia at this time.
OA 1941.5–5.1.

128

129 Belt-clasp Georgia (USSR) about 200 BC–AD 250
Cast bronze belt-clasp. Stylized openwork decoration represents horse with bull above back, bird between legs, another dog-like animal in front, and spiral infill; projecting bosses at corners, and herringbone patterning on sides. Hook attached on reverse, in front of horse, and loop behind. W 13·8.

Bronze belt-clasps of this distinctive kind have only been found in Georgia. They may imitate plaques of thin gold or silver, decorated with twisted wire and filigree, which would have been nailed at the corners to wood or leather backings.
Bibliography: Khidasheli (1972), p. 108, no. 124; Painter (1973).
P & RB 1921.6–28.1. Given by L. C. G. Clarke, Esq., on the occasion of the retirement of Sir Hercules Read.

130 Belt-buckle Central Asian(?)
about 300 BC–AD 300
Cast bronze rectangular plate with central openwork panel depicting quadruped looking backwards over its shoulder, and with pair of decorative rings either side; curved in section on horizontal axis; inlaid with sheet iron. H 8·4; W 14·9; WT 229·1.
P & RB 1936.12–11.3.

129

Celtic Europe

In Celtic Europe during the last few centuries BC, as much care was given to the design and elaboration of brooches as to that of torcs. Brooches are usually of bronze, but many were also made of iron and a few in gold and silver. The bronze brooches were quite often enriched with other materials, such as coral and enamel. Although worn by men, brooches were more usually worn by women; in the graves of women up to a dozen or more brooches are quite often found. During this period brooches were frequently made in pairs, connected by chains.

M.S.

131 Brooch Late Hallstatt period 6th century BC Excavated from the Iron Age cemetery at Hallstatt, Upper Austria.

Bronze, cast, with convoluted, ribbed bow on which are set pair of horns and lateral spoked wheels (latter separately made and riveted on). H 2·5; L 5·9; WT 20·0.

The 'perambulator' variety (Sundwall's III γ) of the so-called 'dragon' type of brooch in fashion in northern Italy, from where it was probably exported to Hallstatt; for the type, see Sundwall (1943), pp. 59–62, 250–1, figs. 416–7.

P & RB 1939.5–1.12.

132 Brooch Early Iron Age about 6th century BC Excavated from the Iron Age cemetery at Hallstatt, Upper Austria.

Silver; semi-circular bow with asymmetrical swelling towards front and longitudinal grooving broken at widest point by plain transverse band defined by pair of grooves; two-coil spring on one side of bow only; recurved ends in stylized ram's head with horns added in filigree technique. H 1·9; L 3·2; WT 2·6.

A North Italic type.

P & RB 1939.5–1.22.

133 Brooch Central European Iron Age about 5th century BC From the Iron Age cemetery at Hallstatt, Upper Austria.

Bronze, modelled as dog either barking at or about to bite an unconcerned duck; badly corroded, pin missing, four-coil spring with internal cord pegged to dog's hind leg; peg probably originally provided with spherical finial at either end. H 2·7; L 4·7; WT 11·1.

One of a small group of *Tierfibeln*, brooches with quadrupeds modelled in the round, from fifth century BC contexts in Central Europe; unusual in its depiction of a scene rather than of a single animal. For the type, see Megaw (1971).

P & RB 1939.5–1.7.

131

132

133

134 Brooches (pair) North Italian Iron Age
5th–4th century BC
Silver; apart from slight damage to catchplates, identical pair in perfect condition; double-coil spring on one side of bow only; bow has knee-like angle and knob with narrow flanking ridges; chased or engraved double chevron on foot at junction with bow; foot has domed finial and slight central keel; pin of each brooch curves down at point and has barely perceptible constriction on upper side 6·5 cm. from point – its purpose apparently to hinder brooch from falling out of garment should it accidentally open when in use. L 16·8; 16·9; WT 48·1; 49·8.

A variety of the 'Certosa' type of brooch developed in the sixth and following centuries in northern Italy and disseminated to the Alpine regions and to the area to the north, where local varieties were developed from the fifth century BC.

Collection of S. Egger of Vienna; Sotheby's, 25 June 1891 (lot 262); Pitt Rivers Collection.
Bibliography: *British Museum Report of the Trustees 1972–1975*, p. 50, pl. 34; for the type, see Primas (1970).
P & RB P1974.12–1.334–5.

135 Brooch Early La Tène about 400 BC
Bronze, with high arching bow of symmetrical rounded profile, four large coils to spring, external cord, decorated domed (?)bone stud attached by gold rivet to circular setting on recurved foot; baluster-finial on foot; chased ribbing on catchplate; pin fractured. L 7·2; H 2·6; WT 25·1.

A fine specimen of the 'Marzabotto' type of brooch, belonging to an early phase of the La Tène Iron Age (in Switzerland, La Tène Ia); one of the most widespread types of La Tène brooches, found as widely apart as Britain and Austria.
Bibliography: Allen (1904), pl. XII, top right.
P & RB 80.8–20.25.

136 Brooch Early La Tène 4th–3rd century BC
Prosne, dép. Marne, France.

Bronze, four-coil spring with external cord, low symmetrical bow, large globe flanked by two smaller, and trilobe finial on recurved foot; large globe, bow and spring embellished in low relief with curvilinear patterns. H 2·1; L 6·3; WT 14·2.

The patterns on the brooch are in the so-called 'Waldalgesheim' style of early Celtic art, which was probably developed in the latter part of the fourth century BC and continued to flourish in the third; see Jacobsthal (1944); Megaw (1970); Jope (1971); essays by J. Driehaus, O.-H. Frey, and F. Schwappach, in

Hamburger Beiträge zur Archäologie 1, ii (1971); and Frey (1976); and notes to no. 114.
Bibliography: Morel (1898), pl. 24.25.
P & RB ML1614. Collection of L. Morel, of Reims, 1901.

137 Brooch Duero Culture about 3rd century BC
Bronze, bow and foot cast in one piece; bow swells in middle and has three large sharply-pointed longitudinal ridges and two small lateral flanges; foot has concave-sided square terminal; foot and terminal decorated front and sides (terminal on top too) using ring-punch; spring has six coils on either side of bow and hollowed biconical terminals; rivet holds terminals on to spring and spring to loop at head of bow; internal cord to spring. H 3·2; L 5·7; WT 81·1.

A variety of *Fusszierfibel* ('decorated foot brooch') characteristic of the Duero Culture of the Iberian Iron Age; the territory of this culture coincided more or less with the basin of the River Duero in north-western Spain and northern Portugal. For the type, see Schüle (1969), pp. 143, 149–50, 152, pl. 163.20–1.
P & RB POA165.

138 Brooch Middle La Tène 2nd century BC
La Tène, Canton Neuchâtel, Switzerland.

Iron, wrought in a single piece, with four-coil spring with external cord, foot with cylindrical knob (which has grooves around it front and back) threaded on and with end expanded and bent round to clasp bow. H 2·3; L 9·7; WT 18·6.
Bibliography: Smith (1905), p. 43, fig. 38; Smith (1925), p. 52, fig. 51.
P & RB 80.12–14.8.

139 Brooch South-east Iberian Iron Age
2nd–1st century BC
Silver, parcel-gilt; slightly asymmetrical curved arched bow of arched section; foot recurved and terminal, shaped like head and neck of horse, soldered to bow; two horses clamped by feet to bow; these two horses and horse-terminal decorated with chased ladder pattern on each side; from head of bow a rod of metal projects and secures arms with horse-head terminals; this rod is ornamented with beasties and is soldered to bow; on bow, which has beaded edges, is dotted zigzag line (made with centre-punch) on either side of beasties-moulding; pin missing. L 6·7; H 3·5; WT 48·0.

Rare type; parallels to it have only been found in hoards of silver from southern and eastern Spain; for the type, see Raddatz (1969), pp. 142, 146, pls. 2.10; 48.1–3; 62.5–6 (type II).
P & RB P1970.9–1.1.

135

137

139

140 Brooch Late La Tène late 1st century BC
Torre Annunziata, Italy.

Bronze, with triple moulding at head of bow, crimped ridge along it, openwork catchplate, and four-coil spring broken and repaired with rod inserted inside. L 10·7; H 3·0; WT 25·2.

A variety of one of the commoner types ('Almgren 65' or *fibula ad arpa*) of Late La Tène brooch; probably brought south from the very north of Italy or beyond.
Bibliography: Walters (1899), no. 2062.
P & RB 1935.10–18.50. Given by Sir William Temple, 1856.

141 Brooch Southern Alpine Late La Tène
late 1st century BC
Bronze; ornate openwork catchplate; duck's head at crest of bow just in front of group of three collar-mouldings separated by two 'cotton-reels'; four-coil spring with high external cord. L 13·2; WT 42·2.

A particularly ornate and rare type of Late La Tène brooch normally found along the southern fringes of the Alps in south Switzerland, north Italy and west Slovenia.
   Found in a cupboard in the Museum in 1907. The suggestion that it might have come from the bed of the River Thames was taken up in publication of the piece, but remains unsupported by any evidence.
Bibliography: Brailsford (1953), p. 64, fig. 24.4; Fox (1958), p. 66, pl. 40a; Krämer (1971), p. 127; Ettlinger (1973), p. 51, pl. 24.2.
P & RB 1907.10–24.2.

142 Brooch Pannonian 1st century AD
Székesfehérvár, prov. Fejér, Hungary.

Silver; arched bow, consisting of convex and concave curves meeting at collar flanked by narrow beaded ridges; on front of bow, just below collar, pair of chased 'eyes'; catchplate ornamented on both faces in pointillé technique, on one with fish (? dolphin), on other with a (?) snake; spring has fifteen coils on each side, external cord and is attached to head of brooch with rod threaded through; domed caps protect ends of spring and secure them to arms that run out laterally from head of brooch. H 7·8; L 12·7; WT 127·1.

This extremely rare type of brooch is closely matched in only one other find – a first century AD hoard containing a silver armlet and seventeen silver brooches of this type from Okorág, prov. Baranya, south-west Hungary (von Patek (1942), pp. 99–100, pl. x); both Okorág and Székesfehérvár lie in the eastern part of the Roman province of Pannonia. So close is the

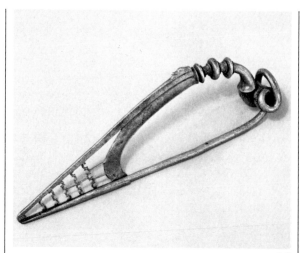

141

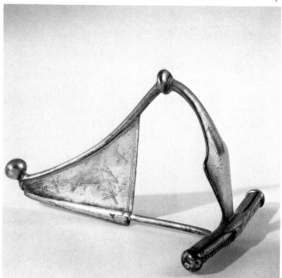

142 △   ▽ 144

resemblance between them that it seems likely that the brooches from both places were made in the same workshop in eastern Pannonia.

P & RB 60.6–9.3. S. Egger collection, Budapest, 1860.

143 Brooch Irish Iron Age
about 1st–2nd century AD
Bondville, near Middletown, Co. Armagh, Northern Ireland.

Bronze, wrought, with double-coil spring and external cord; pin (underneath) bent out of true; bow 'leaf-shaped' and divided into three raised panels by grooves along which run lines of spaced dots made with centre-punch.
L 9·1; WT 24·6.

A unique variety of the Irish 'leaf-bow' brooch.
Bibliography: Jope (1961–62), p. 27, fig. 6.
P & RB 62.6–17.4.

144 Brooch Irish Iron Age 1st–2nd century AD
Clogher, Co. Tyrone, Northern Ireland.

Bronze; two-coil spring with external cord; bow and recurved loop on foot ornamented with three circular recesses for inlay (lost, but probably red enamel) and with fine ridges that grow out of and coalesce into each other. H 2·4; L 8·6; WT 21·1.
Bibliography: Kemble, Latham and Franks (1863), p. 197, pl. XXI.4; Allen (1904), pl. XII, top left; Smith (1905), p. 146, fig. 141; Smith (1925), p. 159, fig. 191; Jope (1961–62), pp. 31–2, fig. 7.
P & RB 54.3–7.2.

145 Armlets (pair) North British Iron Age
1st–2nd century AD
Pitkelloney Farm, near Drummond Castle, Muthill, Perthshire, Scotland.

Brass, cast complete as hoops: one as full circle, only a hair-line crack, developed since casting, separating terminals; one a very poor casting with much metal cast in as repair; relief ornament probably sharpened up in fettling; open terminals of each armlet filled with red and yellow enamelled settings – on one armlet with cruciform design, on other with four-lobe rosette design; enamelling in *champlevé* technique in circle on rounded diamond-shaped brass plate attached at corners by rivets to iron backing-plate; semi-tubular brass frame to each setting attached by rivets to backing-plate; tang projects from each frame and runs down channel between ridges leading up to opening in terminal; over this is cast beaded ridge originally running full length of each groove; at junction of tang with roundel a loop projects from back, through which is threaded brass rod that runs

behind main decorative panels to secure settings in position. D 13·8 by 13·1 and 14·2 by 14·2; H 8·0 and 7·8; WT 1629 and 1730.

Examples of the 'folded' type of 'massive' armlet; these armlets are normally found in pairs. Both types of 'massive' armlet – the 'folded' and 'oval' (the latter represented by no. 146) – were made in Scotland, and all the twenty-one recorded specimens (except for one of 'folded' type from Newry, Co. Down, Northern Ireland) have been found there. All are very similarly ornamented, in native north British style; the two types appear to have been made in different parts of Scotland: the 'folded' in the Angus-Fife-Perthshire region, the 'oval' in the Aberdeenshire-Banffshire region, and possibly also in the Tweed basin.
Bibliography: Kemble, Latham and Franks (1863), p. 183, nos. 23–4; Smith (1905), p. 143, fig. 138; Smith (1925), pp. 155–6, fig. 186; Powell (1966), ill. 245; Simpson (1968), pp. 235–6, 248, 250, 252, fig. 61a,b, pl. X; Megaw (1970), pp. 173–4, pl. VIIIb; Brailsford (1975), pp. 75–81, figs. 106–23; MacGregor (1976), pp. 106–10, 116, nos. 242–3.
P & RB 38.7–14.3a–b.

Colour plate 13

146 Armlets (pair) North British Iron Age
1st–2nd century AD
Castle Newe, Strathdon, Aberdeenshire, Scotland.

Bronze, cast complete as hoops; relief ornament sharpened up in fettling; very finely polished; the pairs of low ridges at base of grooves that separate the three large ribs obliquely nicked (one ridge in one direction, second in other) with tracer in herring-bone style; both armlets originally had enamelled diaphragms in circular openings in terminals; only one of four survives – bronze disc with chequer-pattern of red and yellow enamel squares inlaid in *champlevé* technique; circular double-ridged iron frame, riveted on, holds enamel plate to iron backing which is itself secured to terminal by paste of iron oxide. D 14·6 by 13·3 and 14·0 by 13·6; H 11·0 and 11·3; WT 1604 and 1677.

Examples of the 'oval' type of 'massive' armlet; see notes to no. 145.
Bibliography: Brailsford (1953), p. 64, pl. XIV.1; Powell (1966), p. 244; Simpson (1968), pp. 235, 236, 238, 243, 246, 248, 250, 252, fig. 58b, pl. VI, bottom; Megaw (1970), p. 174; Brailsford (1975), pp. 69–74, 81, figs. 96–105, pl. IX; MacGregor (1976), pp. 106–10, 116, nos. 239–40.
P & RB 1946.4–2.1–2.

Colour plate 13

Mexico: The Olmec

By 1000 BC the Olmec people were already well established in the tropical lowland areas of Tabasco and Veracruz on the Gulf Coast of Mexico. Their ceremonial centres such as that at La Venta, with large temple mounds, platforms, plazas and monumental sculpture, set the pattern for the subsequent Classic period centres throughout Mesoamerica; they also provide the earliest evidence for the use of a calendrical system and hieroglyphic writing.

The Olmec lapidaries were exceptionally skilled in the working of jadeite, nephrite, serpentine and other stones. Caches of small highly polished celts and figurines are found, as well as large ceremonial axes, masks, pendants, ear-flares and the so-called jade 'stilettos' associated with ritual letting of blood. Both in small stone carvings and monumental sculpture the representation of an anthropomorphized jaguar is a recurrent theme. Objects in the highly characteristic Olmec art style are found widely distributed throughout the Mesoamerican area.

E.M.C.

147 Pendant Olmec 1000–100 BC (?)
Jade pendant with human head carved in high relief. Two glyphs are incised on panel to left of the head. Nasal septum is pierced. H 10·5; W 11.

The rounded depressions which appear below the saw cuts representing the eyes are secondary working and thus alter the original character of the face. Traces of four further glyphs can just be seen, two on either side at the extreme edges of the broken panel. These may or may not be contemporary with the original carving.

Bibliography: A Digby, 'The Olmec Jades in the Exhibition of Mexican Art', *Burlington Magazine* (May 1953).

ETH 1929·7–12·1. Given by Mrs Yates Thompson.

147

Peru: The Nazca

The Nazca people of the south coastal region of Peru are best known to us through their elaborately decorated polychrome pottery. As well as stylized bird, fish and animal designs, human figures and severed human trophy heads are quite commonly represented. The so-called 'cat-demons', composite creatures with feline heads, often depicted wearing mouth masks of the kind shown (no. 149) are the most distinctive of the motifs employed. Similar designs decorate the brilliantly coloured textiles and also the metal objects which survive.

Most of the personal ornaments found in graves are made from hammered and cut gold. They include masks, mouth masks, bracelets, etc., but metallurgy was generally less advanced on the south coast than elsewhere in Peru. There is some evidence of metal casting techniques being in use in the latest phases of the Nazca period.

E.M.C.

148 Bracelet Nazca 200 BC–AD 600 (?)
Formed from sheet of hammered and cut gold, with repoussé decoration in form of geometrical shapes and ten feline motifs arranged in pairs. Two perforations, one at each side of bracelet. H 9.
ETH 1921.3–21.1.

149 Nose Ornament Nazca 200 BC–AD 600 (?)
Nose ornament or 'mouth mask' of hammered gold, cut in a semi-circular shape with two extensions terminating in snake-like arms. Further decorated with repoussé work. W 13·5; H 11.
ETH 1952.Am 10.1.

150 Pendant Nazca 200 BC–AD 600 (?)
Half of bivalve shell of *Spondylus* family decorated with mosaic in form of an anthropomorphic figure wearing pectoral and head-dress. Face carved in bone with nose and cheeks in relief. Mouth and eyes of pearl shell. Rest of mosaic consists of different coloured shells, malachite, and black stones. Wax-like substance is used as adhesive. Shell is perforated twice near hinge through which is thread a spun string of cotton for suspension. W 12.5; L 13.5.
ETH 1913.10–20.1. Given by Louis Clarke, Esq.

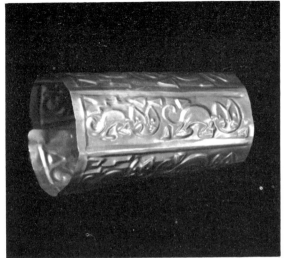

148

149 △   ▽ 150

Peru: The Mochica

The Mochica, or Moche people of the north coastal region of Peru (about AD 300–800) were the inheritors of a cultural tradition extending back to the Chavin period (about 900–300 BC).

The Mochica built large ceremonial centres with elaborate architecture in adobe brick. The best known of these is at Moche itself where two vast pyramids, the *Huaca del Sol* probably a temple pyramid and the *Huaca de la Luna* upon which the houses of the Moche priests or rulers probably stood, rise up out of the now arid valley.

Most of our knowledge of Mochica society is derived from the pottery vessels found in the cemeteries together with examples of Mochica craftsmanship in gold, silver, copper, bone and shell. The jewellery is rich and colourful. The metal-working techniques employed include both simple and lost-wax casting, alloying, gilding and welding as well as cutting, hammering and repoussé decoration.

E.M.C.

151 Ear Ornament Mochica AD 300–800 (?)
Ear ornament consisting of hollow wooden plug and wooden matrix, decorated with mosaic of pearl shell and different coloured stones secured with resin-like substance. Mosaic is in the form of human figure wearing an elaborate head-dress. D 10·5.
ETH 1960.Am 6.1.

151

8

The Mediterranean, Roman Britain, Egypt, Parthia, India and Byzantium

325 BC-AD 600

Hellenistic

The so-called Hellenistic Age lasted, culturally speaking, from about 322 BC until the inauguration of the Roman Empire in 27 BC.

The conquests of Alexander the Great between 333 and 322 BC transformed the Greek world. Vast new territories of the former Persian empire were hellenized by settlements of Greeks, and Greece in return was exposed to influences from the newly conquered territories of Egypt and Western Asia.

So far as jewellery is concerned, the most important fact is the far greater quantity of surviving material, thanks to the greater availability of gold. For the first time since the Bronze Age, gold was plentiful in Greece, partly because of the intensive mining operations in Thrace initiated by Philip II, but mostly from the dissemination of the captured Persian treasures. The general appearance of the jewellery was at first much as before, but by the early second century BC new forms took their place beside the old, and the system of decoration soon radically changed. Then, for about two centuries, there was little further change.

The principal innovations may be classed under three headings: new decorative motifs, new forms of jewellery, and new systems of decoration.

1 *New motifs*. The so-called Heracles-knot (the reef-knot) was introduced at the beginning of this period and retained its popularity as an ornament for jewellery into Roman times. It may be presumed to have come from Egypt, where its history as an amulet goes back to the beginning of the second millennium BC.

The crescent is another foreign import. It was introduced from Western Asia, where it had a high antiquity, and whence it had already reached Greece in the eighth and seventh centuries. In its homeland it was sacred to the Moon-god. It is found in Hellenistic necklaces as a pendant; although its purpose was doubtless primarily decorative, it had a certain amuletic value.

Of purely Greek motifs, figures of Eros are among the most popular, as in all Hellenistic art.

2 *New forms*. The animal- or human-headed hoop-earring was introduced about 330 BC probably from the east, and retained its popularity in certain regions till the Roman period.

Elaborate diadems, frequently with a Heracles-knot as a centre-piece, are first found about 300 BC and lasted for about two centuries. Bracelets in the same general style were also made, doubtless to accompany the diadems.

New types of necklaces are also found from about 330 BC, of which chains with animal-head finials and straps with pendants of buds or spear-heads are the most important. Beads not threaded but linked together are typical of the second and first centuries BC.

3 *New techniques*. The most important innovation, which transformed the appearance of Greek jewellery, is the polychromy provided by the inlay of stones and coloured glass. Of the stones, chalcedonies, carnelians and above all garnets were in use from 330 BC onwards. In the second and first centuries BC we also find emeralds, amethysts, and pearls.

R.H.

152 Diadem Greek 3rd century BC
Found at Melos.

Gold. Composed of three strands of twisted gold bands, central one decorated with rosettes. In centre is reef-knot of gold wire richly enamelled and encrusted with large cabochon garnet. L 27·9.
Bibliography: *BMCJ*, no. 1607; *GRJ*, p. 160, pl. 45A.
G & R 72.6–4.815. Castellani Collection.

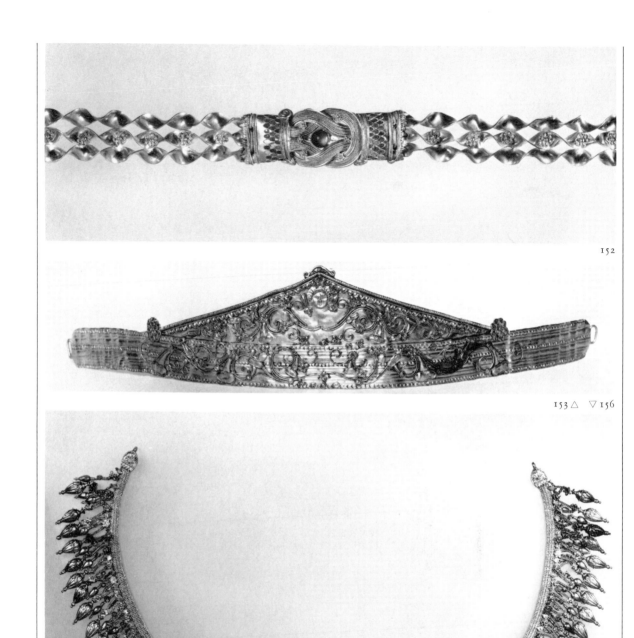

153 Diadem Greek 3rd century BC
Found at Santa Eufemia, the ancient Terina, South Italy, in 1865.

Gold. Rising to point over brow and richly decorated in pictorial style with low relief and filigree. L 17·7.

Probably made at Tarentum. Dated by associated coins.
Bibliography: *BMCJ*, no. 2113; *GRJ*, p. 159, pl. 45B; *L'Antiquité Classique* xlii (1973), p. 552.
G & R 96.6–16.1.

154 Part of Diadem Greek 2nd century BC
Gold. Central portion of diadem in form of reef-knot flanked by squares of decorated gold work. Knot inlaid with garnets, flanking ornaments decorated with enamel and filigree. L 8·6.
Bibliography: *BMCJ*, no. 1608; *GRJ*, p. 159, pl. C.
G & R 67.5–8.537.

155 Pair of Earrings Greek 4th–3rd century BC
Found at Kyme, north-west Asia Minor.

Gold. From disc, richly decorated with filigree, hangs inverted pyramid, also richly decorated. Figure of Victory sits on pyramid, and two other Victories hang by chains from the disc. H 6·5.
Bibliography: *BMCJ*, nos. 1672–3; *GRJ*, p. 165.
G & R 77.9–10.16–17.

156 Necklace Greek 3rd century BC
Found at Melos.

Gold. Strap from which hang miniature gold jars (or flower-buds) on five chains. Points where the chains cross are masked by small enamelled discs. L 33·6.
Bibliography: *BMCJ*, no. 1947; *GRJ*, p. 168, pl. 49.
G & R 72.6–4.660. Castellani Collection.

157 Necklace Greek 2nd century BC
Taormina, Sicily.

Gold. A chain from which hangs a crescent-shaped pendant inlaid with garnets. W 3 (pendant).
G & R 1914.10–16.1.

154

155 △　▽ 157

Roman

For many centuries in the Roman world jewellery was one of those luxuries under official disapproval and surviving examples are very scarce.

However, with the inauguration of the Empire in 27 BC and the annexation by Rome of most of the Hellenistic world, the old austerity was quickly put aside. In artistic matters Rome was always deeply in the debt of Greece, and the jewellery of the early Empire was, in many respects, simply a continuation of Hellenistic. Gradually, however, certain other influences made themselves felt, and by the end of this period, much Roman jewellery was anticipating the Byzantine style which was to follow.

Jewellery at the beginning of this period was essentially gold jewellery. Towards the end of the period, however, an increasing emphasis was placed on stones for their own sake, and less pains were taken over the working of the gold in which they were set. Here for the first time the very hardest stones were used: diamonds occasionally, although uncut; sapphires, and above all, emeralds, from the newly discovered Egyptian mines in the Red Sea hills, which were used in the natural hexagonal prisms in which these stones are found.

One form of gold-working was, however, popular towards the end of this period, and that is a kind of metal-fretwork, called by the Romans *opus interrasile*, in which patterns are cut out of sheet gold with a chisel. This process was further developed in Byzantine jewellery.

Inlaying was still practised. Enamel was sometimes used, especially in the Celtic areas, and a related form of decoration, niello, made its first appearance.

The chief centres of production were probably Alexandria and Antioch, and also Rome itself, whither many immigrant craftsmen from the Greek East had migrated. We have evidence that goldsmiths and silversmiths were now organized in guilds like medieval craftsmen. Their workmanship, though skilled, falls short of the high standards maintained by the Hellenistic goldsmiths.

It is difficult to give a date for the end of the Roman period, but a reasonable date would be AD 313, the year of the Edict of Milan.

R.H.

158 △   ▽ 164

158 Hair-ornament Roman 3rd century AD
Tunis.

Gold. Inlaid with emeralds and set with pearls and a
sapphire. H 10·7.
Bibliography: *BMCJ*, no. 2866; *GRJ*, p. 183, pl. 62C.
G & R 1903.7–17.3.

159 Earrings Roman 1st century AD
Pozzuoli, the ancient Puteoli, in the Bay of Naples.

Gold. Hemisphere masking an S-shaped hook;
smaller boss above. H 3·1.
Bibliography: *BMCJ*, nos. 2618–19; *GRJ*, p. 184, pl. 54E.
G & R 72.6–4.1109. Castellani Collection.

160 Necklace Roman 3rd century AD
Gold. Necklace of pierced work, with emerald inlay
and bezel-set amethysts. L 40.
Bibliography: *BMCJ*, no. 2749; *GRJ*, p. 186, pl. 61B.
G & R 2749F. Franks Bequest, 1897.

161 Necklace Roman 2nd century BC
Gold. Cut-out patterns alternating with emerald
crystals. L 41·6.
Bibliography: *BMCJ*, no. 2731.
G & R 14.7–4.1203. Towneley Collection.

162 Necklace Roman 1st century AD
Rome.

Gold, with sapphires, garnets, rock-crystals. Bezel-set
stones mounted in centre of gold chain, so as to make
a butterfly-shaped pendant. L 32·1.
Bibliography: *BMCJ*, no. 2746; *GRJ*, p. 186, pl. 58.
G & R 72.6–4.670. Castellani Collection.

163 Bracelet Roman 1st century AD
Pompeii.

Gold. Composed of eleven paired hemispheres, linked
together. L 24.

Found at Pompeii and given by the King of Naples to
Sir William Hamilton. Later in the possession of
Viscount Dillon.
Bibliography: *GRJ*, p. 187, pl. 60A.
G & R 1946.7–2.1. Given by Mrs M. Acworth, 1946.

164 Bracelet Roman 1st century AD
Gold. In form of coiled snake. D (external) 8·2.
Bibliography: *GRJ*, p. 187, pl. 61E.
G & R 1946.7–2.2. Given by Mrs M. Acworth, 1946.

161 △   ▽ 162

Roman Britain

Already well before the Claudian invasion of Britain in AD 43, Roman influence becomes apparent in the designs of certain objects made in the British Isles. After the Conquest, it is valid to speak of fully 'Romano-British' styles, particularly in the sphere of jewellery, since native styles of decoration continued to be used on jewellery until well into the second century AD. British enamelwork was particularly esteemed in the ancient world (no. 166). Many finds of more 'mainstream' Roman jewellery have, however, been made in Britain, such as the Backworth bracelet and necklaces (no. 169) and the Moray Firth brooch (no. 171).

M.S.

165 Hair-pin Romano-British late 1st century AD
Bone; head of pin modelled as bust of woman resting on square plinth; elaborate coiffure with little projections around top, presumably representing heads of hair-pins. L (total) 19·4; L (base of plinth to top of coiffure) 5·5; WT 8·2.

This style of coiffure was in vogue in the Flavian period to which the pin may be dated. An identical bone pin has been found in the bed of the River Walbrook in the City of London (now in the Museum of London; Merrifield (1969), p. 156, fig. 41); it is likely that both pins were made in the same workshop in Roman London (*Londinium*).
Bibliography: Brailsford (1964), p. 28, no. 9, fig. 14.9.
P & RB OA245.

166 Brooch Romano-British
Late 1st–early 2nd century AD
Bronze, cast, with blue and white enamel set into the metal in *champlevé* technique; pin missing. L 6·2; WT 16·7.

A specimen of the 'dragonesque' type of brooch, which is principally found in northern England and southern Scotland. The style of its ornamentation is in the Late Iron Age tradition; this specific style was developed in southern Britain in the decades leading up to the Claudian invasion of AD 43, but persisted in almost unmodified form for the ornamentation of small objects, principally jewellery, well into the second century.
Bibliography: Smith (1907–9), pp. 59, 62, fig. 4; Allen (1904), p. 107, pl. XII, bottom left; Bulmer (1938), p. 153, fig. 3.G1; Feachem (1951), p. 42, fig. 3.G1.
P & RB

167 Pin Romano-British 1st–2nd century AD
Bed of River Walbrook, City of London.

Silver; head of pin represents hand holding pomegranate, arising from double-disc moulding; stem of pin bent out of true. L (total) 12·2; L (hand) 2·2; WT 9·4.
Bibliography: Smith (1935), p. 95, pl. XXXI.1; Brailsford (1964), p. 28, no. 12, fig. 14.12.
P & RB 1934.12–10.21.

168 Pin Romano-British 2nd–4th century AD
Excavated in the City of London.

Silver, with head representing nude figure of Venus leaning on pole, adjusting her sandal and standing on Corinthian capital. L (total) 12·8; H (figure) 2·6; WT 12·6.

A common design for a pin in the Roman world, but its crude execution suggests that it is provincial work.
Bibliography: Brailsford (1964), p. 28, no. 10, fig. 14.10.
P & RB 83.5–9.2.

169 Brooches (pair), Necklaces (two), Bracelet
Romano-British late 1st–early 2nd century AD
Found at Backworth, Northumberland, England, before 1812.

(a, b) Pair of identical silver-gilt brooches (mercury-gilded), with chased wave-patterns in two panels on bow, both above and below central acanthus-moulding; head and catchplate have chased or engraved motifs in Late Iron Age style; pin missing from both brooches, and spring from one; spring separately made and hinged to back of head of each brooch; moulded loop and ridged rectangular plate at its base, both separately made, project from head of each brooch; loops formerly used as terminals for chain (lost) that linked brooches together; large circular finial with ridged edge to catchplate. L 10·2 and 10·0; WT 80·3 and 90·6.
(c, d) Gold necklaces, with respectively seventy-two and ninety-six figure-of-eight links twisted through right-angle at neck, and wheel and crescentic pendants; each opens with hook at one end of chain, linked to eye projecting from wheel; wheel on one necklace has central green glass button. D (wheels) 2·3 and 2·2; L (unhooked) 74·3 and 83·3; WT 41·1 and 60·2.
(e) Gold bracelet with wheel pendant and fifteen figure-of-eight links; hollow ball threaded on to lengthened neck of each link; links twisted through right angle at neck. D (wheel) 1·9; WT 16·3.

From a treasure of which the original full contents are not known, but which also contained five gold finger-rings, 280 coins and part of a mirror, all within a silver gilt skillet (handled vessel). The latest coin is alleged to have dated to AD 139, and while the brace-

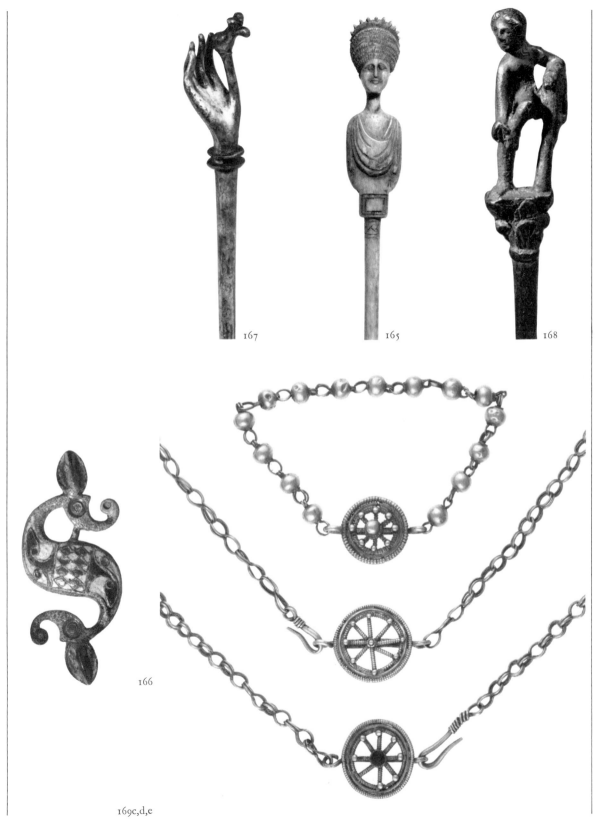

167

165

168

166

169c,d,e

let and necklaces may be late first or early second century in date, the brooches were probably made in the last quarter of the first century. They are of British make, their ornamentation reflecting both native and Roman traditions; the bracelet and necklaces are in purely Roman style, paralleled, for example, at Pompeii.

Bibliography: Allen (1904), p. 103–4 (fig.), 107; Smith (1905), p. 101, fig. 84; Marshall (1911), nos. 2738–40; Smith (1922), pp. 54, 62–3, figs. 62, 79; Smith (1925), p. 96, fig. 102; Collingwood (1930); Corder and Hawkes (1940), p. 351; Charlesworth (1961), pp. 3–5, 20–1, 34–5, pl. VII; Brailsford (1964), p. 14, no. 5, p. 18, no. 17, p. 28, no. 1, figs. 7.5, 9.17, pl. I.1; Henig (1971), p. 322; Boon and Savory (1975), pp. 44, 46, 47, 51; Lins and Oddy (1975), p. 369, no. 33; Pfeiler (1970), pp. 71–2, pl. 19–20.

P & RB 50.6–1.3–5.15–6.

170 **Pendant** Romano-British 3rd–4th century AD
Southfleet, Kent, England.

Gold, consisting of 20 identical composite links, each originally embellished with pairs of pearls and blue-green beads; hook-terminal has beaded gold wire ornamentation; other terminal square with beaded wire around edge, setting containing semi-precious stone, and two (originally three) hexagonal blue-green beads suspended on twisted wires. L 26·3; WT 52·2.

Found with a pair of gold bracelets and a gold finger-ring on the skeleton of a child in a lead coffin in 1801.
Bibliography: Rashleigh (1803), pp. 38–9, pl. VIII,2;

Smith (1922), pp. 50, 65; Brailsford (1964), p. 28, pl. 1.7.

P & RB 1912.6–20.1.

171 **Brooch** Romano-British 4th century AD
Moray Firth, Scotland.

Gold; hollow; at head three faceted hexagonal onion-shaped terminals with beaded collars, one of which (nearside in photograph) screwed into position (on left-hand thread); purpose of screw inside arm was to secure head of (now missing) pin of which point-end was inserted in socket in foot of brooch; pin-head inserted into perforation at back of centre of head of brooch; by unscrewing onion-terminal pin could be released; on top of each lateral arm simple running-scroll in openwork technique; both faces of bow and foot ornamented with friezes of triangles; on bow these alternately filled with leaf-fronds and palmettes, on foot with leaf-fronds only; niello applied to grooves that comprise these filled triangles; foot of lozenge section, plain in lower half, decorated with applied cusped motifs; base of bow wound round several times with length of woven gold wire; above this a beaded collar. L 7·9; WT 39·6.

A fine example of the widespread late Roman 'crossbow' type of brooch. The screw-mechanism is matched on crossbow brooches from Richborough, Kent.
Bibliography: Curle (1931–2), pp. 336 f., 392, no. 77A, fig. 36.4; *GRJ*, p. 192, pl. 64C; Robertson (1970), pp. 212, 223, fig. 11.4.

P & RB 1962.12–15.1 (formerly G & R 1922.4–12.1).

171

172

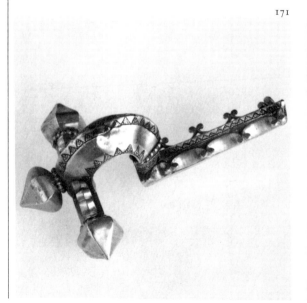

Egypt

After the New Kingdom ended, Egypt underwent a troubled period until order was restored throughout the country by Egyptianized Nubians. The succeeding XXVIth Dynasty marked a return to the style and taste of earlier times but few pieces of jewellery can be dated definitely to this period; only the gold figure of Maat may be of this date.

The glass industry revived under the Ptolemies and glass head-beads are characteristic. Earrings largely disappeared during the Third Intermediate and Saite Periods but later returned, often in forms frequently found throughout the Hellenistic world; animal-headed earrings had no previous history in Egypt. Although cloisonné work remains excellent, the emphasis is on unadorned gold: gold bracelets and bangles made from untraditional strip-twisted wire, necklaces of gold beads resembling Roman work, gold diadem ornaments of Greek origin, are often indistinguishable from Hellenistic or Roman work.
C.A.

172 Necklace with Pendant Egyptian
600 to 100 BC (?)
Saite to Ptolemaic periods
Gold, figure of Maat seated on pedestal, suspended from gold chain. Latter is loop-in-loop made of gold rolled and beaten wire. Figure apparently made of gold foil over core which remains. Details of eyes, nose and mouth carved; mouth slightly twisted, not enough metal having been removed. Striations on wig roughly done. Truth-feather on head made of central piece of sheet gold to which four cloisons soldered on both sides following line of feather. Loop at back of head for suspension. L (chain) 49·5; H (figure) 2·7; L (base) 0·9.

Statuettes of gods in metal as pendants are known particularly from the later periods. Maat was goddess of truth, justice and cosmic order and, according to Diodorus Siculus, small figures of her were worn as the insignia of a judge.
EA 48998. Purchased with the aid of Lady Wantage.

Colour plate 7

173 Pectoral Egyptian about 600–100 BC
Saite to Ptolemaic periods
Gold flying falcon in round with inlay. Details of head, eyes and beak moulded and chased on underside. Legs hollow and gold wire feet probably once added. Back of head, body, wings and tail inlaid with coloured glass set in cloisons. Glass probably blue, green and red (?) in colour but much decayed. Body must have been moulded over core and wings and legs added separately. Wings made of base-plate, rims and cloisons, each made separately. Outer frame thick and cloisons substantial. Wing span 14·8; w (wing 2·2; L (body) 5·8.

This is a very fine piece of workmanship. Presumably it was worn as a pectoral although no suspension loops have survived. Cf. Aldred (1971), pl. 142.
Bibliography: *ILN* (27 October, 1923), p. 741, fig. 5.
EA 57323.

174 Earrings Egyptian about 300–100 BC
Ptolemaic period

(a) Pair of gold, formed from hollow crescent of thin sheet gold with inverted pyramid-shaped pendants. Thin piece of gold wire attached to one end of crescent by pin which allows it to swivel up and down. To close earring free end of wire is pushed into open end of crescent. Three-sided pyramid covered with regularly-placed gold grains; base-plate unadorned. To point of pyramid are attached two gold rings and gold ball, set one above other. External D (shank) 1·7; H (pendant) 1·0.

(b) Pair of gold, with gazelle- or antelope-head terminals. Heads hollow gold foil; twisted wire horns and gold-foil ears added separately and soldered to head. Neck decorated with wire circlets and sleeve which joins neck to shank decorated with twisted wires and loops. Shank made from wire twisted to form coil tapering towards end where it hooks into ring in animal's mouth. External D (shank) 2·6; L (head) 1·4.

(a) Pyramid-shaped pendants of this type are not uncommon on earrings of the Hellenistic period throughout the eastern Mediterranean area. Cf. Vernier (1927), pl. XXXVII, 52.504–7. (b) Earrings with animal-head terminals are widely spread in the eastern Mediterranean world during the fourth to first centuries BC. Those with antelope- or gazelle-heads are apparently not Egyptian in origin and date more precisely to the fourth and early third centuries BC. Cf. Vernier (1927), pl. XXXV, 52.523; H. Hoffman and P. F. Davidson, *Greek Gold, Jewelry from the Age of Alexander* (Mainz, 1965), p. 107, nos. 27–8.

EA 65684, given by the Rt Hon. Viscount Crookshank; 67399–67400, given by Mrs S. Hall (collection of Dr H. R. Hall).

175 Head-beads Egyptian
about 3rd–1st centuries BC
Ptolemaic period
(b) Excavated at Mostagedda, Egypt, grave 801 by British Museum in 1928; (c) Karnak (Thebes), Egypt.

(a) Glass, male head; face and ears in opaque yellow, head-dress in translucent dark blue. Eyes formed from pale-blue rings. Blue suspension loop on head. H 1·8.

(b) Glass, cylindrical form representing negro in opaque bright blue. Large eyes formed from circles of white with bright blue pupils in high relief. Heavy lips also of white glass. Ears represented, one now missing, by loop of bright blue; blob of white below is presumably earring. Suspension loop on top of head in opaque bright blue. Brown core. H 3·0.

(c) Glass, seemingly Hellenistic type. Face in opaque yellow has heavy curled beard in dark blue which is also colour of hair, now almost entirely lost. Small drop of this blue glass is preserved on back of head where mandril was held. H 1·9.

These beads seem to have served as pendants for earrings as well as elements of necklaces. One of the few excavated examples, (b), was found strung with three glass eye-beads. The face of (c) seems to be Greek rather than Semitic and it is possible that a satyr is intended.

Bibliography: (a) *Sale Catalogue of the Athanasi Collection of Egyptian Antiquities* (London, 13 March, 1837), lot 613; Cooney (1976), no. 283; (b) Brunton (1937), p. 137, pl. LXXXIII, 1; Cooney (1976), no. 292; (c) Cooney (1976), no. 293.

EA 2882; 62580; 64220, given by the Rt Hon. Sir W. H. Gregory.

176 Necklace with pendant Egyptian
about 300 BC–1st century AD
Ptolemaic to Roman periods
Said to be from Memphis, Egypt.

Composed of gold segmented, spherical, collared, disc and gadrooned beads and pendant in form of situla or heart. Many of beads made in two halves soldered together. L 33.

The gadrooned nasturtium-seed beads are very similar to those known to be XVIIIth Dynasty in date. But the necklace as a whole resembles fourth century Italian work.

Bibliography: *Salt Collection* (1835), lot 641; *BM Guide* (1874), p. 70; *ibid.* (1922), p. 100, no. 797.

EA 3075.

177 Bangles Egyptian about 100 BC–AD 300
Ptolemaic and Roman Periods
(a) Possibly Luxor (Thebes), Egypt.

(a) Gold, one of pair of twisted wire with snake's head terminals. Wire appears to be beaten and in many places is soldered together. Wound around central solid bronze (?) wire now blackened by corrosion. Coils of wire are larger on side away from terminals. Snake's head terminals appear to be hollow cast and slipped over ends of wires. D (max. outer) 7·2; Maximum D (shank) 0·9.

(b) Gold, made from two pieces of thin sheet gold twisted together. Two long pieces of wire soldered at ends of strips and twisted together in complicated fashion. External D 8·3; D (shank) 0·7.

Gold bangles with terminals formed from animals' heads and those with twisted wire shanks are typical of the Hellenistic Age.

Bibliography: (a) *BM Guide* (1904), p. 215, no. 107;

175a,b,c

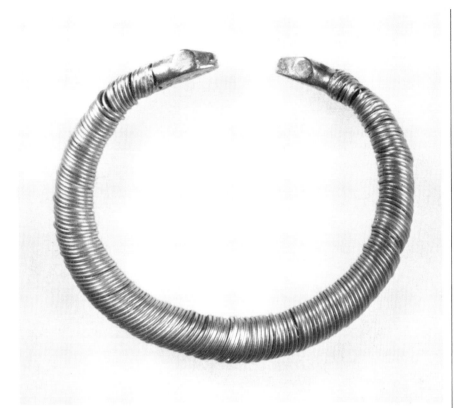

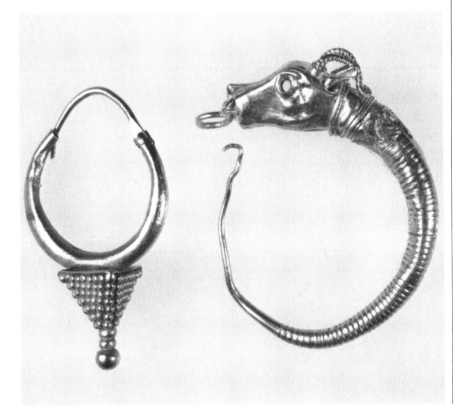

121

ibid. (1922), p. 89, no. 107; (b) H. R. Hall, 'Egyptian Jewellery and Carvings', *BMQ* 3 (1928), p. 41, pl. XXIII,a.
EA 34264; 14457, given by Sir Robert Mond.

178 Diadem Ornament Egyptian
1st–3rd centuries AD
Roman period
Gold, star with eight rays or petals, each made separately and consisting of base-plate containing escape hole for air and curved upper part. Petals soldered to central circular base around central circular boss. Between every two rays are two granules of gold alternating with single granule. Ring for suspension soldered in centre at back. D 3·4.

This ornament is strikingly similar to a seven-pointed gold star worn on the forehead of a bearded man in a Fayumic portrait of the second century AD. See A. F. Shore, *Portrait Painting from Roman Egypt* (London, 1962), pl. 8.
EA 26328.

Colour plate 7

Parthia

179 Buckle Parthian
about 1st century BC–1st century AD
Nihavend area, Iran.

Gold buckle, embossed and chased, showing eagle gripping young goat; inlay, mostly lost, of turquoise and another stone. W 9·34.

179

Buckles of this kind could have been used for fastening belts or cloaks, though it has also been suggested that they may have come from horse harness. This is one of a pair found in a hoard which may have belonged to a principal noble family of Parthia, the Karens; its pair is in the Metropolitan Museum of Art, New York.
Bibliography: Dalton (1928); Herzfeld (1928), p. 22.
WAA 124097.

180 Earrings Parthian about 1st–2nd century AD
(a) Vase-shaped gold pendant, decorated with granulation and filigree, and inlaid with garnets; one loop on top, and seven small loops below. H 6·67.

This earring would have had an additional fitting on top, for attachment to the ear, and extra ornamental pendants below, probably representing bells and pomegranates.
Bibliography: Porada (1967), p. 107.
WAA 135207.

(b) Gold pendant, decorated with granulation and inlaid with garnets and another material; bell-shaped

180a

180b

ornaments of sheet gold attached by chains of gold wire. H 4·62.
Bibliography: Barnett (1963), p. 100.
WAA 132933.

India

181 A Group of Gold Ornaments Indian
about AD 500 (?)
Excavated from burials in the Nilgiri Hills.

181

Pendants, pearled rings, earrings, a ribbed bead, crushed circlet, chains and floral ornaments with strips for attachment at back.

The finds accompanying the burials in the Nilgiri Hills were formerly associated with the 'megalithic' period in South India (end of the first millennium BC) on the most general grounds of resemblance in the form of interment; more recent work attributes the very different cultural equipment of the Nilgiri burials to a somewhat later period, perhaps in the second half of the first millennium AD.
Bibliography: Sir Walter Elliot, 'Ancient Sepulchral remains in Southern India and the Nilagiri Hills' (*International Congress of Prehistoric Archaeology*), *Transactions of the third session . . . 1868* (London, 1869), pp. 240–57 with illustrations.
OA 86.5–15.1–7; 9; 12–16; 18, given by Sir Walter Elliot; 1923.7–12.1, given by Mrs Elliot Lockhart.

182 Group of Gold Objects Indian about AD 500 (?)
Excavated in the Temple of the Enlightenment (Mahabodhi), Bodh Gaya, Bihar, in 1881.

Gold objects consisting of flowers with central sapphire strung with gold conch shells; floral discs, buttons, bracteates, plain or with floral decoration, various fragments and pendant imitating coin.

The earliest Buddhist shrine deposits contained the remains of venerable persons but by the first millennium AD, deposits of coins, gold precious and semi-precious stones, beads and other ornaments are common. The frequently restored temple commemorating the historical Buddha's spiritual enlightenment at Bodh Gaya has yielded such deposits. A ball of clay excavated from in front of the Enlightenment Throne in 1881 contained coins, silver objects and a quantity of precious stones as well as this gold jewellery. Although the pendant imitates a coin of the second century AD and the coins are no later in date the evident possibility of subsequent depositions during the Buddhist period makes the same date for the gold ornaments open to doubt.
Bibliography: Sir Alexander Cunningham, *Mahabodhi* (London, 1892), p. 20, pl. XXII.
OA 92.11–3.13–20; 22–31.

Early Christian and Byzantine Jewellery

The use of gold was widespread in the jewellery of the fourth to the seventh centuries AD; silver is used only rarely, as in the little charm from the Esquiline Treasure (no. 183). A variety of different techniques, all of them derived from the jewellery of the Roman period, continued to be practised, but an essential characteristic of the period was the growth in the use of *opus interrasile*, the technique of chiselling or cutting through a thin sheet of gold in order to produce an openwork pattern (no. 184). Precious and semi-precious stones were also much in vogue and, especially in Egypt, the combination of pearls, sapphires and emeralds was particularly popular (no. 191).

R.C.

183

183 Charm Early Christian Era 4th century AD
Found on the Esquiline Hill, Rome, in 1793.

Silver, in form of mouse eating fruit. L 2·3.

One of fifteen pieces of jewellery found in association with the Esquiline Treasure.
Bibliography: Dalton (1901), no. 239.
M & L 66.12–29.49. Formerly in the collection of the Duc de Blacas.

184 Mount with Lion Hunt Early Christian Era
4th century AD
From Asia Minor.

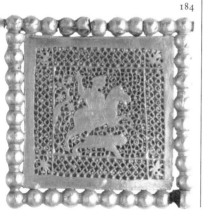

184

Gold mount with, on front, figure of woman on horseback accompanied by lion, and, on back, diaper pattern of leaves. W 5·1.
Bibliography: Dalton (1901), no. 252; W. F. Volbach, *Early Christian Art* (London, 1961), p. 333, pl. 119.
M & L AF332. Franks Bequest, 1897.

185 Pair of Earrings Early Christian Era
about AD 400
From Syria.

Pair of gold earrings; wire of S-shape with three jadeite beads at one end and amythest and pearl suspended from foot. H 5·1.
M & L 1949.10–7.1–2.

185

124

186

186 Carthage Treasure Early Christian Era
about AD 400
From the Hill of St Louis, Carthage, North Africa.

(a) Necklace of emeralds, sapphires and pearls. L doubled 39·4.

(b) Pair of earrings, en suite with necklace. L 5·7.

(c) Gold finger-ring, bezel formed of quadruple claw holding pearl. D 2·2.

(d) Gold necklace of thin wire plaited in herringbone pattern, having at each end lion's head terminal. L 34·9.

(e) Oval plasma intaglio with bust of Hercules. L 2·5.

(f) Octagonal nicolo intaglio engraved with figure of Fortuna aboard ship and inscription 'NAVIGA FELIX'. L 1·6.

(g) Onyx cameo with head of Minerva. L 4·1.

The Carthage Treasure, with which this jewellery is associated, is one of the major hoards of Early Christian silver plate from the period around AD 400.
Bibliography: Dalton (1901), nos. 242–8.
M & L AF323–30. Franks Bequest, 1897.

187 Earring Early Christian Era about AD 500
From Kalymnos in the Aegean.

Gold earring, consisting of ring, fine chain and rectangular domed lantern with pierced sides, from each corner of which hangs pearled pendant. L 9·6.

189

One of a large number of objects excavated in the nineteenth century by Charles Newton, HM Vice-Consul at Mytilene, at various sites on Kalymnos. M & L 56.8–26.721. Given by Lord Stratford de Redcliffe, 1856.

188 Pair of Earrings Byzantine about AD 600
Pair of gold earrings, each consisting of loop of penannular wire to which is attached thimble-shaped cage of filigree, broad end of which is closed and has in centre raised setting, now empty. D 5·3.
Bibliography: Dalton (1901), no. 274.
M & L AF344. Franks Bequest, 1897.

189 Pair of Earrings Byzantine about AD 600
Said to have been found at Lambousa, Cyprus.

Pair of gold crescent-shaped earrings filled with chased openwork floral scroll pattern and border of beaded wire. H 3·5.

Lambousa was the find-spot of the two famous Byzantine silver hoards, known respectively as the 'First' and 'Second Cyprus Treasures', which are now divided between the British Museum, the Metropolitan Museum of Art, New York, and the Cyprus Museum, Nicosia; the treasures were found before the First World War.
M & L 1957.7–4.1 and 2.

190 Breast Chain Byzantine about AD 600
Said to have been found in Egypt.

Four gold chains designed to be worn as an ornament to cover breast and back, each chain of twenty-three openwork discs and attached at both ends to two larger discs of same type. L 73·4.

188

190

191

Although apparently intended to be worn in the same manner as the chains seen on some Romano-Egyptian terracotta figures (1877.11–12.34), the dimensions of the present chain are such as to suggest that it was made either for someone of considerable size or as decoration for a statue.

Bibliography: W. Denison, 'A gold treasure of the Late Roman Period', *University of Michigan Studies, Humanistic Series* XII (1918); O. M. Dalton, *East Christian Art* (1925), p. 320.

M & L 1916.7–4.1. Given by Mrs W. Burns, 1916.

Colour plate 15

191 Gold Parure Byzantine about AD 600
Said to have been found in Egypt.

(a) Gold chain of lengths of plaited wire separated by groups of pearls and emeralds, suspended beneath large openwork disc of pearls, emeralds and sapphires. L 96·5.

(b) Pair of gold earrings, the heads with openwork settings now largely empty and supporting three chains of settings with pearl and sapphire pendants. L 12·4.

(c) Pair of gold bracelets, each with two coils in form of serpent. D 6·6.

This parure is said to have been found in association with the gold breast chain (no. 190).

Bibliography: W. Denison, 'A Gold treasure of the Late Roman Period', *University of Michigan Studies, Humanistic Series*, vol. XII (1918).

M & L 1916.7–4.2–6. Given by Mrs W. Burns, 1916.

Europe, China, Korea and Japan

AD 300-1000

Germanic Jewellery

If anything can banish the old erroneous notion that the Germanic tribes were barbarians, it is surely their jewellery. At its best, it is unexcelled in technical virtuosity and in bold and complex designs. In an age when jewellery was to a large extent portable wealth and the expression of its owner's rank and status, it was natural that it should take on eye-catching forms. To this end, the most striking feature of the Germanic jewellery is its dramatic use of polychrome effects. In particular, the inlay of precious stones, especially garnets, and other materials reaches an importance hardly matched anywhere else before modern times. The gold and garnet dazzle of the Sutton Hoo jewellery (nos. 197 and 198), which is technically unsurpassed in the formal complexity of the cut garnets, its use of new inlay techniques, such as the 'mock-champlevé' or lidded cloison in the zoomorphic interlace on the shoulder clasps, and the virtuoso use of all-over cloisonné inlay, represents a high point. But gem inlay was a technique widespread amongst the Germanic people which attained high standards wherever it was used, as the Ostrogothic necklace and earrings show (no. 192).

Other important aspects of the polychrome style are the various metal finishes such as gilding, silver-plating, tinning, and niello inlay, all of which were used to give rich effects of contrast such as may be seen on the Sarre quoit brooch, with its alternating gilded and plain silver zoning (no. 193) and the Sleaford pin (no. 194). Filigree and granulation in gold are also important techniques for this period and, as on the splendid buckle from Taplow (no. 200), may often be used to develop zoomorphic motifs, the other principal feature of this jewellery.

This type of decoration developed in fifth-century northern Europe from zoomorphic decorative details on late Roman metalwork, notably the metal fittings from military belts which had a wide currency about and beyond the frontiers. It became a highly sophisticated and formalized style, which was to fuel western European art in many ways for the next 600 years. The Sleaford pin with its grotesque mask design (no. 194), the Dover pendant (no. 196) and the Taplow buckle's filigree serpent (no. 200) are examples of Anglo-Saxon treatments of the theme in different techniques, while the Gotlandic bracteates (nos. 195 and 203) and magnificent Lombardic brooch (no. 199) show continental versions.

As with the animal style, the techniques used by Germanic jewellers were mostly learnt from the Roman workshops, and developed to suit their special needs. In form, too, many of the pieces were derived from Roman prototypes. The Sutton Hoo shoulder clasps (no. 197), for instance, are apparently ultimately modelled on Roman shoulder fittings from parade armour; the necklace of inlaid pendants from South Russia (no. 192) owes a clear debt to antique forms, and the Scandinavian gold bracteates derive from the Roman gold solidi which found their way north. The ability to absorb and transform the products and styles of other cultures is a continuing feature of this jewellery.

Finally, this rich and splendid jewellery was not only an indication of wealth and rank, but also very often functional. The paired brooches worn on the shoulders by Anglo-Saxon women were not only decorative; they pinned up and adjusted the tubular dress at the shoulders. The large, handsome buckles worn by men clasped broad belts around the tunic, while very small buckles, sometimes richly decorated, were used on gartering and shoes. Even the magnifi-

cent sword belt mounts from Sutton Hoo (no. 198), the craftsmanship and glamour of which rather obscure their purpose, were strictly functional; the moving parts, some actually inlaid with garnets, operate with perfect smoothness and precision after more than a thousand years.

L.W.

192 Gold and Garnet Jewellery Ostrogothic

3rd–5th century AD
South Russia.

(a) Necklace consisting of eight garnet-set pendants, central green stone pendant and ten transversally ribbed sheet gold spacers in form of triple and quadruple cylinders; garnets both flat and convex. L 16·5.

(b) Earring with heart-shaped garnet cabochon in beaded border, and three pendants set with pebble garnets. L 3·8.

(c) Pendant with central cabochon garnet, border set with cut garnets and one green stone in cloison cells. L 3·6.

(d) Pair of earrings with twisted hoops; each polyhedral head set with twelve pieces of cut garnet. D 3·0.

(e) Jewel, with three cabochon garnets in oval frames, originally mounted with three gold rivets. H 2·8.

This small group shows various basic ways in which garnet was cut, finished and set in gold jewellery. Later, in the fifth, sixth and early seventh centuries the exuberant use of garnet in complex cloison cells, reached a high degree of perfection – a characteristic feature of the Migration Period jeweller's art in western Europe. All the garnet used had to be imported, probably from the area around north-west India and is striking evidence of the long distance 'trade' in luxury goods of the period. Garnet can be split in the horizontal plane, but sheets so formed have to be individually cut to shape for the patterned cells. Cabochon stones are ground and polished to shape; the cabochon setting (b) is an outstanding example of a stone three-dimensionally patterned in this manner.

Bibliography: B. Arrhenius, *Granatschmuck und Gemmen aus Nordischen Funden des Frühen Mittelalters* (1971). M & L 1923.7–16, 8, 13, 55, 64, 65, 111. Delagarde Collection.

193 Brooch Anglo-Saxon (?) mid-5th century AD

From a grave in the Anglo-Saxon cemetery at Sarre, Kent, England.

Silver-gilt quoit brooch decorated with concentric

zones of engraved animal ornament and three-dimensional doves. D 7·8.

This brooch is the finest example of a type associated with a variety of zoomorphic decoration derived from Late Roman ornament, and fashionable in the early years of the Anglo-Saxon settlement of England. *Bibliography*: S. C. Hawkes, 'Jutish Style A', *Archaeologia* XCVIII (1961), pp. 30–2; V. I. Evison, *The Fifth Century Invasions South of the Thames* (London, 1965), pp. 62, 65, 125, pl. 12a.
M & L 93.6–1.219. Durden Collection.

194 Pin Anglo-Saxon late 6th century AD
Excavated at Sleaford, Lincolnshire, England. Grave 95 in the Anglo-Saxon cemetery.

Bronze dress pin with gilded and silver plated terminal in form of stylized animal head. L 15·25.

Found on the chest of a woman's skeleton. Dress pins of this date are relatively rare in Anglo-Saxon contexts, and the use on this example of a decorative motif usually employed on the terminal of the regional brooch type suggests that the craftsman was perhaps working with an unfamiliar type of object.
Bibliography: G. W. Thomas, 'On excavations in an Anglo-Saxon cemetery at Sleaford, Lincolnshire', *Archaeologia*, L (1887), pp. 394, 406, pl. XXIV(1).
M & L 83.4–1.176. Given by Sir A. W. Franks, 1883.

195 Pendant (Bracteate) Migration Period
6th century AD
Probably Gotland, Sweden.

Sheet gold pendant (bracteate) with stamped decoration about central roundel executed in repoussé. Suspension loop and rim enriched with filigree gold wire, and part of surface with filigree wire and granulation. D 3·6.

This piece, and the later bracteate (no. 203), draw inspiration from Late Roman gold coins or medallions; gradually the original horse and rider motif became increasingly stylized, abstract, and combined with elements from Scandinavian mythology. The sixth-century piece clearly depicts a horse galloping left, with an anthropomorphic face in profile above, wearing an elaborate head-dress or coiffure; a bird is seen hovering above, facing right. In the later, eighth-century piece the head-dress element is clearly present, but the facial features have been reduced to groups of dots; the bird and the horse with its galloping hooves have become a group of three creatures with gaping snouts. The class of gold bracteates, widely spread throughout Scandinavia and known in England, were modified to Germanic taste; much Germanic art of the fourth–seventh centuries, like

193

195   196

194

131

these bracteates, drew heavily on a range of Late Roman decorative motifs.
Bibliography: M. Mackeprang, *De Nordiske Guldbrakteater* (1952), no. 197, pl. 14, no. 13.
M & L 1921.11–1.365. Curle Collection.

196 Pendant Anglo-Saxon 7th century AD
Excavated at Buckland, Dover, Kent, England. Grave 20 in the Anglo-Saxon cemetery.

Gold disc pendant with repoussé ornament in design of three birds of prey. D 3·8.

Though technically very closely related to the bracteates, this type of pendant abandons the characteristic ornament based on coin prototypes, employing instead decoration based on native motifs.
M & L 1963.11–8.101.

197 Pair of Shoulder Clasps Anglo-Saxon early 7th century AD
Excavated at Sutton Hoo, Suffolk, England, in 1939.

Gold hinged and curved clasps, each consisting of two halves fastened by pin attached by chain. Clasps decorated with cloisonné garnets and millefiori glass in panelled designs, zoomorphic interlacing ornament, and interlinked boars. Decorative filigree trimmings also present. L 12·7; W 5·4.

From the renowned Anglo-Saxon ship-burial, these shoulder clasps, which were presumably designed to clasp a thick leather or fabric garment on the shoulders, are unique in form and display certain virtuoso decorative techniques, such as millefiori glass inlays and 'mock-champlevé' inlay, which are particular features of the Sutton Hoo school. The decoration of the main panels of the clasps strikingly prefigures an ornamental 'carpet' page of one of the earliest insular manuscripts, the *Book of Durrow*.
Bibliography: R. L. S. Bruce-Mitford, *The Sutton Hoo Ship-Burial: a handbook* (2nd edition, London, 1972), pp. 74–5, pls. F, 34; R. L. S. Bruce-Mitford, *et al., The Sutton Hoo Ship-Burial* (London, 1975), vol. 1, *Excavations, Background, The Ship, Dating and Inventory*, pp. 518–21.
M & L 1939.10–10.4 and 5. Given by Mrs E. M. Pretty, 1939.

Colour plate 11

198 Mounts from a Sword Harness Anglo-Saxon early 7th century AD
Excavated at Sutton Hoo, Suffolk, England, in 1939.

(a) Pair of gold rectangular strap-mounts with all-over cloisonné garnets in mushroom-cell pattern. L 5·1; W 1·8.

(b) Pair of gold rectangular strap-mounts with all-over cloisonné garnets in stepped cells within cabled grid. L 5·1; W 2·0.
(c) Gold T-shaped strap-distributor with all-over cloisonné garnets, designed for junction of two straps of different widths; consists of rectangular mount to which swivelling terminal fitting attached by inlaid hinge. L 6·1; W 5·3.
(d) Gold buckle with rectangular plate, decorated with all-over cloisonné garnets in complex cell-patterns. L 7·6; W 2·5.
(e) Gold triangular curved clasp, dummy buckle with rigid parts, set all over with cloisonné garnets. Tongue cut away to allow free passage of strap. L 7·3; W 2·8.
(f) Gold triangular strap-mount with all-over cloisonné garnets in complex pattern containing zoomorphic elements. L 3·0; W 2·4.

These splendid pieces from the Sutton Hoo ship-burial display a virtuoso command of the difficult technique of cloisonné inlay. In particular, the use of very small garnets, garnets cut to complex and irregular shapes, garnets deployed upon curved surfaces, and (as on the strap distributor) even moving parts, shows the craftsman's genius. Though certain details of the arrangement of mounts on the harness must remain conjectural, the overall arrangement conforms with several other continental harnesses of similar type. Such elaborate suites are, of course, rare and were in life confined to the topmost social strata; the Sutton Hoo suite, the only such harness set to survive in England, is the finest of all.
Bibliography: H. Ament, 'Merowingische Schwertgurte vom Typ Weihmörting', *Germania*, 52 (1974), pp. 153–61; R. L. S. Bruce-Mitford, *et al., The Sutton Hoo Ship-Burial*, vol. 1, *Excavations, Background, The Ship, Dating and Inventory* (London, 1975), pp. 519–21.
M & L 1939.10–10.6–11.17.18. Given by Mrs E. M. Pretty, 1939.

199 Brooch Lombardic 7th century AD
Cast silver, gilt and nielloed brooch with semicircular, radiate head. Around head-plate, row of animal masks; inner field of head-plate contains two intertwined serpents in profile, each biting own body; on each side of bow, abstract interlace pattern; two pairs of interlaced serpents in profile symmetrically set on body of brooch. Two pairs of profile birds' heads with curved beaks set on edge of body, lower pair (of which one survives) biting onto animal mask, as seen from front. Eyes, tusks and muzzle of latter animal strongly defined, but when viewed from side, each half of mask can be seen as head in profile. Pair of conjoined, upward-facing animals at foot of brooch.

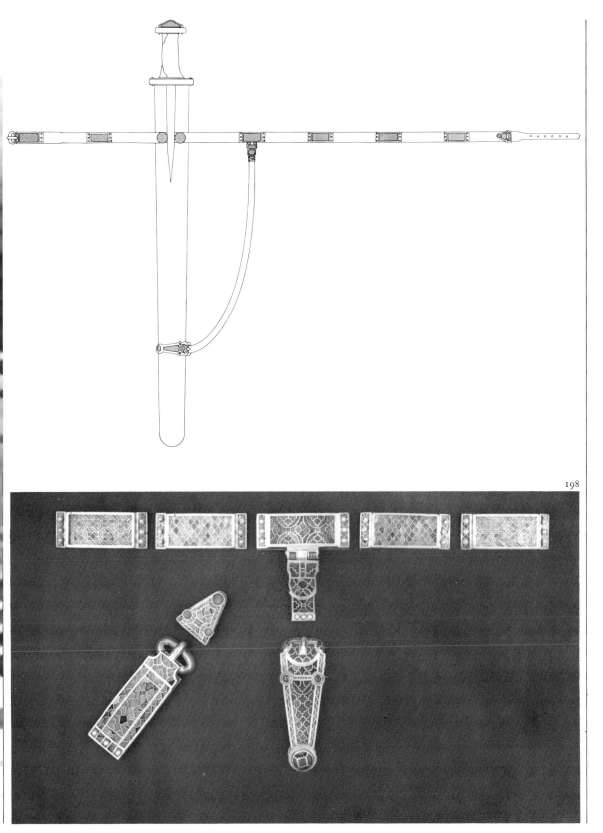

Pin catch on back in form of animal mask and body seen from above. L 16·5.

Possibly from Tuscany. Profusion of animal motifs over the brooch, executed in the 'Animal Style II', fills every available surface. The complex interlacing and the several possible ways of viewing some elements of the design are characteristic of the 'puzzle' quality of much animal art of the period.
Bibliography: B. Salin, *Altgermanische Thierornamentik* (1904); S. Fuchs and J. Werner, *Die Langobardischen Fibeln aus Italien* (1950), pl. 20, A84.
M & L 51.8–6.10.

200 Buckle Anglo-Saxon about AD 700
Excavated at Taplow, Buckinghamshire, England, in 1883.

Gold buckle of sub-triangular shape, set with cloisonné garnets and glass, and embellished with filigree wire and granulation. Centre of plate decorated with zoomorphic design in filigree on repoussé base. L 9·9.

Found with many other items in the burial mound of an Anglo-Saxon nobleman, this buckle is one of the most technically accomplished and sumptuous pieces of Anglo-Saxon jewellery outside the Sutton Hoo group. Buckles of this imposing type are the chief item of male jewellery in the later sixth and early seventh centuries, and were used to clasp a broad belt worn around the waist or hips.
Bibliography: J. Stevens, 'On the Remains found in an Anglo-Saxon tumulus at Taplow, Bucks.', *Journal of the British Archaeol. Assoc.*, XL (1884), pp. 61–71; *VCH Bucks* (1905), vol. 1, p. 199.
M & L 83.12–14.1. Given by the Rev. Charles Whateley, 1883.

201 Pendant Necklace Anglo-Saxon
late 7th century AD
From an Anglo-Saxon grave at Desborough, Northamptonshire, England.

Necklace consisting of gold-mounted garnet pendants, gold wire biconical and cylindrical beads, gold miniature pendant bullae and central pendant cross of gold. L (overall) 25.4.

The later seventh century saw a change in fashions of Anglo-Saxon female jewellery, whereby the long-standing habit of brooches paired with bead necklaces was abandoned, and a new style based on pins and necklaces of pendants replaced it. This necklace is the most sumptuous surviving instance of the new taste.
Bibliography: R. F. Jessop, *Anglo-Saxon Jewellery*

199

200

(London, 1950), p. 121, pl. XXVIII (4).
M & L 76.5–4.1.

202 The 'Castellani' Brooch South Italian (?)
7th or 8th century AD
Canosa, Italy.

Gold filigree, cloisonné enamels and pearls mounted in and on gold casing over mortar-like core; on reverse, sheet silver backing-plate holds pin fittings. In central disc, executed in opaque white and blue cloisonné enamel, portrait of female who wears disc brooch with three suspension loops, similar to Castellani brooch itself. Concentric zones of decoration about central roundel consist of ribbed gold sheet; pairs of pearls strung on bronze or copper wire held in position by gold loops; filigree wire; row of contiguous circles each filled with star composed of four arcs to form series of cloisons filled with red, blue, green and yellow enamels; series of gold loops originally held wire of pearls; border of gold filigree. D 6·0.

The 'Castellani' brooch shows strong Byzantine influence and is outstanding for quality of craftsmanship in enamelling at a comparatively early date. The place and date of manufacture is uncertain, because of a lack of comparable general eighth century Byzantine enamelled pieces. While similar to later material in undiagnostic technical features, the brooch can be best compared with some seventh century enamelled pieces found in South Italy and in the overall arrangement of some Lombardic gold disc brooches. In the circumstances, a date extending into the eighth century for its manufacture cannot be precluded; a later dating, and the broad parallels sometimes drawn between this piece and the famous Alfred Jewel (ninth century), cannot be borne out.
Bibliography: Dalton (1904), p. 65, fig. 1; Y. Hackenbroch, *Italienisches Email des Frühen Mittelalters* (1938), p. 12, pl. 3; P. Lasko, *Ars Sacra 800–1200* (Harmondsworth, 1972), pp. 9 and 269, pl. 5.
M & L 65.7–12.1. Castellani Collection.

203 Pendant (Bracteate) Vendel Period
8th century AD
Sheet gold pendant (bracteate) with concentric stamped decoration about central roundel executed by stamping and repoussé. Suspension loop and part of surface enriched with filigree and granulation. D 5·6.

Probably from Gotland, Sweden. A late example of a specifically Gotlandic type, rarely found outside the island.
Bibliography: B. Nerman, *Die Vendelzeit Gotlands* (1969).
M & L 1921.11–1.363. Curle Collection.

201

202 △   ▽ 203

Celtic Jewellery

This small selection of Celtic jewellery of the post-Roman period contrasts strongly with the Anglo-Saxon and continental Germanic material from the same period. We see here, in forms and techniques very different from those of Germanic jewellery, the continuation of Celtic Iron Age art. The swirling spirals seen on pieces such as the Londesborough brooch (no. 206) go back directly to the curvilinear patterns of La Tène art, while the use of opaque enamel such as we see on the Co. Cavan brooch (no. 205) has a long insular tradition behind it. The penannular brooch type exemplified by these two brooches also derives from earlier versions current in Roman Britain. However, the eighth-century Londesborough brooch, the latest of these Celtic pieces, clearly reflects the growing influence of Anglo-Saxon animal art and cloisonné inlays.

L.W.

204 'Latchet' Irish 6th–7th century AD
River Shannon at Athlone, Northern Ireland.

Bronze 'latchet' with spiral attachments. L 17·5.

The purpose of this class of object is not entirely clear, though it seems that they were dress fasteners of some sort.
Bibliography: R. A. Smith, *British Museum Guide to the Anglo-Saxon and Foreign Teutonic Antiquities* (London, 1923), p. 132.
M & L 54.7–14.96. Formerly in the collection of Mr Cooke of Birr, Co. Offaly.

204

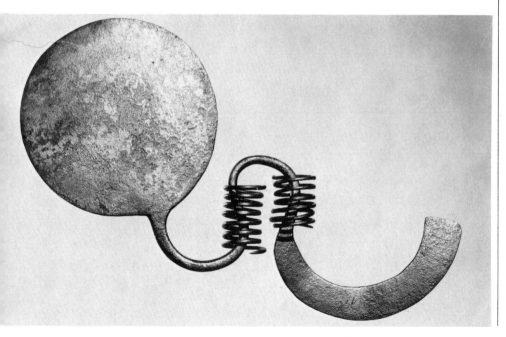

205 Brooch Irish 7th century AD
Co. Cavan, Ireland.

Bronze penannular brooch with developed zoomorphic terminals inlaid with red enamel and millefiori roundels in bronze cells. Pin head also decorated with cast ornament, while hoop and underside of brooch decorated with lightly incised decoration. L (overall) 12·7; D (of brooch) 7·6.
Bibliography: H. Kilbride-Jones, 'The Evolution of Penannular Brooches with Zoomorphic Terminals in Great Britain and Ireland,' *Proceedings of the Royal Irish Academy*, XLIII (1935–37), Section C, pp. 433–4.
M & L 56.3–20.1.

206 The 'Londesborough' Brooch Irish
8th century AD
Silver-gilt penannular brooch with chip-carved and engraved ornament in zoomorphic, interlaced and spiral patterns, and set with blue glass bosses engraved with rectilinear cell-patterns. L (overall) 24·2; D (of hoop) 10·6.

One of the finest brooches of its type to survive. The use of gilding, chip-carving, zoomorphic decoration and the engraved glass inlays show the strong influence of Anglo-Saxon metalwork.
Bibliography: R. A. Smith, 'Irish Brooches of Five Centuries', *Archaeologia*, LXX (1913–14), p. 228, fig. 4; F. Henry, *Irish Art in the Early Christian Period to AD 800* (London, 1965), pp. 113, 116.
M & L 88.7–19.101. From Lord Londesborough's collection.

205

206

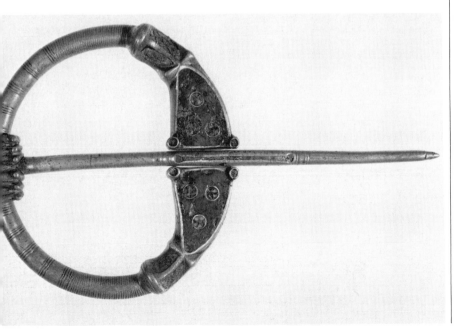

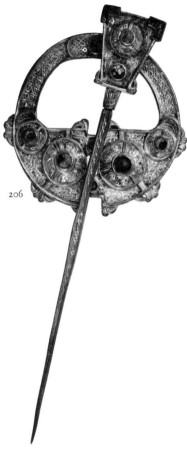

Late Anglo-Saxon and Viking Jewellery

The closing years of the seventh century AD saw a turning point in Anglo-Saxon and continental Germanic jewellery styles. The flow of Byzantine gold into the Western kingdoms had ceased, so that henceforth the predominant medium for jewellery was to be silver, which reached Europe in vast quantities from the Arab empire during the Viking period. Gold remained popular, but in Anglo-Saxon jewellery was conserved chiefly for gilding, inlays and small objects such as finger-rings. At this time the taste for stone inlay is eclipsed by a growing fashion for elaborate designs executed in niello such as can be seen on the Fuller brooch (no. 207). Zoomorphic decoration of various kinds remained a major ornamental feature, particularly on Viking metalwork, for example on the magnificent Swedish brooch (no. 208). L.W.

207 The 'Fuller' Brooch Anglo-Saxon

9th century AD

Silver disc brooch inlaid with niello in design representing the Five Senses against background of animal and plant ornament. D 11·4.

This extremely accomplished piece represents the high point of the 'Trewhiddle style' (named after the hoard of silver and coins found at Trewhiddle, Cornwall, exhibited in the Medieval Room, British Museum), which dominated Late Saxon metalwork in the ninth and early tenth centuries. The use of silver in this piece and other notable jewellery of the later Saxon and Viking period contrasts strongly with the gold-rich ornaments of the sixth and seventh centuries. The great quantities of Arab silver coins imported into western and northern Europe by Vikings, replacing the exhausted supplies of Byzantine gold to the West, were in large measure the source of this.
Bibliography: R. L. S. Bruce-Mitford, 'Late Saxon Disk-Brooches', *Dark Age Britain: studies presented to E. T. Leeds*, ed. D. B. Harden (London, 1956), pp. 171–201; Wilson (1964), pp. 213–4, pl. XLIV.
M & L 1952.4–4.1. Part-gift from Captain A. W. F. Fuller, 1952.

Colour plate 14

208 Disc Brooch Viking

late 9th to early 10th century AD
Sweden.

Cast silver disc brooch with domed section. Surface decorated with lozenges and interlace, made to resemble filigree. Central openwork boss encircled with four animals in the round riveted on to surface. Two human heads cast on edge of brooch, alternating with animal masks. Back has cast pin attachments, loop for securing chain, and bears clear impressions of cloth used in preparing mould for casting. D 7·8.

One of a small group of silver disc brooches similar in design and technique, mostly from mainland Sweden. Both the two-dimensional and plastic elements are in the so-called 'Borre' style of Viking art. Elements of the design are found widely on other artefacts, but the profusion of three-dimensional figures of such quality is not common. The interpretation of the symbolism is unclear.
Bibliography: M. Stenberger, *Die Schatzfunde Gotlands der Vikingerzeit* (1947; 1958), pl. 4; D. M. Wilson and O. Klindt-Jensen, *Viking Art* (London, 1966), p. 91, pl. XXXIa.
M & L 1901.7–18.1. Given by the Friends of the British Museum, 1901.

209 Brooch Viking 10th century AD

Found in a field at Penrith, Cumbria (Cumberland), England, in 1830.

Silver penannular 'thistle' brooch, with engraved terminals in shape of thistle heads. L (overall) 5·15.

This is one of the most extravagant versions of a type of brooch whose distribution centres on the Norse regions of the British Isles.
Bibliography: A. Bjørn and H. Shetelig, *Viking Antiquities in England* (ed. H. Shetelig, *Viking Antiquities in Great Britain and Ireland*, part IV) (Oslo, 1940), pp. 46–7, 50; Olaf Sverre-Johansen, 'Bossed Penannular Brooches: a Systematization and Study of their cultural Affinities', *Acta Archaeologica*, XLIV (1973), pp. 114–15.
M & L 1904.11–2.3. Bequeathed by W. Forster, 1904.

210 Torc Viking about AD 1000

Halton Moor, Lancashire.

Silver torc of interwoven wire, the hooked expanded terminals with stamped decoration. D 18·0.

Found with a silver-gilt bowl, gold repoussé mount, and 860 coins, with a terminal date of AD 1025. The torc is a characteristic Norse Viking example.
Bibliography: T. Combe, 'Account of some Saxon Antiquities found near Lancaster', *Archaeologia* XVIII (1815), 199–202, pl. XVIII; A. Bjørn and H. Shetelig, *Viking Antiquities in England* (*Viking Antiquities in Great Britain and Ireland*, ed. H. Shetelig, part IV), (Oslo, 1940), 45–6, fig. 14.
M & L AF542. Franks Bequest, 1897.

China

In China it is remarkable that as early as the Shang dynasty (about 1500 BC) jewellery to ornament the hair, in the shape of bone or jade hairpins takes pride of place. It must have been the properties of the hair of Far Eastern women, straight because it is round in cross-section, heavy, long, and usually dark in colour, which gave rise to this preoccupation. Poetry throughout many centuries sings of the beauty of women in terms of their hair. Thus it is that among Chinese jewellery hairpins and combs play a very significant part. Gold seems to have become the material preferred for these ornaments in the late Han dynasty and during the Western and Eastern Chin dynasties third–fourth century AD (no. 211). That is not to say that gold had not been used in small quantities at a much earlier date. Excavated examples of appliqué designs and beads are known, but it is only in the Han period that personal ornaments were made in any significant quantities in gold. Early pieces such as the gold hairpin have a certain solidity which by the T'ang dynasty (AD 618–906) blossomed forth in elaborate fantasy (nos. 213 and 215). The vogue for elaborate hair styles in this period is recorded in both poetry and painting. The lady shown in a painting (Stein 47) of the tenth century wears pins and a comb reminiscent of nos. 213 and 215.

What hair ornaments were for women, belt-ornaments seem to have been for men. Early examples have already been encountered in the form of belt-hooks (no. 127). By the T'ang period, the belt-set, which was made from a decorative hardstone, principally jade but occasionally agate (see no. 214), consisted of a group of approximately square plaques and one longer one covering the buckle attached to leather or silk. This particular formula had a long life and no. 278 is a fourteenth century example of this same type of longer buckle plaque.

The Chinese jewellery made between the third century and AD 1000 demonstrates important changes in technique. The solidity and weight of the early plain hairpin (no. 211) is typical of its period, and even throughout the T'ang period many small ornaments were cast rather than worked from the sheet metal. However, towards the end of the T'ang period this changed. The late T'ang comb pin-points this transformation, for here the metal used was very light and thin.

A very important technique which was used in China from the Han dynasty (206 BC to AD 220) until AD 1000 was that of granulation (see no. 212). This is a technique which is so specific that it is highly improbable that it was invented independently in the Far East and must therefore have been introduced from the West. It clearly had an important influence on the north-east area of China and in Korea. The Korean earring (no. 216) is a rich example of its use and can be contrasted with the much finer workmanship of the later T'ang dynasty hairpins (no. 213).
J.M.R.

211 Hairpin China 3rd–5th century AD
Plain gold hairpin, U-shaped with flattened portion at centre; tapering to points at ends. L 8·4.

This is the most typical early form of hairpin in China, and seems to have been widely used in late Han and succeeding periods; it is occasionally found as late as the T'ang dynasty. A similar pin has been excavated from a tomb of the Eastern Chin period (third–fourth century AD) near Nanking: see *Wen-Wu* 1965/10, p. 29, fig. 22(a).
OA 1938.5–24.195.

212 Five Beads China 3rd–5th century AD
Five gold beads, each suspended from double loop of twisted wire; decorated with granulation arranged within triangular borders of wire and enhanced with further granulation in groups of three. L 2·2.

The use of the technique of granulation it must be presumed was derived from western example. Its use on beads and miniature ornaments dates from the Han dynasty and continued until about AD 1000.
OA 1938.5–24.221–225.

213 Pair of Hairpins China 7th–8th century AD
T'ang dynasty
Complicated construction with long, slender, silver gilt pins and broader, flattened section at U-shaped bend forming main framework. Gold foil wrapped around upper part enhanced with bands formed by applied scrolls of wire between rings of wire and granulation. On U-shaped centre-section are five roundels again outlined in wire and granulation. Upper portion of space between prongs filled with granulation held by scrolls or wire and on one side are applied three flowers which formerly held semi-precious stones in centres. Below a dividing horizontal band, decorated with chevrons and row of granulation, a gold sheet is enhanced with four rings which formerly held precious stones, and bird among flowers, which too must have been inlaid, against background of granulation; on reverse is simple scroll design. L 17·0.

Similar to this quite exceptional work is the head from a pin in the Metropolitan Museum of Art, New York. Plain pins of this very long form dating from the T'ang dynasty have been excavated at a number

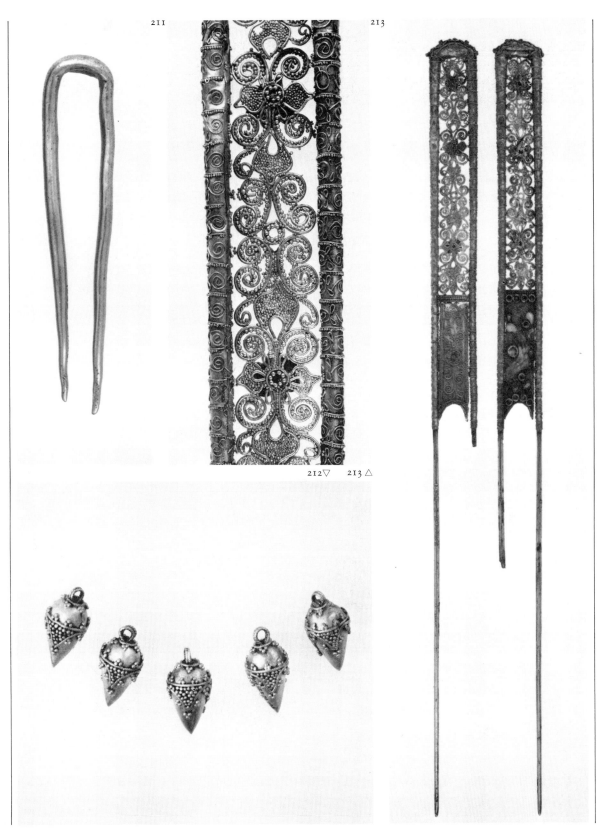

211

213

212▽   213△

215   214▷

of sites in China but examples of this technical complexity have been extraordinarily elusive. Recently a comb-back worked in exactly the same way was found in a hoard excavated at Ho-chia-ts'un near Sian, Shensi province, see Wen Wu Press (1972), p. 61. OA 1938.5–24.252.

214 Set of Nine Belt-Plaques China
7th–8th century AD
T'ang dynasty
Set of pale grey agate belt-plaques, eight approximately square and carved in low relief with musicians seated on mats and playing various pipes, reed-organs and drums; ninth of almost double length and curved at one end, carved in upright rather than horizontal sense with musicians and dancer. Backs of plaques pierced at four corners for attachment to leather belt. H 5·2; W 5·5; large plaque, H 9·8; W 5·5.

A number of sets of belt ornaments of this type, mainly in jade, have been excavated from tombs of the imperial family or high officials. They date from the T'ang to the Ming periods. A set in jade, also carved with musicians but in a style which is evidently later in date than the present example, has been excavated from a tomb of the Sung dynasty (AD 960–1279) in Kiangsi province. See Wen-wu (1964/2), p. 67.

Bibliography: London, Royal Academy (1936) no. 748; Ayers and Rawson (1975), no. 222.
OA 1937.4–16.129–137.
Colour plate 16

215 Comb China 10th century AD
Late T'ang or Liao dynasty
Silver, with gilded upper section; within lower portion teeth cut in graded sequence forming arc; upper portion worked with raised decoration enhanced with chasing, with inner panel of birds among flowers against ring-punched background inside beaded border; further beading and plain border separates this from floral border with ring-punched background; originally final band of beading completed decoration but now in the main missing. W 18·2.

This comb was intended to be worn in the hair and a similar one is shown in the tenth-century painting found at Tun-huang (Stein painting 47). The decoration on this comb derives from the widespread use in the T'ang dynasty of the bird and flower motif. The looseness of the design in this instance suggests the relatively late date. A similar example has been excavated in Hunan province, see K'ao-ku (1957/5), p. 40, pl. 7(9).
OA 1938.5–24.284.

143

Korea and Japan

In so far as jewellery is concerned Korea was, and remained, within the general Chinese sphere of influence but produced her own distinctive style. The relationship between Japan and the rest of the Far East was more unusual. Indeed, later developments on the mainland had a minimal influence on Japan, where from the historical period onwards (mid-seventh century) jewellery scarcely existed at all. Rings, necklaces, bracelets, earrings and the like had no place in traditional dress, and the only adornments approaching jewellery were the lacquered combs and pins and artificial flowers worn in the hair by young women.

In earlier periods there had been a tradition of rather elementary earrings and magatama pendants made from stone, pottery or shell. This began about 1000 BC and eventually developed in the early Great Tombs Period (third–fifth centuries AD) into a very high level of stone carving, probably as a result of the diffusion of Chinese jade-working skills through Northern China and Korea. Apart from the very polished stone bracelets, beads and magatama of this period, some fairly skilful copies were done of the contemporary Korean gilt bronze jewellery in the fifth–seventh centuries.

216

216 Earring Korea 5th–6th century AD
Hanging from two gold rings; from these is suspended a loop covered with granulation joined to a ball on which lozenges demarcated by rows of granulation enclose projecting diamonds; below further loop decorated with granulation passes through three heart-shaped plates outlined in rows of granulation; centre one is largest. L 6·2.

Although this earring and those in no. 217 below are typically Korean and have been excavated from a number of Korean tombs, they were clearly part of a tradition of gold working which was shared with north-east China. The technique of granulation was almost certainly learned from the Chinese and may have reached Korea by way of the Chinese colony in Korea at Lo-lang.
OA 1938.5–24.238.

217 Pair of Earrings Korea 5th–6th century AD
Gold, consisting of openwork roundels from which are suspended small leaf-shaped pendants; roundels separated from one another by bar with rope design; at bottom is large leaf-shaped element with central rib and border which are hatched; neither earring complete. L 5·8; 6·2.

The use of decoration with small suspended pendants

217 △   ▽ 219

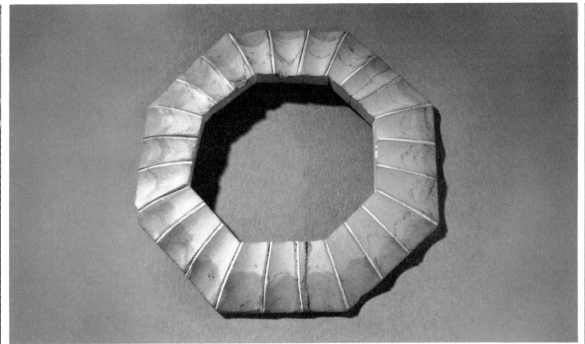

is typical, not only of Korea but of the north-east area of China, and is seen on gold ornaments of this same period excavated in Liaoning province, see *K'ao-ku* (1960/1), p. 24, pl. 3.
OA 1938.5–24.243.244.

218 Bracelet Japan 3rd–5th century AD
Great Tombs period
Said to have come from Yamato province.

Stone ring with eight facets divided radially into twenty-four fluted channels on upper surface, each separated by groove. D 10·5.

Such discs described as bracelets are thought to re-produce the style of metal bracelets worn during a person's lifetime. The stone bracelets must have had a ritual or spiritual significance as they are usually found carefully arranged around the coffin in a tomb.
OA+1140.

219 Magatama Japan 3rd–5th century AD
Great Tombs period
(a) Twenty-five magatama carved from soft grey mottled stone; comma-shaped and pierced at top. L 1·5 to 2·0.
(b) Large magatama in striated grey and green stone; comma-shaped and pierced at top. L 4·5.

Magatama is the name given to this type of bead, which is characteristically comma-shaped and was known in Japan as early as the late Jōmon period (about 1000 BC); as a type it then almost disappeared. Such beads appear again in profusion in the period of the Great Tombs, third–sixth centuries AD, perhaps because they were widely popular in Korea at the same time.
OA (a)+1142; (b) 1940.12–14.320. Given by Mrs B. Z. Seligman.

220 Beads Japan 3rd–5th century AD
Great Tombs period
Fourteen cylindrical beads carved from a dark green hardstone. L 2·0 to 2·4.

Beads similar to these have been found in large numbers in the Great Tombs and were probably thought to have a magical significance, in the sense that the multiplication or increase in their numbers was apparently important, as though they had the force of a repetitive charm, for example.
OA+1141.

221 Glass Beads Japan 3rd–7th century AD
String of blue glass beads of depressed rounded shape. L (approx.) 75·0.

Glass beads are found in large numbers in the Great Tombs but it is not known whether the glass was made in Japan or imported.
OA+1143.

10
Mayan Central America
AD 600-1000

People speaking Mayan languages still live today within the area where their ancestors developed the pre-eminent civilization of Pre-Columbian Mesoamerica. Remains of the great Maya ceremonial centres constructed between about AD 300 and 900 are found throughout parts of southern Mexico, the Yucatan peninsula, Guatemala, Belize and the western fringes of Honduras and El Salvador. Even in their ruined state their magnificence attests the skill of the Maya architects, masons and sculptors of the Classic period. After that time, the civilization was in decline, although even at the time of the Conquest the Spaniards found a pattern of life which still closely followed the forms of the civilization in its heyday. Small scattered settlements of farmers cultivated the maize, beans, squash and other staples which supported the priestly rulers, the specialist craftsmen and merchants living in or near the great centres. This pattern was general in Mesoamerica, but the Classic Period ceremonial centres of the Maya, with their great temple pyramids, ball-game courts, plazas, 'palace' structures and monumental sculptures, are certainly the most impressive of their kind.

Other Mesoamerican peoples too had a knowledge of chronology and writing, but the Maya mathematicians and astronomers evolved calendrical and hieroglyphic writing systems which surpassed all others in the New World. The priest-kings so often represented in Maya sculpture were the custodians of all this knowledge – the interpreters of the lore preserved in the monumental inscriptions and the painted books. They presided over the rituals and ceremonies necessary to satisfy the demands of a complex pantheon of gods led by a principal deity called Itzam Na. The rulers are shown wearing elaborate regalia and jewellery, sometimes so prolific that it all but obscures the form of the man. From such representations and others on painted pottery, in stucco work and in the few extant mural paintings and wood carvings which survive, we have considerable evidence of Maya craftsmanship to add to the tangible evidence uncovered by archaeology. Apart from the sometimes richly carved jades made into head-dresses, ear ornaments, lip plugs, nose pins, necklaces, bracelets and anklets, many of which have survived, we know that the Maya made wide use of other materials, including feathers, flowers, elaborate woven or embroidered textiles, animal skins and shell. Tattooing and body-painting and the filing and inlaying of teeth were other forms of adornment. We also know that artificially deformed skulls and artificially crossed eyes were considered marks of aristocratic beauty, as was a profile with a straight line from forehead to the end of the nose, sometimes produced by the use of an artificial bridge of jade or other material.

Metal-working techniques were not well-developed and apart from copper bells and a few other items, many of which were probably imported from outside the Maya area, gold and other metal ornaments are rarely found.

In the Post Classic period (about the tenth century AD), the Toltecs from central Mexico began to move into the area of Yucatan, eventually taking control and establishing a Toltec/Maya 'kingdom'. In the early thirteenth century the Itza, possibly from Campeche, Mexico, were the next to dominate this area and finally by the middle of the sixteenth century, the Spanish had effectively gained control.
E.M.C. & P.K.B.

222 Jade Jewellery Maya AD 600–800 (?)
Pomona, Belize (formerly British Honduras).

Jade ornaments consisting of
(a) Bead necklace. L 49·0.
(b) Two delicately worked ear-flares with scalloped rims. Approx. D 4·5.
(c) Four small figurine pendants. H respectively 4·8; 4·2. 3·8; 3·5.
(d) Three long tubular beads; L respectively 16·5; 10·2; 9·6.
(e) Small earplug with triangular shaped perforations in rim. H 3·3.

Jade, highly valued by the Maya, was often buried with the dead. An indication of a person's importance or wealth was the number of jade pieces in his tomb. The composite jade ear-flares were either worn through the distended lobe of the ear or, if very large and heavy, were probably attached to a head-dress.
Bibliography: Kidder and Ekholm (1951).
ETH Pomona Loan, 1950

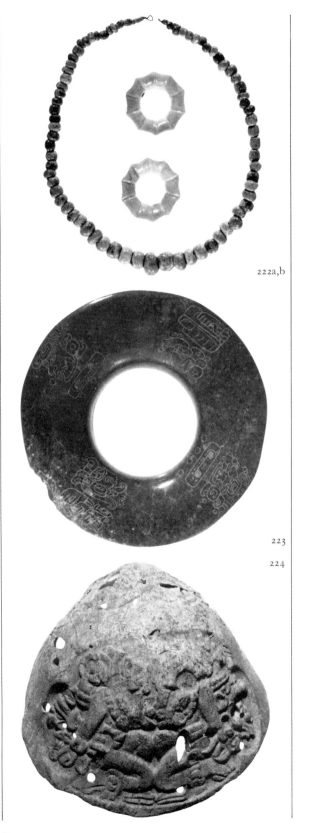

222a,b

223 Ear Ornament Maya AD 600–800 (?)
Pomona, Belize (formerly British Honduras).

Highly polished dark green jadeite, perforated either side of stem; four glyphs incised on face of ornament. D 18·0.

This is one of the largest ear-flares found in Meso-america, and one of the most remarkable examples of jade working in the Maya area. It has been suggested that because of its size, it formed part of a head-dress, or was suspended from the ear rather than inserted through the ear lobe. The glyphs are of an early Maya style but indecipherable.
Bibliography: Kidder and Ekholm (1951); Digby (1972).
ETH Pomona Loan, 1950.

223

224

224 Pectoral Maya AD 600–800 (?)
Pomona, Belize (formerly British Honduras).

One half of bivalve shell (*Spondylus* family) carved with two kneeling human figures (possibly ball players) facing each other, wearing elaborate costumes, head-dresses and necklaces. Carving on upper part of shell also represents two opposing figures, one crouching, one kneeling. L 15·3 (hinge to shell rim).

In addition to the natural perforations in the shell there are a number of drilled perforations including two large holes presumably for suspension at the top of the pendant and four more around the edge. Some depressions which form part of the carving, particularly those at ear, waist and wrist level of the two large figures, were possibly intended for inlay of other materials.
Bibliography: Kidder and Ekholm (1951).
ETH Pomona Loan, 1950.

225

225 Pendant Maya AD 600–800 (?)
Said to have been found at Teotihuacan, Mexico.

Jade, with perforations at top and bottom, shows in bas-relief, large seated figure facing small standing figure. Seated figure has speech scroll issuing from mouth, and wears elaborate regalia including jewelled head-dress, ear-flare and pendant, pectoral ornament and belt with jade mask at centre. L 14·0; W 14·0 (top); 6·5 (bottom).

Probably part of a pectoral ornament, head-dress, or waist ornament. Teotihuacan is outside the Maya area but other Maya trade items have been found there.
Bibliography: Digby (1972); T. Gann, *Mexico* (London, 1936); T. A. Joyce, 'The Gann Jades', *BMQ* 12 (1938–39).
ETH 1938.10–21.25. Dr T. Gann Bequest, 1938.

226

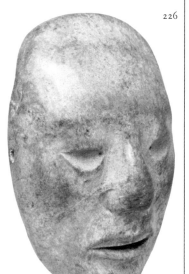

226 Pendant Maya AD 600–800 (?)
Said to have come from Copán, Honduras.

Jade pendant in form of human head with artificially flattened skull. Eye socket left unpolished and small drillings at inner corner suggest that some form of inlay would have been used to represent eye. Back of mask bears incised hieroglyphic inscription. W 10·0; H 15·2.

Although said to be from Copán, this piece is in the style associated with the Maya ceremonial centre at Palenque, Chiapas, Mexico. Such pendants are quite heavy but there is much evidence from sculptures and pottery to show that they were actually worn, even if only on ceremonial occasions.
Bibliography: Digby (1972).
ETH 9599. Given by Sir A. W. Franks.

227

227 Ornament Maya AD 600–800 (?)
Jade, in form of human head. Back is hollowed and three sets of double perforations drilled for attachment of head, which no doubt formed part of larger ornament. L 6·8; W 6·2.
ETH +4076. Given by Sir A. W. Franks, 1889.

228 Pendant Maya AD 600–800 (?)
Jade, with low relief carving of human head; transverse drilling for suspension; and three small pairs of tubular drillings at base indicate that some further ornamentation was attached. L 6·0; W 4·0.

The carved head is said to represent the Maya maize god.
Bibliography: Digby (1972).
ETH 9685. Given by Sir A. W. Franks, 1876.

228

229 Pendant Maya AD 600–800 (?)
Jade, carved with half of seated figure and a scroll design. Figure wears tubular jade bead suspended by cord around neck. H 5·8; W 7·5.

The long transverse tubular drilling through which a cord was passed for suspension represents a considerable technical feat.
Bibliography: T. A. Joyce, 'The Gann Jades', *BMQ* 12 pl. 21 (1938); J. A. Mason, 'Native American Jades', *The Museum Journal*, Museum of Univ. of Pennsylvania, vol. 18 (1927).
ETH 1938.10–21.24. Dr T. Gann Bequest, 1938.

230 Bead or Pendant Maya AD 600–800 (?)
Tikal, Guatemala.

Jade, with transverse drilling for suspension, carved with head and torso of human figure. Pendant is complete and carving has been fitted into contours of irregularly shaped plaque of jade. H 4·5; W 3·0.

ETH 8382. Formerly in the collection of M. l'Abbé Brasseur de Bourbourg, given by Sir A. W. Franks, 1872.

231 Pendant or Plaque Maya AD 600–800 (?)
Jade, showing seated figure in bas-relief wearing ear ornaments, necklaces and armlets. Despite irregular shape, pendant is complete. L 9·5; W 5·0.
Bibliography: T. A. Joyce, *Maya and Mexican Art* (London, 1927); Digby (1972).
ETH 1952.Am 2.1. Given by Mrs T. A. Joyce, 1952.

232 Pendant Maya AD 600–800 (?)
Shell (*spondylus* family), with incised decoration in form of hieroglyph. Two holes drilled for suspension on one side; other holes appear to be natural. L 10·0 (hinge to rim); W 9·0.
ETH 1952.Am11.2. Given by Michael Stuart, Esq., 1952.

233 Necklace Maya AD 600–1000 (?)
Jade and greenstone beads. L 45·0.
ETH 1930.F.459. Purchased with aid of National Art-Collections Fund.

234 Bead Maya AD 600–800 (?)
Tubular jade bead with elaborate relief carving of standing figure with hands held on breast. L 14·2.

The figure has the eye form associated with the sun god. The crossed bands in the mouth also denote this deity. The figure wears an elaborate head-dress and costume. In the style associated with Quirigua, Guatemala.
Bibliography: Digby (1972).
ETH 1938.7–8.1. Given by Mrs T. Gann, 1938.

237

236

235

235 Nose Pin Maya AD 600–800 (?)
Jade pin with spiral decoration in relief. L 9·8.

Pins of this type were worn through the perforated septum.
Bibliography: A. P. Maudslay, *Biologia Centrali-Americana* (London, 1895–1902).
ETH 1938.10–21.51. Dr T. Gann Bequest, 1938.

236 Two Lip-Plugs Maya AD 800–1000 (?)
Obsidian, polished. D (respectively) 2·3; 2·5.

Lip-plugs (or 'labrets') were worn through a perforation in the lower lip. The wider, flattened end was worn inside against the teeth and gums, the rounded boss protruded beneath the lower lip. Although common in Mexico, they are less typical of the Maya area and may have been imported by the Mexicans, who infiltrated the Maya area about AD 900–1000.
Bibliography: W. H. Dall, 'On masks, labrets and certain aboriginal customs, with an inquiry into the bearing of their geographical distribution', *Third Annual Report of the Bureau of American Ethnology* (Washington, 1885).
ETH (a) 1930.F.476. Purchased with aid of National Art-Collections Fund. (b) 1938.10–21.201. Dr T. Gann Bequest.

237 Pendant Maya AD 600–1000
Said to have been found at Palenque, Chiapas, Mexico, by Frederick de Waldeck.

Cast gold; possibly upper part of bell in form of human head. Figure wears ear ornaments, artificial nose bridge and necklace with central pendant. H 4.5; W 2.5.

This is an extremely rare example of fine cire-perdue casting from the Maya area. Cast bronze bells are quite common in the later periods of Maya culture, but probably most were imported from Central America.
Bibliography: T. A. Joyce, 'An example of cast gold work, discovered at Palenque by de Waldeck, now in the British Museum', *Proceedings of the twenty-first International Congress of Americanists*, 1st part (The Hague, 1924); J. E. S. Thompson, 'A copper ornament and a stone mask from Middle America', *American Antiquity*, vol. 30 (1964–65).
ETH 1920–118. Formerly in the collection of the de Waldeck family, given by C. B. O. Clarke, Esq., 1920.

11
Central and South America
AD 500-1500

Accounts by Indian informants of the rich resources and wealth to be found in the Americas enticed the Spanish explorers and conquistadors on into the interior of Middle and South America and hence, eventually, to the great civilizations of the Aztec (in Mexico) and the Inca (in Peru). The conquistadors were not disappointed with what they discovered. The sixteenth-century monk Fray Bernadino de Sahagún describes Cortes's first visit to the treasure house of the Aztec ruler, Moctezuma: 'the quetzal feather head fan, the devices, the shields, the golden discs, the devil's necklaces, golden leg bands, golden arm bands, golden head bands . . . they took all, all which they saw to be good' (Sahagún, 1955). In Peru, the Spanish were even more impressed by the spectacular cities and wealth of the Inca Empire and this encouraged them to continue the search in other regions. Soon few areas of the Andes and Central America were free from Spanish plunder but, sadly, most of the riches found by the Spanish did not survive the Conquest and the examples of Pre-Columbian gold known today come from graves and tombs.

The first evidence of goldworking in the Americas was in the southern highlands of Peru dated at about 2000 BC. In Ecuador and Colombia it was thought to have begun sometime in the last few centuries BC and in Panama and Costa Rica about 500 years later. Metalworking was not evident in Mexico until sometime between AD 700 and 900.

In the Inca Empire, the mining and distribution of gold was under the control of the state. Objects of gold and silver made by hereditary specialists were for the sole use of the Inca ruler, the nobility, and the gods, with the commoners allowed only the use of the baser metals.

There is also evidence in Colombia of specialist craftsmen; the Spaniard Juan de Vadillo, in the early sixteenth century, describes one town, Dabeiba in Antioquia, Colombia, as being a community of specialist jewellers. Mining in Colombia also appears to have been organized within a stratified society of *principales* and slaves. In Mexico, at least in some regions, both gold and silversmiths were organized into distinct communities (Ixtlilxochitl, 1891–92). Their crafts were hereditary and the knowledge and skill acquired were zealously guarded. In Mexico, unlike the Inca Empire, gold jewellery was sold openly in the market place. There were trading networks all over Middle and South America and many items of jewellery, along with other objects, have been found hundreds of miles from their sources of manufacture. It need hardly be said that this vast area was not a single homogeneous unit but consisted of a number of diverse cultures, each with its own distinctive visual art.

A brief description has already been given of the early cultures of Peru (pp. 109–10); in the later pre-conquest period, large 'kingdoms' emerged, such as the vast Inca Empire (AD 1476–1534) and the earlier Chimu 'empire' of the north coast of Peru (about AD 1000–1500) centred on the urban site of Chanchan (see no. 238). In Ecuador, archaeology is still in its infancy, and, with the exception of some parts of coastal Ecuador, the chronology is not yet well established. Most Pre-Columbian jewellery comes from coastal Ecuador, particularly from the north coast, but goldworking centres have also been located in other areas, such as the south Ecuadorian highlands at Sigsig and Chordele. The Ecuadorians did use the technique of casting in metalworking, but there appeared to be a preference for using sheet metal which was cut and embossed in high and low relief.

The dating of the Colombian cultures is also far from well known; however, a number of regional and cultural variations have been distinguished. In the Cauca valley the population lived in small hamlets under the rule of local chiefs, while what is known of the Muisca region, further to the east, suggests that the social organization was somewhat more sophisticated – towns and villages being more common; and towards the north, especially in the Tairona region, there was evidence of a more urban type of settlement with stone architecture. Colombian graves and tombs have yielded an abundance of personal ornaments, many of which are made of a gold-copper alloy known as *tumbaga* and often a form of depletion gilding (surface enrichment) was used. This was a process by which the base metals were removed from the surface, leaving the gold untouched. Hammered sheet gold seemed to be preferred in southern Colombia and was used to create such complex ornaments as the Calima pectorals (no. 241). The technique of *cire-perdue* casting reached refinement in many areas of Colombia, but perhaps the most striking are those from the Quimbaya region, such as the mask shown here (no. 246), and lime bottles in the shape of human figures. The craftsmen of the Sinú valley had perfected the technique of filigree casting which is particularly effective in their delicate crescent-shaped earrings (no. 252).

The Pre-Columbian Panama/Costa Rica cultures, lying directly between Mesoamerica and Andean South America, were influenced by both and is reflected in Isthmian metalwork. For example, there is a similarity in style between the Coclé and Veraguas pieces (Panama) and the Quimbaya goldwork of Colombia. Furthermore, Central American objects have been found in many different areas of Middle and Andean South America, indicating trade over long distances. Among Coclé jewellery (about AD 500–1000) are gold pieces set with precious stones such as emeralds, quartz, jasper, opal, green serpentine, agate, etc. Coclé jewellers also made distinctive twin figure pendants (no. 254), ear ornaments, bracelets, leggings, belts, headbands and finger-rings. In the Veraguas-Chiriquí region (about AD 100–1500), a common type of jewellery was the 'eagle' pendant (no. 255), but many other types of animals such as fishes, turtles, deer, rabbits, jaguars, etc., have also been represented.

The Mixtec, who began to settle in the Oaxaca region of Mexico during the decline of the Zapotec culture (about AD 1000), were among the best craftsmen in Pre-Columbian Mexico. They made finely-worked ornaments and jewels of obsidian, rock-crystal, onyx, jade and turquoise, as well as intricately carved items of shell and bone, and were skilful in the working of gold and silver. Typically Mixtec are the small and delicate personal ornaments cast (using the *cire-perdue* technique) and decorated with false filigree. Cast objects, half of gold and half of silver, with movable parts, illustrate the technical skill of the goldsmiths. There is a distinctiveness and a uniformity in all Mixtec art and, in terms of style and iconography, the surviving jewellery resembles illustrations in many Mixtec manuscripts.

P.K.B.

238 Ear Ornaments (two) Chimu (Peru)
AD 1000–1500 (?)
Hammered gold-copper alloy discs with silver-copper alloy plugs; design of stylized bird in repoussé outlined by incision with chased and repoussé dotted decoration. D 4·2.

Remains of a cotton wrapping are still present around the ear ornaments, probably used as packing in order to secure the plugs in the ear lobes.
ETH 1920.10–13.2a and b. Given by G. Lockett, Esq., 1920.

239 Ear Ornaments (two) Peru (?)
AD 1000–1500 (?)
Gold discs consisting of rings cut from hammered sheet gold and filled with lattice designs of wires soldered together at intervals. At back of each, a silver alloy plug is soldered into position. D 3·5.
ETH 1920.10–13.4a and b. Given by G. Lockett, Esq., 1920.

240 Breast Ornament Coastal Ecuador
AD 500–1500 (?)
Thin hammered gold, cut to shape, in form of mask in high relief surrounded by border decorated with stylized animals, faces and geometrical designs. Nostrils of mask perforated and two holes on each side of head for attachment. D 10·3.
ETH 1904.10–31.1.

241 Breast Ornament Calima AD 500–1500 (?)
Hammered gold in crescentic shape decorated in centre with human face in high relief wearing nose ornament. Necklace of five strands of gold beads suspended below head. W 36·5.
Bibliography: Pérez de Barradas (1954).
ETH 1900.5–17.1.

242 Nose Ornament Calima AD 500–1500 (?)
Cut from sheet gold with appendages attached by means of wires passed through perforations. The whole is in the form of a stylized human face, the nose being emphasized by repoussé work. L 14·4 (centre section); 12·0 (left-hand appendage); 12·4 (right-hand appendage).

The ornament is worn through a perforation in the nasal septum. Because of the thinness of the gold and the attachments the whole piece would have trembled when worn.

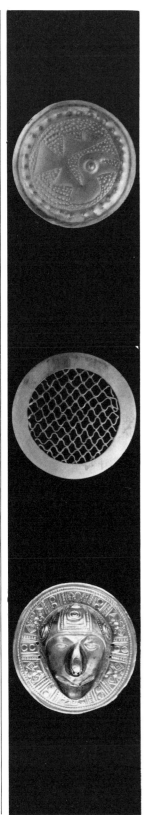

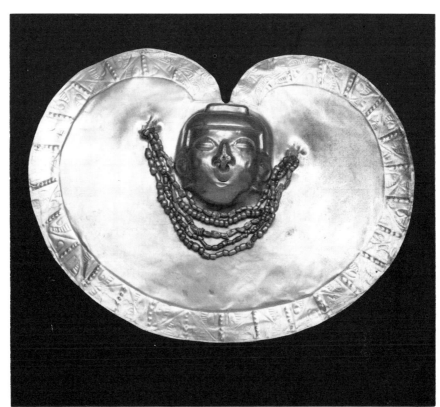

◁ 238,239,240

241 △   ▽ 242

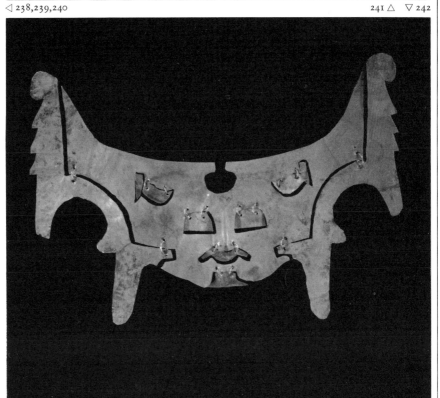

Bibliography: Pérez de Barradas (1954).
ETH + 5802. Given by Sir A. W. Franks, 1892.

243 Pendant Calima AD 500–1500 (?)
Gold-copper alloy, surface enriched, cast in form of standing warrior wearing face mask and carrying club or sceptre in one hand and what appears to be shield in other. H 7·5; W 4·0.
Bibliography: Emmerich (1965); Pérez de Barradas (1954).
ETH 1902.6–23.1.

244 Pin Andean South America AD 500–1500 (?)
Gold, with head section formed by hammering, cutting and repoussé techniques. L 34·0.
ETH 44.7–29.1.

245 Pins (two) Calima AD 500–1500 (?)
Gold, *cire-perdue* cast pins,
(a) With a trumpet-shaped head. L 54·0.
(b) With a head in the form of a bell. L 47·5.
ETH 1904.7–18.2; 1904.7–18.1.

246 Mask Quimbaya AD 500–1500 (?)
Gold, cast in form of human face wearing nose ornament with pieces of gold metal suspended from ears and forehead. H 12·0; W 11·7.
Bibliography: Root (1961).
ETH 1910.12–2.5.

247 Pendant Quimbaya (Popayan) AD 500–1500 (?)
Popayan, Colombia.
Made of surface enriched gold-copper alloy, and *cire-perdue* cast with axe-base probably further stretched by hammering; in shape of an anthropomorphic figure, terminating in axe-like form.

Figure wears large round nose ornament. Four figures with bird-like beaks shown in relief, two at head level and two at legs. Two further animal or reptilian figures with bird heads shown in profile, attached to upper arms of central figure. H 28·2.

The place name 'Popayan' is also used to denote a sub-culture of Quimbaya.
Bibliography: H. J. Braunholtz, 'A Gold Pendant From Ancient Colombia', *BMQ* 13, no. 1.
ETH 1938.7–6.1. Given by National Art-Collections Fund, 1938.

Colour plate 27

248 Pendant Probably Quimbaya (Popayan) AD 500–1500 (?)
Surface enriched, gold-copper alloy, *cire-perdue* casting. In form of stylized bird with outspread wings and tail, which were probably further worked by

243

244,245

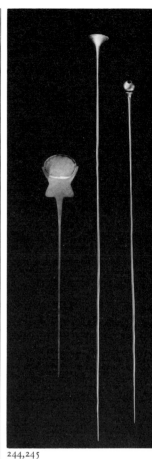

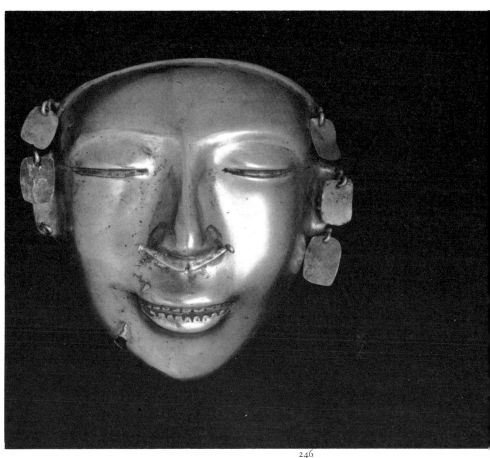

249,248

246

hammering. Figure wears two pairs of plumes and spiral ear ornaments. H 8·0; W 6·0.

The nose ornament worn by the figure is of the type illustrated above it (no. 249).
Bibliography: *El Museo del Oro* (Banco de la Republica, Colombia, 1948).
ETH + 5803.

249 Nose Ornament
Probably Quimbaya (Popayan) AD 500–1500 (?)
Gold; thick drawn wire bent into spiral shape with hammered flat discs attached to each end. L 3·5.
Bibliography: *El Museo del Oro* (Banco de la Republica, Bogotá, Colombia, 1948); Pérez de Barradas (1965).
ETH + 5804.

250 Pendant Cauca Valley, Colombia
AD 500–1500 (?)
Hollow cast gold, in form of male figure; additional crescent-shaped pieces of cut, hammered gold suspended from body of figure, nose ornament and lip-plug (labret). H 9·3.
ETH 1928.12–7.1. Given by H. G. Beasley, Esq., 1928.

155

251 Pendant Tolima AD 500–1500 (?)
Gold, *cire-perdue* cast, stretched by hammering, and polished; in form of stylized figure with axe-shaped base. H 13·5; W 7·0.

These pendants in the shape of flat ceremonial knives decorated with stylized figures are characteristic of the Tolima region, Colombia.
Bibliography: Emmerich (1965).
ETH 1954.W.Am 5.1589.

252 Earrings (two) Sinú AD 500–1500 (?)
Openwork, geometric design cast in gold-copper alloy. W 9·5; H 5·2.

The metalworkers of this region had perfected the art of openwork casting and the use of false filigree. The earrings are typical of this work.
ETH 1955.Am 6.1 and 2. Given by Miss Beatrice A. Bernal through National Art-Collections Fund, 1955.

253 Ear Ornaments Antioquia, Colombia
AD 500–1500 (?)
Ornaments of hammered gold, cut in form of birds with head raised in relief and eyes defined by repoussé work. L 21·0.
ETH +344; +345.

254 Pendant Coclé AD 500–1000 (?)
Gold *cire-perdue* casting representing two standing male figures. H 4·0; W 7·5.

Bibliography: Emmerich (1965).
ETH W364.

255 Pendant Veraguas AD 1000–1500 (?)
Cire-perdue cast gold, in form of bird clutching stylized snake in beak and claws. Outspread wings and tail further worked by hammering. H 7·2; W 9·5.
Bibliography: Root (1961).
ETH 4539.

256 Pendant Mixtec AD 1000–1500 (?)
Tehuantepec, Mexico.
Cast gold; in form of human face wearing articulated earrings. Four chains ending in bells are suspended from main body of piece. Technique of false filigree has been used. L 13·5.
Bibliography: Saville (1920).
ETH +1669.

257 Pendant Mixtec AD 1000–1500 (?)
San Sebastian, Tehuantepec, Mexico.
Cast gold; in form of human figure surrounded by openwork border. Figure carries club, shield and arrows, and wears movable ear ornaments and small mask suspended from lip-plug, bells being suspended in turn from mask. H 8·5.
Bibliography: Saville (1920).
ETH +7834.

254 257▽

252 251 ▷
256 253

156

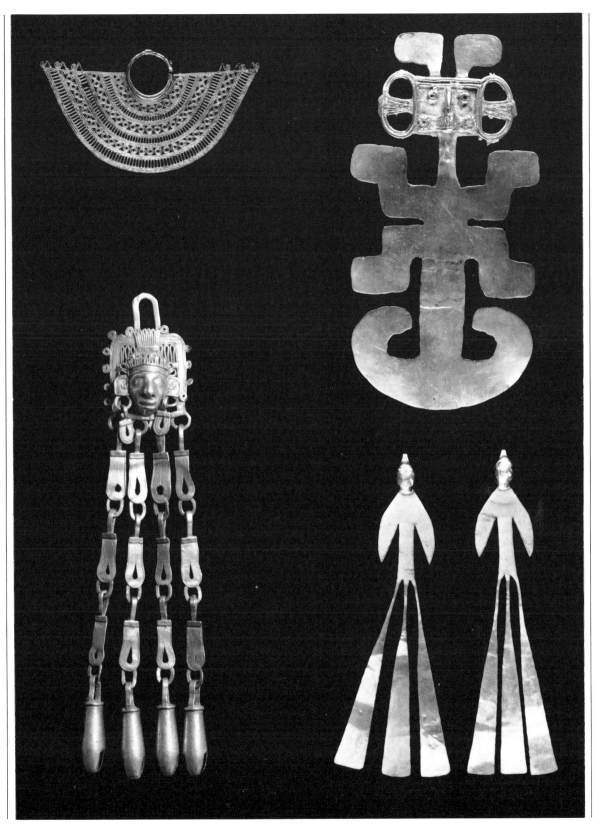

12

Europe, Islam, China, Korea and India

AD 1100-1500

Byzantine Influence

The dominant characteristic of Middle Byzantine jewellery (ninth to thirteenth centuries) was the widespread use of the technique of *cloisonné* enamelling on gold; in this technique the details of the design are defined by narrow bands of metal (called *cloisons* in French), which are then filled with a vitreous glaze. A fine example, probably of Constantinopolitan origin, is the magnificent tenth-century gold and enamelled reliquary cross (no. 359). Provincial imitations, produced in northern and eastern Europe, may be seen in the twelfth-century gold earring (no. 260), which is characteristic of a type produced in the vicinity of Kiev, and in the 'Towneley' Brooch (no. 259), which is probably of German origin, although some authorities consider it a Byzantine original.
R.C.

258 Brooch German (?) about AD 1000
Dowgate Hill, London, England.

Gold filigree openwork circular brooch, with granulation and set with pearls and central enamelled roundel with crowned male full-face bust. D 3·5.

Despite its English provenance, the closest parallels to this brooch seem to lie in the techniques and style of German goldsmiths of the late tenth and eleventh centuries. Certain features of the goldwork, such as the use of double flat filigree wires set edge-on, and raised openwork star-shaped elements, do not occur elsewhere on Anglo-Saxon jewellery, where gold itself is rare enough, but can best be paralleled on German pieces, e.g. the jewelled crown of the Essen Gold Virgin. Pearl settings and the delicate enamelling are also prominent features of German precious metalwork of the period. The crowned figure suggests a king, but it is impossible to make any closer identification from the simplified style of portrait.

From the collection of London and other antiquities formed by Charles Roach Smith.
Bibliography: C. Roach Smith, 'On an Ancient Ouche in Gold', *Archaeologia* XXIX (1842), pp. 70–5; Dalton (1904), pp. 65–6; Smith (1923), p. 101; M. Chamot, *English Medieval Enamels* (London, 1930), pp. 3, 22–3, pl. IC.
M & L 56.7–1.1461.

259 The 'Towneley' Brooch German under North Italian influence (?) 11th century AD
Said to have been found in Scotland.

Circular gold brooch decorated with filigree work and set with pearls and translucent *cloisonné* enamels. D 5·6.
The Towneley Brooch has been considered as German, Italian and Byzantine. In terms of its overall design, its closest affinity is with German jewellery of the eleventh century; both the style and quality of the filigree work have German parallels. The enamels, on the other hand, although based on Byzantine prototypes of the tenth century, appear to be European copies, executed possibly in northern Italy.
Bibliography: Dalton (1904), p. 65, fig. 2; Evans (1970), p. 43, pl. 1; M. M. Gauthier, *Emaux du moyen âge occidental* (1972), pp. 321–2; P. Lasko, *Ars Sacra 800–1200* (1972), p. 87.
M & L Towneley Collection, 1814.

Colour plate 23

260 Earring Russian (Kiev) 12th century AD
Gold, crescent-shaped with ornament in *cloisonné* enamel; on one side, two birds back-to-back with medallion between, on other, two shaped panels with scrolls and circular medallion with quatrefoil in between. L 4·1.

Earrings of this type have been found throughout the

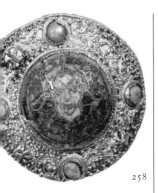

258

Kiev region as well as in excavations near the Cathedral of St Sophia in Kiev. Both the shape and the enamelling technique are derived from contemporary Constantinopolitan jewellery (cf. Marvin C. Ross, *Catalogue of the Byzantine and Early Medieval Antiquities in the Dumbarton Oaks Collection*, II, 1965, p. 112).
M & L 81.8–2.3. Bequeathed by William Burges, Esq., 1881.

261 Part of a Hoard Slav 11th–12th century AD
Found in the Street of the Three Saints, Kiev, USSR, in July, 1906.

(a) Hinged silver bracelet fastened by split pin. Either part decorated with three arcades enclosing nielloed birds and plant motifs. H 5·3.
(b) Silver bracelet of two twisted rods, with pear-shaped terminals decorated in niello. D 6·7.
(c) Pair of silver earrings with openwork border and central zoomorphic motif on niello ground. W 4·7; 4·6.
(d) Two silver filigree earrings. D 4·0; 4·2.
(e) Silver finger-rings decorated with niello and incised designs. D (hoop) 2·1; 2·1; 1·9.

The hoard contained a series of Byzantine gold and enamel medallions, other goldwork and gold coins, as well as a quantity of silver hair-rings, earrings, finger-rings, bracelets and money ingots, some of which were disposed of at the time of discovery. The composition of the hoard is similar to several others from the city of Kiev. The exact nature of the Byzantine influence apparent in some of the nielloed pieces is open to dispute.
Bibliography: *Kratkye Soobschenya* (1972), no. 129, pp. 24–30 with references; G. Korzuchina, *Russkiye Klady* (1954), p. 124, no. 108.
M & L 1907.5–20.1–21. Given by J. Pierpont Morgan Esq., 1907.

261a

261c

261d

260

Medieval Europe

The ring brooch used to fasten the dress is the most common type of medieval brooch. Usually plain, it was occasionally decorated with inscriptions or jewels set around the rim. A most elaborate example of this type of brooch, no. 265, probably from Hungary, is set with jewels and monsters. Later the lozenge and heart increased the range of shapes. The Fishpool hoard provides a fine group of mid fifteenth-century jewellery, and shows the English late-Gothic style of decorating jewellery with inscriptions amidst flowers and foliage. It is possible that some of the Fishpool jewels, like some of the coins in the hoard, may have been imported from the Continent. The jewels from the River Meuse show the three-dimensional quality of the more elaborate late medieval jewels. This is also shown by the Dunstable Swan Jewel, a jewel that indicates the influence of heraldic badges and romance on late medieval jewellery. The use of opaque enamelling on gold is a characteristic of finer jewellery of the later Middle Ages. The jewellery from Chalcis and Venice contrasts with that from North Europe, as the decoration is mainly in niello and filigree enamel.
J.C.

262 Ring Brooches (two) English 13th century AD
Found in 1937 during excavations for extension to Coventry and Warwickshire Hospital, Coventry, Warwickshire.

Two silver ring brooches, larger divided into eight sections alternately plain and decorated. Decoration consists of punched ornament and inlaid bands of niello. D 4·6; 3·8.

The coin hoard was deposited in the last decade of the thirteenth century and so the two brooches were undoubtedly made before that date. Many simple silver ring brooches have been found in hoards in northern England and Scotland deposited at the end of the thirteenth and the beginning of the fourteenth century.
Bibliography: Anon., 'Notes', *Antiquaries Journal* XVII (1937), p. 440; R. A. Smith, 'Coventry Treasure Trove', *BMQ* 11 (1936–37), p. 167; J. D. A. Thompson, *Inventory of British coin hoards* (London, 1956), no. 103.
M & L 1937.6–8.1–2.

263 Brooch English 13th century AD
Found at Writtle, Essex, before 1847.

Gold ring brooch (D 2·0) inscribed on the two sides:
+ IEO : SUI : FERMAIL : PUR : GAP : DER : SEIN :
+ KE : NU : SVILEIN : NIMETTE : MEIN.

The function of this brooch, to close a garment at the neck, is explained by the inscription, which may be translated: 'I am a brooch to guard the breast, that no rascal may put his hand thereon'. The use of the ring brooch in this position may be seen on statues, particularly those of the thirteenth century. In England, the west front of Wells Cathedral provides the best illustration of this use of the brooch.
Bibliography: Mr Neale, 'Proceedings of the Association', *JBAA* III (1848), p. 125; H. Syer Cuming, 'On the Norman Fermail', *JBAA* XVIII (1862), p. 228; Evans (1970), p. 46.
M & L 1929.4–11.1. Given by F. A. Harrison, 1929.

264 Ring Brooch English 13th century AD
Gold ring brooch set alternately with rubies and sapphires *en cabochon*. Pin set with cabochon sapphire. Between stones surface of brooch decorated with punched ornament through which engraved inscription IE IO ∞ VII EMI can be read. On reverse engraved IO SUI ICI EN LIU DAMI : AMO :. D 3·8.

This attractive ring brooch was a lover's gift. The inscription on the reverse means 'I am here in place of the friend I love'.
Bibliography: Evans (1970), pl. 8a.
M & L AF2683. Franks Bequest, 1897.

265 Ring Brooch Hungarian (?) 14th century AD
Gold ring brooch with four raised openwork bosses in form of monsters alternating with sapphires and emeralds. Outside this are eight projections alternately set with sapphires and pearls. D 5·6.

Londesborough collection.

Thought in 1857 to be Merovingian; later thought to be medieval but produced in either northern Europe or even England. It is, however, very similar to jewellery found in Hungary (in the Hungarian National Museum, Budapest) and this suggests that it was probably made in Hungary.
Bibliography: F. W. Fairholt, *Miscellanea Graphica* (1857), pl. XXIX, fig. 5; Evans (1970), pl. 15b; Evans (1921), p. 44, pl. XI, 7; A. Helf-Detari, *Old Hungarian Jewellery* (1965), pl. 4–6.
M & L AF2702. Franks Bequest, 1897.

266 Brooch North-west European
14th or 15th century AD
Lozenge-shaped brooch with incurved sides with raised collets on each side alternately set with spinels and sapphires. At end of pin are three small pearls. Points of lozenge originally set with pearls of which one remains. L 4·0.
Bibliography: Evans (1970), pl. 18b.
M & L AF2703. Franks Bequest, 1897.

263 △   ▽ 262

264△   ▽ 266

267 Brooch North-west European 15th century AD
Gold brooch in form of pelican in her piety standing on scroll: on breast of pelican a ruby: on scroll, a pointed diamond, a smaller bird and letters YMTH. L 3·8.

This jewel in the form of a bird modelled in the round was never intended to be enamelled. It may possibly have been a rich and elaborate pilgrim sign though such signs in the form of a pelican in her piety are unusual. The significance of the letters YMTH is unknown. Said to have been found in the River Meuse in the nineteenth century.
Bibliography: Clifford Smith (1908), p. 111; Evans (1970), pl. 19B.
M & L AF2767. Franks Bequest, 1897.

268 Swan Jewel English or French 15th century AD
Found on site of Dominican Priory at Dunstable in 1965.

Gold jewel modelled in form of swan covered with white enamel on head, body, wings and legs. Traces of black enamel on legs and feet. Around neck there is gold coronet with six fleurs-de-lis to which is attached chain of thirty links ending in ring. At back jewel has original pin and catch. H 3·2.

The Swan Jewel is a fine example of the use of opaque white enamel *en ronde bosse* over gold. This rich technique was used in Paris at the beginning of the fifteenth century for large reliquaries, and it was also probably used in England. The jewel was probably worn by someone of either noble or aristocratic birth. A number of noble families used the swan as a mark of their descent from the Swan Knight of medieval romance. Amongst them were the Tonys, de Bohuns, Beauchamps and Courtenays. The swan was also used as a badge by the Prince of Wales in the fifteenth century.
Bibliography: J. Cherry, 'The Dunstable Swan Jewel', *JBAA* XXXII (1969), pp. 38–53.
M & L 1966.7–3.1.

Colour plate 20

269 Three Brooches North-west European
15th century AD
Gold.
(a) Female figure set amidst foliage and three cabochon rubies holds a faceted sapphire. H 4·0.
(b) Star-shaped with radiating buds containing white enamel; in centre small diamond above pale ruby in midst of foliage. H 2·8.
(c) Cup-shaped flower containing faceted garnet. H 1·9.

These elaborately constructed brooches, which were originally enamelled, provide examples of the richly sculptured jewelry worn at court at the end of the Middle Ages. An inventory of jewels delivered to Henry IV on his accession refers to a jewel with a white angel holding in her hand a sapphire which was probably similar to (a). Said to have been found in the River Meuse in the nineteenth century.
Bibliography: Clifford Smith (1908), p. 143, pl. XX, 10–12; Evans (1970), plate 22f., p. 63; J. Cherry, 'Medieval Jewellery from Fishpool', *Archaeologia* CIV (1973), p. 316, pl. LXXXVI f,g.
M & L AF2768; AF2769; AF2770. Franks Bequest, 1897.

270 'Fishpool Hoard' English (?) 15th century AD
Found at Fishpool, near Mansfield, Nottinghamshire, in 1966.

(a) Two chains. L 31·1; 54·0.
(b) Heart-shaped brooch decorated on front with wreathed bands of opaque blue and white enamel and on back with inscription, 'Je suy vostre sans de partier', divided by flowers and leaves. W 3·8.
(c) Cross. On front is a ruby in centre and arms each engraved with eight-petalled flower. On back are four rectangular amethysts. H 3·0.
(d) Gold rectangular padlock inscribed on one side 'de tout' and on other 'mon cuer' amidst foliage and leaves. L 1·5.
(e) Roundel set with central sapphire surrounded by circle of white enamel beads on stalks. D 1·8.

This jewellery was found with four rings and 1237 gold coins (of which 82% were English and 18% foreign; of the latter 13% were struck for the Dukes of Burgundy). The coins indicate that the hoard was buried early in 1464. The total hoard would have been worth £400 at the time of its burial and it seems likely that the only person who could have afforded such a sum would have been either a very rich merchant or a prominent member of one of the opposing factions in the Wars of the Roses. The jewellery is elaborately decorated with black letter inscriptions and flowers and foliage. The method of construction of the roundel may be compared with the three brooches found in the River Meuse (no. 269) and this has led to the suggestion that it may have been imported from the Continent or possibly made in England by craftsmen working in a Continental style.
Bibliography: M. Archibald, 'Fishpool, Blidworth (Notts) 1966 hoard: interim report', *Num. Chron.* VII (1967), pp. 133–46; J. Cherry, 'Medieval Jewellery from the Fishpool Nottinghamshire hoard', *Archaeologia* CIV (1973), pp. 307–21.
M & L 1967.12–8.5–9.

269a

267 △   ▽ 270c,b,d

271 'Chalcis Treasure' Venetian (?)
15th century AD
Found at Castle of Chalcis on Island of Euboea in Greece in the nineteenth century.

(a) Two silver buckles, one silver-gilt, other having rectangular plate on which is man's helmeted head in profile moulded like a cameo. L 6·2; 9·8.
(b) Two silver-gilt belt terminals consisting of internal silver strip surrounded by silver-gilt frame pieced with openwork tracery. L 12·6; 11·8.
(c) Silver circular medallion. In centre is long-necked bird reserved against background for translucent enamel surrounded by elaborate filigree work. Outer edge of circular frame pierced with eight holes. D 4·2.
(d) Silver chain. L 144·5.
(e) Two belt plaques decorated with brown and green opaque enamel, encircled by filigree in form of flowers and leaves. H 3·6; 3·2.

These selected examples are from a find of silver rings and personal ornaments at Chalcis. The circumstances of the find are not recorded but it has been suggested that the treasure was deposited between 1385 and 1470, when the island was under the undisputed domination of the Venetians. The form of the buckles and belt ends, and use of openwork tracery and grotesque animals recall the Gothic decorative motifs of northern Europe. The cameo-like head on the buckle (a) is more classical in derivation. The find combines both translucent and filigree enamelling. In the latter type of enamelling the wire encloses the enamel in the same manner as the strips of metal in the cloisonné process. This type of enamelling is thought to have originated in or near Venice in the second half of the fourteenth century, and is best known from Hungary in the fifteenth century.
Bibliography: O. M. Dalton, 'Medieval personal ornaments from Chalcis in the British and Ashmolean Museums', *Archaeologia* LXII (1911), pp. 391–404; I. Fingerlin, *Gürtel des Hohen und Späten Mittelalters*

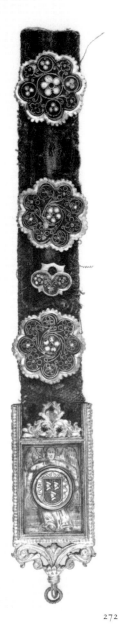

(1971), cat. nos. 150–73.
M & L AF2809; AF2811; AF2820; AF2821; AF2823; AF2824; AF2840; AF2841. Franks Bequest, 1897.

272 Belt Venetian 15th century AD
Two ends of velvet belt: (a) silver-gilt buckle with sunken medallion, with shield of arms on either side of which are initials LB, between male and female bust, all nielloed. Rest of belt has three sexfoil plaques decorated with filigree enamel (L 30·0); (b) belt-end has on one side medallion with shield inset in figure of angel and on other shield surrounded by cherubs, heads and surmounted by legend CON EL TEMPO. Rest of belt has three sexfoil plaques decorated with filigree enamel (L 28·3).

Octavius Morgan collection.

The velvet of the belt has been remounted and the exact original position of the belt fittings is uncertain. The buckle and pendant are fine examples of Italian niello work and the significance of the arms, initials, and motto has not been satisfactorily determined. The back of the buckle bears the silver mark of a horse. The use of filigree enamel on the belt mounts is very close to that on the belt mounts of Chalcis. The arms are probably those of the Malatesta of Rimini and the facing male and female heads on the buckle suggest that it is a betrothal gift.
Bibliography: Octavius Morgan MP, 'Proceedings at Meetings of the Archaeological Institute', *Archaeological Journal* XIX, p. 293; O. M. Dalton, 'Medieval personal ornaments from Chalcis in the British and Ashmolean Museums', *Archaeologia* LXII (1911), p. 399, footnote 3; I. Fingerlin, *Gürtel des Hohen und Späten Mittelalters* (1971), cat. 174.
M & L AF2851. Franks Bequest, 1897.

273 Pendants Venetian 15th century AD
Three circular pendants inset with niello roundels showing on one side – (a) busts of youth and girl in profile; (b) bust of woman within decorative border; (c) bust of woman; on other side – (a) sacred monogram, IHS; (b) interlaced pattern within decorative border; (c) interlaced pattern. D 1·6; 2·3; 2·0.

Pendants decorated with religious imagery and inscriptions often contained consecrated wax medallions. However, the presence of the profile faces on these three medallions suggest that they are more likely to have been secular rather than religious. It is probable that profiles facing one another imply a betrothal medallion.
Bibliography: A. M. Hind, *Nielli in the British Museum* (London, 1936), nos. 113/126; 116/129; 118/131.
M & L AF2894; AF2891; AF2889. Franks Bequest, 1897.

272

272

Islam

The Islamic world inherited the jewellery techniques and styles of Greco-Roman Syria and Egypt and of Sassanian Persia. The earliest surviving examples of jewellery are from Fatimid Egypt and Seljuq Persia. The decorative style, which was developed under the patronage of the Seljuq Turks, can be seen in the fine silver-gilt and nielloed belt trappings (no. 274). Niello seems to have been used fairly extensively in Persia and occurs in the little amulet case which is also decorated with animals in repoussé (no. 379). The gold bracelets (no. 275) chased with benedictory phrases in Arabic are examples of female ornaments. R. P-W.

274 Belt Trappings Islamic 11th–12th centuries AD Nihavand, Western Persia.

Silver, parcel-gilt and nielloed. Thirteen plaques, buckle and five loops. Two plaques square, hollow and open on each of four sides, to allow for passage of leather bands passing at right-angles: each of remaining plaques rectangular with short side of ogival form and provided with pair of studs at back for securing plaque to leather except for terminal plaque which is hollow: two plaques have rings attached to point. Upper edge and sides of square plaques are gilt, upper face decorated with palmette scrolls arranged in cruciform composition and reserved in niello: other plaques decorated with scrolling ornament also reserved in niello. Square plaques, 2·5; plaques with pointed side, L 2·5; W 1·5.

The belt trappings were part of a hoard of silver objects found at Nihavand which included another set of belt trappings and a gold bowl. The hanging straps were used for suspending the sword or quiver.
Bibliography: Basil Gray, 'A Seljuq hoard from Persia', *BMQ* 13 (1938–39), pp. 73–81, pl. XXIIb.
OA 1937.3–13.20–38.

275 Bracelets (pair) Islamic 12th century AD Persia.

Gold with chased decoration. Open circular band with slightly projecting framing bands on outside and strengthening support, triangular in section, in middle. Chased on inside with rosette; and on outside with four panels each containing benedictory phrases in Kufic characters, only partially decipherable, and cartouches variously containing leaves, or knots, or lion. D (max.) 5·5.
OA 1958.10–13.1 and 2. Given by P. T. Brooke Sewell, Esq.

275

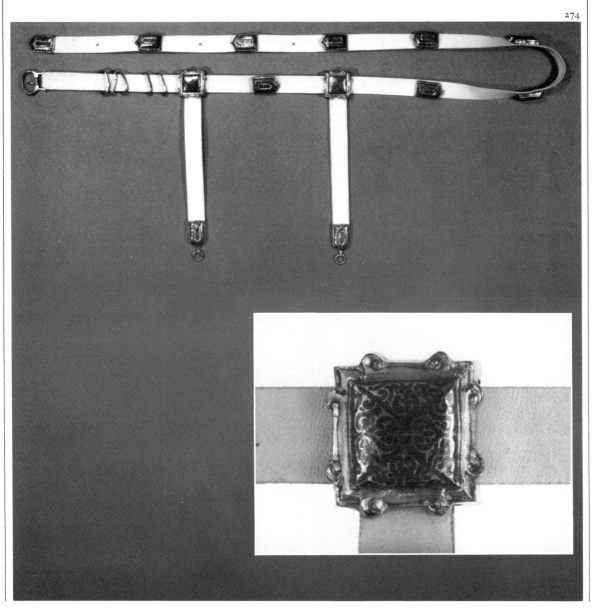

China and Korea

Jewellery of the Sung and Yüan period (eleventh to fourteenth centuries AD) in China shows an interesting emphasis on the animal and flower themes so beloved in the decorative arts of the time. The designs of fish or flowers on the small cast plaques (no. 277), and the scroll designs on the three hairpins (no. 280) can all be paralleled in other materials, particularly porcelain. Although some of the most interesting and rare items, the small silver gilt plaques are cast and are in consequence quite solid; work in thin sheet metal in particular shows great advance at this time. The belt-plaque decorated with fruit (no. 278) is finely and skilfully executed. By comparison with the tenth-century comb (no. 215) the technique of chasing combined with relief is used to much more striking effect and is utterly appropriate to the decorative theme. The control of this technique laid the foundation for the elaborate work of the Ming dynasty in the fifteenth and sixteenth centuries.

J.M.R.

277

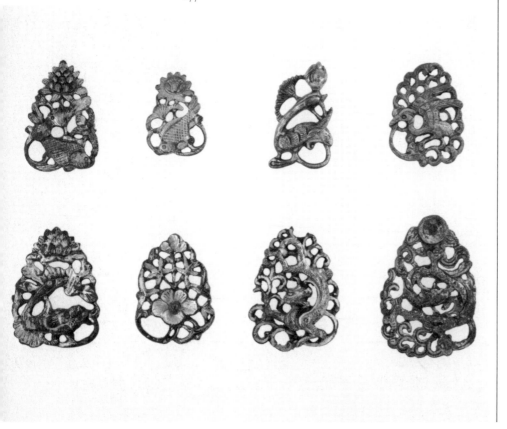

276 | **276 Ornament** China 10th–12th century AD
Silver-gilt appliqué in shape of flying bird with out-
stretched wings, among four flowers in openwork;
worked in relief and enhanced with chasing. L 8·8.
OA 1938.5–24.351.

277 Group of Eight Plaques China
11th–13th century AD
Sung dynasty.
Seven cast silver plaques and one in bronze, gilded;
each with dragon, bird, fish or flower in openwork
among scrolls. H 2·4 to 4·0.

Small openwork ornaments, presumably for attachment to clothing, had been known from the Han
dynasty, first–second centuries AD. As a technique of
ornament, openwork seems to have been popular in
the Sung period and examples of ornaments in other
forms have been excavated in recent years; see
K'ao-ku (1965/1), p. 21, pl. 5(7).
OA 1938.5–24.281; 356; 357; 362; 363; 364; 369; 371.

278 Belt Plaque China 13th–14th century AD
Yüan dynasty.
Silver-gilt, rectangular in shape with one of short
ends curved; main field enclosed in projecting edge
and worked in relief with fruit on climbing plant
against stippled background; at bottom is small cloud
or fungus, and leaf motif similarly placed at centre of
top. L 11·6; W 5·5.

This is the buckle plaque from a set of plaques of
which the others would have been approximately
square. They would probably have been attached to a
leather belt. Belt-plaques of a very similar type, also
decorated with fruit in relief, have been excavated
from a tomb of the Yüan dynasty in Kiangsu province, see *Wen-wu* (1959/11), p. 19.
OA 1938.5–24.328.

278

279 Pair of Armlets China 13th–14th century AD
Yüan dynasty.
Gold, each consisting of loose coil from flattened
gold band; at both ends bands bound with stout wire
which is then looped with three strands on to neigh-
bouring portion of coil. L (approx.) 19·0.

Armlets were certainly used at an earlier date in China
and have been found in tombs of the fifth and sixth
centuries. However this present pair belong to a
tradition of rather longer armlets which was established in the Sung dynasty. Examples similar to the
present pair have been excavated from a Yüan
dynasty tomb in Anhui province: see *Wen-wu*
(1957/5), p. 55.
OA 1938.5–24.204; 205.

280 Three Hairpins Korea 13th–14th century AD
Koryo period.
Silver, with gilded heads. Each consists of two solid
pins, with slight bulge before tapering to point,
jointed to solid hemispherical head, decorated with
small knob (missing on one of pins) at centre of ring
of radiating incised lines and scroll border. Upper
portions of pins decorated with incised chevrons.
L 6·1; 5·4.

This is a very unusual form of pin contrasting with
the more slender types in nos. 281, 282. The scroll
design can be paralleled in other types of metalwork
and on other materials; this suggests the date to
which they are here attributed.
OA +615; 1938.5–24.433; 528.

281

279

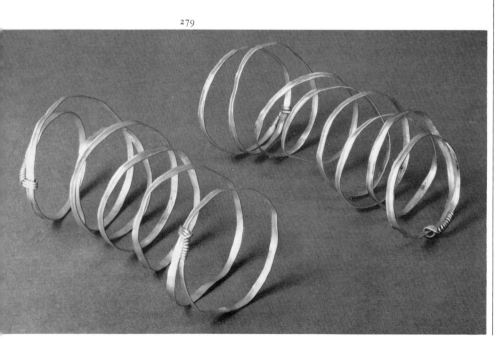

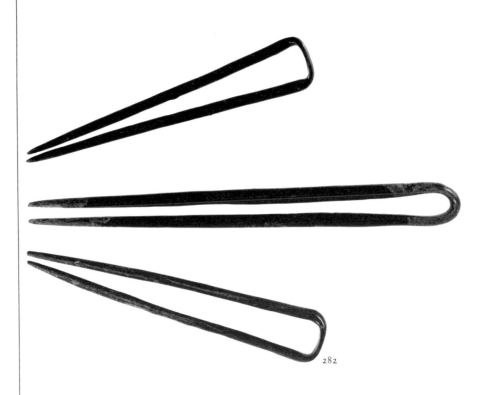

281 **Two Hairpins** China 13th–15th century AD
(a) Gold hairpin, head hollow, worked in shape of
double segmented seed-pod or gourd. L 10·0. Thirteenth–fourteenth century AD.

A similar pin has been excavated from a tomb at
Canton to which a Sung date has been given. It appears from some of the contents of the tomb that it
might be slightly later in date; see *Wen-wu* (1955/10),
p. 50, fig. 3.
Bibliography: Jenyns and Watson (1963), pl. 2.
OA 1938.5–24.210.

(b) Solid gold hairpin with head in shape of phoenix
plumed and crested, holding in beak small round ball
and ring for attachment; incised feathers worked into
upper part of pin. L 10·3. Fourteenth–fifteenth century AD.
Bibliography: Jenyns and Watson (1963), pl. 2.
OA 1938.5–24.264.

282 **Three Hairpins** Korea 10th–12th century AD
Koryo period.
Bronze, U-shaped; two with broad flattened centre
section, third turned in narrower bend. L 8·3; 8·5;
11·9.
OA 1913.7–8.10; 1938.5–24.511; 506.

India

283 Chain (part of) Deccan

12th century AD (?)

Three openwork roundels attached by three short lengths of gold chain; two outer roundels contain plant motif of one trunk or stalk with three branches curving symmetrically outwards on either side and terminating in buds or foliage; open flower (?) surmounts central stalk. Middle roundel contains two figures, probably male and female. Motifs of roundels in low relief and repeated on reverse. Framing roundels are two pearled bands. L 11·0.

OA 1963.5–23.1.

13

Europe

AD 1500-1700

For a brief period lasting little longer than the second half of the fifteenth century, Renaissance Italy seems to have experienced a period of harmony between body, dress and ornament.

The extreme artificiality of the fashions of the French and Burgundian courts of the first half of the century, which were much copied throughout Europe, gave way in Italy to a simplicity and a natural grace that, no doubt, was directly connected with the discovery of human beauty in the nude, even perhaps with the recognition of man as an individual whose natural dignity springs from his qualities and merits, not from his origins and inheritance. From mid fifteenth-century Florence these concepts and ideas flowed through the courts of Ferrara, Mantua and Urbino to the great cities of Italy and found expression in a hundred different ways. Judging by the Italian portraits of the period, jewellery was being worn with discrimination, more in order to enhance the beauty of the female body and less as a symbol of rank.

Despite the official forbidding of 'a display of the neck and shoulders', the neckline steadily fell during the last decades of the fifteenth century until the full décolletage became universal and, with it, the return to the jewelled necklace and choker (or *gorgeret*), which had been such favourite items of jewellery in classical antiquity but which had virtually disappeared during the Middle Ages. Conversely, the ubiquitous medieval brooch fell completely out of fashion.

There was, however, little accurate knowledge of Greek and Roman jewellery and so in a sense could the new Renaissance jewellery be described as a re-birth of the classical tradition, except in cameo carving – though, of course, many of the latter were never intended for jewellery but for the cabinets of connoisseurs and collectors. The Renaissance jewellers and goldsmiths took their designs and decorative motifs from the general repertoire of Renaissance ornament – a new vocabulary built up by the artists of the Quattrocento. Though the forms and techniques were not classical in origin, the jewellery of the Renaissance was visually quite distinct from the Gothic.

The hair, hitherto hidden beneath wimples and coifs or those steeple head-dresses, was now revealed and either entwined with strings of pearls or aigrettes of precious stones. Earrings, especially hung with pearls, came back into fashion, for the hair was often gathered up to reveal the beauty of the neck; unfortunately, few seem to have survived in their Early Renaissance settings.

The bracelet also reappears for the first time in Europe since classical antiquity and ladies of rank took to wearing pomanders (nos. 284 and 297) and tiny prayer-books (nos. 285–6), hanging from the waist on a long chain reaching almost to the floor. Indeed, Henry VIII's great court painter, Hans Holbein, produced at least two alternative designs (no. 287) for one of his English patrons, possibly Thomas Wyatt, but it is doubtful if either met with approval and was ever executed in enamelled gold. The well-known portrait of Mary Tudor by Hans Eworth (in the Fitzwilliam Museum, Cambridge) shows how these miniature girdle prayer-books in their elaborate gold covers were often a prominent item of jewellery.

The men of the Early Renaissance seem to have worn jewellery very sparingly; over the dark close-fitting tunic perhaps a gold chain (no. 291), the belt fastened with a small enamelled buckle (no. 292) and, unlike the medieval fashion, only two – or at most three – finger-rings. The badge or *enseigne*, worn in the hat in the Late Middle Ages was transformed from a modest affair, usually with religious and amuletic overtones, into a totally new and magnificent type of jewel, often with subjects of classical mythology rendered in miniature sculpture. Cellini describes how in 1524 the fashion was for the subject to be chosen by the patron and how he vied with his great rival Caradosso (died 1527) to excel in the modelling and enamelling of these miniature scenes in high relief (nos. 288–90).

The courts of Europe embarked on a new era of formal splendour on an unprecedented scale – led by the Spanish court, rich from its vast possessions in the New World. Bare skin was once more lost behind rich brocades and velvets and mask-like faces and bejewelled hands seem dwarfed amidst stiff ruffs and starched lace collars and cuffs hung with pendant jewels of incredible size and intricate detail (nos. 293, 295). Even the men were encrusted with a profusion of pearls and jewels – as in the full-length portrait of James I (1603–25), in Cambridge University Library.

This King's spectacular present to one of his more humble subjects, a gentleman of Somerset called Thomas Lyte, has survived, complete with the Hilliard miniature of James I inside the locket. It affords an opportunity to assess the high artistic standards being achieved in London at this date (no. 298). By good fortune, the jewel was painted in 1611 as it hung on the chest of the proud Thomas Lyte (no. 299) and, instead of the routine pendant pearl, we can see that the goldsmith had ingeniously devised a most unusual pendant of table-cut diamonds ending in a trilobed drop.

The art of the miniaturist was increasingly in demand in the seventeenth century, partly, no doubt, because of the level of perfection to which it had been brought by artists like Nicholas Hilliard in England and François Clouet in France. Led by Jean Toutin and his son, Henri, the goldsmiths of France developed a wonderful technique for painting miniatures in enamel on gold, and some delicate items of jewellery have survived. The earliest date to appear on any of these pieces is 1636 (no. 301) and is accompanied by Henri Toutin's signature in full. The minute polychrome scenes and floral decorations are often hidden on the backs of the jewels (no. 302) and in England and the Netherlands this style was copied in monochrome on the backs of many items of jewellery during the middle decades of the century (no. 303).

With the change of fashion in the Baroque seventeenth century, vast flowing silken fabrics replaced the stiff tight costumes of the Late Renaissance and its great display of formal ceremonial jewellery. The French court, which now set the fashions, tended to frown on the wearing of much jewellery as vulgar and, once again, jewellery became subordinate to the decoration of beauty.

H.T.

284 Pomander English early 16th century
Found in the Surrey bank of the River Thames in 1854.

Gold, openwork spherical pomander-case, incomplete, only five of the twelve pearls remaining to ornament the top and bottom; at the top, a small ring-topped screw holds the two hemispherical sections firmly together; twisted and coiled gold wire is used to decorate exterior surfaces; no trace of enamel remains on the keyed surfaces. H 5·2; D 4·3.

'Pomander' (from the French *pomme d'ambre*), or 'musk-ball' – a ball filled with scented substances like musk, civet and ambergris (a wax-like substance found in tropical seas and in the intestines of spermwhales, remarkable for its odour; hence its use in perfumery and pomanders).
Bibliography: Evans (1921), p. 84, pl. XVII; *BM Guide* (1924), p. 143, fig. 207; Evans (1970), p. 101.
M & L 54.1–24.1.

285 Pair of Book-covers English about 1520
Gold, enamelled in blue, black and white, representing (a) the Judgement of Solomon, surrounded by black enamelled inscription: +SOLOMONIS IVDITIO PVERI MATER DINOSSETVR VERA; (b) Susanna accused by the Elders and the judgement of the young Daniel, surrounded by black enamelled inscription: +REDITE.IN.IVDITVM QVIA ISTI FALSVM IN ANC TESTIMONIVM.DIX.ERVNT. (Book of Daniel, xiii, 49 – 'Return to the place of judgement, for they have given false testimony against her'.) Parts of background finely engraved but draperies and foreground are keyed to receive enamel, all of which has been carefully removed. H 6·6; W 4·4.
Now unmounted, this pair may have been part of a girdle prayer-book.
Bibliography: Evans (1921), p. 83; Tait (1962), p. 235f, pl. XLIId.
M & L AF2852–3. Franks Bequest, 1897.

286 Girdle Book English about 1540
Gold, enamelled in red, green, black and white, representing (a) on the front, in relief scene of the Brazen Serpent (Numbers, xxi, 8) surrounded by black enamelled inscription: +MAKE.THE.AFYRYE. SERPENT.AÑ.SETITVP.FORA.SYGNE: THATAS.MANY.AS-ARE.BYTĒE.MAYELOKE.VPONIT.AÑ.LYVE.; (b) on the back, in relief scene of the Judgement of Solomon (3 Kings, iii, 27) surrounded by black enamelled inscription: +THEN.THE.KYNG.ANSVERED.AÑ.SAYD. GYVE.HER.THE.LYVYNG.CHILD.AÑ.SLAYETNOT.FOR. SHEIS.THEMOT.HER.THEROE.3 K3C. Arabesque interlaced design in black enamel on spine and two clasps;

two suspension rings enamelled in black. H (of spine) 6·4.

The precise wording – but not the illiterate mis-spelling – of the inscriptions is to be found in two early English translations of the Bible – the Cromwell Bible (or First Great Bible) printed in 1539 in Paris and the Cranmer Bible printed in 1540 in England. Both the earlier and the later printed translations of the Bible have a different form of words. The printed devotional book inside the gold enamelled cover is not original, for it includes the only known example of the 1574 edition of a set of prayers printed by Henrie Middleton for Christopher Barker.

According to Nichols in 1788, the book contained 'on a blank leaf at the beginning this memorandum: *"This Book of Private Prayer was presented by the Lady Eliz. Tirwitt to Queen Eliz. during her confinement in the Tower; and the Queen generally wore it hanging by a Gold Chaine to her Girdle; and at her death left it by will to one of her Women of the Bed-chamber."'* Although the Lady Elizabeth Tirwitt was appointed to the Princess Elizabeth in place of Katherine Ashley in 1548, there is no evidence to confirm this tradition nor does the memorandum survive within the book.

In 1788, in possession of Rev. Mr Ashby, of Barrow, Suffolk, whose mother is said to have received it about 1720 from her husband's father, George Ashby MP, of Quenby, Leicestershire, as a family heirloom.

In 1872, in possession of Mr Farrer, who had it from Sir John Cullum; subsequently in the collection of the Duke of Sussex; in sale of Mr George Field's collection, purchased by Mr Charles Wertheimer and sold to Mr A. W. Franks, who presented it to the Museum in 1894.

Bibliography: Nichols, *Progresses of the Court of Elizabeth*, vol. 1, p. xxxvii; *Notices and Remains of the Family of Tyrwhitt* (reprinted 1872), p. 25; *Gentleman's Magazine*, vol. v (1791), p. 27, pl. III; Evans (1921), p. 82, pl. XVII; Tait (1962), p. 232ff, pl. XLIa and b; Evans (1970), p. 101, pl. 70.

M & L 94.7–29.1. Given by A. W. Franks, Esq., 1894.

Colour plate 24

287 Two Holbein Designs English
probably 1533–40

(a) Pen and ink drawing, with Indian ink and yellow ochre wash, of a girdle prayer-book with an arabesque design enclosing the initials T↓W in the centre and having the initials 'T W' in the upper corners and, in reverse, 'W T' in the lower corners. H 7·9; W 5·9.

(b) Pen and ink drawing of an alternative design for a girdle prayer-book, with an arabesque pattern enclosing the same set of initials but arranged in a different order, i.e. T↓WI (in the upper half of the cover) and, in reverse, I↓WT (in the lower half). H 8·1; W 6·0.

Painted by Hans Holbein the Younger (1497–1543),

284   285

who resided in England from 1526–28 and again from 1532–43, working mainly at the court of Henry VIII. The arabesque designs in these two drawings would have been copied by a goldsmith and probably executed in black enamel on gold, as on the spine of the girdle prayer-book (no. 286). It has been suggested by Dr Joan Evans that 'the initials, T. W. [are] probably for Thomas Wyatt the poet, clerk of the King's jewels' but the meaning of the initial 'I' remains uncertain, although, as suggested in 1782, it might stand for (Thomas Wyatt) Junior or for Jane, his wife, whom he married in 1537. Significantly, the Wyatt family have possessed, at least since 1745 but probably long before, a very similar gold girdle prayer-book with arabesque ornaments executed in black enamel but without any initials incorporated into the design.

Bibliography: Robert Marsham, 'Manuscript Book of Prayers of the Wyatt Family', in *Archaeologia* XLIV (1873), pp. 259–62. L. Binyon, *Catalogue of Drawings by British Artists … in the British Museum* (London, 1900), no. 31a–b; Evans (1921), p. 82, pl. XVII; Paul Ganz, *Die Handzeichnungen Hans Holbein der J.* (Berlin, 1937), nos. 404–5; Evans (1970), p. 101.

P & D Sloane Collection, 1753.

287a,b

288 Hat Badge English about 1540

Gold, enamelled in blue, green, red, black and white, representing Christ talking to the Woman of Samaria at Jacob's Well (St. John iv, 4–42): black enamelled inscription reads: +OF.A.TREWTHE+THOW.ART.THE. TREW.MESSIAS. The repoussé figure-scene, the convex frame and the four projecting loops are attached by clips to the circular gold base-plate, partially punched for ornamentation. D 5·7.

Bibliography: Hugh Tait, 'Tudor Hat Badges', *BMQ* 20 (1955–56), p. 37; Eric Mercer, *The Oxford History of English Art, 1553–1625*, (Oxford, 1962), p. 216, pl. 75a; Tait (1962), p. 228ff, pl. XXXIXa,b and c.

M & L 1955.5–7.1. Purchased with the aid of the National Art-Collections Fund and the Christy Trustees, 1955.

288

289 Hat Badge Italian (?) about 1530–40

Gold, enamelled and set with diamonds and rubies, depicting animated crowded scene of conversion of St Paul, modelled in high relief; on frame, inscription: DVRVM.EST.TIBI.COMTRA. [*sic*] STIMVLVM.CALCITRARE: and five loops for suspension. D 4·8.

The inscription on the back in Italian, of more recent date, states that it was worn by Don John of Austria, who placed it in the hat of Camillo Capizucchi; confirmation of this history is lacking. Don John of Austria (1547–78) was half-brother of Philip II of Spain, the victor of Lepanto (1571) and a most

289

176

popular and chivalrous figure.
Bibliography: Read (1902, rev. 1927), no. 171; Evans (1970), p. 85, pl. 46a.
M & L Waddesdon Bequest, 1898 (no. 171).

290 Pendant English about 1550–60
Gold, enamelled; in centre, oval scene in high relief representing Joseph in the well surrounded by seven of his envious brethren, executed in repoussé work and enamelled in dark blue, red, black and white; enclosed within oval convex inner frame and outer frame of scroll-work, from which hang three pearls in gold enamelled mounts; suspended by means of two gold chains, each with two enamelled beads, from a small gold enamelled quatrefoil plaque, set with a table-cut diamond and having a pendant pearl below and suspension ring above. On the reverse, translucent *basse-taille* enamelled designs – in the centre, a bird pecking at fruit and flowers beneath a baldacchino – in the style of engravings by Jacques Androuet du Cerceau, executed in 1550. W 6·3; H (total) 12·8.

The front of the outer frame reveals a change of plan; the four corners were designed to receive table-cut diamonds but have been covered with blobs of green enamel.
Bibliography: Hugh Tait, 'A Tudor jewel; gold enamelled pendant', *Museums Journal* LVI (1957), p. 233; Tait (1962), p. 241ff, pl. XLVIIa–d.
M & L 1956.10–7.1. Purchased with the aid of the National Art-Collections Fund, 1956.

291 Chain English about 1550
Gold, enamelled in black and white, comprising eleven links of openwork design, each forming an elongated polygon. L (total) 30·5.
M & L 1959.4–3.1. Given by the Worshipful Company of Goldsmiths, 1959.

292 Belt-Buckle English about 1560
Gold, enamelled, in two sections, each ornamented with white enamelled mask within an openwork scroll-work of red and black enamel; the dome-shaped head is enamelled with a red flower and a green foliate border. On the reverse, both sections have two thin raised gold bars, through which the ends of the cloth belt were threaded and stitched. L (total) 7·4.

A portrait of the second Baron Wentworth dated 1568 (National Portrait Gallery) typifies the fashion for wearing the narrow belts fastened with buckles of this design. The dome-shaped head on the one section is designed to slip into the larger loop of the other section; the adjacent smaller loop seems to be purely decorative and to have no practical function.

290 △   ▽ 291

Bibliography: Hugh Tait, 'Tudor gold enamelled buckle', *BMQ* 26 (1962–3), pp. 112–13, pl. LVIII–LIX. M & L 1960.2–2.1.

293 Pendant South German about 1560–70
Gold, enamelled, with figure-group of Charity and three children standing within an architectural frame set with diamonds and rubies, flanked by the figures of Faith and Fortitude; above, an emerald between two music-making putti; below, a larger emerald between two lions. Reverse, enamelled architectural design in low relief. L (with ring) 9·4.
This massive, solid jewel closely resembles engraved designs by Erasmus Hornick, published in Nuremburg in 1565. Trained as a goldsmith in his native Antwerp, Hornick settled in Augsburg, where in 1555 he married the daughter of a patrician family. Later he went to live and work in Nuremburg (1559–66) but returned to Augsburg, where he was granted citizenship. He died in 1583, the year after he had joined the Emperor Rudolf II's court in Prague. No piece of jewellery can be identified as his creation, though some hundreds of drawings and engravings, attributed to Hornick and his workshop, have survived. This jewel, if not by his own hand, is strikingly similar to his style of design.

Bibliography: Read (1902, revised 1927), no. 149; Yvonne Hackenbroch, 'Erasmus Hornick as a jeweller,' *The Connoisseur*, Sept. 1967, pp. 58–9. Evans (1970), p. 113, pl. 85(a) and (b). M & L Waddesdon Bequest, 1898 (no. 149).

294 The 'Phoenix Jewel' English about 1570–80
Gold; bust of Queen Elizabeth I cut out in silhouette; on reverse, in relief, the device of a phoenix in flames under the royal monogram, crown and heavenly rays; enclosed within an enamelled wreath of red and white Tudor roses with green leaves and intertwined stalks. W 4·6.

This jewel is a unique survival and bears every indication of having been freely and individually tooled, engraved and chased. Although said to be cut from a medal, no other matching example is known. Neither the front nor the back corresponds with the surviving examples of the famous medal known as the 'Phoenix Badge' (*Medallic Illustrations*, Elizabeth, no. 70), which was also engraved and published in 1620 by John Luckius in *Sylloge Numismatum Elegantiorum*, where it is dated 'about 1574' but without any justification; a silver impression in the British Museum bears the engraved date '1574', but this has almost certainly been added more recently. The medals, unlike this gold version, bear an encircling legend expressing grief over the celibacy of the Queen. She is said to have adopted the phoenix as an emblem of herself – in one painting, the Queen is portrayed wearing a pendant jewel in the form of a phoenix (see Strong [1963], p. 60, pl. VII) – but firm documentary evidence concerning the use of this emblem is lacking, and Miss Farquhar's reference to the use of the phoenix as 'her Highnesses badge' at Norwich in 1578 seems to be inaccurate and misleading. At present, this jewel can only be dated tentatively to the decade 1570–80, partly because of the similarities between this gold bust of the Queen and Nicholas Hilliard's miniature of the Queen dated 1572 (in the National Portrait Gallery); however, Dr Auerbach's recent attribution of this gold jewel to the hand of Hilliard has yet to be proved.

Bibliography: Evans (1921), p. 91, pl. XIX; Helen Farquhar, 'John Ruttinger and the Phoenix Badge of Queen Elizabeth', *Numismatic Chronicle*, fifth series, III (1923), p. 270f. pl. XIII; *BM Guide* (1924), p. 147; E. Auerbach, *Nicholas Hilliard* (1961), p. 179f, pl. 174a–b; Strong (1963), p. 149; Evans (1970), p. 120. M & L Acquired in 1753 (Sir Hans Sloane's collection).

Colour plate 26

295 Pendant Spanish late 16th century
Gold, enamelled and fashioned in the form of a sea-dragon, the body and part of the tail of this fantastic beast consisting of two large, irregular-shaped pearls, known as 'baroque pearls'. Smaller pearls mask the join of the tail and the body, and decorate the suspension chains. On reverse, enamelled gold strapwork design; below, a pendant pearl. L 10·5 ; W 6·8.

These huge pendants were intended to be worn over rich brocades, particularly for pinning high up on stiff sleeves so that the jewels were free to swing, catching the light as they moved. The engraved designs of Hornick in 1562 and of Hans Collaert of Antwerp in 1581 include large pendants in the form of dragons and sea-horses; however, they do not appear to incorporate the 'baroque pearl', unlike the drawing of a similar jewel by the Spaniard, Pere Juan Bastons in 1593 (in Barcelona). The most comparable jewel to have survived – and certainly from the same workshop – is the sea-horse pendant preserved in the Cathedral Treasury of Santo Domingo.

Bibliography: Read (1902, revised 1927), no. 159; Evans (1970), p. 110f, pl. 79a,b; Muller (1972), p. 88, pl. 135–6. M & L Waddesdon Bequest, 1898 (no. 159).

See frontispiece

296 The Cheapside Hoard English about 1600
Found under a house in Cheapside (near St Paul's Cathedral), London, in 1912.

292 △   ▽ 295

293

296 b
a

296 j

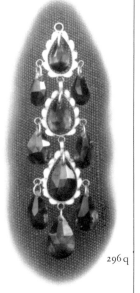

296 q

296 o

296 t

296 s

The major portion of the hoard is preserved in the Museum of London and a further selection in the Victoria and Albert Museum; the following items, preserved in the British Museum, typify the jewellery in the hoard:

(a) Chain, gold, links of alternate flowers and leaves enamelled white and green. L 159·6.

(b) Chain, gold, links alternately quatrefoils in white enamel with blue centres, and double corded rings. L 55·8.

(c) Finger-ring, gold, small circular bezel set with seven cabochon emeralds, the back enamelled. D 2·0.

(d) Finger-ring, gold, circular bezel set with cabochon emeralds (two missing), the hoop and back enamelled. D 2·3.

(e) Finger-ring, gold, small circular bezel set with seven fancy-cut garnets, the hoop and back enamelled D 2·0.

(f) Finger-ring, similar to last.

(g) Finger-ring, gold, circular bezel set with nine cabochon emeralds, part of hoop enamelled. D 2·3.

(h) Finger-ring, gold, circular bezel set with nine cabochon emeralds (three missing), hoop and back enamelled. D 2·4.

(i) Finger-ring, gold, circular bezel set with six fancy-cut sapphires (one missing) and a central pearl. D 2·3.

(j) Finger-ring, gold, oval bezel set with a cat's eye. D 2·2.

(k) Finger-ring, gold, large flat bezel set with a table-cut emerald surrounded by eight cabochon emeralds (one missing), back and part of hoop enamelled. D 2·3.

(l) Pendant fan-holder, gold, enamelled in green and blue, and made in the form of a lotus flower. L 5·1.

(m) Pendant fan-holder of white enamelled gold set

180

296 m

296 n

296 l

with eleven cabochon emeralds (on both sides), and made in the form of a flower. L 6·1.

(n) Pendant fan-holder of gold enamelled in white, green and amber, and made in the form of a caduceus. L 5·6.

(o) Pendant, gold, pear-shaped, openwork set with pearls in alternate vertical rows of small and large settings (nearly all the larger pearls missing), with an upper spray of six pearls (four missing). H 5·6.

(p) Pendant, similar to last, but without upper spray. H 6·1.

(q) Pendant, gold, of three white enamel links with ten rose-cut amethyst drops (briolettes). H 6·4.

(r) Pendant, pairing with last. H 6·6.

(s) Pendant, gold, with white enamel, set with a cabochon garnet and having a pendant water-sapphire (iolite) rough-polished. H 4·1.

(t) Pendant of amethyst set in gold and carved in the form of seven bunches of grapes (two missing), arranged in two rows of triple branches. H 4·1.

(u) Button, gold, enamelled in white, blue and green, in the form of a 5-petal rosette. D 2·0.

(v) Button, gold, enamelled in white and blue (traces only) set with four table-cut rubies and a central diamond (missing). D 1·3.

(w) Button, similar to last, but one ruby and setting missing.

(x) Button, similar.

(y) Button, similar.

The Cheapside Hoard was apparently part of a jeweller's stock, probably hidden about 1640, perhaps because of the Civil War. It contains few items of outstanding value, the bulk being of moderate intrinsic worth and, presumably, suited to the purse of the successful merchant-class of late Tudor and early Stuart London.

Bibliography: *The Cheapside Hoard of Elizabethan and Jacobean Jewellery*, London Museum Catalogues, No. 2 (1928); *Exhibition of Gemstones and Jewellery*, City Museum and Art Gallery, Birmingham (1960).

M & L 1912.7–24.1–5 and 1914.4–23.1–20. Partly purchased in 1912 and partly given by the Rt Hon. Lewis Harcourt and the Corporation of the City of London in 1914.

297 Pomander Spanish about 1600

Gold, enamelled in white and red, the mount fitted with suspension loop; gum benzoin ball studded with small cabochon emeralds set in gold in a star-shaped design. H 4·4.

Gum benzoin is an aromatic resin; no other example of this type has been recorded.

Bibliography: Muller (1972), p. 66, fig. 89.
M & L AF2863. Franks Bequest, 1897.

297

298 The 'Lyte' Jewel English 1610–11

Gold enamelled locket set with twenty-five square table-cut diamonds and four rose-cut diamonds; cover of pierced openwork design incorporating the monogram 'IR' (in Latin, 'IACOBUS REX', for King James VI of Scotland and I of England, who succeeded Queen Elizabeth in 1603); reverse of hinged cover is brilliantly enamelled in red and blue; inside, miniature portrait of James I; back of jewel is mainly white enamel with design in fine gold lines and ruby enamel. H 6·2.

Miniature of James I is by Nicholas Hilliard (1547–1614), painter, limner and engraver to Queen Elizabeth and, later, to James I – the first English-born artist to gain this recognition at court.

Given by James I in 1610 to Mr Thomas Lyte, of Lytescary, Somerset, as a reward for drawing up an illuminated pedigree of the King, in which the royal ancestry was traced back without a break to the mythical founder of the British nation, Brut, the Trojan. This genealogy was presented to the King at the Palace of Whitehall in the year 1610 in the presence of the Prince of Wales and the principal personages at court, and doubtless it was on that occasion that the King 'gave the said author his picture in gold set with diamonds, with gracious thanks'. The portrait of Thomas Lyte dated 14 April 1611 shows him wearing the Jewel and provides a *terminus ante quem* (see no. 299). In 1747, Thomas Lyte, of New Inn, a great-grandson of the author, bequeathed both the Lyte Jewel and the portrait of 1611 to his daughter, Silvestra Blackwell, who bequeathed them to her daughter, Silvestra, who married James Monypenny, of Maytham Hall, Kent, and so to their descendant, Thomas Gybbon Monypenny (died 1854). Sold through a London dealer to the Duke of Hamilton; *The Hamilton Palace Collection*, illustrated priced Catalogue, London, 1882, lot 1615, fetched £2,835; Baron Ferdinand Rothschild.

Bibliography: Anthony à Wood, *Athenae Oxonienses* (ed. 1813), vol. ii, p. 649; *Notes and Queries*, 1st Series, vol. vii, p. 570; Sir Henry Maxwell Lyte, KCB, 'The Lytes of Lytescary', *Proc. of the Somerset Archaeological Society* (1892), vol. 38, pp. 60ff; Read (1902, revised 1927), no. 167; Evans (1921), p. 120; *BM Guide* (1924). Evans (1970), p. 134, pl. 117a.
M & L Waddesdon Bequest, 1898 (no. 167).

Colour plate 25

299 Portrait of Thomas Lyte English 1611

Painted on panel, half-length, three-quarters face, wearing a white lawn collar and a wide red ribbon around his neck from which hangs on his chest the 'Lyte Jewel', closed but complete with its original pendant in the form of a trilobed drop set with diamonds suspended from the tiny loops at the base of the oval locket. Inscription (in upper right-hand corner): AETATIS SVAE 43; 14° DIE APRILIS, 1611; in upper left-hand corner, a shield of arms of the Lyte family: gules, a chevron between three swans argent. H 58·4; W 45·1.

Thomas Lyte (1568–1638); the portrait remained in the family of the Lytes, of Lytescary, Somerset, until in 1774 it was bequeathed by Thomas Lyte, great-grandson, to his daughter, Silvestra Blackwell, who left it to her daughter, Silvestra Monypenny, of Maytham Hall Kent. It was sold at Sotheby's, 3 February 1960, lot 70, by a member of the Lyte family.

Bibliography: Sir Henry Maxwell Lyte, KCB, 'The Lytes of Lytescary', *Proc. of the Somerset Archaeological Society* 38 (1892), pp. 60ff.

Lent by the Somerset County Museum, Taunton Castle.

298 ▷

▽ 299

182

300

300 Pendant Medal Netherlands (?) 1627
Gold, cast and chased, set in enamelled gold frame; *obverse*, bust of Frederick V, King of Bohemia (1619–20), laureate and legend: FRIDERICVS.D.G.REX.BOHE.ELECT.PALAT; on the truncation, s.d.r.f.1627; *reverse*, a crowned lion sejant with orb and sceptre, above, a crown held by five hands issuing from cloud. L 4·25; W 3·35.

The reverse is decorated with Frederick's crest as Count Palatine and the five hands represent Bohemia and the four Protestant provinces (Moravia, Silesia, Upper and Lower Lusatia), which elected him King in August 1619 in opposition to the Emperor Ferdinand II. The imperial army defeated Frederick's forces at the famous battle of the White Mountain, near Prague, in 1620 and forced Frederick and his 'Winter Queen', Elizabeth, daughter of James I of England, to seek asylum in the Netherlands. Prince Rupert of the Rhine, the famous Cavalier, was their son. Neither the maker's initials, s.d.r.(f?), nor the date '1627' have been satisfactorily explained and a Netherlandish, rather than a German, origin may be the explanation. Although several other examples of this medal, both in gold and silver, have survived, none is framed and mounted as a pendant jewel, though the gold example, which was already in George III's collection by 1771 (now in the British Museum), has a suspension loop. The practice of setting gold medals in pendants was popular in Germany (examples can be seen in the Waddesdon Room, British Museum, and in the Grünes Gewolbe in Dresden).

Bibliography: C. G. Heraens, *Bildnisse der regierenden Fursten* . . . (Vienna, 1828), pl. 44, no. 26; *Medallic Illustrations of British History* (London, 1911), vol. 1, pl. XVIII, no. 2.
M & L AF2876. Franks Bequest, 1897.

301 Locket French 1636
Gold, enamelled with miniature scenes; on front of cover, a naval engagement, inscribed 'H Toutin' on flange at top; inside of cover, Diana and Actaeon; on back of locket, a military siege; inside, the enamelled inscription: *Henry Toutin Mt. orphevre A Paris fecit 1636.* (Henri Toutin, master-goldsmith at Paris made it, 1636.) H (including suspension ring) 4.5

This piece, and the miniature portrait of Charles I of England (Rijksmuseum, Amsterdam), are the earliest dated and signed works by Henri Toutin (b. 1614). His father, Jean Toutin (1578–1644), a goldsmith of Chateaudun, has been credited with the discovery of this new technique of fine miniature painting in enamel colours on a white enamel ground; no authenticated work of this master has survived. From about 1630, Toutin's workshops in Blois and Paris were producing these gold plaques 'émaillées à figure' for jewellery, watches, etc.

Bibliography: H. Clouzot, *Dictionnaire des Miniaturistes sur Email* (Paris, 1924); H. Clouzot, *Histoire de la Miniature sur Email en France* (Paris, undated); Pierre F. Schneeberger, *Les Peintres sur Email Genevois au XVIIe et au XVIIIe Siècle* (Geneva, 1958), p. 90.
M & L BL3470. Bernal Collection, 1855.

302 Slide for Ribbon French about 1630–40
Gold, set with engraved onyx intaglio gem depicting a male nude figure; reverse, enamelled with miniature painting of different flowers in many colours on white ground, including the two raised 'bars' for the ribbon to slide through. L 3·2.

An oval locket enamelled in this manner and signed 'H. Toutin' (in the Kunsthistorisches Museum, Vienna) is datable to 'around 1640'. This style of floral enamelling became extremely popular with jewellers and goldsmiths in France, the Low Countries and Germany.
Formerly in the Arundel and Marlborough collection.
Bibliography: Story-Maskelyne (1870), no. 612.
M & L 1924.3–8.1.

303 Necklace Low Countries (?)
mid 17th century AD
Gold, thirty-five links, each set with a table-cut diamond; in the centre, a larger link set with a diamond, from which hangs a pendant jewel set with a flat octagonal sapphire and surmounted by an open-work bow set with three rose-cut diamonds. Reverse, painted enamelled decoration in black and pink on a white ground; on reverse of pendant, a tulip. L (total 35·4; L (of pendant) 2·5.

'Tulipomania', the veneration of the tulip, reached its climax in the Low Countries around 1635 and spread throughout Europe. Necklaces of similar character are to be seen in Dutch portraits, including Rembrandt's picture of Saskia, but an English or French origin for the necklace cannot be excluded.
Bibliography: Y. Hackenbroch, 'A jewelled necklace in the British Museum', *Antiquaries Journal* XXI (1941), p. 342.
M & L 1941.7–7.1. Given by the National Art-Collections Fund, 1941.

304 Pendant Spanish late 17th century AD
Gold, set with emeralds; added on reverse, in open-work gold the insignia of the Holy Office of the Inquisition. Two stamps: a lion rampant. L 6·4.

In 1603, Philip III decreed that ministers of the Holy Inquisition should exhibit its insignia on their clothing during religious functions and public acts; this order was not universally respected throughout Spain. By 1680, however, members of the Court attending the Inquisition's *auto-da-fé* in Madrid appear to have worn pendants of this kind (see Muller [1972], p. 117).
M & L 1951.10–9.1. Bequeathed by Miss Mary Bidwell, 1951.

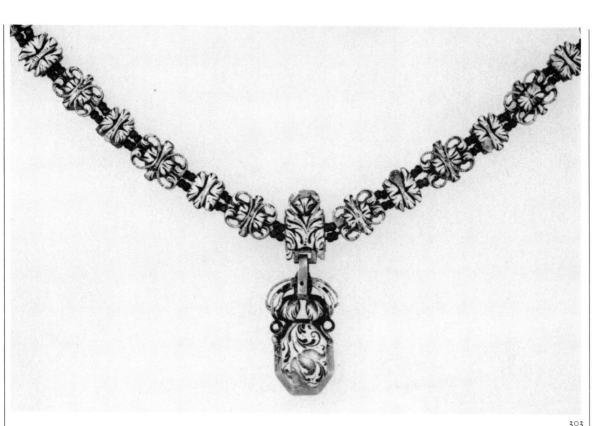

14
China, India and Tibet
AD 1500-1800

This section has been devoted entirely to jewellery from China, India and Tibet, as it is less fruitful to explore similarities and comparisons with jewellery from the West at this later period than it was for earlier sections. With the jewellery from Tibet a completely new style is introduced, while the Chinese, on the other hand, elaborate the themes already initiated (see sections 7, 9, 12 above). From China, prominent as before are hairpins, and accompanying them are the ornaments in which a man would enclose his knot of hair (no. 305). Such small caps in jade or gold are known from paintings and from a few excavated examples of the fourteenth–sixteenth centuries. From the Ming period likewise, date the excavated examples of the crowns worn by women which are here represented by a miniature and late example (no. 315). A full-size nineteenth-century example is shown on the woman in a painting (Chinese painting A173). Although only comparatively late examples survive some early paintings suggest that such crowns were worn before the Ming periods. They bear a close resemblance to the crowns which adorned Bodhisattvas shown in both paintings and sculptures in the elaborate forms current from the late T'ang period (tenth century AD). It is perhaps the growth in importance of the crowns which accounts for the relatively small size of the hairpins of the Ming and Ch'ing periods.

The other major genre of Chinese jewellery, belt ornaments, continues to play an important part. Up to the fifteenth century the main form of the belt set continued to consist of a group of plaques and a buckle ornament. However, while this remained in vogue new forms were introduced in the Yüan period, which resulted in a greater diversification in general from the later Ming period. The jade belt ornaments (no. 310) illustrate some of the variety which evolved. In the sense that these belts were an important article of dress, and became almost an integral part of the magnificent robes worn by officials and princes, two large gold plaques can be considered in association with them (no. 309). The design of dragons is of exceptionally high quality and can be dated quite confidently to the fifteenth century by analogy with designs on blue and white porcelain. It is instructive to compare the detail and high quality of the chased and relief work on the plaques with the much bolder and less refined treatment of the hair ornament (no. 306) which is somewhat earlier in date. Important too is the addition of polished gems in rather primitive settings, a characteristic of the Ming dynasty. The use of such boldly placed stones is rare before the Ming period but thereafter becomes an important element in Chinese jewellery.

The most important technical change to take place in the Ming and Ch'ing dynasties is from working predominantly in thin sheets of metal to the use of wire filigree. The two plaques illustrate a stage in this development: on the one hand there is great precision and detail in the execution of the dragons and on the other the effort to achieve an open light effect is arrived at by the pierced work around the clouds and the dragons producing a scroll effect. In the late fifteenth and early sixteenth centuries this trend to finer and more detailed work was continued until in the second half of the sixteenth century such pierced work was replaced by wire mesh and filigree. An area where this transition can be dated quite accurately is in Kiangsi province in central China. Here two tombs at Nan-ch'eng, one dating to the second quarter of the sixteenth century, with gold jewellery mainly worked from sheets of gold with pierced details can be contrasted with a tomb dating from the later part of the sixteenth century in which a magnificent group of jewellery was found. In this latter group the fine detail is executed in elaborate wire mesh. During the seventeenth and eighteenth centuries such wire mesh was used both as a filler in the main elements of the design (no. 312) and as the structure of the whole piece (no. 313). The silver lion dog (no. 317) represents the culmination of this development of the potential of coiled and meshed wire.

J.M.R.

China

305 Hair Ornament China 14th–15th century AD Ming dynasty

Carved from rectangular block of jade and hollowed out; enhanced with five raised ribs in relief running over central portion and joined on both sides by horizontal rib midway up side of ornament. At sides rib runs up from lower front corner and makes spiral against both ends. Ornament pierced below spiral for insertion of pin. L 5·7; 18·8 (pin).

This ornament, worn by a man, was intended to hold a small bun of hair in place. Similar items are shown in paintings of the Sung period but the majority of excavated examples, usually in metal, are of the Yüan and Ming periods. The ribbed design on this piece can be compared with an ornament from a Ming tomb near Nanking, see *K'ao-ku* (1962/8), p. 470, pl. 5(1). The pin does not belong to this present example.

OA 1910.12–24.3.

306 Hair Ornament China 14th–15th century AD Ming dynasty

Gold, hollow, with chased decoration and semi-circular ribs rising from sequence of arcs which step up from horizontal division in lower portion of ornament formed by band with leaf design; below lower section again divided by border formed by arcs; headdress pierced with four holes in lower section. Different segments of head-dress decorated by coarse ring-punching and two side sections with floral diaper. Plain area on back of ornament suggests further element was attached through four holes at this point. H 8·4; W 9·5.

This ornament, like the previous jade example, was used to enclose a knot or bun of hair. It is very similar in form to the hair ornament excavated from the tomb of the Prince Chu T'an who died in the fourteenth century AD, see *Wen-wu* (1972/5), p. 25, fig. 20.

OA 1938.5–24.247.

307 Pair of Earrings China 14th–15th century AD Ming dynasty

Gold, with S-shaped loops decorated with five oval-shaped seed-like elements beaten out from body of gold. H 2·8.

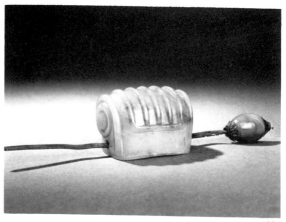

305

306 △   ▽ 307

189

Several unusual hairpins decorated by a very similar method have been excavated from an early Ming tomb near Nanking, see *K'ao-ku* (1962/9), p. 470, pl. 5(4).

OA 1938.5–24.239.

308 Pair of Earrings China 15th–16th century AD
Ming dynasty
Gold, suspended from S-shaped loops worked in relief with openwork showing phoenix in profile perched on flower with back to sunflower. H 5·0.

OA 1938.5–24.217; 218.

309 Pair of Plaques China 15th century AD
Ming dynasty
Gold, rectangular, with two dragons and flaming pearl among clouds worked in relief with chased detail, joined by scrolls in openwork formed by piercing metal; set in centre of clouds and in double row around borders of plaques are semi-precious stones in settings formed by upright enclosures; plaques pierced around edge for attachment. H 15·0; L 18·0.

These plaques were probably attached to official or ceremonial robes.
Bibliography: Jenyns and Watson (1963), pl. 4.
OA 1949.12–13.1–2.

Colour plate 17

310 Four Belt Ornaments China
14th–18th centuries AD
Ming and Ch'ing dynasties
(a) Rectangular grey jade plaque with brown areas, corners rounded and pierced at centre; on one face in high undercut relief two dragons with branching tails, following each other head to tail. L 8·4.
Early Ming Dynasty, fourteenth–fifteenth century AD.
Bibliography: Ayers and Rawson (1975), no. 349; London, Royal Academy (1936), no. 606.
OA 1930.12–17.39. Bequeathed by James Hilton, 1930.

Colour plate 16

(b) Square green jade plaque pierced transversely to allow leather belt to pass through with oval loop below for suspension of subsidiary portion of belt at right angles; outline of main plaque pinched in at four corners; enclosed in plain border is a dragon in high relief with bifurcating tail and head turned towards smaller dragon poised on one foot of larger one. H 7·6; W 6·3.
Ming dynasty, fifteenth–sixteenth century AD.
OA 1930.12–17.37. Bequeathed by James Hilton, 1930.

(c) Belt ornament of bluish green jade in shape of two lotus leaves, one seen from top and other from

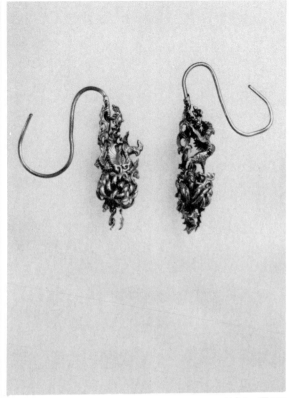

308 △   ▽ 310

side, with elaborately intertwined stalks in openwork. L 9·5.

Late Ming dynasty, sixteenth–seventeenth century AD.
OA 1930.12–17.34. Bequeathed by James Hilton, 1930.

Colour plate 16

(d) Pale greenish white jade belt-clasp in two parts; one side pierced with rectangular hole to take projecting hook of other part; both decorated with crouching dragons curled around with tails touching heads in high undercut relief. L 10·3.

Ch'ing dynasty, eighteenth century AD.
OA 1930.12–17.36. Bequeathed by James Hilton, 1930.

This group of four belt ornaments illustrates both the different forms used and also the stylistic development which took place during the period. An early example of belt ornaments decorated with undercut relief has been excavated from an early Ming dynasty tomb near Nanking, *K'ao-ku* (1972/4), p. 31, pl. 7.

311 Three Hairpins China 17th–18th century AD
Ch'ing dynasty

(a) Gold hairpin tapering from square cross-section near head above which is ringed section forming stalk of flower; five petals of flower made from woven and coiled filigree and alternate with wires culminating in small heads which represent stamens; red semi-precious stone enclosed. L 10·2.
OA 1938.5–24.262.

(b) Pin of openwork gold culminating in lizard's head of filigree gold wire with bulging eyes; below head further portion of filigree work enhanced with floral scroll in gold wire. L 13·2.
OA 1938.5–24.209.

(c) Gold hairpin, U-shaped and linked by two roundels and scrolls in openwork; head in form of flowers executed in fine wire filigree enclosed in wire framework with further details executed in wire; inlaid with red semi-precious stone and pearl. This portion formed independently of pin and attached to it. L 12·6.

Filigree hairpins which may be compared with this one have been excavated from a seventeenth century tomb near Peking, see *Wen-wu* (1969/1), p. 50.
Bibliography: Jenyns and Watson (1963), pl. 2.
OA 1938.5–24.273.

312 Pair of Bracelets China 18th century AD
Ch'ing dynasty
Gold, each constructed in two parts hinged at centre, and fastened by catch beneath flower with four small petals; same floral motif repeated at three more points on bracelets; between flowers is a channel probably formerly inlaid and bordered by scrolls in filigree

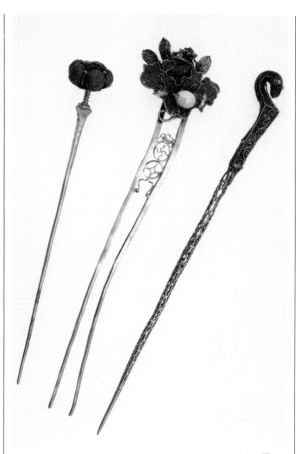

311 △   ▽ 312

191

315

work; inside of bracelet covered by diaper ground;
cloud scrolls on filigree ground decorate upper and
lower edges of bracelets. W 7·8.
OA 1937.4–16.237; 238.

313 Collar China 17th–18th century AD
Ch'ing dynasty
Gold; made of three sections worked in filigree,
joined in two places with balls in foil with chased design; terminating in two balls worked in filigree and
decorated with scrolls in wire. Main part of collar is
decorated with vases of flowers, ceremonial axes and
musical stones among cloud scrolls executed in wire.
At back main semicircle open, bordered by gold wire
showing reinforcing of different elements joined with
wire. At joints reverse enhanced with plaques with
scroll design composed of filigree with wire. W 20·0.
OA 1937.4–16.236.

314 Ornament China 17th–18th century AD
Ch'ing dynasty
Gold, in shape of flower, outer ring of wire petals in
beaten gold enhanced with veins in twisted wire;
inner ring of eighteen petals with small petals of
beaten gold outlined in twisted wire alternating with

314

192

petals in filigree; in centre hollow calyx surmounted by border of wire loops. At back double tube of rectangular cross-section for attachment. W 5·5.
OA 1938.5–24.270.

315 Head-dress China 18th–19th century AD
Ch'ing dynasty

Miniature silver head-dress consisting of domed cap with five ribs between sections decorated with triangles: crown wrapped around this, front section has five *ju-i*-shaped projections over scene which shows three Sages among trees; behind, on either side, plume rises with shaped edge curving backwards and joined to band which forms back of crown; projecting over this back portion is fan-shaped element decorated with a bat, and from each of five arcs pendants are suspended; around base of crown is ring of small bosses of which a portion now missing, on either side a dragon attached by coiled wire and dragon head placed on top of cap; flaming pearl attached to front by length of coiled wire and at back similarly attached are decorations made up of flowers and butterflies. Whole decorated in relief with chased details and pierced extensively. L (front to back) 12·0.

This is a late example in miniature of the elaborate head-dress worn particularly by women from the Sung period onwards.
OA 1938.5–24.340.

316 Ornament China 17th–18th century AD

Silver-gilt, composed of butterflies, flowers and fruits surmounted by knot of eternity; mounted on framework consisting of oval or flat wire in back with two small rings for attachment; detail executed in twisted wire. L 13·2.

316

This ornament is part of an elaborate head-dress and would probably have been attached towards the back of such a complex. On the miniature silver head-dress (no. 315) similar compositions of flowers and butterflies can be seen at the back.
OA 1938.5–24.341.

317 Lion-dog China 18th century AD
Ch'ing dynasty

Ornament in shape of lion-dog executed in silver-wire filigree; head formed from small coils with projecting spirals, large bulging eyes and mane of broad coils; body and legs in borders of looped wire with tail in broader coils and strands; creature standing on cloud scrolls of silver sheet bordered with twisted wire which was formerly inlaid with blue possibly in form of enamel. Small hook on back for attachment to larger complex of ornament. L 5·0.
OA 1938.5–24.373.

317

India

In the martial society of Mughal India the goldsmith's art was applied to the decoration of dagger and sword hilts which were often of hardstones such as jade and rock crystal, carved and encrusted with gold and precious stones. The archer's thumb-ring was also treated in this manner (no. 428). Jewellery was as much an adornment of men as of women and the enamelled gold armlet (no. 318), worn on the upper arm, is commonly depicted in portraits of the Emperor, princes and great officers of the imperial household.

R. P-W.

318 Armlet India 18th century AD
Probably Jaipur, India.

Gold, enamelled and encrusted with precious stones. Central oval medallion set with green stone on one side and on other decorated in champlevé enamels with central flower and leaf sprays: hinged to each end of medallion is lotus flower, on one side decorated with cloisonné enamels and on other encrusted with greenish yellow stones, possibly tourmalines. Silk cords bound with seed pearls. L (with cord) 39·6; L (jewelled ornament) 9·3.

Armlets consisting, like this, of three elements secured by silken cords are commonly depicted in portraits of the Mughal emperors, princes and nobles where they are worn on the upper arm.

318   OA 1961.10–16.3. Bequeathed by Louis C. G. Clarke.

Tibet

Where Chinese jewellery of this late period is increasingly detailed, the appeal of Tibetan jewellery lies primarily in its bold handling of metal and semi-precious stones. Among the Tibetans the use of jewellery was not confined to women, but 'ladies of good position', wrote Sir Charles Bell, '(are) known as *gyen-sang-ma* (literally "she with good ornaments")'. Their liberal use of self-adornment, indeed, extended to head-dress, and facial and bodily decoration. The effect of Tibetan jewellery is achieved by an interplay of predominant turquoise incrustation, sometimes forming elaborate patterns, and metalwork devices such as scrolling with pearled wire and the decoration of settings with abundant false granulation. The metals range from copper alloy, sometimes gilded, through low-grade silver to gold. Turquoise, which had talismanic properties, was often of local origin; like the scarcely less popular coral, the use of which was already noted by Marco Polo (1254–1324), turquoise was also imported. Pearls, beads of various stones, coloured glass and lapis-lazuli are also used; the inlaid stones, being fixed with a weak adhesive resembling sealing wax, are frequently lost.
w.z.

319

319 Ornamental Plaque Tibetan 18th century AD
Gold, square, backed with silver and pierced with five tubular passages for threading or attachment with chains. Top consists of leaf- and petal-shaped turquoises set in raised mounts decorated with borders of pearled gold wire and globules and forming design of four trefoils radiating from central rosette. Borders of turquoise and gold florets and three pearled gold wires. H 5·8.
OA 1964.10–15.1.

320

320 Pair of Earrings Tibetan 18th century AD
Bronze composed of three main sections each having turquoises set in bronze mounts with coarse beaded borders. Top section oval and surmounted by three small turquoise stones, middle section has roughly circular turquoise surrounded by two rows of pearled wire and below a floral motif consisting of three turquoise petals. L 10·5.

Ear pendants of this type are reported as having been worn formerly by Lhasa women on festive occasions but were also generally common in Tibet. When worn they are turned to the front.
Bibliography: T. H. Hendley, 'Indian Jewellery, Part X', *Journal of Indian Art and Industry* XII (1909), p. 137, pl. 114, no. 789.
OA 1905.5–18.75.

Colour plate 17

195

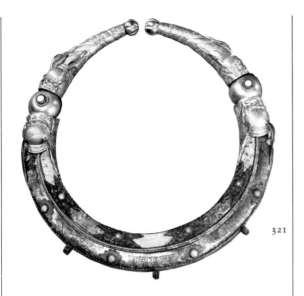

321

321 Ornamental Collar Tibetan
18th–19th century AD
Gilt bronze, consisting of segment of circle ending in globes to which are attached curved hinged terminals in form of horned Chinese dragons represented as swallowing globes; two similar horned dragon's heads on the segment also shown in act of swallowing globes. Between the globes, the top of the collar is divided along its length into two bands separated by pearled wire. The inner zone is set with strips of turquoise, lapis-lazuli and coral separated by gilt-bronze plaques decorated with vegetal scrolls and with a round turquoise or coral set in the centre above the pin. The outer zone consists of a gilt-bronze band of curved section decorated with incised floriated scroll patterns and magical letters, in the *lantsa* character, separated at intervals by a flower with a central coral or turquoise set in petals of cloisonné enamel. The two zones are set in walls of raised scrolled and pearled decoration and the flat bottom of the collar is also decorated with raised designs. Along the outer edge are three loops. The precise function is not clear but the form suggests use as a collar. D 22·0.
Bibliography: T. H. Hendley, 'Indian Jewellery, Part X', *Journal of Indian Art and Industry* XII (1909), p. 137, pl. 114, no. 792; G. Tucci, *Tibet, Land of Snows* (London, 1967), p. 200, fig. 9.
OA 1905.5–31.1.

322 Waist Ornament Tibetan 19th century AD
Cruciform ornament consisting of three strips made up of silver links joined at middle by hinges to central plaque studded with tiered turquoises and extended on top by crest-like ornament also studded with turquoises, pattern on both being outlined in pearled silver wire. Two horizontal strips end in hinged leaf-shaped buckle set with turquoise and attached to hook; pendant strip has ribbed silver ring hanging from leaf-shaped terminal. Central plaque has small hooked chain. Strips decorated with small copper cartouches enhanced with pearled wire scrolling and floral device in turquoise. W (span) 50·8; H 35·0.
Bibliography: L. A. Waddell, *The Buddhism of Tibet or Lamaism* (London, 1895), p. 572, for an illustration showing such a belt in use.
OA 1905.5–18.74.

323 Head Ornament Mongolian 19th century AD
Circlet of silver, wider at the front with two hinged attachments and two openwork pendants; decorated with elaborate scrolling of pearled silver wire and set with coral, turquoise and other stones, chiefly circular and oval. Two separate silver hair attachments are decorated with pearled silver wire scrolling enclosing silver granules and corals and turquoises. These attachments were fitted to each of two large stiffened braids of hair. D (circlet) 15·9; L (pendants) 10·2; L (attachments) 7·6.

It is said to remind married women of the Mongols' descent from a nature spirit and a cow, the stiffened braids of hair representing cow's horns. This headdress was acquired in Urga by the donor from a Mongol woman who was actually wearing it.
Bibliography: T. H. Hendley, 'Indian Jewellery, Part X', *Journal of Indian Art and Industry*, vol. XII (1909), p. 138, pl. 120, no. 832; *Catalogue of the Tibetan Collection and other Lamaist articles in the Newark Museum* . . ., vol. IV (Newark, N.J., 1961), p. 59. pl. XXX, for a similar parure and the explanation quoted above.
OA 1903.10–6.12–13. Given by C. W. Campbell, Esq., 1903.

15
West Africa
AD 1500-1850

Benin

Benin is the capital of a kingdom in the humid tropical forest region of southern Nigeria. Its present king, Akenzua II, is the thirty-eighth of a dynasty which has ruled for 600 years or more. At the height of its power, by the mid sixteenth century AD, the imperial authority of Benin was extended by military conquest far beyond the 'tribal' boundary of the kingdom as far as Lagos to the west and the River Niger to the east, incorporating substantial groups of Yoruba and Ibo peoples. Throughout this area the King was able to enforce the payment of tribute, the performance of military service and the safe passage of Benin traders as well as his own personal monopoly of the coastal trade with Europeans. The internal structure of this empire was inevitably complex, with various orders, grades and titles of nobility, a system of territorial administration, trading companies and so on. Considerable skill was demanded of the King in balancing the frequently opposing interests of different factions competing for political favours and power. The King was, however, no ordinary mortal for at his installation he became the vehicle for those mystical powers by which his dynasty had ensured the survival and continuity of the kingdom.

The production of works of art was organized among various guilds in the capital and their professional activities were controlled by the King. In particular the casting of brass by the *Iguneromwon*, the brass-workers guild, and the carving of ivory by the *Igbesamwan*, the sculptors guild, are said to have been carried out only with the King's permission for the exclusive use of the royal court, either as ornaments and furniture for the palace and the royal ancestral shrines, or as regalia for the King and the nobility. Only the King himself wore and used regalia of ivory. (He claimed the right to one tusk from each elephant

killed in the kingdom and the option to purchase the other. Ivory surplus to his ceremonial needs would have been traded with Europeans.)

The late fifteenth to early sixteenth century was the period of greatest military success in the history of the kingdom with increasing power, prestige and wealth at the centre, and it was also during this time that Europeans, beginning with the Portuguese, first established contact. These developments inevitably had their effect on Benin art which, in this period, displays great originality and skill. Portuguese influence was indirect though none the less profound, for Benin artists were clearly stimulated to introduce new forms and motifs by the sight of these exotic human beings with their long hair and long noses. They were stimulated too, perhaps, by the sight of goods in the baggage which can be expected to have included armour and illustrated books from Europe as well as a variety of wares from India and the Far East.

J.P.

324 Armlets Benin 16th century AD
(a) Ivory, carved with figures representing the King and other courtly persons, surrounded by a profusion of motifs representing attributes of royal power, including Portuguese, leopard and elephant heads. L 11·2.
ETH 1949.Af46.179.
(b) Ivory inlaid with brass; a pair, each carved from a single piece of ivory to form two separate but interlocking cylinders with figures in high relief; on the outer cylinder, figures of the King; on the inner cylinder, elephant heads. L 13·3.
ETH 1910.5–13.2 and 3.
Colour plate 12
(c) Ivory inlaid with brass; a pair, both carved with

groups of Portuguese bearded heads alternating with ceremonial swords. L 12·5.

ETH 1922.3–13.3 and 4.

(d) Ivory, carved with Portuguese heads: inlaid with cast ornaments of gilt-brass of European origin. L 13·0.

ETH 1922.7–14.1.

Bibliography: R. E. Bradbury, *Benin Studies* (London, 1973); P. Dark, *Benin Art* (London, 1960); P. Dark, *An Introduction to Benin Art and Technology* (Oxford 1973); W. B. Fagg, *Nigerian Images* (London, 1963); W. B. Fagg, *Divine Kingship in Africa* (London, 1970); A. F. C. Ryder, *Benin and the Europeans* (London, 1969).

Ashanti

The kingdom of Ashanti was one of the most successful imperial powers to arise in West Africa. Between 1700 and 1900 this state dominated the central area of the Gold Coast (modern Ghana) and its influence was felt over a far wider area. Its power and prestige were founded upon the vast gold resources it controlled. Gold-dust was the sole currency for internal trade and it was also used to obtain European-made goods, such as fire-arms, which served to increase the power of the state.

By the beginning of the nineteenth century the Ashanti had developed an elaborate system of centralized government based on the capital, Kumasi, and linked to local chiefs and provincial administrators. Each level of the political and military hierarchy from the Asantehene (overall king) to local chief had its peculiar insignia and regalia. The creation and use of these were, therefore, directly related to the state's political order; and their redistribution followed changes in the pattern of rule. The wearing of gold jewels and gold decorated regalia was restricted to the King and major chiefs and certain of their senior officials and servants. Gold-dust which had been accumulated during a successful career could only be turned into regalia with the King's permission. All goldwork was produced by professional smiths, some descended from those captured from defeated states in the early days of Ashanti expansion. In Kumasi they worked under the strict supervision of a senior court official. Working for the King and for senior chiefs, they were expected to be inventive and to produce a steady flow of new and striking work. It is even possible that some of the King's gold was recast annually to impress visitors to the yearly yam festival by its seemingly infinite variety.

Ashanti goldsmiths were particularly skilled in lost-wax casting; the technique was probably first introduced into the area, perhaps as early as the thirteenth

century; by traders from the north travelling in search of gold. By this technique, and by chasing and repoussé work, they produced a wide variety of forms nearly all of which show their liking for elaborately decorated surfaces. Some of the patterns they used seem to have been adapted from imported European silverware and, possibly, ceramics. Their representational work, and in particular the finger- and toe-rings worn by chiefs, was often made to call to mind well known proverbs or aphorisms. To the Ashanti, therefore, this art has a verbal dimension.
M.M.

325 Gold jewellery Ashanti 18th–19th century AD
(a) Hammered and chased disc, with a conical centre and semi-circular ornament at one side made by lost-wax casting. D 9·0.
ETH 1900.4–27.11.
(b) Hammered with chased and repoussé ornament. D 9·5.
ETH 1900.4–27.25.
(c) A lost-wax casting. D 6·4.
ETH 1900.4–27.28.
(d) Hammered with chased and repoussé ornament, and cast semi-circular ornaments top and bottom. D 8·6.
ETH 1942.Af9.1.

Items (a)–(d) were worn as insignia by senior servants of the Ashanti king.

(e) Three beads, gold, lost-wax castings; probably from a chief's anklet or wristlet. Circular. D 6·2. ETH 55.12–15.1; in the form of a shell. L 4·7. ETH 98.6–30.6; L 7·3. ETH 1900.4–27.37.
(f) Gold, in form of scorpion. L 4·7.
A lost-wax casting, probably broken from finger- or toe-ring.
ETH 1900.4–17.44.
(g) Gold, in form of three elephants surmounted by six birds. D 4·7.
A lost-wax casting; possibly either broken from a finger- or toe-ring or intended for mounting upon a cap.
ETH 1900.24–7.44.
(h) Gold ring, lost-wax casting, with three cannon. D 2·0.
ETH Q74.Af2922.

Bibliography: A. A. Y. Kyeremeten, *Panoply of Ghana* (London, 1964); R. S. Rattray, *Ashanti* (Oxford, 1923); R. S. Rattray, *Religion and Art in Ashanti* (Oxford, 1926).

◁ 325a,b,c,d

325e

325f

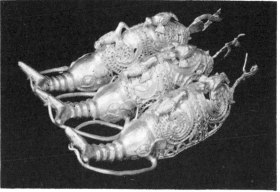

325g △   ▽ 325h

16

Amuletic Jewellery

China

Jade, the name we give to the mineral nephrite, had a very special significance in ancient China. It was not only valued as a precious and beautiful stone but it was believed to have spiritual and even magical qualities. The suits made of jade plaques in the Han dynasty (200 BC–AD 220) which, it was thought, would preserve the bodies of the dead, are the most striking examples of this faith in the magical qualities of jade. But as early as the neolithic period the Chinese must have attached such spiritual or magical properties to jade for thèy went to great lengths to transport jade thousands of miles and to manufacture it into discs, rings, and arc pendants which are clearly not functional, but must have had some ceremonial purpose. It is impossible here to illustrate the full range of Chinese jades, particularly the ceremonial sceptres, discs and tubes, but a representative group of early carvings in the shape of animals (no. 326) is shown. These particular creatures also appear on Chinese ritual bronzes and must therefore have played a parallel role in the elaborate cult of the dead for which the vessels were used. The jade animals are all pierced so that they could have been attached to robes and presumably they were worn as pendants.

The second group of jades are of a type which are definitely known to have been worn as pendants (nos 328, 330). An exceptional early painting from a tomb of the second century BC has provided important evidence as to the purpose of this type of pendant. Shown in the centre of the painting is a ring similar to no. 327 and below· it a jade arc similar to no. 329. Above, there is a portrait of the occupant of the tomb, the wife of the Marquis of Tái, and then in a complicated picture of dragons, the sun and the moon, the heavens are portrayed and the occupant of the tomb is shown having reached this abode. The jades thus seem to be an important instrument in enabling the dead woman to ascend to the heavens, and to avoid the terrors of the underworld which are shown with horrifying monsters below. Such jades are often found placed in the coffin of the dead but they were also worn as part of formal or ceremonial dress, for the clinking sound which they made as the wearer walked is vividly described in contemporary texts. The three pendants are all decorated with spirals and scrolls which are the hall-mark of the late Chou period. Derived ultimately from bronze designs, such decoration sparkles in the light and was clearly intended to bring out the qualities of this otherwise subtle and subdued stone.

J.M.R.

326 Five Animal Pendants China
13th–10th century BC
Shang and Western Chou periods
(a) Jade buffalo, calcified and buff in colour, carved in the round standing on its four legs, head facing forwards crowned with horns; body and legs decorated with meander in pairs of incised lines; pierced at mouth. L 5·2.
Shang dynasty, thirteenth–eleventh century BC.
Bibliography: Ayers and Rawson (1975), no. 46; Jenyns (1951), pl. XXII (B); London, Royal Academy (1936), no. 275.
OA 1947.7–12.468. Bequeathed by H. J. Oppenheim.
(b) Cicada carved in the round from turquoise matrix, with prominent eyes and on upper side neatly curving wings; underneath segmented body is shown; pierced at front. L 3·1.
Shang dynasty, thirteenth–eleventh century BC.
Bibliography: Ayers and Rawson (1975), no. 54.
OA 1945.10–17.162. Bequeathed by O. C. Raphael.
(c) Jade fish, grey-green in colour: long and slender and with slightly curving cross-section; incised detail of eye, head and fins on both sides: pierced at mouth. L 12·5.

Western Chou period, eleventh–tenth century BC.
Bibliography: Jenyns (1957), pl. XXVIII (G).
OA 1937.4–16.77.

(d) Flat translucent green jade pendant in shape of bird in silhouette with large up-curving wings and heavy tail curving downwards. Detail of eye, crest wings and tail executed in pairs of incised lines of which one is often slightly bevelled; pierced at breast. L 5·7.
Western Chou period, eleventh–tenth century BC.
OA 1945.10–17.37.

Colour plate 16

(e) Flat grey-green jade pendant in form of stag in silhouette; with large horns swept back to touch body at rear and with legs held as if braced against ground; detail of eye and legs executed in single broadly incised lines. L 6·0.
Western Chou period, eleventh–tenth century BC.
Bibliography: Ayers and Rawson (1975), no. 62; Jenyns (1951), pl. XXCII (H); London, Royal Academy (1936), no. 339; Palmer (1967), pl. 4; Pelliot (1925), pl. XXX (5).
OA 1947.7–12.466. Bequeathed by H. J. Oppenheim.

Colour plate 16

Such small pendants, both three-dimensional and flat, have been found in many burials of the Shang and early Chou period. They are usually of the same general size and represent the same range of animals. It is argued that they must have had some significance in the very powerful beliefs of these periods in which the cult of the dead played a prominent part.

327 Ring China 3rd century BC
Eastern Chou period
Pale translucent grey-green jade ring with brown markings, incised on both sides with lines around inner and outer edges, enclosing bands of slightly raised spirals linked by incised C-scrolls. D 10·2.

Such rings are part of a long tradition from the neolithic period of discs and rings which were believed to have supernatural powers to summon the spirits and later to aid the soul of the dead. A small ring such as this one might have been worn as part of a pendant set hanging from the waist, as well as being buried with the dead. It would have been strung in combination with arc-shaped jades such as no. 329 below.
Bibliography: Ayers and Rawson (1975), no. 93; Jenyns (1951), pl. XXI (upper); Palmer (1967), pl. 6.
OA 1947.7–12.510. Bequeathed by H. J. Oppenheim.

Colour plate 16

328 Dragon China 4th–3rd century BC
Eastern Chou period
Brownish-grey jade pendant in form of S-shaped dragon with projecting fins and with small bird joined to body below neck; decorated on both sides with incised scrolls. L 7·9.

Dragons in jade clearly had a significance related to that of the ring (no. 327) and arc-shaped pendant (no. 329). Dragons were benign spirits and in some tomb-paintings of a slightly later date are shown carrying souls of the dead on their backs.
Bibliography: Jenyns (1957), pl. XXXVII (B).
OA 1947.7–12.516. Bequeathed by H. J. Oppenheim.

Colour plate 16

329 Arc-shaped Pendant, Huang China
3rd–2nd century BC
Eastern Chou period or Han dynasty
Pale translucent grey jade arc with red-brown markings terminating at two ends with worked dragon heads; pierced at upper centre; between heads pendant decorated on both sides with linked incised C-scrolls between plain borders. L 13·0.

As with the ring (no. 327), this type of jade had a long history in China. Both as an ornament and with a ritual significance it was worn in combination with other jades in pendant sets. Drawings of the arc pendant on coffins of this period suggest that it also was believed to have the power to summon spirits to assist the souls of the dead.
Bibliography: Ayers and Rawson (1975), no. 109; Jenyns (1951), pl. XXXVII (D).
OA 1945.10–17.49.

330 Pendant China 8th century AD
T'ang dynasty
Calcified white jade plaque with bronze attachment; arc with shaped and notched outline; three small holes for suspension, fourth used for attachment of bronze bar broken off at other end. W 10·8.

This type of pendant is descended from the arc (no. 329) and was worn in combination with other plaques of the same type. The complete combination, together with beads, is often seen in tomb paintings of the time. This piece can be compared with plaques from the tomb of the Princess Yung-t'ai, AD 706; see *Wen-wu* (1964/1) p. 22, fig. 31.
Bibliography: Ayers and Rawson (1975), no. 226.
OA 1938.5–24.383.

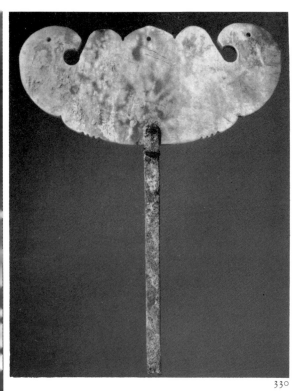

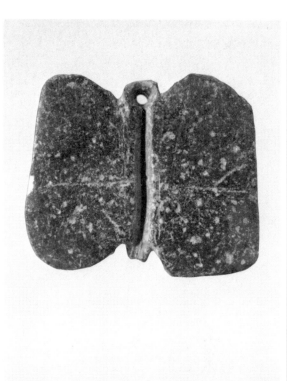

330

331 △　▽ 329

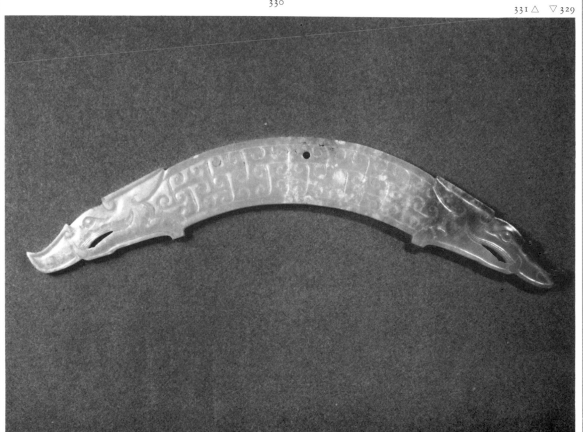

Western Asia

331 Pendant Halaf period about 5000 BC
Arpachiya, Iraq.

Pendant of black stone. W 3·3.

This may be a version of the later double-axe motif.
Pendants representing animals and objects are often
regarded as amuletic, but this can seldom be demonstrated without supporting written or archaeological
evidence. Many presumably had decorative and social,
amuletic or religious functions at one and the same
time.
Bibliography: Mallowan and Rosa (1935), pp. 95–6
(A864).
WAA 127676.

332 Animal pendants Jamdat Nasr period
about 3000 BC
Tell Brak, Syria.

Stone pendants representing pig; bear or baboon;
ram; fox. Each has stamp-seal design cut into base or
back. L 3·75; 2·4; 4·45; 4·05.

Animal pendants of this kind, and cheaper imitations
in faience, were found in great numbers during
excavations at the Tell Brak temple. They may have
been left there as votive offerings, but some were
actually embedded in the brickwork.
Bibliography: Mallowan (1947), pp. 40–3; 102–7.
WAA 126251; 126407; 126445; 126448.

333 Pendants Mesopotamia about 2500–2000 BC
Diqdiqqeh, Ur, and Nineveh, Iraq; Tell Brak, Syria.

Two pendants of white stone, from Nineveh, one
showing two-headed bull or ram and other perhaps
bear; two-headed animal pendant of black stone,
from Tell Brak; shell hand, from Diqdiqqeh; shell
leg, and lapis-lazuli frog and fly, from Ur. Maximum
dimensions, L or H: 3·47; 3·08; 1·63; 2·23; 1·74; 1·67;
1·97.

The double-headed animal was an old Mesopotamian
device, and the wild bull often symbolized brute
strength. Frogs and flies were common amulets, and
were found in the Ur graves: a Babylonian myth
records that a goddess used to wear lapis-lazuli flies to
remind her of the flood that had almost destroyed
mankind.
Bibliography: Beck (1931), p. 434; Woolley (1934),
p. 375; Mallowan (1947), p. 112.
WAA 1930.5–8.137–8; 125770; 116772; 118655;
120650; 122848.

332

333

Egypt

Most Egyptian jewellery has a magical significance and it is therefore almost impossible to distinguish purely amuletic from ornamental. Moreover, since the Egyptians took their everyday jewellery with them to the grave it is not always possible to distinguish even funerary jewellery, always amuletic, from secular.

Predynastic amulets are recognizable but it is not until the late Old Kingdom and First Intermediate Period that amulets increase substantially in range of subject and material. Apart from the forms represented, materials also had significance: green felspar or turquoise was the colour of new life, red carnelian the colour of life-blood, blue lapis-lazuli the colour of the heavens. Amulets such as the falcon or bull gave the owner certain powers by assimilation. Others, such as the turtle or scorpion, represent the very thing to be avoided. Parts of the body endowed the wearer with their particular bodily functions or could act as substitutes. The cowrie shell and fish, and such deities as Thoeris and Bes, gave protection; sometimes the identity of a deity with their special powers could be assumed.

The scarab was a very potent amulet signifying regeneration. Apart from its special funerary use, it was often set as a ring bezel, sometimes inscribed with further amuletic signs. Other amulets such as the frog and cat also acted as bezels. Some types of amulets are peculiar to particular periods: faces, legs and hands are typical of the late Old Kingdom and First Intermediate period, oyster-shells, cylinder-amulets and knot-clasps are especially Middle Kingdom in date. Flies are a New Kingdom decoration, small metal figures of gods are of the Late Period.

C.A.

334 Amulets Egyptian about 2300–2100 BC
Old Kingdom to First Intermediate period

(a) Carnelian, left-hand amulet with suspension loop at top. Flat back. L 1·8.

(b) Carnelian, leg with foot. Pierced from front to back. H 1·9.

(c) Dark green jasper turtle. Pierced behind neck for suspension. D (body) 1·1; H 1·3.

(d) Carnelian in form of two lions' heads and forepaws set back to back; pierced through centre for suspension. H 1·0; L (base) 1·2.

(e) Amethyst falcon in profile; pierced from chest to back. H 1·3.

(f) Pink limestone human face, bearded with pro-

truding ears and incised details. Suspension loop on top of head. Flat back. H 1·6; W 1·1.

All these amulets are typical of the period. The hand, foot and face amulets were presumably intended to give the owner the power of action, walking and use of the senses but as funerary amulets could also serve as substitute limbs and head. Hand amulets were usually found at the wrist and legs at the ankles. The other amulets all have funerary significance. The double lion amulet is rare; it represents the regions where the dead are reborn to a new life. The turtle was the animal of death and darkness; an amulet in its form would give protection against evil. The falcon amulet may be connected with Chapter LXXVII of the Book of the Dead, 'Spell for taking on the form of a falcon of gold'.
Bibliography: (a) Petrie (1914), pl. I,11,d; (b) *ibid.*, pl. I,15,b; (c) *ibid.*, pl. XLI,239,a; (d) G. Brunton, *Qau and Badari* II (London, 1928), pl. XCV, class 17; (e) Petrie (1914), pl. XLI,245,l; (f) *ibid.*, pl. I,2,d.
EA 14703; 54747; 57710; 57773; 57803; 57812.

335 Goddess Pendant Old Babylonian
about 2000–1600 BC
Gold figure worked on bitumen core; suspension loop at back. H 3·55.

The figure, with her horned cap and flounced dress, can be identified as the goddess Lama, who was regarded as an intercessor, able to speak with higher gods and convey petitions.
Bibliography: Wiseman (1960), p. 168; Maxwell-Hyslop (1971), p. 89.
WAA 103057.

335

336 God Pendant Hittite about 14th century BC
Solid gold pendant of god wearing pointed cap, kilt, long boots, and carrying short staff; loop for suspension at back. H 3·94.

This may represent a Hittite weather-god. Comparable amulets have been found near the Hittite capital of Hattusa (Boğazköy) and elsewhere in the empire.
Bibliography: Barnett (1940), p. 32.
WAA 126389.

337 Amulets of Deities Egyptian
about 1200–100 BC
XXth dynasty to Ptolemaic period
(a) Gold, pendant figure of goddess Mut in the round wearing Double Crown of Upper and Lower Egypt, long wig with two lappets and close-fitting dress to her ankles. Left leg is advanced, arms at sides. Figure stands on base-plate. At back of head is soldered loop for suspension with two smaller gold loops attached. Apparently cast; details of face and

336

337

wig incised. About 1200–1100 BC. H 2·9; L (base) 1·0.
(b) Gold, pendant figure of ibis-headed Thoth in the
round holding *udjat*-eye before him. He wears long
wig with two lappets and short kilt with ornate belt.
Left leg advanced. Presumably it was cast with all
details including those of minute size on *udjat* being
incised. Suspension loop at back of head. About
1000–900 BC. H 2·4; L (base) 1·0.
(c) Gold, pendant figure of Amun, seated, in profile,
with flat back. He wears usual crown with two tall
feathers and collar with counterpoise. His hands rest
on his knees. There is suspension loop at back of
feathers. Face is worked on front and back. Figure
appears to be cast and worked by hand in one piece.
Feathers, decorated on one side only, may have been
added later. About 600–300 BC. H 2·5; W (base) 0·7.
(d) Gold foil figure of Ptah made over core and
standing on base-plate. As usual he is shaven-headed,
wears beard and is enveloped by long cloak from
which only his hands emerge, holding *was*-sceptre.
Foil is in two halves with join down each side. To
judge from lightness of figure, core is probably wood.
About 300–100 BC. H 3·1; L (base) 0·8.

(a) Mut, a local goddess of Thebes, became important
as wife of Amun the great imperial god of the New
Kingdom. She was a protecting goddess, especially in
vulture form. (b) Thoth was essentially the scribe of
the gods but here he is acting as mediator between
Horus and Set, returning the *udjat*, the eye of Horus,
to its owner. (c) The seated amulet is identified as
Amun because of its distinctive feather head-dress but
the pose is that of the Assessors of the Dead or the
Underworld Guardians of the Gates as depicted in
Book of the Dead vignettes. (d) Ptah was the great
creator god of Memphis who enjoyed a return to
supreme power under the Saite Dynasty.
Bibliography: (a) Petrie (1914), pl. XXX, 164, c; (d)
Vernier (1927), pl. XCI, 53.203.
EA 33888, given by Mrs G. Ashley Dodd; 23426,
given by Dr J. Anthony; 65330, Sir Robert Mond
Bequest; 65401, bequest of Mrs A. M. Favarger.

338 Bangle Egyptian about 2000–1750 BC
Middle Kingdom
Flat openwork, gold, with inset figures of various
amulets and animals in gold and silver alternating.
Composed of flat almost circular band of gold tapering to point at each end and overlapping for short
distance. Both ends are beaten thinner than main
part of object. Between these two margins are soldered animals and amuletic signs, increasing in size
from points towards centre. Beginning from point of
lower overlap they are: silver snake gripping silver
turtle or tortoise by neck, gold *udjat*-eye, two silver
two-finger amulets with gold *Bat*-amulet between,
gold *udjat*, silver *ankh*, another gold *Bat*, silver *udjat*,
gold and silver running hares, two gold *ankhs* and two
silver seated baboons alternately, three gold *djed*-
pillars (the last with only two arms), with two silver
falcons between, one silver and one gold running
hare, silver *udjat*, gold *djed*, silver *ankh*, gold draughtsman, silver draughtsman and silver headless serpent.
Two margins of band are joined together rather
clumsily, one side being folded over other at one
point. At other point join was not so successful and
one side of band was cut off and piece of gold added.
Udjat-eyes made in two parts: upper and lower,
former probably cast, latter of wire. There is central
knob for eyeball. Hares probably also cast and ears
added separately. All other elements cast and soldered. D (external) 8·3; D (internal) 5·8; maximum H
(inset band) 0·6.

This is a rare form of Egyptian jewellery. The only
other comparable form of bangle is dated to the First
Intermediate Period (see G. Brunton, *Qau and Badari*,
I (London, 1927), pl. XLVIII, 1030). This frieze-like
procession of animals and amulets is similar to those
found on amuletic ivory wands of the same period.
The style of the *Bat* amulets and *udjat*-eyes also sug-
gests a Middle Kingdom date.
Bibliography: BM Guide (1904), p. 216, no. 140; *ibid.*
(1922), p. 90, no. 140; H. G. Fischer, *Ancient Egyptian
Representations of Turtles* (New York, 1968), no. 102.
EA 24787.

339 Necklace or Girdle Egyptian
about 1900–1800 BC
Middle Kingdom
Said to be from Thebes, Egypt.

Composed of six cowrie shell beads, cowrie shell
clasp, two beard pendants and two fish pendants (all
of electrum), silver lotus-flower pendant with glass
and carnelian inlays, electrum *heh*-amulet and spherical, oblate and truncated convex bicone beads of
carnelian, amethyst, lapis-lazuli, green felspar and
electrum. Hollow cowries, fish and beard pendants
were made in two halves, probably each half being
stamped out, and soldered around edges. Each half of
cowrie shell clasp was closed by flat electrum plate,
one containing slot, other a flanged bar which slipped
into slot to close clasp. Flat sheet electrum tail and
fins of fish were slipped between two halves of body.

Details of face and scales shown partly by repoussé and partly by chasing. Eyes probably once inlaid. Covering plate at top of beard pendant carries suspension ring. *Heh*-amulet made from repoussé front attached to flat back-plate. *Heh*, wearing kilt and wig, kneels on wire base and holds wire palm ribs in his wire arms. Lotus-flower pendant has silver base-plate with edge made from sheet metal and cloisons arranged in design comprising two parts: upper complete lotus flower and two lotus flowers set side by side below. Inlays are blue and green glass and carnelian. There is suspension ring soldered to top of base-plate and double ring at base, now broken. L 46·3; L (beards) 3·6; H (lotus pendant) 1·6.

Metal cowrie shells as beads and clasps are typical of the Middle Kingdom, being worn apparently in girdles rather than necklaces, to judge from several female statuettes. The shell was regarded as a bringer of fertility and perhaps as an averter of the evil eye from pregnant women (see Wilkinson (1971), pp. 80–1). Metal fish pendants are equally typical, being attached usually to the side-locks of children and called *nekhaw* (see Aldred (1971), p. 141). The form of the beard amulet is described by a word variously translated as beard or tail, the word for side-lock is quite different, therefore it seems that this amulet represents a beard rather than a side-lock as has been sometimes suggested. *Heh*-amulets are common from the Middle Kingdom until Roman times: the pictogram in which he is incorporated wishes the wearer millions of years.

Bibliography: *Salt Collection* (1835), lot 763; *BM Guide* (1922), p. 100, no. 760; H. Ranke, *The Art of Ancient Egypt: architecture, sculpture, painting, applied arts* (Vienna and London, 1936), no. 330; Budge (1925), p. 267.

EA 3077.

Colour plate 6

340 Amulets Egyptian about 2000–1800 BC
Middle Kingdom

(a) Green felspar *ba*-amulet in round in form of crouching sphinx with human head wearing striated lappet wig. Details incised and piece pierced from chest to back for suspension. H 1·6; L (base) 1·2.

(b) Carnelian crouching baboon in round, pierced through shoulders for suspension. H 1·7; maximum W 1·0.

Both in form and material these amulets are typical of the Middle Kingdom. Petrie calls the *ba*-amulet a female sphinx with cat body; the baboon was the sacred animal of the god Thoth.

Bibliography: (a) Petrie (1914), pl. XXXIII, 185, f–h; (b) *ibid* pl. XXXVII, 206.

EA 14754; 57715. Given by Sir Alan Gardiner.

341 Fish Pendant Egyptian about 1900–1800 BC
Middle Kingdom

Pendant made of gold with green felspar inlay. Open on both sides and made of central cloison formed from a strip of sheet metal curved around to make oval shape. Disc of sheet gold on each side of inlay represents head; on one side ring has been soldered for eye. Tail and fins scored to represent natural markings and soldered onto cloison. One of lower fins lost. On one side small oblong of sheet gold has been soldered to tail to strengthen it. Suspension ring soldered at tip of face. L 2·9; L (cloison) 1·6; W (cloison) 0·7.

The fish amulet was usually attached to the side-lock of children and was called *nekhaw*. It seems most often to have been made from a green stone to judge from the number of known examples and a well-known story about king Sneferu (see Aldred (1971), p. 141 and Wilkinson (1971), p. 75).

Bibliography: *BM Guide* (1904), p. 220, no. 386; *ibid*. (1922), p. 93, no. 386; J. Garstang, *el Arabah* (London, 1901), p. 4.

EA 30484.

Colour plate 6

342 Cylindrical Amulets Egyptian
about 1900–1800 BC
Middle Kingdom

(a) Pendant made of tube of sheet gold decorated with granulation in ten double rows of chevron pattern, bordered at top and bottom by six triangles composed of granules. At each end: conical cap formed from hollow cone of sheet gold with flat top. Upper cap removable and has striated tube soldered along it for suspension thread. Joins between individual granules are visible. Possibly granules were fixed together before being arranged on tube. Suspension tube made from sheet gold rolled up and scored with nine lines cut with chisel. L 6·8; D (lid) 2·7; D (body) 2·5; L (suspension tube) 2·2.

(b) Cylindrical pendant composed of three short cylindrical amethyst beads alternating with three similar beads formed from sheet gold over core. At each end a gold cap from piece of sheet gold folded over to make cone, soldered along one edge and disc of sheet gold added at top. On upper cap tube for suspension is soldered with nine lines cut on it imitating beads. Copper pin runs down centre of pendant. Two of amethyst beads are bored horizontally as well as vertically but horizontal boring does not meet central vertical boring. L 5·0; D (lid) 1·5; D (body) 0·8; L (suspension tube) 1·1.

342a

342b

343a

(a) These all-metal cylindrical pendants first make their appearance in the Middle Kingdom but continue into the New Kingdom and later. In this instance the quality of the granulation suggests a Middle rather than a New Kingdom date. When hollow it is highly probable that they were used as amulet cases: one example of late date still contained three amulets, others contain spells written on papyrus.

(b) There are in existence very many similar cylindrical pendants of metal and stone, all of Middle Kingdom date. They, like their hollow counterparts, when excavated have come mainly from female burials. There is apparently no example of their being worn.

Bibliography: *BM Guide* (1904), p. 216, no. 137, and p. 220, no. 389; *ibid.* (1922), p. 89, no. 137 and p. 93, no. 389; J. D. Cooney, *Five Years of Collecting Egyptian Art* (New York, 1956), pp. 42–3, no. 49, bibliographical footnote; Wilkinson (1971), p. 55.
EA 24774; 30478.

343 Two Pendants Palestine about 1600 BC
Tell el-'Ajjul, Palestine.

(a) Gold, lightly embossed and incised, in form of a female figure. H 8·9.

(b) Gold, lightly embossed and incised. H 6·33.

(a) The naked female figure, crudely stylized, with emphasis on the face, breasts, and sexual organs, represents a fertility goddess, Astarte, who was worshipped extensively in the lands along the eastern Mediterranean coast.

(b) The eight-pointed star is recorded in prehistoric Palestine; its significance as a symbol is unclear, but it may be related to the naked goddess.

Bibliography: Petrie (1952), p. 10, no. 13; (1934), p. 6, no. 14; Stewart (1974), pp. 42–4.
WAA 130761; 130766.

344 Two Scarab Finger-Rings Egyptian
about 1800 and 1550 BC
XIIth and XVIIIth Dynasties
(a) Excavated at Abydos, Egypt, tomb G 62.

(a) Obsidian scarab mounted in sheet gold funda which is made in two parts: rim and base-plate, latter uninscribed. Shank made from tube of gold joined along inside. Ends are drawn out into fine wire which passes through scarab and then is wound around shank on both sides. Scarab itself is carved with details of head, divisions of wing cases and scratches on sides indicating legs. External D (shank) 2·0; L (scarab) 1·1.

(b) Gold, with green jasper scarab bezel, its base inscribed with central knot of four uraei; their heads at each corner and four *ankh*-signs in cartouches between heads. Shank is hollow tube of gold with gold

212

bead and collar with milled edge soldered at each end. Gold wire wound around top of shank passes through collar and scarab and is wound around shank on opposite side. External D (shank) 2·6; L (scarab) 1·7.

(a) In material and form this scarab is typical of the late Middle Kingdom. Since the base of the funda is uninscribed the bezel could only have functioned as an amulet and not a seal. The scarab was the symbol of resurrection in the Other World and one of the most potent amulets.
(b) The style of this scarab is characteristic of the early XVIIIth Dynasty. Although the base is incised the scarab here, as in the case of (a) is acting as a powerful amulet. The signs on the base are the *ankh*-sign which gives eternal life and the uraeus which could represent a number of goddesses, all beneficent.
Bibliography: (a) *BM Guide* (1922), p. 291, nos. 26–57; (b) *ibid*. (1904), p. 218, no. 225; *ibid*. (1922), p. 91, no. 225; Hall (1913), pl. no. 4.
EA 37308. Given by Egypt Exploration Fund; 36466.

344a,b

345 Heart Scarab Egyptian about 1640 BC
XVIIth Dynasty, Sobkemsaf
A tomb at Thebes, Egypt.

Green jasper heart scarab with rounded back carrying human face, set in gold plinth with rounded back edge. Legs made from sheet gold strips with striations representing hairs and splayed out on base. Scarab is set in cloison with beaded top. Around edge of plinth and on base are roughly chased hieroglyphs from Chapter XXXB of the Book of the Dead: 'Spell for preventing the heart from opposing the deceased'.
L (mount) 3·6; W (mount) 2·4; H (mount) 0·7; L (scarab) 2·2.

The text mentions King Sobkemsaf and the king in question is assumed to be the second of that name because the scarab entered the collection with the coffin of Nubkheperre Inyotef, one of the later XVIIth Dynasty kings. In the inscription the legs of the birds are missing: this is a common custom in magical texts to prevent them from running away or, in the case of larger and more dangerous birds, to prevent them from attacking the dead person. The heart scarab, which should be of green material, was placed over the heart of the mummy and the spell on it ensured that the heart did not give adverse witness against its owner when weighed in the balance to decide whether the deceased should enjoy everlasting happiness in the other world.
Bibliography: *Salt Collection* (1835), lot 209; Hall (1913), p. 22, no. 211; Budge (1925), p. 293.
EA 7876.

Colour plate 6

343b

346 Two Finger-Rings Egyptian
about 1380–1350 BC
XVIIIth Dynasty, Amarna period
(b) Said to be from Alexandria, Egypt.

(a) Gold, with oval bezel surmounted by frog and inscribed on base with scorpion. Shank of sheet gold over core; thicker at side opposite bezel. Sides of shank bound with wire which passes through cups at shank's ends and through length of bezel. Collars are soldered to shank-ends to act as additional pivot. Bezel is oval lozenge, its edge decorated with double row of beading. At one side is soldered protective socket for swivel; other is missing. Frog on top has solid body and wire legs. External D (shank) 2·4: L (bezel) 1·3.

Colour plate 7

(b) Gold, with seated carnelian cat as bezel. Sheet gold of shank is drawn out at ends into wire which is threaded through length of bezel from each end and wound around opposite end of shank. Cat sits on rectangular base, its face turned to one side. Underside of bezel has incised *ankh*-sign. External D (shank) 2·0; L (bezel) 0·8.

Perhaps both of these rings were once worn by women. The frog was the emblem of Heqat, goddess of childbirth and fertility. The cat was the sacred animal of Bastet, goddess of festivity and sometimes too of fertility. A scorpion represented on the underside of the bezel (a), is a symbol of Selkit, one of the four protecting goddesses of the dead. The *ankh*-sign on the base of (b) is the sign for life.
Bibliography: (a) *BM Guide* (1904), p. 217, no. 199; *ibid.* (1922), p. 91, no. 199; Aldred (1971), pl. 69.
EA 2923, Anastasi Collection; 54547, Franks Bequest, 1897.

347 Pendant Egyptian and Mesopotamian
about 1300–1100 BC
XIXth–XXth Dynasties
Said to be from Dahshur, Egypt.

Gold in form of lapis-lazuli bull's head set above gold papyrus head on basket, flanked by two lotus buds and two uraei wearing sun-discs. Gold base-plate is cut in shape of aegis. To it is soldered shallow collar onto which bull's head is cemented. Other elements soldered below head were made separately but it is difficult to tell whether they are hollow or cast. Gold wire loops are soldered to sun-discs and threaded through loops soldered on base-plate, outside collar, at level of ears. H 2·3; W (maximum) 1·7; H (bull's head) 1·2.

The gold mount is Egyptian, the papyrus head, lotus, uraei and basket forming a well-known Egyptian motif. The bull's head is not of Egyptian style or workmanship. The treatment of the muzzle and eyes with multiple folds is distinctly Mesopotamian in character. The returning spiral on the forehead is also non-Egyptian. There is no doubt that this is an imported object belonging to a foreign art, either Babylonian or more probably akin to the Babylonian, possibly Elamite or Urartian, mounted in an Egyptian setting. This is a unique piece.
Bibliography: H. R. Hall, 'Egyptian Jewellery and Carvings', *BMQ* 3 (1928), p. 41; pl. XXIII,a.
EA 14456. Given by Sir Robert Mond.

348 Necklace with Pendants Egyptian
about 1500–1400 BC
XVIIIth Dynasty
Composed of long truncated convex bicone beads and Thoeris amulets, all of gold. Beads are made in two halves; amulets also made from two pieces. Onto flat back-plate of gold foil was soldered moulded or stamped front piece of Thoeris in profile. Suspension loop added at top. L 41·8; L (pendants) 1·8.

Thoeris was the goddess of childbirth and always appears in the form of a standing hippopotamus. She was, of course, the special protectress of women and thus it is not surprising that an identical necklace with gold foil Thoeris amulets was found in the burial of the three wives of Tuthmosis III (see Aldred (1971), pl. 86).
Bibliography: H. R. Hall, 'Egyptian Antiquities from the Maxwell Collection', *BMQ* 4 (1930), p. 104; pl. LVIII.
EA 59418. Given in memory of Sir John Maxwell by Committee members of Egypt Exploration Society.

349 Finger-Rings Egyptian about 1100–800 BC
Late New Kingdom
(a) Blue glazed composition with openwork design consisting of five figures of Bes standing on each other's heads. As usual he wears tall feathered head-dress, has strongly lion-like features, is naked and shown completely frontally. D 2·4; H 1·1.
(b) Blue glazed composition. Top is decorated with openwork aegis of Bastet holding long-stemmed papyrus-headed sceptre. Underside divided into five long narrow strips with pointed ends; these divisions do not go through to inner surface. D 2·3; H 1·8.

(a) Bes was a beneficent demon who scared away malevolent forces at childbirth. Such a ring may well have been worn by a woman.
(b) The aegis is a deep collar of beadwork surmounted

by a lioness' head; here the sun-disc and uraeus are also worn. Although Bastet was usually a cat-goddess and not a lioness, when such an aegis carries an inscription it nearly always refers to Bastet and not Sekhmet as might be expected. Such a ring would have protective qualities.

EA 59850, bequeathed by Lady Maxwell; 66620, given by Mrs M. E. A. Wallis.

350 Lamashtu Amulet Mesopotamian
about 7th century BC
Uruk, Iraq.

Green stone plaque incised with cuneiform signs and figure of demon. H 6·25.

This is an unusually crude example of an amulet intended to protect the wearer against the evil demon, Lamashtu, and send her back to the underworld. Lamashtu, who was a particular threat to women in childbirth, is represented as a female with the head and claws of a hawk. The writing, on both sides of the plaque, is an illiterate attempt at cuneiform.

Bibliography: Loftus (1857), p. 236; Thureau-Dangin (1921), pp. 161–89.

WAA 51.1–1.18.

351 Pazuzu Head Mesopotamian
about 7th century BC
Lapis-lazuli head of demon, with vertical perforation. H 1·46.

Pazuzu was a wind demon whose assistance was particularly valuable in driving away Lamashtu.

Bibliography: Thureau-Dangin (1921), pp. 189–94.

WAA 116228.

350 △ ▽ 347   △351   349 △ ▽ 348

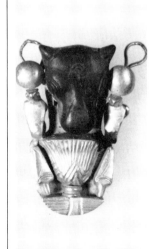
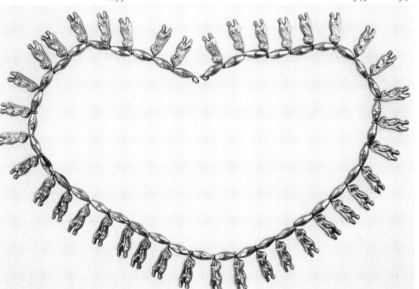

215

352 Necklace Phoenician about 6th century BC
Tharros, Sardinia.

Necklace of carnelian and gold beads, with stone pendants. Central pendant consists of hollow box in gold, representing eye of Horus, contours being defined by cloisons which would once have been inlaid; from this hangs seated stone cat, to which is attached pendant consisting of two plaques soldered together back to back; front represents female head, wearing wig, with pattern of granulation below. Other stone pendants, fastened with gold wire, represent cats, hawks, Egyptian sign for heart, and woman with children on either side. L 32.

This is a typically Phoenician mixture of amuletic symbols adapted from Egyptian prototypes. Many of the Tharros graves contained necklaces of this general nature.
Bibliography: Marshall (1911), pp. 156–7, no. 1546; Pisano (1974), pp. 58–9.
WAA 56.12–23.789.

353 Amulet Case Phoenician
about 7th–6th century BC
Tharros, Sardinia.

Gold amulet case embossed with 'aegis of Bastet', head of lioness, surmounted by disc with uraeus cobra in front, and decorated with granulation and cloisons for inlay. Cylindrical section below is hollow. H 4·53.

Pendants of this kind were probably intended to hold magic charms or talismans.
Bibliography: Marshall (1911), p. 159, no. 1560; Pisano (1974), p. 62.
WAA 135781.

353

352

Early Christian Amulets

Christian motifs (no. 354), used either for purposes of identity or, more commonly, for protection against sickness or ill-fortune, made their appearance on jewellery at least as early as the beginning of the third century AD. After the official recognition of Christianity by Constantine the Great in the fourth century, such images became very much more numerous and frequently appeared on secular jewellery of considerable lavishness (no. 355). New shapes and new types of jewellery were also devised in order to satisfy the demand for a specifically Christian form of amulet: the pectoral cross (no. 356) and the reliquary pendant (no. 359) were the most notable.

R.C.

354 Brooch Romano-British about AD 400
Probably found in Sussex.

Silver, parcel-gilt; bow ornamented with head and mane of boar; eyes of boar of blue glass; disc at head of brooch has Chi-Rho monogram chased on to it in spaced dots (made with centre-punch). L 6·6.

354

The Greek letters *chi* and *rho* are the first two letters of Christ's name in Greek (*Χριστος*). Though originally used in monogram form as an abbreviation for other words beginning with these two letters, by the fourth century AD when Christianity was the official religion, the monogram was specifically Christian, and often associated with *alpha* and *omega*, the first and last letters of the Greek alphabet ('I am alpha and omega, the beginning and the end'). There are numerous examples of the use of the Chi-Rho monogram in fourth-century Roman Britain: most notable are the mosaic pavement from the villa at Hinton St Mary, items in the silver treasures from Mildenhall and Water Newton, and the wall-paintings from the Christian chapel at the Lullingstone villa (all of which are in the British Museum).
Bibliography: Toynbee (1964), p. 344, pl. LXXIX, c.
P & RB 1954.12–6.1.

355 Bracelet Byzantine about AD 600
Said to have been found in Syria.

Gold bracelet, front opening on hinge and decorated with bust of the Virgin in relief with both hands raised; design on hoop consisting of confronted pairs of swans and peacocks within vinescroll. D 7·2.

355

Formerly in the collection of Count Tyskiewicz.

The pair to this bracelet was in the Dzialinski Collection at Goluchow Castle, Poland, until 1939 (W. Froehner, *La collection du château Goluchow* (1897), no. 198).

356

Bibliography: Dalton (1901) no. 279; Ross (1965), p. 21. M & L AF351. Franks Bequest, 1897.

356 Pectoral Cross Byzantine 7th century AD
Said to be from Athens.

Gold pectoral cross with arms rounded at ends; in centre figure of crucified Christ and in medallions personifications of sun and moon, figures of Virgin and St John, and scene showing soldiers casting lots. H 7·9.
Bibliography: A. B. Tonnochy, 'A Byzantine Pectoral Cross', *BMQ* 15 (1941–50), p. 76; Ross (1965), p. 22. M & L 1949.12–3.1.

357 Signet-Ring Byzantine 9th–10th century AD(?)
Silver signet-ring, hoop crudely engraved with Greek inscription decipherable as 'Lord protect the wearer' and bezel with Medusa-like face from which radiate seven serpents. D 2·0.

357

The design on the bezel is common on amulets used for protection against disease or accident.
Bibliography: Dalton (1901), no. 142. M & L AF242. Franks Bequest, 1897.

358 Brooch Ottonian about AD 1000
Gold brooch of pyramidal form, apex set with onyx with cameo inscription in three lines:
ΕΥΤΥΧΩC ΠΡΟΚΟΠΤΕ Ο ΦΟΡΩΝ (Good luck to the wearer). L 3·3.

Frequently considered as being a good luck charm of the fourth or fifth century AD it seems probable that only the cameo is of antique origin; the goldwork has close medieval parallels, particularly to a brooch of about AD 1000 now in the Museum für Kunst und Gewerbe, Hamburg (E. Steingräber, *Antique Jewellery* (London 1957), p. 24, fig. 13).
Bibliography: Dalton (1901) no. 280; A. Alföldi, 'Ein Glückwunsch aus der römischen Kaiserzeit', *Festschrift Hans R. Hahnloser* (1961), p. 11 and Abb. 3. M & L AF352. Franks Bequest, 1897.

358

359 Reliquary Cross Byzantine 10th century AD
Believed to have been found in the Great Palace at Istanbul.

Gold and cloisonné enamelled pectoral cross opening in two halves: enamelled decoration on front missing, but probably originally showed figure of Christ crucified; back shows figure of the Virgin *orans* between busts of St Basil and St Gregory Thaumaturge. Cross suspended from chain apparently contemporary with it. H 6·1; L (of chain) 62·2.

Formerly in the collection of Adolphe Stoclet,

Brussels; sold at Sotheby's, 27 April 1965, lot 34.

There is a similar but somewhat larger cross of the same period in the Cleveland Museum of Art which is also said to have been found in Constantinople (*Early Christian and Byzantine Art*, The Walters Art Gallery, Baltimore, 1947, no. 524).
Bibliography: John Beckwith, 'A Byzantine Gold and Enamelled Pectoral Cross', *Beiträge zur Kunst des Mittelalters* (Festschrift für Hans Wentzel zum 60 Geburstag) (Berlin 1975), pp. 29–31.
M & L 1965.6–4.1.

Colour plate 22

360 Reliquary Byzantine 12th–13th century AD
Gold, circular; back enamelled with half-figure of St George, front with gold hinged half-cover with Georgian inscription and circular opening inset into which is hinged enamel panel of St Demetrius in his tomb which covers gold relief of same subject. D 3·7.

One of a pair of pendant reliquaries thought to have been made at Saloniki in the twelfth or thirteenth century (the other is in the Dumbarton Oaks Collection, Washington DC). Although in all probability originally intended to hold a relic of St Demetrius, the patron saint of Saloniki, the Georgian inscription states that it also contains a relic of the True Cross once belonging to Saint Kethevan. The reliquary was, therefore, possibly at one time in the possession of Saint Kethevan, Queen of Georgia (d. 1624).
Bibliography: O. M. Dalton, 'An enamelled gold reliquary of the Twelfth Century', *BMQ* 1 (1926–27), pp. 33–8; Ross (1965), p. 111; Klaus Wessel, *Die byzantinische Emailkunst vom 5 bis 13 Jahrhundert* (1967), pp. 192–3, fig. 63.
M & L 1926.4–9.1.

360

361 Bead Anglo-Saxon about AD 500
From the Anglo-Saxon cemetery at Kings Field, Faversham, Kent, England.

Crystal, faceted bead, disc-shaped. D 4·4.

Rock crystal was commonly believed in antiquity and medieval times to have amuletic properties and, in the medieval period at least, to be particularly efficacious in ensuring a copious lactation after childbirth. Large crystal beads occur both on the Continent and in England at this period, when their relative scarcity and occurrence in rich graves indicate their importance.
M & L 1216 70.

362 Tooth Pendant Anglo-Saxon 7th century AD
From an Anglo-Saxon grave at Wigber Low, Derbyshire, England.

362

Animal tooth set in gold mount with suspension loop. L 3·8.

Tooth pendants are a rare but fairly widespread feature of Migration period culture.
Bibliography: A. Ozanne, 'The Peak Dwellers', *Medieval Archaeology*, 6–7 (1962–3), pp. 29–30, pl. III(a).
M & L 73.6–2.95.

363 Two Finger-Rings Anglo-Saxon
9th or 10th century AD
(a) Found at Grey Moor Hill, Kingmoor, Carlisle, Cumbria (Cumberland), England, in 1817 during fencing work, it passed into the ownership of the Earl of Aberdeen. (b) Unknown find-place.

(a) Gold band, inscribed on outer and inner face of hoop in runes with untranslatable magical formula. The runic inscription inlaid with niello may be transliterated: '+ærkriufltkriurithonglæstæpontol'. D 2·7.
(b) Agate ring, plano-convex in section, and engraved on outer face of hoop with runic formula closely similar to (a). The letters filled with white chalky material read: 'eryriufdolyriuritholwlestepotenol'. D 2·9.
These rings, together with another with the same inscription from Bramham Moor, Yorkshire (now in the National Museum of Antiquities in Copenhagen), form a remarkably homogeneous group. The meaning of the inscription, which is presumably amuletic in intent, is not understood, but it has some points of resemblance to phrases in certain Old English manuscript charms.

Bibliography: Bruce Dickins, 'Runic Rings and Old English Charms', *Archiv für das Studium der neueren Sprachen*, CLXVII (1935), p. 232; D. M. Wilson, 'A Group of Anglo-Saxon Amulet Rings', *The Anglo-Saxons: Studies Presented to Bruce Dickins,* ed. P. Clemoes (London, 1959), pp. 159–70; D. M. Wilson, *Catalogue of Antiquities of the later Saxon Period I: Anglo-Saxon Ornamental Metalwork 700–1100 in the British Museum* (London, 1964), pp. 138–9. and Appendix A, R. I. Page, 'The Inscriptions', pp. 73–5.
M & L (a) Ring Cat. no. 184, given by the Earl of Aberdeen before 1823; (b) 73.2–10.3. found before 1824 and given by Sir A. W. Franks.

364 Pendant Cross Anglo-Saxon 7th century AD
Wilton, Norfolk, England.

Gold, mounted in centre with gold solidus of Heraclius I and Heraclius Constantine (AD 615–32), and set with cloisonné garnets. L 4·5.

This important piece was a chance discovery from a gravel-pit. The use of distinctive mushroom- and arrow-shaped cells on this piece, and the 'long and short' cells framing the central coin link it closely to the workshop that produced the Sutton Hoo jewellery. Like a number of other jewels of the middle and later seventh century, it proclaims a Christianity newly introduced to Anglo-Saxons (see also the Desborough necklace, no. 201).
Bibliography: Jessop (1950), pp. 120–1, pl. XXVIII(3); R. L. S. Bruce-Mitford (1974), pp. 29–31.
M & L 1859.5–12.1.

363a
b

364

Medieval Amulets

There are five classes of medieval jewellery which may be considered amuletic:

1 Jewels (no. 366) sometimes held relics, such as the Holy Thorn Reliquary (no. 368), the Clare Reliquary (no. 366) or the Devizes Reliquary (no. 367).

2 Pendant jewels also possessed an amuletic significance derived from the scene depicted on the pendant, such as the Crucifixion (no. 372), or, in the case of the coin pendant, the inscription around the edge of the coin (no. 373).

3 Religious inscriptions were thought to be particularly efficacious, and the octagonal brooch inscribed with the name of Jesus (no. 369b) and the Glenlyon brooch with the names of the Three Kings illustrate this (no. 369c).

4 Precious stones were thought to possess particular qualities which would help the wearer, and these were often set in rings (no. 370).

5 Pilgrim signs (no. 365) were worn by pilgrims on their return from shrines, but it is doubtful whether the lead badges themselves were considered amuletic. J.C.

365a

365 Pilgrim Badges English and French 14th–15th century AD

(a) Lead bust of St Thomas à Becket. H 6·2.

(b) Lead badge showing shrine of St Thomas à Becket at Canterbury. Body of saint lies beneath shrine. Kneeling man points to large jewel in centre of shrine. L 5·1.

(c) Silver badge of the shrine of Our Lady of Hal (Belgium). D 3·8.

Pilgrim badges were sold at shrines for pilgrims to wear on their return. Canterbury was a shrine of international repute. The second badge is remarkable since it shows the actual shrine at Canterbury, which was elaborately decorated with jewels. The large jewel in the centre was probably the famous jewel 'the regale of France' given by Louis VII to the shrine.
Bibliography: (a) B. W. Spencer, 'Medieval pilgrim badges', *Rotterdam Papers*, I (1968), pp. 137–53.
M & L 56.7–1.202; 1971.6–3.5; 47.8–29.1.

365b △   ▽ 365c

366 Reliquary Cross English 15th century AD
Found during the construction of the railway station on the site of Clare Castle, Suffolk, in 1866.

Suspended from chain; on front, a cruciform panel of Crucifixion, reserved on ground showing traces of red enamel, with inscription INRI in black. Cross contains fragment of wood and granite – perhaps those of True Cross and Rock of Calvary. H 3·8.
Bibliography: A. Way, 'Gold pectoral cross from

Clare', *Arch. Journal* XXV (1868), pp. 60–71; A. B.
Tonnochy, *BMQ* 11 (1936–37), p. 1, fig 1.
M & L On loan from HM the Queen.

367 Reliquary English (?) 15th century AD
Found near Devizes, Wiltshire, before 1848.

Gold reliquary with three lobes at top and one lobe
on each side. Both sides originally enamelled with engraved standing figures in reserve each between two
flowers enamelled white: on one side, archbishop
with cross on other, St John the Baptist with Lamb of
God. Underneath the legend, A MON DERREYNE in
black enamel. On each side are eight engraved tears
and along bottom are six engraved tears, all originally
enamelled. H 4·6; W 3·3.

In the collection of Revd. William Maskell in 1848.

The word 'derreyne' (a form of *derrière*) signifies the
last moment of existence and the words imply an
invocation of St John the Baptist and another saint
for help at the moment of death. It may have contained a consecrated tablet of wax, the Agnus Dei,
which was blessed by the Pope at Easter in the first
year of his pontificate and every seventh year subsequently. These were thought to be of special efficacy

366

368

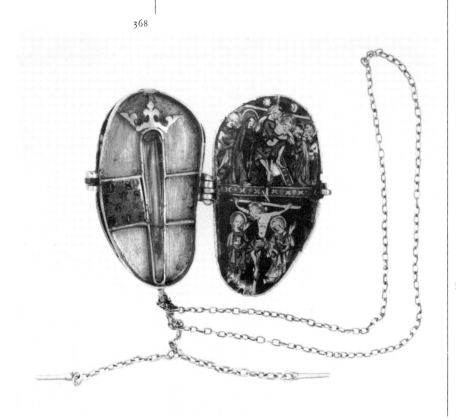

367

against sudden death. The containers for such tablets are usually circular.

Bibliography: Anon., 'Archaeological Intelligence', *Arch. Journal* V (1848), pp. 156–7.

M & L AF2765. Franks Bequest, 1897.

368 Reliquary of the Holy Thorn French
14th century AD

Gold, with two large cabochon amethysts on exterior. Consists of central leaf and two covers. On inside of covers and on one side of central leaf are six scenes in translucent enamel: a King and Queen beneath the Virgin and Child, the Presentation, the Flight into Egypt, the Descent from the Cross, and the Crucifixion. On other side of central leaf is a manuscript illumination of the Nativity and the Annunciation to the Shepherds. Behind this, thorn mounted in crystal and has on one side inscription DE SPINA : SĀNCTE : CORONE (Thorn of the Holy Crown). H 3·8.

369a

The Holy Thorn was taken from the Crown of Thorns purchased by St Louis from Baldwin, the Emperor of Byzantium. The setting, with its enamelled scenes, probably dates from the second quarter of the fourteenth century. Said to have been in the Pichon collection in Paris in the nineteenth century.

Bibliography: Clifford Smith (1908), p. 119; Evans (1970), p. 50.

M & L 1902.2–10.1. Given by G. Salting, Esq., 1902.

369 Three Brooches English and Scottish
13th–15th century AD

(a) Gold ring brooch, set with ruby and opal in pair of projecting hands, inscribed + AVE I MARIA G. D 1·9.
(b) Silver octagonal brooch, inscribed on one side. IHESUS and on other NASERRENE. D 4·0.
(c) Silver ring brooch, with transverse bar and two pins. On back nine engraved arches with inscription IASPAR MELCHIOR BALTAZAR CONSUMATUM in black letters. On bar are two trees growing out of vases. D 13·3.

369b

Brooch (a) is inscribed with the Angelic Salutation to Mary, (b) with the name of Jesus, and (c) with the names of the three Kings and the last word of Christ. The name of Jesus and the three Kings were thought to be of special value against epilepsy. The last brooch, (c), was formerly in the family of the Campbells of Glenlyon, and so known as the 'Glenlyon' brooch; (sold at Christies, 21 May 1897).

Bibliography: (a) J. Cherry, 'A ring brooch from Waterlooville, Hants.', *Medieval Archaeology*, XIII (1969), p. 225. (c) Clifford Smith (1908), p. 132; Evans (1970), pl. 16 and p. 59.

M & L 49.3–1.33, collection of Mr Cowen, 1849; AF2711, Franks Bequest, 1897; 97.5–26.1.

369c

370 Four Rings Medieval 12th–15th century AD
(c) Found in the cutting for the railway at Colchester;
(d) Found at Cannington, near Bridgwater, Somerset, in 1924.

(a) Gold, bezel set with toadstone. D 2·9.

(b) Silver-gilt, rectangular bezel set with carbuncle. D 2·9.

(c) Gold, quatrefoil bezel set with jacinth. D 2·5.

(d) Gold, hoop engraved AVE GRATIA PLENA DM, and ending in two animal heads supporting high openwork bezel decorated with birds and set with cabochon sapphire held by four claws. D 3·3.

Rings (a)–(c) illustrate the use of precious stones in rings as amulets: the jacinth increases riches, the carbuncle inspires, and the toadstone, so called because it was thought to have been found in the head of a toad, remedies many afflictions; (d) the 'Cannington' ring is a fine religious ring inscribed with the Angelic Salutation.

Bibliography: Dalton (1912), nos. 895; 1826; 1916; O. M. Dalton, A medieval gold ring found at Cannington, *Antiq. Journal* V, (1925) pp. 298–9; Oman (1974) pl. 26a.

370d

M & L AF1023; AF1865; AF1930; 1925.1–13.1.

371 Ring English 15th century AD
Found in Coventry, Warwickshire, near the medieval town wall, in 1802.

Gold; hoop is engraved on exterior with Christ standing in the tomb with the instruments of the Passion behind. Around hoop (D 2·7) are engraved the Five Wounds of Christ described as follows in black letter:

371

the well	*the well*	*the well*
of pitte	*of comfort*	*of ever*
the well	*the well*	*lasting*
of merci	*of gracy*	*lyfe*

Inside, engraved in three lines:

Wulnera quinq̄ dei sunt medecina mei
crux et passio xti sunt medecina mei jaspar
melchior balthasar ananyzapta tetragrammaton

The Five Wounds of Christ were a popular subject for personal devotion at the end of the Middle Ages. Instructions for making rings of this type are referred to in at least three wills beginning with that of Sir Edmund Shaw who died on 20 March, 1487. The end of the inscription is magical rather than devotional.

Bibliography: E. in *Gentlemans Magazine*, LXXIII (Jan. 1803), p. 497; T. Sharp, 'An account of an ancient gold ring found in Coventry Park in the year 1802', *Archaeologia* XVIII (1817), pp. 306–8; Dalton (1912), no. 718; Oman (1974), pp. 116–17.

M & L AF897. Franks Bequest, 1897.

372 Pendant English early 14th century AD

Gold lozenge-shaped pendant with standing Virgin and Child on one side and Crucifixion on other. Figures reserved against background keyed for enamel and background of both sides scattered with six petalled flowers. H 2·2.

This is a rare example of a simple religious pendant. It was originally decorated with translucent enamel but every trace of this has been removed. The engraving is of very high quality and the figure style and drapery have been described as typical of the East Anglian school of manuscript illumination at the end of the thirteenth and the beginning of the fourteenth century.

Bibliography: Anon.; Connoisseurs Notes', *Connoisseur* CXLVII (no. 591), Feb. 1961, p. 41.

M & L 1959.7–6.1. Given by Richard and Martin Norton in 1959.

372

373 Coin Pendant English 15th century AD

Gold coin (a rose noble) of Edward IV (1461–83) set in cabled border with loop for suspension. On one side is inscription IHC + AUT + TRANSIENS + PER + MEDIUM + ILLOR IBAT. D 4·1.

This coin was worn as an amulet on account of the text which is taken from Luke iv.30: *Ipse autem transiens per medium illorum ibat* (But he, passing through the midst of them, went his way). The words were very generally used as a charm against the dangers of travel by sea and land, especially against attack by robbers. The text was often used on the gold nobles of Edward III and may refer to his victory in the naval battle off Sluys in 1340.

M & L AF2772. Franks Bequest, 1897.

373

374

374 Ivory Amulet Spanish 16th century AD

In form of a right hand, thumb and first finger making a loop. First and third fingers wear gold rings housing single garnet and single emerald. Gold mount forms part of sleeve with cuff enamelled in the cloisonné technique, red, blue and green, and ruff of silver. Amulet hangs from gold suspension loop with quatrefoil attachment. H 6·7.

This was known in the sixteenth-century in Spain as a 'higa', a fist-shaped amulet directed against the 'evil eye', with the characteristic position of the thumb and first finger forming the 'mano cornuta', a 'potent gesture directed against evil'. A similar hand-shaped pendant of wood and enamelled silver has been considered an 'ex-voto' of Charles V of Spain (see *Carlos V y su ambiente,* (Madrid, 1958), pl. CCXCIV of the quatercentenary exhibition catalogue).

Bibliography: W. Bode, *Die Sammlung Oscar Huldschinsky* (Frankfurt, 1909), no. 124, p. 49; Muller,

375△   ▽376

(1972), pp. 68–70 and pl. 97; F. T. Elworthy, *The Evil Eye* (1895), p. 258; L. Hansmann and L. Kriss-Rittenbeck, *Amulett und Talisman* (Munich, 1966), p. 192ff.

M & L 1941.10–7.1. Formerly in the Huldschinsky collection.

375 Reliquary Cross Pendant Spanish
early 17th century AD
Gold cross, enamelled, of hollow, box-like construction, the reverse panel lifting to allow the placing of relics, mounted on white cloth, in the oval vitrines of the obverse. Superimposed on the black-and-white enamelled moresque pattern on the reverse are individual red, green and blue enamelled plaquettes with symbols of the Passion. The sides bear alternate lozenges and ovals enamelled in black on a white ground. Suspension loop at the top and fleur-de-lys terminals to the arms. H 10·2.
Bibliography: Muller (1972), pp. 61–3. A very similar example is illustrated on pl. 72.
M & L AF2867. Franks Bequest, 1897.

376 Coral Pendant Italian early 17th century AD
In a silver-gilt mount, carved in relief on one side the Annunciation, and on the other the Return of Jesus with Mary and Joseph to Nazareth after the Dispute in the Temple. H 4·3.

The identification of this latter scene, rare in European art, is proved by the presence of the Holy Ghost above the group – St Joseph is actually pointing to the Dove – as in the painting of this subject by Rubens in the Jesuit College in Antwerp. Although the mount could date to the second half of the sixteenth century, it would appear to have been made specifically for this carving and to be contemporary with it.

Coral was thought to have great amuletic powers having originated, according to Greek mythology, as the spurts of blood that had gushed forth when the Medusa's head was cut off by Perseus. As a protection against magic spells, it was believed to be highly efficacious.
Bibliography: *Burlington Magazine* CVIII (January, 1966), p. 24, figs. 31 and 33.
M & L 1965.6–1.1.

377 Monogram Pendant Spanish
late 17th century AD
Gold, openwork, set with table and cabochon emeralds forming the monogram of the Virgin Mary, crowned above, and with a small rosette below. On reverse, gold engraved in places with details, e.g. the

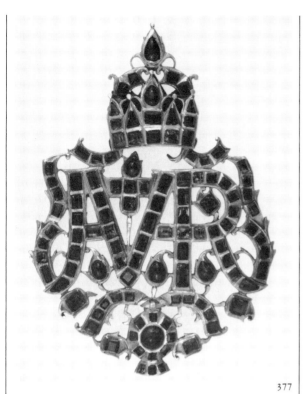

377

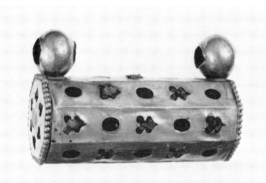

378 △　▽ 379

crown and the flower buds; small quatrefoil carved in relief on back of rosette. Gold suspension loop. H 9·3.

A jewel of the type known as a 'venera' was worn by members of Spanish religious confraternities throughout the seventeenth century.
Bibliography: Muller (1972), pp. 117–24, cf. pls. 189 and 191.
M & L AF2957. Franks Bequest, 1897.

378 Amulet Case Gandhara 2nd–3rd century AD
From *stupa* at Ahin Posh near Jalalabad, Afghanistan.

Ten-sided hollow gold cylinder with alternating oval and leaf-shaped openings, five along each of ten faces of case. All oval openings backed with garnets and one leaf-shaped opening still contains green-black stone. Each end of cylinder has flat cap with pearled border and seven openings, six leaf-shaped centred on one round, last still set with a garnet. Globular suspension ring at both ends of one of the faces. One cap can be withdrawn. W 3·0; L 7·3.

Gandhara sculptures of Bodhisattvas show cylindrical attachments strung on a cord running over the left shoulder and passing beneath the opposite armpit. There seems little doubt that the same type of amulet case is depicted. Two somewhat similar gold amulet cases, cylindrical and plain except for incised parallel lines, are reported from Sirkap at Taxila (Marshall, *Taxila* II, p. 631, no. 84 and III, pl. 191, fig. q.)
OA 1880–29.

379 Amulet Case Persia
late 12th–early 13th century AD
Persia.

Silver, parcel-gilt and nielloed. Hexagonal in section, ends convex and bordered by diamond-shaped facets, three suspension loops attached to upper panel. Three of five remaining panels decorated in gilt-repoussé with hound, hare and ibex respectively, each on matted ground: other two panels inscribed in naskhi script with Arabic words *al-'izz wa'l-iqbāl wa* ('Glory and prosperity and . . .') reserved in niello: each end decorated with hexagram in gilt repoussé and foliate elements reserved in niello in facets. L 2·7.
Bibliography: R. H. Pinder-Wilson, 'A silver-ladle and amulet case from Persia', and R. M. Organ and D. E. Bisset, 'Notes on the restoration of a Persian silver-gilt amulet case', *BMQ* 25 (1961), 32–6, pl. IXa-h.
OA 1960.8–1.1. Brooke Sewell Bequest, 1960.

380 Amulet Box Tibetan 18th century AD
Oval box, lid of gold and fitting closely over sides. Sides of lid decorated with floral filigree pattern and

flower design encrusted with turquoise. One side has long hollow tube for suspension consisting of four 'balusters' decorated with turquoise and on opposite side is similar tube closed at each end with spiked terminals and enhanced with pearled wire and turquoise. Top of box has central turquoise boss set in oval mount with surrounding petals of turquoise. L 7·0; W 5·1.

Tibetan Buddhism is notable for the great prevalence of magic deriving from native tradition about malignant spirits responsible for illness and other misfortunes. The imported Tantric Buddhism of Eastern India itself enshrined practices of a magical nature. Reflecting this background is the charm box, worn for protection, especially when travelling. These boxes are sometimes in the form of miniature shrines and contain stamped plaques with Buddhist images; otherwise they may contain woodblock-printed charms on paper, grains, pebbles and pieces of cloth or silk. In the case of this box it is recorded that it was worn on the pigtail of an official's servant.

Bibliography: T. H. Hendley, 'Indian Jewellery, part X', *Journal of Indian Art and Industry*, vol. XII (1909), p. 137, pl. 114, no. 793.
OA 1905.5–18.77.

Colour plate 17

380

17

Cameos in Jewellery

Cameos are precious, or semi-precious, stones on which the design has been carved in relief – the exact opposite of the much older engraved (or intaglio) gem, which is also frequently set in jewellery, especially in signet-rings. Both cameos and engraved gems were mostly cut in the same method (i.e. on the wheel), but, instead of hollowing out the design, the stone of a cameo was cut away to leave the design standing in relief. Whereas the engraved gem was highly functional, since it could be impressed into damp clay and wax to indicate ownership of the sealed goods, etc., the cameo was purely ornamental, and so it is perhaps not surprising that, although the engraved signet-stone (in some form or another) can be traced back to the Sumerian period in Mesopotamia and even back to about 5000 BC in some parts of Western Asia (no. 399), the cameo does not make its appearance until the Hellenistic period (about third century BC).

Its emergence in the Greek world following the conquests of Alexander the Great (333–322 BC) has led to the suggestion that it may be due, in part, to influences from the newly acquired territories of the former Persian Empire. Certainly, at this time, the Greeks acquired the Oriental fashion for mounting precious stones in their jewellery and both the onyx and sardonyx were stones admirably suited for cameo treatment, since both have stratified layers of light and dark stone. The opportunity to create decoration in relief – albeit in miniature – would have accorded with Greek taste and may, therefore, account for the flowering of the cameo as an art-form in the Hellenistic Age. Unfortunately, none of the Hellenistic cameos in the Museum is set in contemporary jewellery.

To demonstrate the long-standing interest in banded stones in Western Asia, two early examples (one from Sumeria, about 2000 BC, the other from the

Persian Empire, about 500 BC) have been selected (nos. 381, 382). Both are set in jewellery, but, although both demonstrate a simple form of cutting and polishing to accentuate the concentric circles, neither has been cut away to leave a surface-pattern in relief. This smooth polished treatment of the banded stones remained popular in the eastern Mediterranean; for example, a massive Late Antique gold finger-ring (cat. no. 459), set with a colourful sardonyx of this type, was found at Tarvis in Illyria and probably dates from the third century AD. There is even evidence among the jewellery from Ur (about

2500 BC) that some of the carnelian beads had been artificially given white patterns, reminiscent of the white strata in a banded stone. The effect was produced by drawing a pattern on the bead with an alkaline solution, generally soda, and subsequently heating it; the alkali would then penetrate the stone, leaving the pattern indelibly marked upon it in white. Either the beads or this technique of bleaching the carnelian beads may have been brought to Ur from the east but, even at this early date, it is indicative of the oriental fascination with the natural beauty of stones and their variegated markings, which is most fully realized in the cameo technique at its best.

By the end of the second century BC, the cameo had been generally accepted by the Romans, both as an ornament, especially for furniture, and as personal adornment – the Roman Emperors wore them, according to Pliny, as *insignia* with ceremonial dress. Stylistically, the Roman cameo is a direct continuation of the Hellenistic, and for about 200 years the art flourished; by the end of the second century AD the Roman cameo begins to disappear except for one class with inscriptions, mainly dedicatory but sometimes amuletic (no. 358). The master of the art of cameo carving in the Augustan period was Dioskorides, to whom the Museum's great Augustus cameo (no. 383) has been attributed; certainly, the skilful handling of the three stratas of the sardonyx and the artistic modelling of the head exemplifies the high standards achieved during the early Imperial period. Although without any antique setting, the cameo has been included, partly because its exceptional size permits a more ready appreciation of the skilful cutting and partly because it still retains a medieval jeweller's embellishment – the gold diadem set with precious stones and two small cameos (restored in the eighteenth century).

Curiously, the Museum's fine collection of classical cameos contains few that have survived in their original mounts and settings – indeed, the only items of jewellery set with cameos are finger-rings. A typical example is the ring set with an onyx cameo of a Gorgon's head, which was reputedly found near Patras and dates from the second century AD. A slightly later example (no. 384) found near Cardiff, Wales, is one of only eighteen cameos known to have a Romano-British origin – and, significantly, the only ones found mounted in jewellery are those set in finger-rings. Furthermore, this ring is also set with a Medusa or Gorgon's head – a subject that seems to have been much the most common among the Roman cameo finger-rings, due to some amuletic belief.

After the Roman period, cameos were evidently highly prized and very rarely are to be found in gold settings, like the 'Epsom' cameo (no. 385). During the Middle Ages, as the late Professor Hans Wentzel has shown, the carving of cameos was not as rare as previously thought. However, much uncertainty remains about the location of the workshops and the date of their productions – as, for example, in the case of the magnificent 'Noah' cameo (no. 386) that had entered the Medici collections before 1465.

With the Italian Renaissance in the fifteenth century, the art of the cameo blossomed under the patronage of eager collectors, like Pope Martin V (1417–31), Leonello d'Este of Ferrara (1407–50), Dandolo of Venice, Giustiniani of Genoa, Cardinal Francesco Gonzaga, Pope Paul II (1464–71) and per-

haps the greatest of all, Lorenzo de' Medici. The names of the gem-engravers begin to be known, though more is known about those of the sixteenth century. By that time every court in Europe had followed the Italian fashion, and many employed Italian artists for this purpose. Matteo del Nassaro, of Verona, worked in France for François I, training both Italians and Frenchmen, while Jacopo de Trezzo became gem-engraver to Philip II of Spain.

Of course, many of these creations were not intended to be worn as jewellery, and of those that were mounted a fair proportion have since been separated. Consequently, the number of cameos in the Museum that remain in their original settings as items of jewellery is not large. A selection of the most interesting, spanning approximately 400 years, follows (nos. 387–98).

H.T.

381 Beads Sumerian about 2200–2000 BC
Ur, Iraq.

Group of agate, gold, and carnelian beads. L 9·0.

Banded stones became increasingly popular in the later third millennium, and the central bead here, cut so as to give concentric circles of different colours, may be regarded as a distant ancestor of the cameo.
Bibliography: Woolley (1934), p. 587 (U13509).
WAA 122720.

382 Pendant Persian Empire about 500 BC
Ur, Iraq.

Embossed gold pendant, with carnelian beads fixed around it by gold pins, and single agate in centre. W 3·9.

The dark layer of stone on the agate has been partially removed so as to accentuate the pattern of concentric circles.
Bibliography: Woolley and Mallowan (1962), p. 106 (U459C).
WAA 116563.

383 Cameo Roman 1st century AD
Sardonyx (three-layered). Bust of the Emperor Augustus in profile to left, wearing aegis with Gorgon's head. In background, part of lance. H 12·8; W 9·3.

In the Middle Ages a diadem of gold and precious stones was attached. It was restored in the eighteenth century.
Bibliography: *BMC Gems*, no. 3577.
G & R BL484. Formerly Strozzi and Blacas Collections.

383

381

382

384 Two Finger-Rings Roman

2nd–3rd century AD

(a) Found in a tomb near Patras.

Gold, hoop of eight flattened beads separated by two narrow rings in relief, with oval bezel set with a sardonyx cameo of head of Medusa to front. D 2·5.
Bibliography: BMCR no. 467.
G & R 476F. Franks Bequest, 1897.
Colour plate 10

(b) Sully Moors, near Cardiff, Wales.

Gold, shoulders of ring modelled as stylized vine-leaves, with onyx cameo depicting head of Medusa surrounded by wreath of serpents, in foliate setting. D 2·4; WT 6·86.

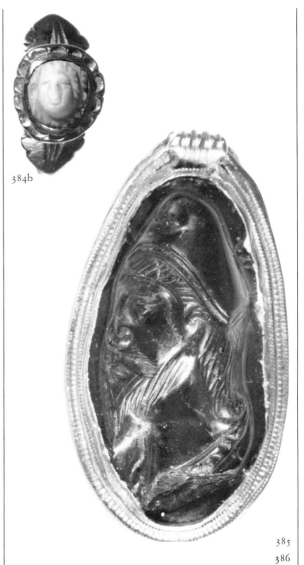

384b

One of four gold finger-rings found with a hoard of silver and gold coins (latest issue AD 306) in October 1899. One of only eighteen cameos known from Roman Britain; the commonest design on these cameos is of Medusa.
Bibliography: Marshall (1907), no. 544; Smith (1922), pp. 65–6, fig. 82.2; Walters (1926), no. 3547; Henig (1970), p. 339, no. 1; Henig (1974), no. 729.
P & RB 1900.11–23.3.

385 Pendant Anglo-Saxon late 7th century AD

Epsom, Surrey, England.

Gold, with beaded wire edging and grooved suspension loop, containing irregularly-shaped garnet cameo carved in high relief with head of bearded man in Phrygian cap, facing left. L 3·85.

This pendant belongs typologically to a group of Anglo-Saxon pendants, set with cabochon garnets, which appear towards the end of the seventh century as one of the latest types of object to be found with the dead before Christian practice finally put an end to this pagan custom. Similar examples may be seen on the Desborough necklace (no. 201).

The presence of a cameo in such a pendant is unique, and though the material, garnet, is characteristically Germanic, cameo-carving is certainly not. Stylistically, it seems possible that this is a late Antique cameo reset in the seventh century.
Bibliography: Henig (1974), no. 734, pl. xlvi.
M & L 1970.3–1.1.

385
386

386 The Noah Cameo Sicily or Southern Italy

about AD 1204–50 (?)

Onyx, carved with representation of Noah and his family leaving the Ark, about which are birds and other animals; incised on doors of the Ark, 'LAVR MED' (the mark of Lorenzo de'Medici). L 5·3.

This gem has been attributed to antiquity, to the

court workshop of Frederick II Hohenstaufen (1194–1250), to the circle of Ghiberti (1378–1455) and to a Florentine gem-cutter of the time of Lorenzo de' Medici (1449–92). It is now accepted that it cannot be antique, but opinions still differ as to its true date; although by no means universally accepted, the least controversial view is that it is a product of the court workshop of Frederick II Hohenstaufen. The gold mount with its finely pounced floral motifs on the reverse is characteristic of French metalwork of the late fourteenth and early fifteenth century.

Listed in the inventories of Piero de' Medici (1465) and Lorenzo de' Medici (1492); purchased in Paris in the eighteenth century by the fourth Earl of Carlisle.

Bibliography: Dalton (1915), no. 18; E. Kris, *Meister und Meisterwerke der Steinschneidekunst in der italienischen Renaissance* (1929), pp. 25–6 and 153; H. Wentzel, 'Staatskameen im Mittelalter', *Jahrbuch der Berliner Museen*, IV (1962), p. 67, figs. 21, 22, 23; N. Dacos, A. Giuliano, U. Pannuti, *Il Tesoro di Lorenzo il Magnifico*, I (1973), no. 37 and figs. 33–4. M & L 90.9–1.15. Carlisle Collection.

Colour plates 18, 19

387 Double Cameo Pendant Italian
about AD 1520–30

Onyx; (a) bust of Hercules with lion's skin tied round neck, cut entirely in dark blue stratum; (b) reverse, Omphale wearing lion's skin on head, cut in creamy-white/brown strata; set in gold and black enamelled mount, enriched on both faces with diamonds and rubies and appliqué vine leaves and bunches of grapes arranged in 'fleur-de-lis' form. w 4·5 (with frame).

Given by the Emperor Charles V to Pope Clement VII (died 1533), who presented it to the Piccolomini family; in the Piccolomini cabinet in Rome; subsequently, in the Medina, Bessborough and Marlborough collections.

Bibliography: Borioni, *Museum Piccolomini, Collect. ant.*, pl. iii, no. 45; Montfaucon, *L'antiquité expliquée et représentée en figures, Supplément*, i, p. 141, pl. liii, fig. i; Story-Maskelyne (1870), no. 309, and the original *Marlborough Gems* (1791), vol. ii, no. 18; S. Reinach, *Pierres gravées* (1895), pl. 114, no. 18; Dalton (1915), nos. 109–10, p. 18, pl. VI. M & L 99.7–18.2.

388 Pendant French (?) mid-16th century AD
Onyx bust of Diana facing right, bow and quiver appearing behind shoulder, mounted in enamelled gold frame; on reverse, gold plate, engraved with floral designs, has been added at a more recent date. L 4·8 (with frame).

387 △   ▽ 388

233

389

Above the head is visible the beginning of a perforation vertically piercing the stone and issuing beneath the bust; this may be due to the fact that the stone originally came from the East in the form of a bead.
Bibliography: C. Davenport, *Cameos* (1900), p. 18; Clifford Smith (1908), pl. xxix, fig. 6; Dalton (1915), no. 73, p. 13, pl. vi.
M & L. Payne-Knight Bequest, 1824.

389 Pendant Italian (?) about AD 1560–80
Onyx cameo of the Pietà at the foot of the Cross and accompanied by kneeling angels, mounted in enamelled gold triptych, in the form of a miniature altarpiece; on the inside of doors, the emblems of the Passion, enamelled in black; on the outside, SS Peter and Paul, also enamelled in black; on the reverse, a cabochon of rock-crystal beneath which is painted the head of Christ in profile. H 1·5 (cameo); H 4·9 (pendant).
Bibliography: Dalton (1915), no. 22, p. 6, pl. i.
M & L AF2869. Franks Bequest, 1897.

390 Pendant Italian (?)
second half of 16th century AD
Heliotrope bust of Christ wearing Crown of Thorns; red marks of stone utilized to indicate drops of blood on head and face; set in gold, enamelled and jewelled frame with chains for suspension; the opals and the *memento mori* may be later additions; on the reverse, the oval gold back-plate enamelled with flowers and insignia of the Society of Jesus (founded 1540), i.e. the sacred monogram 'IHS' (in red translucent enamel) surmounted by a white cross and below the three nails (also in white enamel). W 4·9.

Vasari relates that Matteo dal Nassaro, of Verona (died 1547), executed a Descent from the Cross in heliotrope, in which he took advantage of the red marks for the same purpose; in Italy it became popular among cameo carvers during the sixteenth century.
Bibliography: Dalton (1915), no. 23, p. 7, pl. i.
M & L AF2673. Franks Bequest, 1897.

390

235

391 Pendant English late 16th century AD
Onyx bust of Queen Elizabeth I, wearing high ruff, and mounted in the centre of gold pendant of radiate openwork design, set with garnets and decorated with white and red enamelled ornamentation. W 2·4 (total).
Bibliography: Dalton (1915), no. 379, p. 51, pl. XV; Strong (1963), p. 132, no. 19.
M & L AF2654. Franks Bequest, 1897.

392 'Commesso' Pendant French (?)
late 16th century AD
Gold frame and suspension ring, enamelled mainly with translucent floral scrolls on white ground; against thin onyx background, nude female figure of white chalcedony seated with back to spectator upon edge of bath, her drapery, modelled in burnished gold, beside her. L 7·0 (with frame).

The Italian term, *commessi*, is generally applied to a rare class of Renaissance jewel comprising a combination of gold and cameo elements unified into a single composition. Fewer than twenty of these distinctive jewels are known to have survived, and, although it has been suggested that they are French and perhaps all from one workshop, the variations in quality and in design are too great. This pendant, although damaged and incomplete, remains a strikingly beautiful example from the end of the 16th century; as in the case of the famous Leda and the Swan *commesso* in the Kunsthistorisches Museum, Vienna, there may have been originally a miniature necklace of gold and jewels fitted around the neck of the nude figure.
Bibliography: Dalton (1915), no. 209, p. 32.
M & L 90.9–1.42. Carlisle Collection.

Colour plate 21

393 'Commesso' Jewel French (?)
late 16th century AD
Gold, enamelled bust in armour decorated with masks at the shoulders and on the breast; the bearded head, three-quarters, executed in shell-cameo. Back made of plain gold with three loops for attachment. H 3·1 (total).
Bibliography: C. Davenport, *Cameos* (London, 1900), p. 17; Dalton (1915), no. 408, p. 56, pl. XV.
M & L 90.9–1.11. Carlisle Collection.

394 Pendant Locket Spanish about AD 1600–20
Gold, enamelled and jewelled heart-shaped locket, set with jacinth cameo bust of woman; surmounted by figure of youthful Christ, holding cross and blessing, encircled by openwork enamelled Crown of Thorns set with diamonds; reverse, enamelled hinged

391 △   ▽ 393

236

back reveals gold plate engraved and enamelled in black with three-quarters bust of lady, and initials 'A' 'A' (on either side of the head). H 5·7.

This cameo may have been carved as a secular subject earlier in sixteenth century, and given a religious interpretation when this jewel was made – perhaps as a representation of a saint.
Bibliography: Dalton (1915), no. 28, p. 8.
M & L AF2651. Franks Bequest, 1897.

395 Pendant Cameo French about AD 1630
Onyx bust of Lucius Verus in openwork gold frame, enamelled and jewelled; on back, enamelled design of stylized flower in white, blue and green. H 2·4.

The design of the pendant is in the style of engravings by Pierre Marchant of Paris (1623) and illustrates the new vogue for stylized naturalism.
Bibliography: Story-Maskelyne (1870), no. 478; L. Natter, *Catalogue des pierres gravées de Mylord Comte de Bessborough* (1761), no. 7; Clifford Smith (1908), pl. xliv, fig. 17; Dalton (1915), no. 336, p. 45, pl. XII; Evans (1970), p. 134, pl. 118c–d.
M & L 99.7–19.1. Given by Charles Butler, Esq., 1899.

396 Finger-Ring French about AD 1720
Gold, enamelled; bezel set with ruby cameo of bust of Mme de Maintenon (1635–1719), who was secretly married to Louis XIV in 1684. H 1·8 (bezel); D 2·2 (hoop).
Bibliography: *Catalogue of the Hertz Collection* (1859), no. 2744; Dalton (1915), no. 389, p. 53, pl. XVI.
M & L AF1467. Franks Bequest, 1897.

Colour plate 10

397 'The Flora of Pistrucci' Italian about AD 1810
Gold finger-ring set with a carnelian breccia; carved as head of Flora in high relief, wearing wreath of roses, poppies and marguerites(?). Roses in red stratum; what remains of lowest stratum is cut very thin. L 2·3.

The Italian engraver Benedetto Pistrucci (1784–1855), while still living in Italy, had engraved gems – including 'antiques' – for the dealer Bonelli; among them, according to his own account, was this head of Flora. Not long after his arrival in this country, in 1815, he recognized the gem at Sir Joseph Banks's house in London; it had been purchased from Bonelli by Mr Payne-Knight, who, to the day of his death, treasured it as an antique, despite Pistrucci's claim to its authorship. Though the secret mark which Pistrucci stated that he engraved on the back of the stone cannot be discerned, there can be little doubt that the work is modern; and, as it is in the style of the early

394

395

396 △   ▽ 397

237

nineteenth century, there seems no reason to question Pistrucci's statement. Pistrucci, to support his contention, made several other 'Floras' – without convincing Mr Payne-Knight, whose manuscript catalogue contains a depreciatory comment on Pistrucci, vigorously expressed in Latin. From 1817–49 Pistrucci was Chief Engraver at the Mint.

Bibliography: A. Billing, *The Science of Gems, Jewels, Coins and Medals* (1867), pp. 86, 189ff; L. Forrer, *Biographical Dictionary of Medallists* (1904), iv, pp. 582ff; Dalton (1915), no. 176, p. 26, pl. VII.

M & L Payne-Knight Bequest, 1824.

398 Brooch English mid-19th century AD
Gold, enamelled and set with chalcedony head of Ceres; on reverse, behind glass, plaited hair. H 6.5 (with frame).

Bibliography: Dalton (1915), no. 165, p. 24.

M & L 96.2–7.1. Bequeathed by Mrs Anne Servantes, 1896.

398

18

Finger-Rings

The difficulties of classifying finger-rings have been recognized and stressed by eminent authors in the past, for the ring often serves more than one purpose and its appearance frequently does not proclaim them. The further back in time, the less documentation about the use of rings has survived and their function becomes increasingly conjectural.

Probably the most ancient purpose of the finger-ring was simply to be decorative – and, to this day, finger-rings have been made for this, and no other, purpose. On the other hand, there have been, at different times through the ages, finger-rings specifically designed for a particular function: for example as signet-rings; archers' thumb-rings; rings for the measurement of time; marriage, betrothal and love rings; mourning and commemorative rings; and amuletic rings. All these rings were essentially personal and are, therefore, included here; there were, however, others – official rings, rings of investiture, etc. – that have been excluded for the reasons given in the Introduction.

Although many of these functional rings have also been designed to be highly decorative, their use has been the primary consideration; others, made as purely decorative rings, have subsequently been given a special use, as in late medieval and Elizabethan England when rings set with gems were frequently used by the rich as 'marrying' rings – no doubt, quite indistinguishable from the purely decorative rings of the same type.

Nevertheless, some brief outline of these main types of finger-ring seems justified, despite the fact that clear divisions frequently do not exist and, in the absence of reliable documentary evidence, many finger-rings in the Museum's collections cannot now be reliably classified under specific headings, although there is a strong possibility that they had a special function at one time.

The three most securely identifiable categories are discussed first, followed by the problems concerning the other three categories, and mention is made of a few significant examples. Finally, a brief mention of some aspects of the purely decorative ring indicates the extent of this one subject and the impossibility of doing justice to it within the present limitations of space.

Signet Finger-Rings

Although the finger-ring designed to be used as a signet does not seem to have emerged until much later, the wearing of small pendants, which could be used as stamp-seals, seems to date back in parts of Western Asia to about 5000 BC, and one such stone pendant (no. 399) from Arpachiya (Iraq) is included. Cylindrical seals (no. 400) were soon to become the standard form of signet in southern Mesopotamia; on them, the incised inscription would give the name, family name and profession of the owner, and, by rolling it on the damp clay, goods could be sealed and identified. These cylinder-seals were hollowed out and worn on a cord or chain around the neck or attached to the large toggle-pins (no. 14a), as in some of the graves at Ur, about 2500–2100 BC. Occasionally these cylinder-seals have been found with gold mounts, which, as in the case of the lapis-lazuli example from Ur, transform an essentially functional object into a highly decorative and attractive piece of jewellery (no. 400).

That their cylindrical form was found attractive as well as practical is demonstrated by a massive and beautiful Egyptian gold ring (about 1400 BC), which is set with a revolving glass cylinder in place of the bezel (no. 401). The blue glass, which imitates the lapis-lazuli stone, is not engraved and was evidently intended to be worn purely as an ornament.

The cylinder-seal was unknown in the Minoan and

Mycenaean civilizations, although Babylonian and Hittite cylinders were clearly imported in considerable numbers and later placed in the tombs, as the excavations in Crete and Cyprus have shown. Minoan craftsmen engraved the gold bezels of their fine rings, and the signet-ring (no. 402) demonstrates the high quality achieved at this early date, around 1600–1500 BC.

In Egypt, even as early as the XIIth Dynasty (about 1800 BC), the scarab had become the bezel of the finger-ring (see no. 344). By mounting the scarab so that it could be swivelled round, the Egyptians made it ideally suited to the signet-ring, for it could not only be worn as a potent amulet (the scarab was the symbol of the resurrection in the Other World) but it could also be engraved on the flat underside and so serve as the signet of the owner whenever required; an example bearing the prenomen of Queen Hatshepsut dates from the beginning of the fifteenth century BC (no. 403a). By engraving on the underside of the scarab, a further advantage is gained because the signet is worn against the skin and, therefore, protected from the risk of scratches and surface damage.

About this time the swivelling bezel became a fashionable element in the design of Egyptian finger-rings, and the fine engraving on both sides of the thin glass plaques that were set into these bezels is a remarkably skilful feat (no. 403b). The deeply engraved bezels of gold and other metals also make their appearance about 1400 BC and, simultaneously, a new and inexpensive technique of setting into the bezel an inlay of a different material (no. 405) also makes its début in Egyptian signet finger-rings of the XVIIIth Dynasty. Although the latter may have been intended for use, it is less likely that the cheap glazed composition rings of Tutankhamun and his wife, Ankhesenamun, (no. 406) were functional; if, as has been suggested, they were merely intended for distribution at festivals or court occasions, then these so-called 'signet-rings' would not really qualify for inclusion in this section.

A new form of signet-ring is introduced into Egypt during the Saite period (around 600 BC), in which the thick bezel is raised above the shank and cut away on the underside to allow room for the finger (no. 407). As might be expected, the two contemporary Phoenician signet-rings (no. 408) are clearly much influenced by the older Egyptian tradition of the swivel bezel set with an engraved stone.

In the Greek world, the art of engraving the bezel was re-introduced by about 600 BC and a beautiful Hellenistic example (no. 411) shows the skill to perfection. The Greek tradition for engraving gemstones goes back to about 700 BC but it was not before about 600 BC that the practice of mounting them in finger-rings became general. Like the Greeks, the Etruscans mounted engraved gems in the bezels of finger-rings, but sometimes subordinated the gems within ostentatious and elaborately worked gold settings, using them less as signets and more as ornamental additions to the purely decorative ring (no. 410). However, in Rome the practice of wearing finger-rings for sealing purposes is well documented and, for example, by the end of the third century BC, Roman consuls were wearing signet-rings with a distinctive device. It was about this time that the sardonyx and garnet became popular in Rome as a seal-stone, but many signet-rings (no. 412) continued to have intaglios cut in metal bezels (gold, silver or base-metal); Romano-British finds include three silver rings found at Amesbury in Wiltshire with a hoard of coins, the latest having been issued in AD 402–50 (no. 413). In the Early Christian era there was no break in the tradition (no. 415) and, although the bezels were occasionally set with intaglio gems, more frequently the flat surface of a metal bezel was engraved; such signet-rings were much favoured at the Byzantine Imperial court in Constantinople (no. 416).

The Roman practice lived on in Gaul under Frankish rule, often reaching the highest levels of craftsmanship – the nielloed signet-ring is an exceptionally elaborate survival (no. 417). The fashion for engraved gems set in the bezels of signet-rings did not die in the Eastern Empire as it had in Rome during the Imperial period; the use of garnet combined with an openwork design in the gold hoop (no. 418) is but one example of the elegant style in fashion during the sixth or seventh century AD. An even richer effect is achieved by a contemporary goldsmith north of the Alps, who used filigree and granulation to enrich the gold hoop of the 'Snape' ring with its Late Antique intaglio gem (no. 419). In this period, widespread illiteracy made the seal indispensable, and the signet-ring continued without a break through the Early Middle Ages in the West.

With the development of heraldry in the later Middle Ages in Europe as a means of identification, all who were entitled to bear arms wore signet-rings engraved with their armorial bearings. Thus, the signet-ring gained a new lease of life. By the fourteenth century, very fine examples from Italy occur frequently (no. 427), but not until the following century do English armorial signets of comparable quality appear (nos. 420, 421). A great refinement among armorial signets was to reproduce not only the coat-of-arms but the correct tinctures; this was achieved by engraving the coat-of-arms in crystal, and, on the reverse side, they were repeated in colour;

the crystal would then be set in the gold bezel, and although the engraved surface could be used for impressions, the colours would not wear away. The signet of Mary, Queen of Scots, is probably the most interesting example of this type (no. 422), though whether it was made in France or in this country, where this technique was especially practised and popular, has still to be resolved.

Men who were not entitled to bear arms were allowed to seal with a simple device, and many merchants' rings in bronze and base-metal have survived, engraved on the bezel with a merchant's mark (no. 423).

Although the need for the signet-ring gradually became less essential after the eighteenth century, there remains even to this day a vogue for them, however rarely they are actually put to use (no. 425).
H.T.

399 Seal Pendant Halaf period about 5000 BC
Arpachiya, Iraq.

Black stone pendant incised on one side with geometric pattern. H 2·25.

Seals of this kind were impressed into damp clay to indicate ownership or responsibility for sealed goods. Stamp-seals worn as pendants remained popular in parts of Western Asia throughout the prehistoric and early historical periods.
Bibliography: Mallowan (1935), pp. 92, 98 (A553).
WAA 127650.

400 Cylinder-Seal Sumerian about 2100 BC
Ur, Iraq.

Lapis-lazuli cylinder-seal with gold mounts at either end. Seal carved with two scenes of combat between heroes and animals. Inscription, intentionally erased, would have given name, father's name, and profession of original owner. H 4·3.

Seals of this kind, which could be rolled on damp clay, were the standard form of signet in southern Mesopotamia from the Sumerian period until the middle of the first millennium BC. This example was buried in grave PG1422 (see no. 16). Such seals were sometimes attached to large toggle-pins, e.g. no. 14a, an arrangement which accounts for the statement in a Babylonian text that Rimush, a king of about 2300 BC, was 'murdered with cylinder-seals'.
Bibliography: Woolley (1934), p. 185 (U12470).
WAA 122216.

401 Finger-Ring Egyptian about 1400 BC
XVIIIth dynasty
Gold, massive with lapis-lazuli coloured blue glass

399 △

400 △   ▽ 401

cylinder as bezel. Shank cast solid and beaten out towards ends. Gold wire wound around one end of shank, passes through cup-shaped terminals, through bezel and wound on other end of shank. Cylinder is capped at each end by gold to which are soldered collars which rotate against cups at ends of shank. Maximum external D (shank) 3·1; L (cylinder) 1·3; D (cylinder) 0·9.

This type of metal ring with glass cylinder as bezel is rare in the XVIIIth dynasty.
Bibliography: Hall (1913), pl. 3; Budge (1925), p. 268; Wilkinson (1971), p. 130.
EA 2922.

Colour plate 7

402 Signet-Ring Minoan 16th century BC
Crete.

Gold. Engraved with scene of two wild goats mating. D (hoop) 1·9.
Bibliography: *BMCR*, no. 14.
G & R 42.7–28.127. Burgon Collection.

Colour plate 10

403 Two Signet-Rings Egyptian
about 1500–1450 BC
XVIIIth dynasty
(a) Queen Hatshepsut: gold, with scarab of green glazed composition as bezel, underside inscribed with prenomen of Queen Hatshepsut and flanked by hieroglyphic signs; whole reads 'The Good Goddess, Maat-ka-Re, may she live'. Shank made of piece of gold foil folded over wire. Wire wound around top of shank passes through scarab and gold balls and is wound around opposite end of shank. Scarab set in gold mount. External D (shank) 2·7; internal D 2·1; L (scarab) 1·8.
(b) Tuthmosis III: gold with bezel composed of rectangular plaque of dark blue glass set in gold mount. Plaque bound with gold with extra thinner casing of sheet gold over first. From outer casing protrude necks which hold rings attached to inside of cups soldered to ends of shank and form swivel for bezel. There are inscriptions on both faces of plaque: (i) Tuthmosis III in form of sphinx wearing *atef* crown and trampling prostrate enemy, with hieroglyphs reading: 'The Good God Men-kheper-Re, trampling down every foreign land'; (ii) the reverse inscribed with another of the king's official names: 'The Golden Horus, Wielder of Power'. External D (shank) 2·5; internal D 2·1; W (plaque) 1·6.
(a) The form of the scarab is typical of the early part of the fifteenth century BC. (b) Rings with a swivelling

403a,b

402

rectangular bezel came into fashion in the early New Kingdom.

Bibliography: (a) Hall (1913), p. 298, no. 2831; pl. 5. (b) F. Lenormant, *Catalogue d'une Collection d'Antiquités égyptiennes, rassemblée par M. D'Anastasi*, Paris 1857, lot 712; *BM Guide* (1904), p. 217, no. 202; *ibid.* (1922), p. 91, no. 202; Hall (1913), p. 99, no. 1016; pl. 8.

EA 49717, given anonymously; 14349.

404 Two Signet-Rings Egyptian

about 1417–1362 BC
XVIIIth dynasty

(a) Amenophis III: gold, of stirrup-shape with thin shank and oval bezel inscribed with hieroglyphs for 'Amenhotep, Prince of Thebes'. Maximum external D (shank) 2·0; W (bezel) 0·9.

404a

(b) Akhenaten: gold, massive ring of stirrup-shape with oval bezel deeply incised with central seated figure holding maat-feather, flanked by ceremonial fan and *ankh*-sign, uraeus-flanked sun-disc at top and signs for Lord of the Two Lands below. Maximum external D 2·4; T (shank) 0·7; W (bezel) 1·4.

404b

(a) The epithet 'Prince of Thebes' makes it certain that this ring belonged to Amenophis III. (b) The seated figure seems unmistakably to be Akhenaten: the long head, spindly arms and legs and swollen stomach are unique in Egyptian art. He also based his religious beliefs on the concept of maat – truth or divine order, and the figure holds a maat-feather. This ring was made by the *cire-perdue* or lost wax process.

Bibliography: (a) *BM Guide* (1922), p. 93, no. 266; Hall (1913), p. 275, no. 2665; Wilkinson (1971), p. 129. (b) Hall (1913), p. 278, no. 2688; Wilkinson (1971), p. 129.

EA 30446. Bequeathed by Mr Ernest Hart; 32723.

405

405 Signet-Ring Egyptian about 1379–1362 BC

XVIIIth dynasty

Akhenaten: ivory, roughly-cut ring of stirrup-shape with inlaid blue glazed composition oval bezel in which is incised prenomen of Akhenaten, Neferkheperu-Re Wa-en-Re. Maximum external D (shank) 2·7; T (shank) 0·6; L (bezel) 2·2.

This shape of ring and this method of inlaying the bezel with another material make their first appearance at the beginning of the XVIIIth dynasty. The bezel's inscription gives a good impression and the piece could clearly have been used as a seal as well as being decorative.

Bibliography: Hall (1913), p. 277, no. 2683.

EA 54578. Franks Bequest, 1897.

406 Two Signet-Rings Egyptian
about 1361–1352 BC
XVIIIth dynasty

406a

(a) Tutankhamun: bright blue glazed composition, stirrup-shaped with long oval bezel bearing name of Tutankhamun, Prince of Hermonthis. Maximum external D 3·0; L (bezel) 2·8; W 1·5.

406b

(b) Ankhesenamun: brick-red glazed composition, stirrup-shaped with oval bezel bearing name of Ankhesenamun. The ring has a very small diameter. Maximum external D 2·4; L (bezel) 2·2; W 1·4.

Such glazed composition signets were probably distributed at festivals or court occasions. The nomen of Tutankhamun in (a) is written with the sign of a standing man holding a stave in his hand, the usual determinative of the word for statue. Here it acts as ideogram for *twt*, the part of Tutankhamun's name which means statue or image. This syllable of the name is more usually written out alphabetically. Ankhesenamun was the wife of Tutankhamun.

Bibliography: (a) Hall (1913), p. 280, no. 2705.

EA 17897, Blacas Collection; 65110, Acworth Collection.

407 Signet-Ring Egyptian about 600 BC
XXVIth dynasty

407

Silver, with thick oval bezel raised well above shank with curved section cut away on underside. Bezel inscribed with hieroglyphic inscription: 'The fourth priest of Sheshonq, *wab*-priest of Psamtek, *sma*-priest of Coptos, Scribe of the divine book of Isis, Chief of the Libationers of Min (?), Overseer of God's Land'. External D (shank) 2·6; H (bezel) 2·3.

This form of signet-ring with the underside of the bezel cut away is characteristic of the XXVIth dynasty. Its owner was apparently both a priest of one of the XXIInd dynasty Sheshonqs, presumably Sheshonq I, and of Psammetichus I, founder of the XXVIth dynasty. It is noteworthy that the funerary cult of a revered king who died 300 years earlier was still being maintained.

Bibliography: *BM Guide* (1904), p. 220, no. 392; *ibid.* (1922), p. 94, no. 392; Budge (1925), p. 269; Wilkinson (1971), p. 195.

EA 24777.

408 Two Finger-Rings Phoenician
about 6th century BC

(a) Elliptical gold hoop with carnelian scarab in gold setting. Stone shows Isis suckling Horus, with Osiride figures on either side and winged disc above. W 3·02.

This signet was probably not worn on a finger, but was attached to a string or necklace.

408a,b

Bibliography: Marshall (1907), p. 51, no. 284; Walters (1926), p. 33, no. 273.
WAA 136027.

(b) Gold hoop consisting of three wires ending in discs through which passes swivel of gold wire. Scaraboid of green glass representing two winged sphinxes on either side of sacred tree. L 1·3.

This could be worn on the finger, with the design against the skin, if so desired, to prevent it from becoming chipped.

Bibliography: Marshall (1907), p. 52, no. 293; Walters (1926), p. 33, no. 270.
WAA 136028.

409 Finger-Ring Etruscan 6th century BC
Gold; rectangular bezel with rounded ends, engraved with winged horse and sphinx. L 2·4.
Bibliography: *BMCR*, no. 23.
G & R 1926.4–7.3.

410 Finger-Ring Etruscan 5th century BC
Gold, set with engraved sard gem. Bezel is large and in form of oval dome, decorated in repoussé with animals and dolphins, and by filigree ornaments; ground finely granulated. Gem-stone engraved in 'globolo' style with a man on a horse. L 4·0.
Bibliography: *BMCR*, no. 354; *BMC Gems*, no. 897.
G & R 354F. Franks Bequest, 1897.

Colour plate 10

411 Finger-Ring Greek 4th century BC
Gold. Engraved scene of Aphrodite, naked, holding dove. D 2·1.
Bibliography: *BMCR*, no. 58.
G & R 65.7–12.59.

412 Signet-Ring Egyptian about 250–200 BC
Ptolemaic period
Gold, stirrup-shaped with long bezel inscribed with
hieroglyphs reading 'The Son of Re, Ptolemy, Living
forever, Beloved of Ptah'. The name is contained in a
cartouche. Maximum external D 2·7; L (bezel) 2·9.

The name on the ring is presumably that of Ptolemy
III Euergetes. The epithet 'Living forever' and 'Beloved of Ptah' is borne by four of the Ptolemaic rulers
but the lack of any further titles to distinguish the
owner from an earlier ruler with the same epithet
suggests it dates to the reign of Ptolemy III.
Bibliography: Hall (1913) p. 283, no. 2739.
EA 36468.

413 Finger-Rings (three) Romano-British
about AD 400
Amesbury, Wiltshire, England.

Silver; flat hoops with square bezels with chased and/
or engraved designs:
(a) Four helmeted heads; hoop with slight keel on
exterior; D 2·5.
(b) Recumbent stag looking over shoulder at bird;
bunch-of-grapes motif (made as granulated beads)
and chased dotted lines on hoop either side of bezel;
D 2·5.
(c) Griffin looking over shoulder; simple chased
and/or engraved ornament on hoop either side of
bezel; D 2·5.

The similarities in style and technical execution suggest that the three rings were made by the same craftsman, perhaps for the same customer on commission.
Found in 1843 inside a pot together with a hoard of
coins, the latest being issues of Theodosius II (AD
402–50).
Bibliography: *Proceedings of the Society of Antiquaries of
London* [first series], 4 (1856–59), pp. 27–8, figs. 1–3;
Marshall (1907), nos. 1205–7; Smith (1922), p. 67,
fig. 85; Brailsford (1964), p. 26 no. 6, fig. 13.6; Henig
(1974) nos. 801–3.
P & RB 57.6–30.1–3.

246

414

414 Finger-Ring Sasanian about 4th century AD
Agate ring representing wolf suckling two children
with, above, Pahlavi inscription *b'nwky*, perhaps
proper name. D 2·1.

The design recalls the story of Romulus and Remus,
founders of Rome, and is one of many Sasanian bor-
rowings from the west; the use of stone rings themselves, however, is characteristically Sasanian.
Bibliography: Bivar (1969), pp. 23, 76, no. EA1.
WAA 119353.

415

415 Signet-Ring Early Christian
5th century AD
Found at Usküdar (Scutari) near Istanbul.

Gold signet-ring with solid square bezel crudely engraved in intaglio with Orpheus seated near tree
playing lyre to two recumbent animals. Around edge
of bezel, a Greek inscription which may be deciphered
as reading: 'Seal of John the crowned saint'. D 2·54.

Bibliography: Dalton (1901), no. 123; H. Stern,
'Orphée dans l'art paléochrétien', *Cahiers Archéolo-
giques* (1974), p. 16.
M & L AF228. Franks Bequest, 1897.

416 Signet-Ring Byzantine early 6th century AD
Gold ring, the bezel engraved with a seated female
personification flanked by two Greek monograms.
D 2·8.

416

The female personification is to be identified as the
tyche of Constantinople, which might indicate that
this was the personal ring of an official at the Imperial Court. The monograms have not yet been
positively deciphered, but that on the left appears to
read 'Paul' (*ΠΑΥΛΟΥ*) and that on the left 'Euthemia'
(*ΕΥΘΕΜΙΑ*).

M & L 1964.12–4.1. Bequeathed by Sir Allen George
Clark, 1964.

417 Signet-Ring Frankish 5th century AD
Mulsanne, Sarthe, France.

Heavy gold and niello signet ring with warrior and woman incised on bezel. One side of bezel incised and nielloed DROMACI, on other US BETTA (the names were Dromacius and Betta). On shoulders of ring are cast animal masks, with niello borders. Diamond-shaped reserve set on hoop opposite bezel. D 2·5 (hoop).

The ring is an early Frankish piece displaying Romano-Gallic traditions and innovating tendencies. It is possible that this ring could also have served as a betrothal or marriage-ring. The more common form of Frankish signet-ring is slighter, with a simple monogram on the bezel. Heavy rings set with a stone or an imperial coin are also known in Frankish contexts. In contemporary Anglo-Saxon England rich finger-rings are very rare, being known, for example, from the ship burial at Snape in Suffolk, but not from Sutton Hoo. In Frankish areas some noble burials contain signet-rings.
Bibliography: *Sotheby Sale Catalogue* (11 November 1937), pl. XVII, no. 512.
M & L 1937.11–18.1. Guilhou Collection.

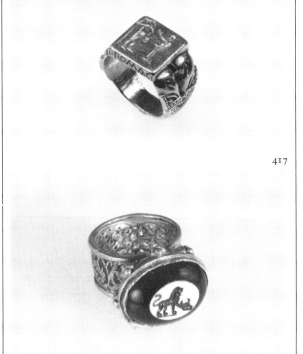

417

418 Signet-Ring Byzantine 6th–7th century AD
Gold ring with openwork hoop, bezel set with garnet intaglio engraved with figure of lion facing bull's head. L (bezel) 2·2.
Bibliography: R. A. Smith, 'Seventh Century Jewellery', *BMQ* (1930–1), p. 84.
M & L 1930.11–7.1.

418

419 Signet-Ring Anglo-Saxon or Frankish
6th century AD
From an Anglo-Saxon ship burial excavated at Snape, Suffolk, England, in 1862.

Gold ring set with Roman nicolo intaglio engraved with figure of *Bonus Eventus*. Hoop beaded and shoulders enriched with filigree and granulation. D (max.) 2·2; WT 14·0.

Simple rings are fairly common in early Anglo-Saxon contexts, but this example is of rare magnificence, befitting the important status of an owner buried in his ship. For the re-use of an Antique gem in Anglo-Saxon jewellery, see also the Epsom cameo pendant (no. 385).
Bibliography: R. L. S. Bruce-Mitford (1974), pp. 126–31, pl. 21a–d; M. Henig (1974), vol. i, p. 197, vol. ii, no. 205, p. 33.
M & L 1950.12–6.1. Given by Mrs H. M. Davidson on behalf of her late husband, H. M. Davidson.

Colour plate 10

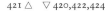

421 △   ▽ 420,422,424

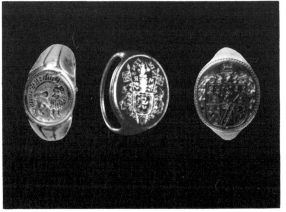

420 The 'Percy' Signet-Ring English
15th century AD
Found by a ploughman at Towton near Tadcaster, Yorkshire, in or before 1789.

Gold hoop cut into six channels, circular bezel engraved with lion passant and inscription: *now : ẏs : thus*. D 3·0.

This very fine, massive signet-ring has been ascribed to the Percy family and may have been lost by a member of the Percy family at the battle of Towton on 29 March 1461. Henry Percy, the sixth Earl of Northumberland, fought on the Lancastrian side and was killed in the battle. A lion passant was certainly a Percy badge in the sixteenth century and may have been adopted in the preceding century; there is, however, no definite evidence that they used this motto. Formerly in the Durlacher and Braybrooke collections.
Bibliography: Isaac Tyson, *Gentlemans Magazine*, vol. lix (1789), p. 616; R. J. T., *Gentlemans Magazine*, vol. lxxiii (Jan 1803), p. 17; Dalton (1912), no. 536; Oman (1974), pl. 41D.
M & L AF771. Franks Bequest, 1897.

421 Signet-Ring English about AD 1400–50
Found at Fishpool, near Mansfield, Nottinghamshire, in 1966, along with other jewellery and coins (see no. 270).

Gold; bezel engraved with the device of a hawk's lure with the wings bound with cords, above the letter 't' with a fleur-de-lis on either side, and flowers beside the lure; inside the hoop inscribed '*de bon coer*'. D 2·5.

The device has not been identified; lures are rare heraldic charges (the Fitzpayne, Seymour, Wakering and Aldrington families); used as a crest by the Sacheverell family of Kirby-in-Ashfield (Nottinghamshire), but, as the lure between two fleur-de-lis was certainly used by the Wowen family of London at a later date, it may have been adopted by them as early as the fifteenth century.
Bibliography: J. Cherry, 'The Medieval Jewellery from the Fishpool, Nottinghamshire, Hoard', *Archaeologia* CIV (1973), pp. 310–11, pl. LXXXVIIA.
M & L 1967.12–8.4.

422 Signet-Ring of Mary, Queen of Scots
AD 1548–58 (?)
Gold, the shoulders and the underside rim of the bezel ornamented with flowers and leaves formerly enamelled, oval bezel containing crystal (?) engraved with the achievement of Mary, Queen of Scots. The shield is that of Scotland surrounded by the collar of the Thistle, with the badge, and supported by two unicorns chained and ducally gorged. The crest on a helmet with mantlings and ensigned with a crown, is a lion sejant affronté, crowned and holding in the dexter paw a naked sword; in the sinister a sceptre, both bendwise. Legend: IN DEFENS, and the letters M. R. On the dexter (right) side is a banner with the arms of Scotland; on the sinister (left) side another, with three bars and over all a saltire. The metals and tinctures appear through the crystal on a field of blue. On the underside of the bezel is engraved a cipher formed of the Greek letters Φ and M, within a circular band and surmounted by a crown, formerly enamelled; traces of black, red and white enamel remain. D 2·25.

The Greek letters which compose the cipher stand for the names Francis (Francis II of France, to whom she was married, aged sixteen, in 1558) and Mary. Since after her marriage she no longer bore the arms of Scotland alone and after the death of Francis in 1560 she would no longer have used the cipher with his name, it has been assumed that the ring was made in France shortly before 1558, probably during the decade between 1548 when she first went to France following her betrothal to the Dauphin and their marriage in 1558.
  Its history is unknown during the period between Mary's death in 1587 and the year 1792 when it belonged to Queen Charlotte. It subsequently passed into the possession of the Duke of York, who sold it in 1827 to Mr Richard Greene, from whom it was purchased in 1856 by the British Museum.
Bibliography: Dalton (1912), no. 316; Oman (1974), p. 32, pl. 46–7.
M & L 56.10–15.1.

Colour plate 10

423 Merchant's Signet-Ring English
16th century AD
Found at Gloucester.

Brass, formerly gilt; flanged hoop engraved on the sides with leaves and flowers filled with black enamel. Oval bezel engraved with a merchant's mark including the letters R, S, P, E and A, within a punched border. The inside of the hoop bears the legend 'Y leve yn hope' (I live in hope).
Bibliography: F. A. Girling *English Merchants' Marks* (London, 1962), pp. 22–3; Dalton (1912), no. 559.
M & L AF783. Franks Bequest, 1897.

424 Ravenscroft Signet-Ring English
late 16th century AD
Gold; plain hoop, oval bezel engraved with a shield

of arms with six quarterings, and crest with mantling, inside a punched border. (1) and (6) are Ravenscroft – argent, a chevron between three ravens' heads erased sable; (2) Holland – azure semée-de-lis, a lion rampant guardant argent; (3) Skevington – argent, three bulls' heads erased sable (wyverns); (4) Brickhill – sable, three garbs, a bordure or; (5) Swettenham – argent, on a bend vert, three spades of the first, a martlet in chief. The martlet appears to be a mark of difference. The crest: on a cap of maintenance gules turned up ermine, a lion statant guardant argent. On the underside of the bezel are four punched marks formed by combination of two punches, one producing an impression in the shape of a shield, and the other an arrangement of five spots as on a die. D 2·7; L (of bezel) 2·2.

This ring belonged to a member of the Ravenscroft family of Bretton in Flint (with a junior branch in Sussex), perhaps to Thomas Ravenscroft recorded as head of the family in the 1580 Visitation of the County of Cheshire (Harl. MS. 1424 fo. 120).

Bibliography: 'The Visitation of the County of Cheshire in 1580', and 'The Visitation of the County of Sussex in 1530 and 1633–4', *Publications of the Harleian Society* (London, 1882), pp. 194–5 and (London, 1905), p. 171; Dalton (1912), no. 601; Oman (1974), p. 32, pl. 48b.

M & L AF811. Franks Bequest, 1897.

425 The Browning Finger-Rings English
AD 1846–61

(a) Gold; oval bezel engraved 'Ba', two oval indentations in the bezel above and below the inscription, the shoulders simply chased, on the underside of the bezel a circular panel of glass now cracked and with no hair set behind. On the inside of the hoop the inscription 'God bless you June 29. 1861'. D 1·9.

(b) Silver-gilt; octagonal bezel, the sides slightly indented, set with an amethyst intaglio inscribed with the initials, 'E BB'. D 1·5.

Their daughter-in-law, Fannie Browning, writing in 1913 notes: 'The one with "Ba" I used to see my father-in-law wear on his little finger – but it was only the other day I noticed the touching inscription and date, and no doubt her hair is in it. The E BB amethyst-seal, one he enlarged for me to wear – but *now* I cannot begin to get it on.'

The enlargement can clearly be seen as a small insert of a slightly different coloured metal in the bottom of the hoop.

Elizabeth Barrett was married to Robert Browning in 1846, and died in 1861; Robert was buried in Westminster Abbey in 1889.

M & L 1952.10–2.2–3. Bequeathed by Sir Frederic G. Kenyon, GBE, KCB.

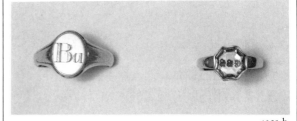

425a,b

The Archer's Thumb-Ring

Another type of finger-ring which was primarily functional – but often very decorative as well – was the bow-ring worn by archers on the thumb. Again, there is a long history attached to these rings, for with the early development of the crossbow thumb-rings of this shape often appear, but in certain countries and at certain periods they are especially beautifully worked and designed. Three have been selected, spanning more than 2000 years and offering three very different solutions (nos. 426–8).

The three accompanying line-drawings (based on illustrations in Sir Ralph Payne-Gallwey, *Appendix to the Book of the Crossbow* (1907), p. 14) show how the wearing of a thumb-ring alters – and, indeed, improves – the archer's handling of the bow and the arrow: (1) the bow-string is at first hitched behind the pointed lip of thumb-ring, the nock of the arrow being close against the lip of the ring and hence very close to the angle formed by the bow-string when it is fully drawn. (2) At this stage, the forefinger is pressing tightly against the sloping surface of the thumb-ring. (3) This detail indicates how the ring (A) is worn on the thumb and shows, in section, the bow-string (B) hitched behind the lip of the thumb-ring; the forefinger (C) is beginning to move towards the sloping surface of the lip of the thumb-ring as the bow is being bent.

By this method, no part of the hand has to hold the ring in position and only the thumb and the forefinger are used in drawing the bow-string.

When the pressure of the forefinger on the ring is removed by separating the forefinger and thumb, the bow-string immediately drags the projecting lip of the thumb-ring forward and it slips off with a sharp 'click'.

If the thumb-ring is worn in any other way, it will fly off the hand when the bow-string is released and the thumb will be hurt; or, of course, the bow-string will not remain hitched in position and will escape when only partially drawn.

The advantage of this method over the comparatively slow, dragging action associated with the release from the leather-covered tips of three fingers in the European practice is that the range of a flight arrow is far greater and far steadier, for there is no need to leave so much space between the nock and the feathers of the arrow so as to avoid crushing the feathers with the three fingers holding the bow-string. Experience has shown that the closer the feathers are to the nock, the greater the distance the arrow will travel and the steadier its path will be.

H.T.

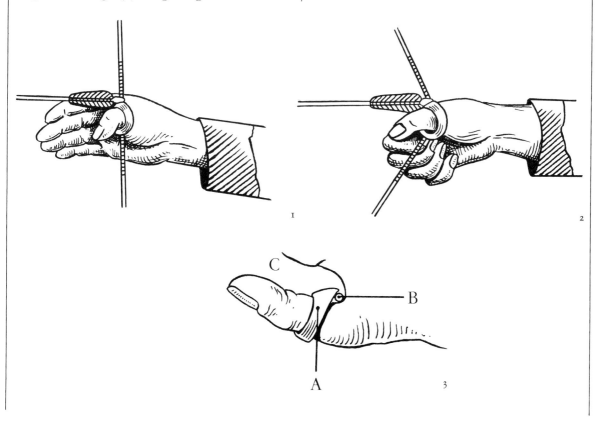

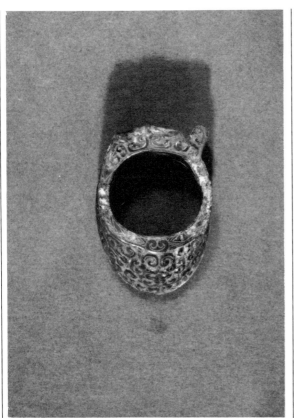

426 Archer's Thumb-Ring China 5th century BC
Eastern Chou period
Brownish green jade ring with traces of pigment; oval and spreading in shape with projection on one side; pierced through back; decorated with dragons' heads in profile formed by modelled C-scrolls with detail of eye and lines on scrolls incised; border of chevrons and C-scrolls incised around ring. L 4·5.

From the period of the development of the cross-bow archer's thumb-rings of this shape seem to have been general in ancient China. A similar example has been excavated at Loyang, Honan province, see Chung-kuo k'o-hsüeh yüan k'ao-ku yen-chiu-so (1959), pl. LXXII.
Bibliography: Ayers and Rawson (1975), no. 171; Jenyns (1951), pl. XXXIII (1).
OA 1945.10–17.61.

427 Archer's Thumb-Ring Venetian (?)
14th century AD
Found at Aegium in the Peloponnese.

Gold signet-ring, octagonal bezel engraved in intaglio with shield of arms: per bend, a column and three bends, surmounted by a helm and crest and surrounded by the legend S DE ZENO DONAT. Exterior decorated with the inscription + IEXUS * AUTEM * TRANSIENS * PER * MEDIUM ILLORUM * IBANT * ELOI reserved on a ground of niello. On inside is engraved a column upon a mount cut by a scythe from which issues a scroll with the legend AIDA MEDIO. D 3·8.

The arms have been identified as those of the Donati, an old Venetian family. For the inscription on the exterior, see no. 373.
Bibliography: Dalton (1912), no. 239.
M & L AF568. Franks Bequest, 1897.

428 Archer's Thumb-Ring India
17th–18th century AD
Mughal period
Jade, inlaid with gold and precious stones. L 4·2.
Bibliography: Dalton (1912), no. 2383.
OA Franks Collection.

426 △   ▽ 428

427

Rings for the measurement of time

In Europe, during the second half of the sixteenth century and in the early part of the seventeenth century, finger-rings were made for the purpose of discovering the hour of the day, albeit without great accuracy or precision. The simplest version, the so-called 'shepherds' dial', is a diminutive form of the well-known ring-dials and is used in the same way (no. 429). The dial takes the form of a metal ring, in which one or more holes are pierced to admit the sun-rays when it is suspended from the fixed ring at its top. The rays of the sun, passing through the pin-hole, shine on the hour-scale which is engraved on the inner surface of the ring. If only one hole is provided the hour-lines have to slope steeply; whereas, if two holes are provided, one for the summer half-year and the other for the winter six months, each hole can face its own hour-scales.

A more accurate type (no. 430) had the pin-hole in a sliding ring within the finger-ring itself; when in use, the hole in the moving ring is brought level with the month in which the observation is being taken and the hour-lines are made parallel to the axis of the ring.

Another group of finger-rings of this period used for measuring time have a locket-like bezel set with a compass, around the edge of which are engraved the hours 1 to 12 and in which the lid of the locket served as a gnomon (no. 431). Perhaps the most sophisticated of these scientific finger-rings is the kind that opens to form an astrological sphere, marked with the signs of the zodiac and of the planets (no. 432).

By the eighteenth century, the greatly improved performance of watches killed the market for ring dials but the application of the mechanical watch to the finger-ring has never been wholly successful. A sixteenth-century striking-watch, designed as a finger-ring and beautifully executed in enamelled gold, survives in the Bavarian royal collection in the Residenz in Munich, and the great English precision watch-maker, John Arnold (1736–99), is known to have presented George III with a repeating watch set in a finger-ring in 1764, but it is now lost. French and Swiss makers also aspired to make attractive and efficient ring-watches (no. 433) in the late eighteenth century but with only limited success; the fashion has continued up to the present day.

H.T.

429 Finger-Ring Dial English (?)
early 17th century AD
Bronze hoop representing a buckled strap, engraved on the outside with a leafy spray and with the initial letters of the names of the months arranged in two rows, viz: I,–, M, A, M, I, I, A, S, O, N, D; also the letters AM and OV somewhat crudely engraved. On the inside, a set of hour numerals in roman IIII to XII and in reverse I to VIII well engraved.

There are three punched holes, of which the one nearest the buckle would serve the early and late summer months approximately, the other two holes being too near the hour-scale to allow light to reach it. D 2·2; W (of band) 0·5.
Bibliography: Dalton (1912), no. 1699, pl. XXIII.
M & L AF1758. Franks Bequest, 1897.

430 Finger-Ring Dial German
late 16th century AD
Gold finger-ring incorporating a ring dial; a single pin-hole is in a sliding ring, and is set according to scales of the months on either side of it, the months being identified by their initials. The equinoxes are at 10 March and 10 September approximately. The hour-marks on the inside of the ring are individual dots, numbered with pairs of hours, a.m. and p.m. On a shield, applied to the outside of the ring, a demi-bull rampant surrounded by the initials H/G V/B. D 2·5; W (of band) 0·8.
Bibliography: Dalton (1912), no. 1698, pl. XXIII.
M & L AF1757. Franks Bequest, 1897.

431 Compass Dial Finger-Ring German (?)
late 16th century AD
Gold; the shoulders and sides of the bezel chased with scrolls enamelled blue, green and white; oval locket bezel, the lid set with a ruby surrounded by five crystals; inside, a compass with flange marked as a horizontal sundial with hours 6 – 12 – 6, with holes at centre of 6 – 6 line and near the edge of the lid for the insertion of a string gnomon. D 2·2; D (of compass) 0·8.
Bibliography: Dalton (1912), no. 1703, pl. XXIII.
M & L AF1762. Franks Bequest, 1897.

432 Astrological Sphere Finger-Ring German
AD 1555
Gold; the sphere is formed of an outer hoop in two parts, working like a gimmel, and three interior hoops almost concealed when the ring is closed and worn on the finger. The exterior hoop is chased on the outer side with scrolls on a ground once enamelled black, and each part has on the flat surfaces concealed when the ring is closed a section of an inscription enamelled black: VERBO DEI CELI / FIRMATI SUNT / DIXIT ET FACTA / SUNT IPSE MANDAVIT ET CREATA SUNT. The figures 1555, indicating the date, follow the words *firmati sunt*. The three interior hoops are plain flat bands engraved and enamelled in black with the signs of the zodiac, stars, and other figures. D 2·5.
Bibliography: Dalton (1912), no. 1700.
M & L AF1759. Franks Bequest, 1897.

433 Finger-Ring Watch French
late 18th century AD
Gold, with a subsidiary seconds dial and date indication; the movement, with cylinder escapement, is
signed: *L'Epine à Paris*. L 2·6.
M & L CA1292. Formerly in the Ilbert Collection.

433

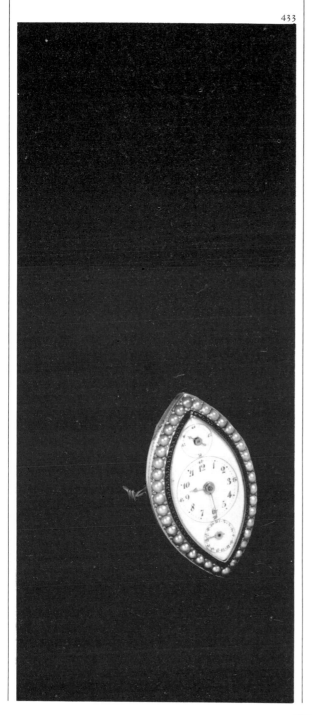

Marriage, Betrothal and Love Rings

The *fede*, or hand-in-hand, ring appears in Roman times, when the two clasped hands, DEXTRARUM IVNCTIO, represented a contract. The Roman symbolism of two hands clasped in troth was, of course, highly applicable to the Christian betrothal or marriage-ring and the magnificent gold example excavated at the late Roman fort of Richborough, Kent, in 1935 is thought to be no earlier than the fourth century AD and, therefore, probably a betrothal finger-ring (no. 434).

Fede-rings have continued in use throughout Europe up to the present day and sometimes they bear a religious, or even magical, inscription, making them fall into both the amuletic and betrothal categories, for it is impossible to know which had the greater significance for the original owner.

Another late Roman innovation was the openwork finger-ring incorporating letters which form an appropriate inscription. From the second century AD onwards, the Christian betrothal-ring was usually made of gold and the delicate polygonal example excavated at the Roman fort at Corbridge, Northumberland, in 1935 is a rare survival from Roman Britain (no. 435). Although the interior is smooth, the sixteen openwork panels are each divided into three horizontal zones, the middle containing a letter; the Greek inscription, which indicates that it was a betrothal-ring, suggests that it was made in the Eastern Roman Empire.

Byzantine marriage-rings of the sixth and seventh centuries are often elaborately engraved, filled with niello or enamel, and depict the bride and bridegroom (no. 436); on one example they are being blessed by the figures of Christ and the Virgin, and accompanying Greek inscription may be read as 'Concord' (no. 437).

There is no reliable information about the form of wedding-ring used in Britain during the early Middle Ages but it is interesting to note that in medieval times the wedding ceremony took place at the church door – not at the entry to the chancel, as is normal today. The custom of the bride to give, as well as to receive, a wedding-ring is another obscure aspect, and certainly few such rings can now be recognized.
H.T.

434 Finger-Ring Romano-British 4th century AD
Excavated at the late Roman fort of Richborough, Kent (*Rutupiae*) in 1935.

Gold; hoop composed of three wires, central twisted, outer pair beaded and terminating in spirals; on each shoulder complex design, symmetrical about circumferential axis, of paired asymmetrical double spirals of beaded wire with globules in interstices; oval bezel with twisted ribbon border, recessed with plaque with embossed clasped right hands motif at base.
D 2·8; WT 13·6.

The clasped hands, DEXTRARVM IUNCTIO, represent a contract, most likely in this context betrothal; therefore probably a betrothal ring.

Bibliography: Smith (1936), p. 161, pl. LI.10–12; Bushe-Fox (1949), p. 126, pl. XXXV.93; Brailsford (1964), p. 26, no. 7, fig. 13.7; Henig (1974) no. 775.
P & RB 1936.2–4.1.

Colour plate 10

434

435 Finger-Ring Eastern Roman Empire
4th century AD
Excavated at the Roman fort at Corbridge, Northumberland, England (*Corstopitum*) in 1935.

Gold; polygonal, divided into sixteen openwork panels by vertical ribs; interior smooth; each panel divided into three zones by two horizontal bars, with a pelta-motif in upper and lower zone; in middle zone a letter, except for one panel which has a cruciform motif with lozenge-shaped arms; inscription reads *ΠΟΛΕΜΙΟΥ ΦΙΛΤΡΟΝ* ('the love-charm of Polemios'); ring made, decorated and inscribed, with punches, as a strip, then coiled round with joint at panel with cruciform motif which was slightly distorted in the process. D 2·5; WT 11·8.

Finger-rings in openwork technique are a late Roman innovation, but ones with inscriptions are rare finds. The Greek inscription suggests that it was made in the Eastern Roman Empire, and indicates that it was a betrothal ring. Another inscribed ring of this type has been found at Corbridge, a remarkable circumstance in view of the rarity of the type.
Bibliography: Cowen (1936); Cowen (1948); Charlesworth (1961), pp. 9–10, 24, no. 6, pl. 1.6.
P & RB Deposited on permanent loan by H.M. Ministry of Works in 1947.

Colour plate 10

435

436 Marriage-Ring Early Christian about 500 AD
Gold ring, the bezel rectangular and engraved in intaglio with a male and female bust confronted, the hoop forming seven circular medallions engraved alternately with male and female busts. D 2·8.

The portraits on this ring are almost identical with those on a less elaborate marriage-ring in the Dumbarton Oaks Collection, Washington DC. It has been suggested that such rings were at times made in pairs, one for the husband and one for the wife.
Bibliography: Dalton (1901), no. 207; Ross (1965), p. 50.
M & L AF304. Dimitri Collection; Franks Bequest, 1897.

436 △   ▽ 437

437 Marriage-Ring Byzantine 7th century AD
Gold ring with octagonal hoop and lobed bezel. On the bezel are engraved the figures of Christ and the Virgin blessing the bridegroom and bride respectively, beneath a Greek inscription which may be deciphered as reading 'Concord'. On the seven free faces of the hoop are engraved scenes from the Life of Christ. These, together with the scene on the bezel, were originally filled with niello work. D 1·6; D (of bezel) 1·2.

This ring is closely related in type to two others, one in the Dumbarton Oaks Collection, Washington DC, and the other in the Museo Nazionale Archeologico at Palermo from the ruins of a Byzantine bath at Syracuse. The latter has been associated with the Emperor Constans II (641–68), who was killed in the baths of Daphne at Syracuse.

Bibliography: Dalton (1901), no. 129; Ross (1965), pp. 58–9.

M & L AF231. Franks Bequest, 1897.

438 Finger-Ring English early 15th century AD
From Godstow Nunnery, near Oxford.

Gold; broad hoop, formerly enamelled, the outside chased with flowers and foliage surrounding three lozenges in which are engraved the Trinity, the Virgin and Child, and a male saint. In the interior is engraved the Legend: 'Most in mynd and in myn herrt/Lothest from you ferto departt'. D 1·9; W (of hoop) 1·1.

This ring was evidently a love-ring, although the ornament is more iconographic in style. It was long described as 'Fair Rosamond's ring'.

Bibliography: Dalton (1912), no. 962; *Arch. Journ.*, XX, p. 195; *Cat. of Antiquities, etc. exhibited in Ironmongers' Hall, 1869*, ii, p. 487.

M & L AF1075. Franks Bequest, 1897.

439 Finger-Ring Italian 15th century AD
Gold; the hoop expanding to the shoulders which bear the legend: 'Lorenso * a Lena Lena' enamelled in black; quatrefoil bezel set with a crystal of diamond. D 1·8.

Bibliography: Dalton (1912), no. 984.

M & L AF1090. Franks Bequest, 1897 (formerly in the Castellani Collection).

440 Two Finger-Rings German 16th century AD
(a) Gold; gimmel ring, enamelled, the bezel in the form of quatrefoil, the leaves enamelled in black, blue, and white, set with a ruby and an emerald; the shoulders moulded with scrolls, also enamelled. On the inner surfaces, when the ring is opened, the enamelled inscription: WAS GOT ZV/SAMEN FIEGT DAS SOL DER MENSCH NIT SCHAIDEN. D 2·3.
(b) Another similar ring set with a ruby and an aquamarine; the legend: QUOD DEUS CONJUNXIT HOMO NON SEPARET. D 2·3.
This type of interlocking ring is composed of two elements which cannot be separated, thus confirming the legend.

A ring of this symbolic type bearing the same legend as (b), the wedding-ring of Sir Thomas Gresham (1519?–79), is in the Victoria and Albert Museum.

Bibliography: Dalton (1912), nos. 991, 992; W. Jones,

Finger-ring Lore (London, 1877), p. 319.

M & L AF1096, AF1097. Franks Bequest, 1897. Formerly in the Braybrooke Collection.

441 Two Finger-Rings English (?)
18th century AD
(a) Gold; puzzle *fede*-ring; fine hoops interlacing at the back, two faceted alternating with three engraved with floral scroll work; all are held together in front by the applied ornament of two hands clasped over a heart. D 2·6.
(b) Another similar of seven interlacing hoops; the two outer ones plain. D 2·7.

Bibliography: Dalton, (1912), nos. 1072, 1075.

M & L AF1155, AF1158. Franks Bequest, 1897.

442 Finger-Ring French 18th century AD
Gold; slender hoop; large oval bezel bordered with pearls alternating with gold bosses and containing under glass (?) a white plaque painted in brown with two hearts on which stand two doves supporting a crown; below, a wreath; above, the legend: L'AMOUR NOUS UNIT. D 2·0; L (of bezel) 1·3.

Bibliography: Dalton (1912), no. 1000.

M & L AF1105. Franks Bequest, 1897.

443 Finger-Ring German 16th century AD
Gold; the hoop a broad band with cabled borders, having on the outside five bosses of filigree ornamented. with pellets, between the bosses enamelled ornament in blue and green with four loops enamelled in apple-green on each side of the bezel, which is a pyramidal gable with enamelled imbrications in dark blue hinged to reveal on its gold base-plate the initial letters of the words 'Mazzāl tōb'. D 3·0; H (of bezel) 1·4.

The engraved legend signifies 'Good luck', and the projecting building most probably represents the synagogue. This large type of Jewish marriage-ring was only worn during the wedding ceremony when the bridegroom placed it upon the middle finger of the bride's right hand.

Bibliography: Dalton (1912), no. 1339.

M & L AF1417. Franks Bequest, 1897.

444 Finger-Ring German (?) late 16th century AD
Gold; with high twisted borders. The broad hoop has, in openwork applied to a silver ground, the Creation of Eve, the Fall, and the Expulsion from Eden, with the sun, the moon, and various animals, the whole enriched with blue, green and white enamels. D 2·5; W (of hoop) 2·1.

See no. 443 for note regarding Jewish wedding-rings.

Bibliography: Dalton (1912), no. 1331.

M & L AF1411, Franks Bequest, 1897.

Mourning and Commemorative Rings

Since the fourteenth century – and probably even earlier – the practice of wearing rings as a memento of a deceased relative or friend has existed. These rings are usually easily recognized by the wording of the inscriptions, but there remains great uncertainty about the classification of two remarkable early Anglo-Saxon rings with royal associations.

The beautiful gold ring inlaid with niello and decorated with the *Agnus Dei* flanked by the letters, 'A D' (no. 446) is inscribed on the inner face of the hoop: EAÐELSVIÐ REGNA. This name has been identified as Queen Ethelswith of Mercia (853–89), sister of Alfred the Great. It was ploughed up in 1870 at Aberford, near Sherburn, in Yorkshire, but nothing of its earlier history is known.

Similarly, the exceptional gold ring with a mitre-shaped bezel decorated with a nielloed design of peacocks and the personal name: '+ ETHELVVLF R.' has been associated with King Aethelwulf of Wessex, the father of Alfred the Great and Ethelswith. The purpose of the ring, perhaps commemorative, remains conjectural. This ring (no. 445) was found in 1780 in a cart-track between Laverstock and Salisbury, and was given to the Museum in 1829 by the Earl of Radnor.

A particularly interesting group of commemorative rings were worn by the adherents of the royal house of Stuart and these 'Jacobite' rings usually have set in the bezel a portrait of one of the Stuart kings – Charles I (the Martyr), Charles II, James II or the Old Pretender.

More often rings in this category are of a highly personal character and it may be supposed, for example, that the extremely fine gold enamelled finger-ring set with a ruby cameo portrait of Madame de Maintenon (no. 396) was a very special commission. The hoop has enamelled pierced shoulders in the form of fleur-de-lis and the style suggests that it may have been made soon after her death in 1719.

The fashion for mourning rings began to fade during the second half of the nineteenth century, largely because it had become thoroughly debased and universal. The cheap versions, mass-produced in centres like Birmingham, often designed to hold an imperfect photograph in the bezel, represent the last phase in the story.

H.T.

445 Finger-Ring Anglo-Saxon 9th century AD
Found in a cart-rut between Laverstock and Salisbury in 1780, the ring passed afterwards into the possession of the Earl of Radnor.

Gold ring with mitre-shaped bezel, inlaid with niello in a design of peacocks, and with the inscription: +ETHELVVLF R. D (maximum) 2·8.

The ring is probably to be associated with King Æthelwulf of Wessex, father of Alfred the Great and of Queen Ethelswith of Mercia (see no. 446).
Bibliography: Dalton (1912), no. 179; Wilson (1964), pp. 22–9, 141–2, pl. XIX(31).
M & L 1829.11–14.1. Given by the Earl of Radnor, 1829.

445

446,447,451

446 Finger-Ring Anglo-Saxon 9th century AD
Ploughed up in 1870 at Aberford, near Sherburn, West Yorkshire.

Gold ring inlaid with niello, with the *Agnus Dei* flanked by the letters AD, and incised on the inner face of the hoop with the words EAÐELSVIÐ REGNA. D 2·6.

The name on the ring may be identified as that of Queen Ethelswith of Mercia (853–89), sister of Alfred the Great. With King Æthelwulf's ring (no. 445), it is a remarkable instance of an object with clear royal associations at this period. The ring passed into the possession of the well-known northern antiquary, Canon Greenwell, and thence to Sir A. W. Franks.
Bibliography: Dalton (1912), no. 180; Wilson (1964), pp. 117–19, pl. XI(i).
M & L AF458. Franks Bequest, 1897.

Colour plate 10

447 Finger-Ring English 17th century AD
Gold; the hoop engraved with a wreath on a ground of black enamel; oval box bezel with a rosette on the underside, and a band of ovals around the side enamelled in black and white set with a miniature portrait of Charles I (executed in 1649), in enamel on a blue ground. D 2·0; L (of bezel) 1·5.
Bibliography: Dalton (1912), no. 1363.
M & L AF1437. Franks Bequest, 1897.

448 Finger-Ring English early 18th century AD
Gold; oval bezel containing, under glass faceted round the edges, a profile portrait of Queen Anne (d. 1714), embossed in gold foil, on a ground of black hair, flanked on each shoulder by a square setting containing a diamond. D 2·0; L (of bezel) 1·1.
Bibliography: Dalton (1912), no. 1379.
M & L AF1453. Franks Bequest, 1897.

449 Finger-Ring Portuguese early 19th century AD
Silver gilt; slender hoop, the shoulders in the form of leaves where they meet the underside of the large oval bezel, engraved at the back with sprigs down the sides, and set with a cameo portrait of Maria I, Queen of Portugal (d. 1816). In porcelain, surrounded by a border of crystal pastes. D 1·9. L (of bezel) 2·6.
Bibliography: Dalton (1912), no. 1392; Sir A. W. Franks, *Catalogue of a Collection of Continental Porcelain* (1896), no. 511.
M & L AF1466. Franks Bequest, 1897.

450 Finger-Ring English early 19th century AD
Gold; the hoop channelled at the shoulders. Large oval bezel, set with a cameo bust of King George III

(d. 1820), facing to right, in white glass-paste on a blue ground, probably by William Tassie (1777–1860), nephew of James Tassie. D 2·1; L (of bezel) 2·3.
Bibliography: Dalton (1912), no. 1385.
M & L AF1459. Franks Bequest, 1897.

451 Finger-Ring English early 19th century AD
Gold; small oval bezel set with onyx cameo of an urn; round the broad hoop on a ground of black enamel in filigree between chain borders, a royal crown, twice repeated, with supporters lions crowned rampant, and monogram of the letters L R, three times repeated, two more lions crowned rampant flank the bezel; on the back of the bezel is engraved: 'GIII Obt. 1820'. D 2·8; W (of hoop) 0·9.
Bibliography: Dalton (1912), no 1437.
M & L AF1509. Franks Bequest, 1897.

452 Finger-Ring English 17th century AD
Gold; the bezel contains an irregular pearl ('baroque pearl'); the inside of the plain hoop is engraved: 'None can prevent the Lord's intent', and the underside of the bezel with the name and date of death of a man whose name can no longer be fully discerned. D 2·0.
Bibliography: Dalton (1912), no. 1437.
M & L AF1528. Franks Bequest, 1897.

453 Finger-Ring English AD 1773
Gold; oval bezel containing a skull and crossbones in black and white enamel on plaited hair under glass surrounded by diamonds; shoulders ornamented with skulls and crossbones reserved on a ground of black enamel, rest of hoop formerly enamelled. On back of bezel is engraved the inscription: 'H.G. the D. of Kingston ob. 23. Sep. 1773. Aet 62. Not lost, but gone before'. D 1·7; L (of bezel) 1·4.

Sir Evelyn Pierrepont, 2nd Duke, KG (1711–73), raised a regiment of horse to oppose the Jacobites in 1745, and was nominated Lieutenant-General in 1759.
Bibliography: Dalton (1912), no. 1443.
M & L AF1514. Franks Bequest, 1897.

454 Finger-Ring English about AD 1788
Gold; slender hoop chased with simple floral and geometric ornament on the shoulders; very large marquise bezel containing beneath a convex glass urn in high relief enamelled gold, white and blue on a white ground, inscribed: IN MEMORY OF A FRIEND; surrounded by a border of black enamel with the inscription reserved in gold: WILL-M HANDLEY. ESQ: OB: 11. MAR: 1788. Æ: 69. D 2·4; L (of bezel) 3·2.
Bibliography: Dalton (1912), no. 1651.
M & L AF1720. Franks Bequest, 1897.

Amuletic Rings

This enormous and complex category has been touched upon briefly in the section dealing with amuletic jewellery, where a few finger-rings have been included. The belief that the wearing of certain kinds of rings would protect the wearer remained strong throughout the centuries, be it because of the inscription or figure engraved on the ring, or the kind of stone or substance set in the bezel, or, occasionally, the holy relic it contained. It was probably not until the end of the seventeenth century that these beliefs began to be abandoned, though even today some gem-stones are still associated with their supposedly good- or ill-luck properties.

The Decorative Ring

Probably as long as man has adorned himself with jewellery, he has worn rings on his fingers. Certainly, on the hands of Queen Pu-abi, as she was placed in her grave at about 2500 BC, there were ten rings (no. 455). The gold band, remaining the same width all the way round, is decorated with a scale-pattern of 'cloisons' which are inlayed with lapis-lazuli cut to the shape of the cells.

These ten Sumerian royal rings would seem to have been decorative and, of course, every country and every age has produced endless variations. Decorative rings, literally in their hundreds, are preserved in the Museum and no more than a comment or two can be made on a few early examples.

The simple Mycenaean gold ring, which was found in Rhodes (no. 456), dates from the fourteenth century BC and its oval bezel can be compared with a contemporary mould (excavated at Enkomi, Cyprus), which is part of a three-piece steatite mould for a finger-ring with a similarly shaped bezel.

In Northern Europe in the Middle Bronze Age (about 1300–1200 BC) an equally simple form of finger-ring was being made with three or four coils, tapered towards the ends and giving a rather tubular effect. Like the example found in a mound at Hollingbury Hill, Brighton, Sussex, in 1825 (no. 457), all those so far found in Britain have come from south-east England.

Thereafter, the evolution of the decorative finger-ring demonstrates the versatility and ingenuity of craftsmen, who continued to introduce into their designs a seemingly endless variety. The Persian goldsmith who around 400 BC made the gold ring in the Oxus Treasure (no. 109f), created one of the most highly stylized animal designs for the bezel of a finger-ring, whereas the Celtic La Tène craftsmen who were making silver finger-rings of a rudimentary form of U-shaped type (no. 458) in Switzerland were probably active about a century later.

Skilful use of natural phenomena, particularly the inexhaustible supply of gem-stones of various hues and patterns, proved especially rewarding, and the massive Roman gold ring from Tarvis, in Illyria (no. 459) is an exceptionally handsome example of good design, uniting a simple but highly polished sardonyx with a rich but uncluttered gold setting.

An even greater simplicity of design, in which the weighty treatment of the gold balances the strength of the penetrating colour of the sapphire, can be seen in a number of English stirrup-shaped rings dating from around 1200 AD, of which the finest is perhaps the one found at Wittersham, Kent (no. 462).

More usually, the decorative ring has been designed to excite amazement on account of its intricacy and technical brilliance and in so far as the goldsmith has been following fashion rather than creating it, the decorative ring through the ages may be said to reflect an aspect of the society in which it was worn.
H.T.

455 Finger-Ring Sumerian about 2500 BC
Ur, Iraq.

Gold ring decorated with scale-shaped lapis-lazuli inlay in gold cloisons. D 2·38.

This was one of ten rings worn on the hands of Queen Pu-abi. While finger-rings occur both in the Ur graves and subsequently elsewhere in Western Asia, they play a relatively minor part in the history of jewellery there before the invention of the signet-ring.
Bibliography: Woolley (1934), p. 88 (part of U10950); Maxwell-Hyslop (1971), p. 14.
WAA 121378.

456 Finger-Ring Mycenaean 14th century BC
Found in Rhodes.
Gold, with oval bezel at right-angles to hoop.
H (bezel) 2·1.

The bezel is similar to that produced by casting from the steatite mould (G & R 1897.4–1.1422) from Enkomi, Cyprus; this three-piece mould is approximately the same date as this gold ring.
G & R 1929.4–17.1.
Colour plate 10

457 Finger-Ring Southern British Middle Bronze Age 13th century BC
Found in a mound at Hollingbury Hill, Brighton, Sussex in 1825.

Bronze; four-coil ring, tapered at ends, with chased

nicks along one edge; of wrought metal. H 1·9; D 2·7; WT 31·1.

One of three coiled finger-rings found with a hoard of bronzes including 'Sussex loop' arm-rings; a type only found in south-eastern England in the 'Ornament Horizon' of the Middle Bronze Age. Similar rings occur in contemporary Northern Europe, where the type may have originated.
Bibliography: *Archaeological Journal* 5 (1848), pp. 323–5; Kemble, Latham and Franks (1863), p. 200, pl. xxv.4; Curwen (1937), pp. 218–19, Table 1, no. 5; Brown and Blin-Stoyle (1959), p. 203; Smith (1959), p. 153.
P & RB 53.4–12.15.

455

458 Finger-Ring Swiss about 3rd century BC
Early La Tène
Excavated on an Iron Age settlement on Park Brow, near Worthing, Sussex, England.

Silver wire oval ring bent to a U-shape. 1·8 by 1·8 by 1·8; WT 2·4.

Since this type of ring is predominantly found in Switzerland, it is likely that this specimen, the only known one from Britain, was imported from there. In Switzerland such rings belong to phase 1c of the La Tène period, as worked out by Wiedmer and Viollier. Objects of silver were very rare in Britain before the first century BC.
Bibliography: Wolseley, Smith and Hawley (1927), pp. 19–20, fig. J; Hodson (1962), pp. 146, 150; Hodson (1964), p. 135.
P & RB 1926.3–13.12.

457

459 Finger-Ring Roman 3rd century AD
Said to be from Tarvis in Illyria.

Gold ring of massive proportions, set with plain sardonyx. D 4·0.
Bibliography: BMCR, 802.
G & R 802F. Franks Bequest, 1897.

Colour plate 10

458 △   ▽ 459

460 Finger-Ring Anglo-Saxon 8th–9th century AD
Found in the River Nene at Peterborough, Northamptonshire.

Gold ring with a flat roundel on either side of the hoop, flanked by bead clusters. The outer face of one roundel is engraved with an 'endless knot' design centring on a cross, the other with a pattern of double-contoured interlacing triangles. The outer face of the hoop is decorated with linear interlace. All the incised decoration is inlaid with niello. D 2·7.

This unusual ring has no close parallel. The motifs

on the two roundels share an ambiguity and indivisibility of pattern which suggests that they probably had some unknown further significance for the wearer. It is perhaps worth noting in this context, that an 'endless knot' formed from a pentacle (itself a figure based on three triangles) was in later medieval times seen as a potent symbol of the Trinity. The three-triangle pattern seen on the River Nene ring also occurs on a group of Swedish carved stones of the Viking period, and is sometimes thought to be a symbol associated with Odin.

Bibliography: Wilson (1964), pp. 56, 158–9, pl. XXVII. M & L 55.11–15.1.

461 Finger-Ring Viking 11th century AD
Found near Waterford, Ireland.

Gold ring of twisted wire. D 3·05.
Bibliography: J. Bøe, *Norse Antiquities in Ireland* (*Viking Antiquities in Great Britain and Ireland*, ed. H. Shetelig, Part III) (Oslo, 1940), p. 105, fig. 72.
M & L 49.3–1.20.

461

462 Finger-Ring English about AD 1200
Found at Wittersham, Kent.

Gold with massive stirrup-shaped hoop containing a sapphire at the bezel. D 3·7.

This is an extremely fine example of the stirrup-shaped type of decorative ring. The type was already in use in England in the middle of the twelfth century since one was found in the grave in Chichester Cathedral attributed to Bishop Hilary (d. 1169).
Bibliography: Dalton (1912), no. 1782; Oman (1974) pl. 15D.
M & L 85.6–15.1. Bequeathed by the Revd E. H. Mainwaring Sladen, 1885.

462

Colour plate 10

463 Six Finger-Rings English 12th century AD
Found wrapped in cloth at Lark Hill near Worcester in 1854 together with coins of Henry II.

Silver; three have rectangular bezels and are set with (a) crystal, (b) amethyst, (c) yellow paste; (d) has long rectangular bezel divided into three panels decorated with niello; (e) formed of two twisted silver wires; (f) has bezel in form of clasped hands.

The hoard was probably deposited in *c.* 1180 and so the rings date from the middle or latter half of the twelfth century.
Bibliography: *Archaeologia* XXXVI, pl. XVII, fig. 4; Dalton (1912), nos. 1743, 1744, 1745, 1740, 1025 and 1741; J. D. A. Thompson, *Inventory of British Coin*

Hoards, 1956, no. 381; Oman (1974), 14D.
M & L 54.8–20.1–6.

464 Finger-Ring Persia 11th–12th centuries AD
Persia.
Gold filigree enhanced with granulation. High bezel with concave sides curving outwards to shoulders: hoop triangular in section. Face inscribed with name *'Uthmān'* in Kufic characters within guilloche border, bezel and hoop decorated with foliate scrolls. H 3·0; W 2·3.
OA 1954.4–12.1. Given by P. T. Brooke Sewell, Esq.

464

465 Finger-Rings Javanese
Mojopahit period, about AD 1293–1520; or perhaps later.
(a) Hollow gold ring decorated at the shoulders by pearled transverse ribs making three sections; bezel a lozenge shaped setting with a crystal mounted *en cabochon*. D 3·0; WT 222.
Bibliography: Dalton (1912), p. 338, no. 2441.
OA 2441/AF2392. Franks Bequest, 1897.
(b) Gold, with the hoop decorated with chased scrolling, the broader bezel likewise in very high relief. D 3·5; WT 695.
Bibliography: Dalton (1912), p. 339, no. 2451.
OA 2451/AF2402. Franks Bequest, 1897.
(c) Gold, plain hoop, shoulder chased with foliage; bezel a plain bud set in a double row of lotus leaves. D 3·0; WT 518.
Bibliography: Dalton (1912), p. 340, no. 2452, pl. xxx.
OA 2452/AF2403. Franks Bequest, 1897.

466 Finger-Ring Mixtec AD 1000–1500
Gold *cire-perdue* cast ring with feline head, flanked by serpent heads and geometrical designs. D 2·0; H 1·0.

Although finger-rings are not common in Pre-Columbian America, the Mixtec did produce some very fine ones including some with attached pendants. Many of the designs are in false filigree work such as the one shown here.
Bibliography: Emmerich (1965); T. A. Joyce, *Mexican Archaeology* (London 1914); Saville (1920).
ETH 1914.3–28.1. Given by Miss Thornton.

466

465c,b,a

Select Glossary

Ajouré work *see* Openwork.

Annealing Removing the brittleness of worked metal by reheating.

Bicone beads Beads in which the profile is convex, acute- or obtuse-angled; when convexed the curved or angled profile meets the perforation; in truncated convex bicones the curved or angled profile does not meet the perforation and the bead has two flat ends.

Bracteate Sheet metal disc whose main decoration is executed in repoussé. Often suspended by means of a cylindrical attachment and worn as a pendant.

Bulla A gold pendant of Etruscan origin, worn as an amulet.

Cabochon A precious or semi-precious stone when merely polished, without being cut into facets.

Champlevé A variety of inlaid work in which the inlays are fixed into channels carved, or occasionally cast, into the metal background.

Chasing Technique of working metal from the front so that the pattern is indented in the surface.

Chip-carving Deeply cut designs, often geometric, deriving much effect from the interplay of light and shadow on their angled surfaces, the latter being frequently gilded.

Cire-perdue The 'lost-wax' process of casting: a wax or wax-coated model is imbedded in clay which is then baked so that the wax melts and is lost, leaving a mould into which molten metal can be poured. The mould has to be broken to retrieve the object.

Cloisonné A variety of inlaid work in which the inlays are fixed into a network of cells or cloisons formed by thin strips of metal which are themselves soldered to a base-plate or flat sheet of metal backing.

Electrum An alloy of gold and silver.

Embossing *see* Repoussé.

Enamel A coloured glass fused on to a metallic base.

Engraving Technique of cutting patterns in a surface with a sharp tool.

Faience a) Conventionally used for ancient glazed compositions with a quartz base; b) in Europe after the medieval period, used to describe tin-glazed pottery.

Fibula A brooch of safety-pin form, often made of bronze.

Filigree A decorative pattern made of wires, usually soldered to a background but occasionally left as openwork.

Gadroons A decoration consisting of joined arcs or curves.

Granulation Decoration consisting of minute balls or grains of metal soldered to a background.

Huang An arc-shaped pendant of ritual significance in China.

Inlay Shaped pieces of material, usually stones, glazed composition or glass, fixed into the surface of another material, usually metal, to give a polychrome effect.

Ju-I A fungus which was thought to confer immortality.

Loop-in-loop chain A type of chain made by folding oval links of metal in half, and hooking them through one another.

'Lost-wax process' *see* Cire-perdue.

Lunula A crescent-shaped sheet of gold.

Millefiori glass insets Multi-coloured glass insets in chequerboard pattern. Formed by fusing together glass rods of different colours and cutting slices across the section.

Niello A black composition consisting of metallic alloys used to fill in engraved designs on silver or other metals.

Obsidian A natural glass, generally black, found in volcanic regions.

Openwork (or ajouré) Any variety of open pattern, such as one formed by cutting holes through a piece of sheet metal.

Opus interrasile Patterns made in sheet gold by cutting out portions of the metal with a chisel.

Palstave A form of European Bronze Age axe with side flanges, stop-ridge, and sometimes one or two loops attached.

Pectoral A form of ornament worn on the chest.

Penannular brooch Discontinuous, ring-shaped brooch with two terminals which are often flattened and highly decorative.

Repoussé (or embossing) Technique of working sheet-metal from behind with punches to raise the pattern which stands out in relief on the front.

Runes Characters composing the earliest Teutonic alphabet.

Spacer A bead or bar pierced at intervals and threaded so as to ensure that multiple strings of beads remain correctly spaced in relation to one another.

Terminal bead A kind of spacer positioned at the end of a multiple string of beads, often semicircular in shape, and perforated both along its straight edge to take the ends of the strings and also along its rounded edge for the tie-strings.

Bibliography

AE: *Ancient Egypt* (London).

ALDRED (1971): C. Aldred, *Jewels of the Pharaohs* (London, 1971).

ALLEN (1961): D. F. Allen, The Origins of Coinage in Britain, in S.S. Frere (ed), *Problems of the Iron Age in Southern Britain*, University of London Institute of Archaeology Occasional Paper no. 11 (London, 1961).

ALLEN (1904): J. R. Allen, *Celtic Art in Pagan and Christian Times* (London, 1904).

ALMAGRO GORBEA (1962): J. Almagro Gorbea, 'Dos nuevos torques de oro, de tipo gallego, ingresados en el Museo Británico', *Ampurias* 24 (1962).

ARMSTRONG (1917): E. C. R. Armstrong, 'The great Clare find of 1854', *Journal of the Royal Society of Antiquaries of Ireland*, 47 (1917).

ARMSTRONG (1933): E. C. R. Armstrong, *Catalogue of Irish Gold Ornaments in the Collection of the Royal Irish Academy*, second edition (Dublin, 1933).

ARSANDAUX and RIVET (1920): H. Arsandaux and P. Rivet, 'Contribution a l'étude de la métallurgie Mexicaine', in *Journal de la Societé des Americanistes de Paris*, nouvelle série, XII (Paris, 1920).

AYERS and RAWSON (1975): J. Ayers and J. Rawson, *Chinese Jade throughout the Ages: Catalogue of an exhibition held at the Victoria and Albert Museum* (London, 1975).

BALTIMORE (1947): *Early Christian and Byzantine Art, The Walters Art Gallery* (Baltimore, 1947).

BARNETT (1940): R. D. Barnett, 'Hebrew, Palmyrene and Hittite Antiquities', *BMQ* 14 (1940).

BARNETT (1960): R. D. Barnett, 'Ancient Oriental Goldwork', *BMQ* 22 (1960).

BARNETT (1963): R. D. Barnett, 'A review of acquisitions 1955–62 of Western Asiatic Antiquities (I)', *BMQ* 26 (1963).

BARNETT (1968): R. D. Barnett, 'The Art of Bactria and the Treasure of the Oxus', *Iranica Antiqua* VIII (1968).

BARNETT and CURTIS (1973): R. D. Barnett and J. E. Curtis, 'A review of acquisitions 1963–70 of Western Asiatic Antiquities', *BMQ* 37 (1973).

BAUDOU (1960): E. Baudou, *Regionale und chronologische Einteilung der jüngeren Bronzezeit im nordischen Kreis* (Stockholm, 1960).

BECK (1931): H. C. Beck, 'Beads from Nineveh', *Antiquity* V (1931).

BERNAL (1965): I. Bernal, 'Archaeological Synthesis of Oaxaca', in G. R. Willey (ed.), *Handbook of Middle American Indians*, III (Austin, 1965).

BERNAL (1969): I. Bernal, *The Olmec World* (Berkeley, California, 1969).

BIRCH (1846): S. Birch, 'On the Torc of the Celts', *The Archaeological Journal* III (1846).

BIVAR (1969): A. D. H. Bivar, *Catalogue of the Western Asiatic Seals in the British Museum: Stamp Seals II: the Sassanian Dynasty* (London, 1969).

BIVAR (1971): A. D. H. Bivar, 'A hoard of ingot-currency of the Median Period from Nūsh-i Jān, near Malayir', *Iran* IX (1971).

BOON and SAVORY (1975): G. C. Boon and H. N. Savory, 'A Silver Trumpet-Brooch with Relief Decoration, Parcel-Gilt, from Carmarthen, and a Note on the Development of the Type', *The Antiquaries Journal* 55 (1975).

BRADLEY (1971): R. Bradley, 'Stock Raising and the Origins of the Hill Fort on the South Downs', *The Antiquaries Journal* 51 (1971).

BRAILSFORD (1953): J. W. Brailsford, *Later Prehistoric Antiquities of the British Isles* (London, 1953).

BRAILSFORD (1964): J. W. Brailsford, *Guide to the Antiquities of Roman Britain,* third edition (London, 1964).

BRAILSFORD and STAPLEY (1972): J. W. Brailsford and J. E. Stapley, 'The Ipswich Torcs', *Proceedings of the Prehistoric Society* 38 (1972).

BRAILSFORD (1975): J. W. Brailsford, *Early Celtic Masterpieces from Britain in the British Museum* (London, 1975).

BRAY (1971): W. Bray, 'Ancient American Metalsmiths', in *Proceedings of the Royal Anthropological Institute of Great Britain and Ireland for 1970* (London, 1971).

BRAY (1974): W. Bray, 'Gold Working in Ancient America' and 'The Organization of the Metal Trade', in *El Dorado/The Gold of Ancient Colombia* (Bogotá, 1974).

BMC Gems: H. B. Walters, *Catalogue of the Engraved Gems and Cameos, Greek, Etruscan, and Roman, in the British Museum* (London, 1926).

BMCJ: F. H. Marshall, *Catalogue of the Jewellery, Greek, Etruscan, and Roman, in the Departments of Antiquities, British Museum* (London, 1911).

BMCR: F. H. Marshall, *Catalogue of the Finger Rings, Greek, Etruscan, and Roman, in the Departments of Antiquities, British Museum* (London, 1907).

BM Guide (1874): *Synopsis of the contents of the British Museum. Department of Oriental Antiquities: Egyptian Galleries. Vestibule* (London, 1874).

BM Guide (1879): *Synopsis of the contents of the British Museum. Department of Oriental Antiquities: First and Second Egyptian Rooms* (London, 1879).

BM Guide (1904): *British Museum. A Guide to the Third and Fourth Egyptian Rooms* (London, 1904).

BM Guide (1922): *British Museum. A Guide to the Fourth, Fifth and Sixth Egyptian Rooms and Coptic Room* (London, 1922).

BM Guide (1924): *British Museum. A Guide to the Medieval Antiquities and Objects of Later Date* (London, 1924).

BM Guide (1964): *British Museum. A General Introductory Guide to the Egyptian Collections in the British Museum* (London, 1964).

BMQ: *British Museum Quarterly* (London).

BROWN and BLIN-STOYLE (1959): M. A. Brown and A. E. Blin-Stoyle, 'A Sample Analysis of British Middle and Late Bronze Age Materials using Optical Spectrometry', *Proceedings of the Prehistoric Society* 25 (1959).

BRUNTON (1920): G. Brunton, *Lahun, I, the Treasure* (London, 1920).

BRUNTON and CATON-THOMPSON (1928): G. Brunton and G. Caton-Thompson, *The Badarian Civilisation* (London, 1928).

BRUNTON (1937): G. Brunton, *Mostagedda and the Tasian Culture. British Museum Expedition to Middle Egypt, First and Second Years, 1928, 1929* (London, 1937).

BRUNTON (1948): G. Brunton, *Matmar* (London, 1948).

BUDGE (1925): Sir E. A. Wallis Budge, *The Mummy, A Handbook of Egyptian Funerary Archaeology* (Cambridge, 1925).

BULMER (1938): W. Bulmer, 'Dragonesque Brooches and their Development', *The Antiquaries Journal* 18 (1938).

BURGESS (1974): C. Burgess, 'The bronze age', in C. Renfrew (ed.), *British Prehistory: A New Outline* (London, 1974).

BURNS (1971): J. Burns, 'Additional torcs from Snettisham', *Proceedings of the Prehistoric Society* 37, i (1971).

BUSHE-FOX (1949): J. P. Bushe-Fox, 'Fourth Report on the Excavations of the Roman Fort at Richborough, Kent',

Reports of the Research Committee of the Society of Antiquaries of London 16 (1949).

BUSHNELL (1963): G. H. S. Bushnell, *Peru* (London, 1963).

BUTLER (1963): J. J. Butler, 'Bronze Age Connections across the North Sea: A study in prehistoric trade and industrial relations between the British Isles, the Netherlands, North Germany and Scandinavia, *c*.1700–700 B.C.', *Palaeohistoria* 9 (1963).

CAH: *Cambridge Ancient History* (3rd edition, Cambridge, 1970–).

CALLANDER (1915–16): J. G. Callander, 'Notice of a jet necklace found in a cist in a Bronze Age cemetery, discovered on Burgie Lodge Farm, Morayshire, with notes on Scottish prehistoric jet ornaments', *Proceedings of the Society of Antiquaries of Scotland* 50 (1915–16).

CANBY (1965): J. V. Canby, 'Early bronze "trinket" moulds', *Iraq* XXVII (1965).

CASO (1965): A. Caso, 'Lapidary work, Goldwork and Copperwork from Oaxaca', in G. R. Willey (ed.), *Handbook of Middle American Indians* III (Austin, 1965).

CASPERS (1972): E. C. L. D. Caspers, 'Etched Cornelian Beads', *Bulletin of the Institute of Archaeology*, no. 10 (London 1972).

CHARLESWORTH (1961): D. Charlesworth, 'Roman Jewellery found in Northumberland and Durham', *Archaeologia Aeliana*, fourth series, 39 (1961).

Chung-kuo ko-hsüeh yüan k'ao-ku yen-chiu-so, *Lo-yang Chung-chou-lu* (Peking, 1959).

CLARKE (1954): R. R. Clarke, 'The Early Iron Age Treasure from Snettisham, Norfolk', *Proceedings of the Prehistoric Society* 20 (1954).

CLIFFORD SMITH (1908): H. Clifford Smith, *Jewellery* (London, 1908).

COE (1971): M. D. Coe, *The Maya* (London, 1971).

COLES (1959–60): J. M. Coles, 'Scottish Late Bronze Age Metalwork: Typology, Distributions and Chronology', *Proceedings of the Society of Antiquaries of Scotland* 93 (1959–60).

COLLINGWOOD (1930): R. G. Collingwood, 'Romano-Celtic Art in Northumbria', *Archaeologia* 80 (1930).

COONEY (1976): J. D. Cooney, *Catalogue of Egyptian Glass in the British Museum* (London, 1976).

CORDER and HAWKES (1940): P. Corder and C. F. C. Hawkes, 'A Panel of Celtic Ornament from Elmswell, East Yorkshire', *The Antiquaries Journal* 20 (1940).

COVARRUBIAS (1966): M. Covarrubias, *Indian Art of Mexico and Central America* (New York, 1966).

COWEN (1936): J. D. Cowen, 'An Inscribed Openwork Gold Ring from Corstopitum', *Archaeologia Aeliana,* fourth series, 13 (1936).

COWEN (1948): J. D. Cowen, The Corbridge Gold Ring: A Footnote', *Archaeologia Aeliana*, fourth series, 26 (1948).

CRAW (1928–9): J. H. Craw, 'On a Jet Necklace from a Cist at Poltalloch, Argyl', *Proceedings of the Society of Antiquaries of Scotland* 63 (1928–9).

CRAWFORD (1911–12): O. G. S. Crawford, 'Notes on a gold torc and a double two-looped palstave, *Proceedings of the Society of Antiquaries of London*, second series, 24 (1911–12).

CULICAN (1964): W. Culican, 'Spiral-end beads in Western Asia', *Iraq* XXVI (1964).

CURLE (1931–2): J. Curle, 'An Inventory of Objects of Roman and Provincial Roman Origin found on Sites in Scotland not definitely associated with Roman Constructions', *Proceedings of the Society of Antiquaries of Scotland* 66 (1931–2).

CURWEN (1932): E. C. Curwen, 'Excavations at Hollingbury Camp, Sussex', *The Antiquaries Journal* 12 (1932).

CURWEN (1937): E. C. Curwen, *The Archaeology of Sussex* (London, 1937).

DALTON (1901): O. M. Dalton, *Catalogue of Early Christian Antiquities in the British Museum* (London, 1901).

DALTON (1903–5): O. M. Dalton, 'On some brooches of cloisonné enamel in the British Museum', *Proceedings of the Society of Antiquaries* XX (1903–5).

DALTON (1904); O. M. Dalton, 'Some early brooches of cloisonné enamel in the British Museum', *Proceedings of the Society of Antiquaries*, 2nd series, XX (1903–5).

DALTON (1912): O. M. Dalton, *Catalogue of Finger Rings in the British Museum* (London, 1912).

DALTON (1915): O. M. Dalton, *Catalogue of the Engraved Gems of the Post-Classical Periods in the British Museum* (London, 1915).

DALTON (1925): O. M. Dalton, *Post Christian Art* (Oxford, 1925).

DALTON (1928): O. M. Dalton, 'A Scythic gold ornament', *BMQ* 2 (1928).

DALTON (1964): O. M. Dalton, *The Treasure of the Oxus* (London, 3rd edition, 1964).

DAVIES (1949): E. Davies, *The Prehistoric and Roman Remains of Flintshire* (Cardiff, 1949).

DIGBY (1972): A. Digby, *Maya Jades* (London, 1972).

EASBY (1968): E. K. Easby, *Pre-Columbian jade from Costa Rica* (New York, 1968).

Egypt Exploration Society, *Exhibition of Antiquities from Abydos and Tell el-Amarna 1925–6. Exhibited at the Rooms of the Society of Antiquaries, Burlington House. July 5th–24th, 1926* (London, 1926).

ELLIS (1849): H. Ellis, 'Account of a Gold Torquis found in Needwood Forest in Staffordshire, *Archaeologia* XXXIII (1849).

EMMERICH (1965): A. Emmerich, *Sweat of the Sun and Tears of the Moon* (Seattle, 1965).

EMRE (1971): K. Emre, *Anatolian Lead Figurines and their Stone Moulds* (Ankara, 1971).

ENGELBACH (1915): R. Engelbach, *Riqqeh and Memphis* VI (London, 1915).

EOGAN (1964): G. Eogan, 'The Later Bronze Age in Ireland in the light of recent research', *Proceedings of the Prehistoric Society* XXX (1964).

ETTLINGER (1973): E. Ettlinger, *Die römischen Fibeln in der Schweiz* (Bern, 1973).

EVANS (1921): Joan Evans, *English Jewellery from the Fifth Century A.D. to 1800* (London, 1921).

EVANS (1953): Joan Evans, *A History of Jewellery, 1100–1870* (London, 1953).

EVANS (1970): Joan Evans, *A History of Jewellery, 1100–1870* (London, 2nd edition, revised and reset, 1970).

FAVRET (1950): P. M. Favret, 'La nécropole gauloise de Villeseneux (canton de Vertus, Marne)', *Bulletin de la Société Préhistorique Française* XLVII (1950).

FEACHEM (1951): R. W. Feachem, 'Dragonesque Fibulae', *The Antiquaries Journal* 31 (1951).

FEUCHT-PUTZ (1967): E. Feucht-Putz, *Die Königlichen Pektorale. Motive, Sinngehalt und Zweck* (Bamberg, 1967).

FOSHAG (1951): W. F. Foshag, 'Mineralogical studies on Guatemalan jades', in *Smithsonian Miscellaneous Collection*, CXXXV, no. 5 (Washington, 1951).

FOSHAG and LESLIE (1955): W. F. Foshag and R. Leslie, 'Jadeite from Manzanal, Guatemala', *American Antiquity*, XXI (Salt Lake City, 1955).

Fox (1958): C. Fox, *Pattern and Purpose: A Survey of Early Celtic Art in Britain* (Cardiff, 1958).

FREY (1976): O. H. Frey, 'Du Premier Style au Style de Waldalgesheim: Remarques sur l'évolution de l'art celtique ancien', in P.-M. Duval and C. F. C. Hawkes, (eds.), *Celtic Art in Ancient Europe Five Protohistoric Centuries* (London, 1976).

FROEHNER (1897): W. Froehner, *La collection du château Colischan* (Paris, 1897).

GAGE (1836): J. Gage, 'A Letter . . . accompanying a Gold British Corselet . . .', *Archaeologia* XXVI (1836).

GAUTHIER (1972): M. M. Gauthier, *Emaux du moyen âge occidental* (Fribourg, 1972).

GHIRSHMAN (1950): R. Ghirshman, 'Notes iraniennes IV: le trésor de Sakkez, les origines de l'art mède, et les bronzes du Luristan', *Artibus Asiae* XIII (1950).

GODARD (1950): A. Godard, *Le trésor de Ziwiye* (Harlem, 1950).

GRJ: R. A. Higgins, *Greek and Roman Jewellery* (London, 1961).

GRIMES (1951): W. F. Grimes, *The Prehistory of Wales* (Cardiff, 1951).

GURE (1964): D. Gure, 'Selected Examples from the Jade Exhibition at Stockholm 1963: A Comparative Study', *Bulletin of the Museum of Far Eastern Antiquities* 36 (1964).

HALL (1913): H. R. Hall, *Catalogue of Egyptian Scarabs, etc. in the British Museum, vol. 1. Royal Scarabs* (London, 1913).

HANČAR (1934): F. Hančar, 'Kaukasus-Luristan', *Eurasia Septentrionalis Antiqua* IX (1934).

HANSFORD (1957): S. H. Hansford, *The Seligman Collection of Chinese Art*, I (London, 1957).

HARTMANN (1970): A. Hartmann *Prähistorische Goldfunde aus Europa: Spektralanalytische Untersuchungen und deren Auswertung* (Berlin, 1970).

HAWKES (1932): C. F. C. Hawkes, 'The Towednack Gold Hoard', *Man* 32 (1932).

HAWKES (1936): C. F. C. Hawkes, 'The Needwood Forest Torc', *BMQ* 11, i (1936).

HAWKES (1942): C. F. C. Hawkes, 'The Deverel Urn and the Picardy Pin: A Phase of Bronze Age Settlement in Kent', *Proceedings of the Prehistoric Society* VIII (1942).

HAWKES (1961): C. F. C. Hawkes, 'Gold Ear-rings of the Bronze Age, East and West', *Folklore* LXXII (1961).

HAWKES (1971): C. F. C. Hawkes, 'The Sintra Collar', *BMQ* 35 (1971).

HAWKES and CLARKE (1963): C. F. C. Hawkes and R. R. Clarke, 'Gahlstorf and Caister-on-Sea: Two Finds of Late Bronze Age Irish Gold', in I. L. Foster and L. Alcock (eds.), *Culture and Environment: Essays in Honour of Sir Cyril Fox* (London, 1963).

HAYES (1953, 1959): W. C. Hayes, *The Scepter of Egypt*, 2 vols. (Cambridge, Mass., 1953, 1959).

HEMMING (1970): J. Hemming, *The Conquest of the Incas* (London, 1970).

HENCKEN (1932): H. Hencken, *The Archaeology of Cornwall and Scilly* (London, 1932).

HENIG (1970): M. Henig, 'A new cameo from Lincolnshire', *The Antiquaries Journal* L (1970).

HENIG (1971): M. Henig, Review of Pfeiler (1970). *Britannia* II (1971).

HENIG (1974): M. Henig, 'A Corpus of Roman Engraved Gemstones from British Sites, *British Archaeological Reports* 8 (Oxford, 1974).

HERZFELD (1928): E. Herzfeld, 'The hoard of the Karen Pahlavs', *The Burlington Magazine*, 52, 298 (1928).

HILDBURGH (1922): W. L. Hildburgh, 'A Find of Ibero-Roman Silver at Cordova', *Archaeologia* LXXII (1922).

HODSON (1962): F. R. Hodson, 'Some Pottery from Eastbourne, the 'Marnians' and the Pre-Roman Iron Age in Southern England', *Proceedings of the Prehistoric Society* XXVIII (1962).

HODSON (1964): F. R. Hodson, 'La Tène Chronology, Continental and British, *Bulletin of the Institute of Archaeology University of London* IV (1964).

ILN: *Illustrated London News* (London).

IXTLILXOCHITL (1891–92): 'Fernando de Alva Ixtlilxochitl', *Obras históricas* (Mexico, 1891–2).

JACOBSTHAL (1944): P. Jacobsthal, *Early Celtic Art* (Oxford, 1944).

JARCE: *Journal of the American Research Center in Egypt* (Boston).

JEA: *Journal of Egyptian Archaeology* (London).

JENYNS (1951): R. S. Jenyns, *Chinese Archaic Jades in the British Museum* (London, 1951).

JENYNS and WATSON (1963): R. S. Jenyns and W. Watson, *Chinese Art, the Minor Arts*, I (London, 1963).

JETTMAR (1967): K. Jettmar, *The Art of the Steppes* (London, 1967).

JONES (1974): J. Jones, 'Gold and the New World' and 'Precolumbian Gold', in *El Dorado/The Gold of Ancient Colombia* (Bogotá, 1974).

JOPE (1961–2): E. M. Jope, 'Iron Age Brooches in Ireland: A Summary', *Ulster Journal of Archaeology*, third series, XXIV–XXV (1961–2).

JOPE (1971): E. M. Jope, 'The Waldalgesheim Master', in J. Boardman, M. A. Brown and T. G. E. Powell (eds.), *The European Community in Later Prehistory: Studies in honour of C. F. C. Hawkes* (London, 1971).

KEMBLE, LATHAM and FRANKS (1863): J. M. Kemble, R. G. Latham and A. W. Franks, *Horae Ferales; or, Studies in the Archaeology of the Northern Nations* (London, 1863).

KHIDASHELI (1972): M. Khidasheli, *A Contribution to the History of Bronze Decorative Work in Ancient Georgia* (in Georgian) (Tbilissi, 1972).

KIDDER and EKHOLM (1951): A. V. Kidder and G. F. Ekholm, 'Some Archaeological Specimens from Pomona, British Honduras', in *Notes on Middle American Archaeology and Ethnology*, no. 102, Carnegie Institution of Washington (Washington, 1951).

KITCHEN (1973): K. A. Kitchen, *The Third Intermediate Period in Egypt* (Warminster, 1973).

KRÄMER (1971): W. Krämer, 'Silberne Fibelpaare aus dem letzten vorchristlichen Jahrhundert'. *Germania* XLIX (1971).

LANDA (1941): Diego de Landa, *Relación de las cosas de Yucatan: a translation*, edited with notes by A. M. Tozzer (Cambridge, Mass., 1941).

LEEDS (1933): E. T. Leeds, 'Torcs of the Early Iron Age in Britain', *The Antiquaries Journal* XIII (1933).

LINS and ODDY (1975): P. A. Lins and W. A. Oddy, 'The Origins of Mercury Gilding', *Journal of Archaeological Science* II (1975).

Liverpool Annals: University of Liverpool, Annals of Archaeology and Anthropology.

LOFTUS (1857): W. K. Loftus, *Travels and Researches in Chaldaea and Susiana* (London, 1857).

London, Royal Academy (1936): London, Royal Academy, *International Exhibition of Chinese Art, Catalogue of an exhibition held at Burlington House* (London, 1935–6).

LÓPEZ CUEVILLAS (1951): F. López Cuevillas, *Las Joyas Castreñas* (Madrid, 1951).

MACGREGOR (1976): M. MacGregor, *Celtic Art in North Britain: a study of decorative metalwork from the third century B.C. to the third century A.D.* (Leicester, 1976).

MALLOWAN and ROSE (1935): M. E. L. Mallowan and J. C. Rose, 'Excavations at Tall Arpachiyah, 1933', *Iraq* II (1935).

MALLOWAN (1947): M. E. L. Mallowan, 'Excavations at Brak and Chagar Bazar', *Iraq* IX (1947).

MARSHALL (1907): F. H. Marshall, *Catalogue of the Finger Rings, Greek, Etruscan, and Roman, in the Departments of Antiquities, British Museum* (London, 1907). Also referred to as *BMCR*.

MARSHALL (1911): F. H. Marshall, *Catalogue of the Jewellery, Greek, Etruscan, and Roman, in the Departments of Antiquities, British Museum* (London, 1911). Also referred to as *BMCJ*.

MARYON (1938): H. Maryon, 'The Technical Methods of the Irish Smiths in the Bronze and Early Iron Ages', *Proceedings of the Royal Irish Academy* XLIV (1938).

MAXWELL-HYSLOP (1960): K. R. Maxwell-Hyslop, 'The Ur jewellery: a re-assessment in the light of some recent discoveries', *Iraq* XXII (1960).

MAXWELL-HYSLOP (1971): K. R. Maxwell-Hyslop, *Western Asiatic Jewellery, c.3000–612 B.C.* (London, 1971).

MEGAW (1965–6): J. V. S. Megaw, 'Two La Tène finger rings in the Victoria and Albert Museum, London: an essay on the human face and Early Celtic Art', *Praehistorische Zeitschrift* XLIII–XLIV (1965–6).

MEGAW (1970): J. V. S. Megaw, *Art of the European Iron Age: A study of the elusive image* (Bath, 1970).

MEGAW (1971): J. V. S. Megaw, 'An unpublished early La Tène Tierfibel from Hallstatt, Oberösterreich in the Naturhistorisches Museum, Vienna, *Archaeologia Austriaca*, L (1971).

MEGGERS (1966): B. J. Meggers, *Ecuador* (London, 1966).

MIFAO (1902–): *Mémoires publiés par les Membres de l'Institut français d'Archéologie orientale du Caire* (Cairo, 1902–).

MOOREY (1971): P. R. S. Moorey, *Catalogue of the Ancient Persian Bronzes in the Ashmolean Museum* (Oxford, 1971).

MOOREY (1974): P. R. S. Moorey, *Ancient Bronzes from Luristan* (London, 1974).

MOREL (1898): L. Morel, *Album de la Champagne souterraine: période gauloise d'avant la conquête romaine* (Reims, 1898).

MORLEY (1956): S. G. Morley, *The Ancient Maya*, third edition, revised by G. W. Brainerd (California, 1956).

MULLER (1972): Priscilla E. Muller, *Jewels in Spain* (New York, 1972).

NISSEN (1966): H. J. Nissen, *Zur Datierung des Königsfriedhofes von Ur* (Bonn, 1966).

OMAN (1974): C. Oman, *British Rings, 800–1914* (London, 1974).

OWLES (1969): E. Owles, 'The Ipswich Gold Torcs', *Antiquity* XLIII (1969).

PADDOCK (1966): J. Paddock (ed.), *Ancient Oaxaca* (Stanford, 1966).

Painter (1971): K. S. Painter, 'An Iron Age gold-alloy torc from Glascote, Tamworth, Staffs', *The Antiquaries Journal* 51 (1971).

PAINTER (1973): K. S. Painter, 'Four bronze belt-clasps from Georgia, U.S.S.R.', *The Antiquaries Journal* 53 (London, 1973).

PALMER (1967): J. Palmer, *Jade* (London, 1967).

PEET and WOOLLEY (1923): T. E. Peet and C. L. Woolley, *The City of Akhenaten*, I (London, 1923).

PELLIOT (1925): P. Pelliot, *Jades Archaiques de Chine appartenant a M.C.T. Loo* (Paris and Brussels, 1925).

PELTENBURG (1971): E. Peltenburg, 'Some early developments of vitreous materials', *World Archaeology*, 3, 1 (1971).

PENDLEBURY (1951): J. D. S. Pendlebury, *The City of Akhenaten*, III (London, 1951).

PÉREZ DE BARRADAS (1954): J. Pérez de Barradas, *Orfebreria Prehispanica de Colombia, Estilo Calima* (Madrid, 1954).

PÉREZ DE BARRADAS (1965): J. Pérez de Barradas, *Orfebreria Prehispanica de Colombia, Estilos Quimbaya y Otros* (Madrid, 1965).

PETRIE (1900): Sir W. M. F. Petrie, *Dendereh 1898* (London, 1900).

PETRIE (1901): Sir W. M. F. Petrie, *The Royal Tombs of the Earliest Dynasties* (London, 1901).

PETRIE (1914): Sir W. M. F. Petrie, *Amulets* (London, 1914).

PETRIE (1934): Sir W. M. F. Petrie, *Ancient Gaza*, IV (London, 1934).

PETRIE (1952): Sir W. M. F. Petrie, *City of Shepherd Kings* (London, 1952).

PFEILER (1970): B. Pfeiler, *Römischer Goldschmuck des ersten und zweiten Jahrhunderts n. Chr. nach datierten Funden* (Mainz, 1970).

PISANO (1974): G. Q. Pisano, *I Goielli Fenici di Tharros nel Museo Nazionale di Cagliari* (Roma, 1974).

PORADA (1967): E. Porada, 'Of deer, bells, and pomegranates', *Iranica Antiqua* VII (1967).

PORADA (1976): E. Porada, 'New Galleries at the British Museum', *Archaeology*, 29 (1976).

POWELL (1953): T. G. E. Powell, 'The Gold Ornament from Mold, Flintshire, North Wales', *Proceedings of the Prehistoric Society* XIX (1953).

POWELL (1966): T. G. E. Powell, *Prehistoric Art* (London, 1966).

PRIMAS (1970): M. Primas, Zur Verbreitung und Zeitstellung der Certosafibeln. *Jahrbuch des Römisch-Germanischen Zentralmuseums Mainz,* 14 for 1967 (1970).

PROUDFOOT (1955): V. B. Proudfoot, 'The Downpatrick Gold Find: A Hoard of Gold Objects from the Cathedral Hill, Downpatrick', *Archaeological Research Publications (Northern Ireland)* no. 3 (Belfast, 1955).

RADDATZ (1969): K. Raddatz, 'Die Schatzfunde der Iberischen Halbinsel vom Ende des dritten bis zur Mitte des ersten Jahrhunderts vor Chr. Geb.: Untersuchungen zur hispanischen Toreutik', *Madrider Forschungen* 5 (Berlin, 1969).

RASHLEIGH (1803): P. Rashleigh, 'Account of Antiquities discovered at Southfleet, in Kent', *Archaeologia* XIV (1803).

READ (1902): C. H. Read, *The Waddesdon Bequest* (London, 1902), revised by O. M. Dalton (London, 1927).

READ and SMITH (1916): C. H. Read and R. A. Smith, 'On a Collection of Antiquities from the Early Iron Age Cemetery of Hallstatt presented to the British Museum by Lord Avebury, 1916,' *Archaeologia* LXVII (1916).

REICHEL-DOLMATOFF (1965): G. Reichel-Dolmatoff, *Colombia* (London, 1965).

RIEFSTAHL (1968): E. Riefstahl, *Ancient Egyptian Glass and Glazes in the Brooklyn Museum* (New York, 1968).

RIVET (1924): P. Rivet, 'L'orfevrerie colombienne', *Proceedings of the Twenty-first International Congress of Americanists*, 1st part (The Hague, 1924).

ROBERTSON (1970): A. S. Robertson, 'Roman Finds from Non-Roman Sites in Scotland', *Britannia* I (1970).

ROOT (1961): W. C. Root, 'Pre-Columbian Metalwork of Colombia and its Neighbours', in S. K. Lothrop and others (eds.), *Essays in Pre-Columbian Art and Archaeology* (Cambridge, Mass., 1961).

ROSS (1965): M. C. Ross, *Catalogue of the Byzantine and Medieval Antiquities in the Dumbarton Oaks Collection,* II (Washington D.C., 1965).

ROWLANDS (1971): M. J. Rowlands, 'A group of Incised Decorated Armrings and their significance for the Middle Bronze Age of Southern Britain', *BMQ* 35 (1971).

SAHAGÚN (1950–59): Bernadino de Sahagún, *Florentine Codex: General History of the things of New Spain*, Trans. from the Aztec into English, with notes and illustrations, by A. J. O. Anderson and C. E. Dibble (Santa Fé, 1950–59).

Salt Collection (1835): Sotheby and Son, *Catalogue of Mr. Salt's Collection of Egyptian Antiquities, 28th June to 8th July, 1835* (London, 1835).

SANDARS (1968): N. K. Sandars, *Prehistoric Art in Europe* (Harmondsworth, 1968).

SAVILLE (1920): M. H. Saville, *The Goldsmith's Art in Ancient Mexico* (New York, 1920).

SAVORY (1958): H. N. Savory, 'The Late Bronze Age in Wales: Some New Discoveries and New Interpretations', *Archaeologia Cambrensis* CVII (1958).

SCHÜLE (1969): W. Schüle, 'Die Meseta-Kulturen der iberischen Halbinsel: Mediterrane und eurasische Elemente in frü-heisenzeitlichen Kulturen Südwest-europas', *Madrider Forschungen* III (Berlin, 1969).

SIEVEKING (1971): G. de G. Sieveking, 'Prehistoric and Roman Studies commemorating the opening of the Department of Prehistoric and Romano-British Antiquities, *BMQ* 35 (1971).

SIMPSON (1968): M. Simpson, 'Massive armlets in the North British Iron Age', in J. M. Coles and D. D. A. Simpson (eds.), *Studies in Ancient Europe: Essays presented to Stuart Piggott* (Leicester, 1968).

SMITH (1865): W. Smith, *Dictionary of Greek and Roman Antiquities,* second edition (London, 1865).

SMITH (1905): R. A. Smith, *A Guide to the Antiquities of the Early Iron Age of Central and Western Europe (including the British Late-Keltic Period) in the Department of British and Mediaeval Antiquities* (London, 1905).

SMITH (1907–9): R. A. Smith, 'Notes on a Romano-British hoard of bronze objects found on Lamberton Moor, Berwickshire', *Proceedings of the Society of Antiquaries of London,* second series, XX (1907–9).

SMITH (1920): R. A. Smith, *A Guide to the Antiquities of the Bronze Age in the Department of British and Mediaeval Antiquities,* second edition (London, 1920).

SMITH (1922): R. A. Smith, *A Guide to the Antiquities of Roman Britain in the Department of British and Mediaeval Antiquities* (London, 1922).

SMITH (1925): R. A. Smith, *A Guide to Antiquities of the Early Iron Age in the Department of British and Mediaeval Antiquities,* second edition (London, 1925).

SMITH (1930–1): R. A. Smith, 'Seventh century jewellery', *BMQ* 5 (1930–1).

SMITH (1931): R. A. Smith, 'A Celtic Gold Torc and Armlets', *BMQ* 5 (1931).

SMITH (1935): R. A. Smith, 'Relics of Londinium', *BMQ* 9 (1935).

SMITH (1936): R. A. Smith, 'Roman and Anglo-Saxon Jewellery', *BMQ* 10 (1936).

SMITH (1959): M. A. Smith, 'Some Somerset Hoards and their place in the Bronze Age of Southern Britain,' *Proceedings of the Prehistoric Society* XXV (1959).

SPRATLING (1973): M. G. Spratling, 'The Iron Age settlement of Gussage All Saints, part II. The bronze foundry', *Antiquity* XLVII (1973).

STEINGRÄBER (1957): E. Steingräber, *Antique jewellery* (London, 1957).

STEWARD (1946–50): J. H. Steward, (ed.), *Handbook of South American Indians* (Washington, 1946–50).

STEWART (1974): J. R. Stewart Tell el 'Ajjul: the Middle Bronze Age remains, *Studies in Mediterranean Archaeology* XXXVIII (Göteberg, 1974).

STORY-MASKELYNE (1870): M. H. N. Story-Maskelyne, *The Marlborough Gems* (London, 1870).

STRONACH (1965): D. Stronach, 'Excavations at Pasargadae, third preliminary report', *Iran* III (1965).

STRONACH (1969): D. Stronach, 'Excavations at Tepe Nūsh-i Jān, 1967', *Iran* VII (1969).

STRONG (1963): Roy Strong, *Portraits of Queen Elizabeth I* (Oxford, 1963).

SUNDWALL (1943): J. Sundwall, *Die älteren italischen Fibeln* (Berlin, 1943).

TAIT (1962): Hugh Tait, 'Historiated Tudor Jewellery', *Antiquaries Journal* 42, pt. 2 (1962).

TALBOT RICE (1957): T. Talbot Rice, *The Scythians* (London, 1957).

TAYLOR (1970): J. J. Taylor, 'Lunulae Reconsidered', *Proceedings of the Prehistoric Society* XXXVI (1970).

THOMPSON (1966): J. E. S. Thompson, *The Rise and Fall of the Maya Civilization* (Norman, 1966).

THOMPSON and HUTCHINSON (1931): R. C. Thompson and R. W. Hutchinson, 'The site of the palace of Ashurnasirpal at Nineveh, excavated in 1929–30 on behalf of the British Museum', *Liverpool Annals of Archaeology and Anthropology,* XVIII (1931).

THUREAU-DANGIN (1921): F. Thureau-Dangin, 'Rituel et amulettes contre Labartu', *Revue d' Assyriologie et d'archéologie orientale,* XVIII (1921).

TOYNBEE (1964): J. M. C. Toynbee, *Art in Britain under the Romans* (Oxford, 1964).

VERNIER (1927): E. Vernier, *Catalogue générale des antiquités égyptiennes du Musée du Caire: Bijoux et orfèveries,* 2 vols. (Cairo, 1927).

VCH: Victoria County History (London, 1900–).

VINSKI (1959): Z. Vinski, 'O prethistorijskom zlatnim nalazima u Jugoslaviji (Die urgeschichtlichen Goldfunde in Jugoslawien)', *Arheoloski radovi i rasprave,* 1 (1959).

VON PATEK (1942): E. von Patek, 'Verbreitung und Herkunft der römischen Fibeltypen von Pannonien', *Dissertationes Pannonicae,* 2nd series, 19 (Budapest, 1942).

WALTERS (1899): H. B. Walters, *Catalogue of the Bronzes, Greek, Roman, and Etruscan, in the Department of Greek and Roman Antiquities, British Museum* (London, 1899).

WALTERS (1926): H. B. Walters, *Catalogue of the engraved Gems and Cameos, Greek, Etruscan, and Roman, in the British Museum* (London, 1926). Also referred to as *BMC Gems.*

WATSON (1963): W. Watson, *Handbook to the Collections of Early Chinese Antiquities* (London, 1963).

WAUCHOPPE (1964): R. Wauchoppe (ed.), *Handbook of Middle American Indians* (Texas, 1964).

WEN WU PRESS (1972): *Wen-hua Ta-ko-ming ch'i-chien ch'u-t'u wen-wu.*

WHEELER (1925): R. E. M. Wheeler, *Prehistoric and Roman Wales* (Oxford, 1925).

WILDE (1862): W. Wilde, *Descriptive catalogue of the antiquities of gold in the Museum of the Royal Irish Academy* (Dublin, 1862).

WILKINSON (1971): A. Wilkinson, *Ancient Egyptian Jewellery* (London, 1971).

WILLEY (1966, 1971): G. R. Willey, *An Introduction to American Archaeology* I and II (Englefield Cliffs, New Jersey, 1966 and 1971).

WILSON (1964): D. M. Wilson, *Anglo-Saxon Ornamental Metalwork 700–1100 in the British Museum* (London, 1964).

WINLOCK (1932): H. E. Winlock, *Studies Presented to F. Ll. Griffith* (London, 1932).

WINLOCK (1947): H. E. Winlock, *The Rise and Fall of the Middle Kingdom in Thebes* (New York, 1947).

WINLOCK (1948): H. E. Winlock, *The Treasure of Three Egyptian Princesses* (New York, 1948).

WISEMAN (1960): D. J. Wiseman, 'The goddess Lama at Ur', *Iraq* XXII (1960).

WOLSELEY, SMITH and HAWLEY (1927): G. R. Wolseley, R. A. Smith and W. Hawley, 'Prehistoric and Roman Settlements on Park Brow', *Archaeologia* LXXVI (1927).

WOOLLEY (1934): C. L. Woolley, *Ur Excavations II: the Royal Cemetery* (London and Philadelphia, 1934).

WOOLLEY (1955): C. L. Woolley, *Ur Excavations IV: the Early Periods* (London and Philadelphia, 1955).

WOOLLEY and MALLOWAN (1962): C. L. Woolley and M. E. L. Mallowan, *Ur Excavations IX: the Neo-Babylonian and Persian Periods* (London, 1962).

WOOLLEY and MALLOWAN (1976): C. L. Woolley and M. E. L. Mallowan, *Ur Excavations VII: The Old Babylonian Period* (London, 1976).

Index

Index of Donors and Loans